IF A WICKED MAN

Endorsement

'There are those who argue that hardened criminals and gangsters are irredeemable – that we should simply lock them up and chuck away the keys. They are wrong. I have visited many prisons over the last few years, and worked with some pretty tough characters through prison charity organisations. In doing so I have met a number of men like John whose lives have been challenged and turned around in prison by the same message and dramatic encounter that he experienced, in that sense John's story is not unique – but it is nonetheless a truly powerful account of a life changed by the seemingly impossible.'

Major General Tim Cross CBE

IF A WICKED MAN

John Lawson

With

John Sealey

RoperPenberthy

RoperPenberthy Publishing Ltd

Published by RoperPenberthy Publishing Ltd,
19 Egerton Place, Weybridge,
Surrey KT13 0PF

ISBN 978 1 903905 92 0

DISCLAIMER
The names of certain people have been changed to
protect their identity.

Cover design by Esther Kotecha

Typeset by Avocet Typeset, Somerton, Somerset TA11 6RT

Printed and bound by CPI Group (UK) Ltd, Croydon, CR0 4YY

Contents

CONTENTS

Dedication

I would like to dedicate this book to my mother Josephine, who never failed to believe in me. To my brother Alex, for his loyalty, to Pastor Duncan Strathdee for his dedication to come into a high security prison week in week out to reach people like me. To my children Daniel, Siobhan, Arran and Lewis whom I love dearly, I am sorry for all you were put through on my account. To their mother Jenny for always maintaining contact and bringing them to see me in prison. To Tony Anthony for the years of mentoring since I was released from jail. And my thanks to John Sealey for a year and a half of hard work whittling down my life story. And with all my gratitude to Carolyn, for loving me with all her heart, and my step-children Mya and Brandon for accepting me into their family despite my past.

Foreword

I was groomed as a Mafia Prince in "Little Chicago" and grew up to become an enforcer in the underworld of the Mob before switching sides to become crooked cop and bent politician. I was embroiled in world of corruption, even planning murder to become a 'made man in the Mafia' before being sent to the State Penitentiary.

If A Wicked Man is book I can easily relate to, I was captivated as I saw elements of my own life in many of the pages. The story of how the breakdown of a marriage can turn a quiet and polite boy into a violent and dangerous criminal is a reflection of the lost and fatherless generation of today. Social deprivation and the destruction of a family can have profound effects on our children that may never surface until years later.

The love of money and a cold heart can drive violent men like us to take by force what we feel society owes us. Taking the law into your own hands is a recipe for disaster with dire consequences for all involved. This book will take the reader on a journey where they will love, hate, empathise, laugh and cry with John Lawson as he rises through the ranks of serious crime before the police finally catch up with him. While serving five years for attempted extortion in a Scottish prison a dramatic encounter took place that revolutionised his life and changed him forever.
Brutally honest, deadly serious and yet strangely funny at times.

A compelling story of a Wicked and violent man that will take you on an emotional roller coaster with an unexpected twist that will leave you challenged.

Rocco Morelli, Author of 'Forgetta 'bout It,' www.roccomorelli.org

FOREWORD

We have all made mistakes at one time or another, and struggled to overcome them, but with some people it can become a lifestyle. John Lawson was a man who had profiteered on the weakness, fear and vice of others. Vividly told, this frank account of a life of twists and turns is a captivating and at times shocking insight into another world where there are no rules, no remorse and no regrets.

This is the true story of how one man, immersed in a world of crime and violence found a turning point in his life in the most unlikely of places, his prison cell. A radical change that forced him to admit for the first time in his life that he was lost and headed for destruction. Nothing fundamental is easy, but this story proves that change is possible even for those written off by society.

If A Wicked Man is told faithfully, in simple language, no excuses. Read it, and believe that there is always hope.

Anne Perry, Best-selling author

Writer's Preface

In writing *If a Wicked Man* I have endeavoured to write the biography of John Lawson as accurately as possible, of his gradual progression into serious criminal activity, in an attempt to draw the reader into a good story while at the same time not shying away from the historical realities of what he did.

All the information in this biography is as related to me by John Lawson and some of those who knew him. I have made every effort to link the stories and events into a disturbing, yet entertaining story. A subject that by its very nature should not be entertaining, but even in criminality there is often humour and empathy that I hope will engage the reader through the pages to the surprising ending.

Most readers will not have heard of John Lawson or his activities, unless they had chanced to read some of the newspaper reports at the time. It is because of this that I felt compelled to write his biography and what has emerged is more than a story of an ex-villain, more than a story of the sex industry, prostitution, trafficking, extortion, loan sharks, gang warfare, kidnapping, beatings, prison life, and the corruption of public officials. It is also a story of abject poverty and hunger, of having to resort to thieving simply to stay alive or to go without food to buy coal to heat the freezing rooms during the bitter winters.

If A Wicked Man is a story that, although shocking in parts it will speak of all these things.

John Sealey, January 2016

Disclaimer:
Some of the names and places have been changed to protect the innocent.

Prologue

GOING DOWN

1989

'THE DEFENDANT WILL RISE,' the clerk of the court ordered. A murmur buzzed around the courtroom as the judge was about to pass sentence. John Lawson, dressed in a smart tailored suit, slowly got to his feet. At twenty one with his square face and strong nose he was a handsome man. Extremely fit, standing five feet ten tall, he had an athlete's build, very muscular with broad shoulders and not an ounce of fat on any part of his body. His curly gingery hair was cut short, giving his face an added fierceness.

He stared around the courtroom, an expression of casual arrogance. The court officials and prosecuting barristers were dressed in their silks and wigs. Members of the jury appeared satisfied with the outcome of the trial, which surprised John a bit as Cecil Watkins his solicitor seemed to be smiling. He also noticed Inspector Ronald Atwell slouching back in his seat in the row behind the prosecuting counsel with one of those *'I said I'd get you and I'm here to see you go down,'* looks on his face.

None of this fazed John, for he still felt bullish as he stood in the dock at Southwark Crown Court, the court where many criminals before him had awaited sentence. The judge gave a little cough as if to draw attention to the seriousness of the pronouncement he was about to make.

'John Lawson' the judge began his face implacable. 'It is my opinion you are a violent man who intimidated an innocent tourist. This man came here seeking our culture, hoping to meet people and take home some good memories, but he was not given this opportunity. Instead, he was forced to pay an extortionate amount of money to you, whilst terrified and fearful. In this country everyone has the right to walk

11

the streets and enter our establishments without fear or menace. We cannot allow our society to evolve, to breed, to infect the good, led by the unscrupulous. We will not tolerate this kind of behaviour, and for this you will be punished with a custodial sentence. I sincerely hope that this case will help to expose and warn people of the unscrupulous methods you and others employ to rob unsuspecting tourists. The fact that you have changed your plea to guilty has been taken into account. However, that does not diminish the gravity and impact of your behaviour, so I sentence you accordingly, you will serve nine months imprisonment. Take him down.'

John fought to suppress a grin, a mixture of relief and guilt sweeping over him as the two prison officers cuffed him and led him down the steep stairwell, their heavy boots echoing all the way to the holding cells.

'I don't know what you're smiling at, you've just been given nine months,' one of the prison officers remarked.

'I'm grinning because I was expecting to get at least two years,' John wanted to tell him, but decided it was smarter not to antagonise him. This was his first conviction and he had no idea what he was in for.

'Your solicitor will come and see you as soon as he's finished his other cases,' the other prison officer informed him, removing the handcuffs before he marched out with the other prison officer, slamming the cell door shut behind them.

John slumped down on the hard bench and looked around at the miserable surroundings wondering what it was going to be like in prison. As he rested his head against the hard concrete wall, he thought about how the Crown Prosecution Service had gone to infinite lengths to fly the gullible American tourist all the way from the States, just to make sure Inspector Atwell got him as he had sworn he would. He shook his head thinking, *If they hadn't gone to those lengths there would have been no case to answer and I wouldn't be sitting here.*

Suddenly the cell door opened and the prison officer announced.

'Right, your solicitor is ready to see you. Get to your feet and put your hands out,' he ordered.

'Well, we didn't do too badly, did we?' Cecil Watkins said cheerfully, as soon as John was seated the other side of the table and the prison officer had left.

'Yeah, I thought I was going to get longer,' John sighed, with an air of relief.

'You would have, if we had not changed your plea to guilty and a few words had been said in the right ears,' Cecil Watkins said, sitting there with his incipient paunch bulging out over the top of the waistband.

'The right ears?'

'The evidence was stacked against you. I never thought for one moment they would fly the witness from the States. With his statement you were going to be looking at more than two years if I hadn't done a deal with the prosecuting counsel,' he said, with a satisfied grin, dandruff flying out of his unruly hair as he involuntarily scratched his head, the flakes falling like snow down over the shoulders of his crumpled dark blue pin striped suit.

'You have to understand, the rule of law is about money. Money makes the law and the law protects money that makes the law. The law has been after the Lawsons for a very long time, without managing to nail them. But, they managed to nail you. You're the first and you only got nine months. With good behaviour you'll finish up doing no more than four and a half months, which won't have pleased the likes of Inspector Ronald Atwell, who for some reason has got it in for you. Keep your nose clean and you'll be out before you know it. Don't worry, your uncles and I will take care of everything and see your mother and your son Daniel are taken care of,' Cecil assured him, as he got to his feet, crossed to the door and tapped on it.

John looked at Cecil as he walked out, the dandruff still sprinkled over his shoulders, wondering why no one has ever bothered to tell him about using a medicated shampoo.

The sweat box was aptly named John thought as he sat with his broad shoulders pressing against either side of the small confined space. The only light coming from a small blacked out window next to his head. The shaky uneven journey of stop and start, as the prison van manoeuvred its way through the evening rush hour traffic, caused him to feel sick, and eventually throw up into a plastic bag the guard shoved under the door. Suddenly, hearing voices, John craned his neck to look out of the blacked out window and saw the large foreboding wooden gate and surrounding heavy stone walls of Her Majesty's Prison Brixton.

The first thing that hit John as he and the other prisoners were let out of the van, was the acrid smell that pervaded the air. He looked around at the ancient concrete walls topped with barbed wire and his face filled with uncertainty. A sense of disgust, horror and regret washed over him as he looked up at the rows and rows of barred windows that had dirty brown streaks running down from them.

John looked curiously at a group of prisoners walking around with shovels picking up all sorts of newspaper wrappings, plastic bags and what looked like odd socks littered about the ground.

'What are they doing?' he asked one of the prisoners standing with him.

'They're the bomb squad,' the prisoner replied.

'What do you mean the bomb squad?'

'Obviously your first time in here,' the prisoner remarked capriciously. 'When you need a crap at night, you don't want it lying around stinking the cell out, so you do it on some newspaper or in an old sock or whatever else you can find, wrap it in a parcel and toss it out the window, these poor buggers have the job of clearing it up. It's the worst job in the prison. Some of the real nasty pieces of work up there try and throw parcels at them while they're cleaning up the mess. Whatever you do, make sure you don't get yourself on the bomb squad.'

'Thanks for the tip,' John replied as the prison officers began to move him and the other prisoners off for induction.

The induction area had a very large cell that could accommodate up to forty prisoners and half a dozen single cells to contain those likely to cause trouble. The room stank of a mixture of sweat and stale tobacco which made John want to puke again.

'Right Lawson, you're next,' a prison officer called out, his manner brusque his voice devoid of emotion.

John followed him to a desk where another prison officer took his photograph, checked his details, handed him a prison rule book and instructed him on the basics of how to behave while serving his sentence and the consequences of failing to obey the rules.

One of the other prison officers guided him over to another counter, where he was issued with the standard prison uniform, two blue and white striped shirts, one pair of jeans, two vests, two underpants, two pairs of socks and a pair of black boots. He was also issued with a pack containing a toothbrush, paste, towel, soap, plastic disposable razor and a set of eating implements consisting of a blue plastic mug, bowl, plate, knife, fork and spoon.

'Right, bring that lot with you, move over to that cubicle, empty your pockets and place everything in the large brown envelope inside the cardboard box, then remove all your clothes,' the prison officer ordered. There were no doors on the cubicle and the prison officer watched as John slowly emptied his pockets, of keys, wallet, loose change and wristwatch and placed them in the envelope which the prison officer sealed. 'Hurry up we haven't got all day,' the prison officer barked, irritatingly as John started to undress. 'And then hand me each article of clothing as soon as you have removed it,' he added.

John watched annoyingly as the prison officer searched through every pocket and lining of his new suit.

'You've just seen me remove everything,' John said, upset he was rumpling up his expensive tailored suit.

'Just checking you haven't got any illegal substance sewn into the linings or pockets,' he said gruffly, before handing the suit back. Now put it in that box,' the prison officer instructed him.

John carefully folded his suit, shirt and tie and the rest of his clothes in the box and then reached for the underwear he had been issued with.

'Right before you do that, I want you to squat and give me a loud cough,' the prison officer ordered him.

'What?' John exclaimed, indignation brimming in his voice.

'Just want to make sure you're not concealing any illegal substances in unusual places,' the prison officer explained, his voice unwavering.

'I don't use drugs,' John said, assertively.

'Yeah, that's what they all say. Just do what I say and cut the chat,' the prison officer said, gruffly.

John squatted and gave a loud cough, anger rising at the humiliation of having to squat like a common criminal, but then the tension eased and he allowed a half smile accepting he was now a common criminal.

'I don't know what you're grinning at Lawson, but I tell you, it won't be there for long, once you're banged up in your cell,' the prison officer rebuked him, a cruel smile playing on his face. 'Right put your prison gear on and join the line to be examined by the doctor.'

John inspected the underpants before putting them on, worrying they had probably been worn by previous prisoners. But they looked reasonably clean, so slipped into them and put on the rest of the prison issue.

'Do up the top button of your shirt and keep it buttoned. That is a strict rule and you'll find yourself in trouble if you don't,' the prison officer said, with a sharp edge to his voice.

John fastened the top button of the striped blue and white shirt, picked up his pack and followed the prison officer out of the cubicle. His boots sounded heavy on the concrete floor as they walked along the corridor to join the line waiting to be examined by the doctor.

The doctor gave him a perfunctory once over and announced him fit and healthy. The prisoners were then marched off to their various allotted wings. As John entered B wing, he looked up dauntingly at the enormity of it, a sense of foreboding tightening in his chest. There were four landings with rows of cells. Wire netting suspended across each landing like a trapeze artiste's safety net to avoid anyone jumping, falling or being pushed over. The noise was deafening, a cacophony of mugs banging on the cell bars, prisoners yelling to each other, music from portable radios blaring out. Some prisoners were leaning over the rails wanting to look at the new fish as they were led to their cells.

The prison officer guided John to a caged staircase that led up to fourth landing and led him to a cell which had been turned into a storeroom stacked with bedding, mops, buckets, brushes and other cleaning materials.

'Right, this is where you pick up your bedding,' the prison officer told him and John watched as an inmate gathered up two bed sheets, two blankets, one pillow, and handed them to him.

'Don't we get a pillow case?' John asked rhetorically, already guessing the answer.

The inmate just glared blankly at him and turned away.

'Let's get you to your cell,' the prison officer said, as he ushered him along to the last cell at the end of the landing.

'Bates, here's your new cellmate,' the prison officer announced, with a mischievous grin shoving John into the cell before stepping out, slamming the door shut with more force than was necessary.

Bates looked at John impassively, waiting until he heard the prison officer's footsteps fading into the distance, before saying anything.

'Me name's Alfie. This yer first time in prison, boy?' he asked, in his broad cockney accent. There was a brooding intensity about him as he slowly swung his legs off the bunk and took a good look at John.

'Yes, first time,' John answered nervously, as he looked around the tiny cell which was no more than ten feet by eight. There were two single beds placed either side with a barred window high up on the rear wall. The walls which had been originally painted cream were now a faded dirty yellowish brown from tobacco stains. There was a rectangle board above each bed for pasting pictures and photos. In the left corner of the cell stood a small table that had a jug of water on it.

'That's yer bed over there boy,' Alfie said, indicating the other bed as though there was a choice.

John plonked his belongings down on the bare mattress.

'So what yer in fer boy?' Alfie asked, his eyes sweeping over him dark and assessing.

'Robbery,' John told him, exuding a hint of pride.

'And what did yer get fer that?'

'Nine months.'

'Bleedin' eck, only nine munfs, what did yer rob, a bleedin' piggy bank? There are blokes in ere that got five years fer robbery. Yer must av ad a bleedin' good brief or bent judge.' Alfie said, sarcastically.

'Yes, I think I had a good solicitor.'

'Well, give me his address, he sounds a lot better than the idiot I ad, didn't know his arse from his elbow. Did yer av to pay fer yer brief or did yer get legal aid?'

'No, his fees were taken care of by the family.'

'There yer go, yer know what they say? It's not ow guilty yer are, but ow much money yer got. Yer won't even av done yer apprenticeship by the time yer get out. Yer not in ta drugs are yer boy?' Alfie said, searching John's face intently looking for any signs of drug abuse.

'I don't have anything to do with any of that stuff. Never have, never will,' John quickly assured him.

'I see,' he said, but there was doubt in his voice. 'I bleedin' 'ope so, cos I can't stand any of those junkies, bleedin' morons. Yer can ear the bleedin' idiots, out of their minds screaming their bleedin' eads off and kicking the bleedin' cell doors. It's bleedin' difficult to get ta sleep sometimes,' Alfie said, disparagingly.

John could see the doubt on his face and was anxious to reassure him.

'Anyone that mucks around with drugs is a fool, a dangerous fool. It's something I've never been tempted to try, I don't even smoke.'

'Ah well baccy, that's anuvver fing, baccy's a valuable currency in ere. So when yer eventually get yer canteen money, make sure yer buy some baccy, because yer can use it ta trade for somefink yer really want.'

'What about you, what are you in for?' John asked, anxious to know a little about the man. John reckoned by his appearance he was in his late fifties, worn down by prison life, but there seemed a brutish masculinity about him. He was of average height and appeared to be a little round shouldered giving him a slight stoop; otherwise he seemed in reasonably good shape. He had a rugged weather beaten face with dark piercing green eyes that seemed to stare out, watching every move you made, his thinning black hair was greased straight back.

'Burglary, fraud, bit of tea leafing, nuffink too eavy, just enuff ta earn a living as it were, nuffink violent. I've been in and out of prison fer most of the last seventeen years. I mean yer av to keep working uvverwise yer bleedin' starve, yer know ow it is. The trouble wiv money is yer never av enuff, and when yer do get enuff, there's always some bleedin' bastard trying ta take it off yer. Doing a twelve munfs stretch this time,' Alfie said, with a nonchalant air.

John felt a sense of admiration for him and became a little more at ease.

'I guess you know your way around the prison,' he said, meaning it as a compliment.

'Yeah, bin in enuff of em, and one fing I've learnt is, yer av ta try not ta fink of what's appening on the outside. Yer world for the next four and alf munfs is prison, and the bleedin'g day ta day routines yer just av ta get used ta. Yer start finking about anyfink else and it'll start ta drive yer bleedin' crazy. Keep yer ead down and do yer bird and that way yer survive. That's how I've always got frew it, which brings me ta the point. As yer can see, toilet facilities in ere are at a bare minimal. That's yer slop bucket there, but if yer av to av a crap in the middle of the night, don't use the bleedin' bucket. Get a couple of sheets of newspaper, lay em on the floor, crap on it, then wrap it up in a parcel and frow it out the window. That way the cell don't stink all bleedin' night,' Alfie explained, irritation suddenly creeping into his voice.

'Yeah, I was told about it when we came in and saw the poor guys going around with shovels picking the parcels up.'

'Yeah well, make sure yer don't get put on the bomb squad. Anyway the best fing of course, is ta train yer bowels as I don't wanna be woken up in the middle of the bleedin' night and see yer squatting with yer trousers round yer bleedin' ankles,' Alfie said, his voice unwavering.

Just then the cell door was unlocked and the prison officer shouted in.

'Right, come and get your meal.'

'We have to take these with us?' John asked as Alfie gathered up his blue plastic bowl and plate.

Alfie gave him one of his long suffering looks as he said.

'Unless yer wanna carry the food back in yer bleedin' ands.'

'You mean they don't have a canteen where we sit down and eat?'

'Sure, with waiter service as well. Where do yer fink yer are boy, the bleedin' Ritz?' he chided good naturedly.

John sorted out his plate and bowl and followed Alfie along the landing to the wire enclosed staircase, the noise was intensified by the clanging of heavy boots on the metal steps as the prisoners from the other levels filed down to the ground floor.

'Bleedin' joke really, the ones on the lower landings get theirs before us and by the time we get ours and carry it back up ta the cell, it's bleedin' cold,' Alfie said, ruefully.

Having got their food they made their way back to the staircase.

'Make sure you don't spill anyfink off yer plate as yer carries it up, as they'll have yer scrubbin the bleedin' stairs from top to bottom,' Alfie warned him.

'You're right the food is cold,' John said, taking his first mouthful as soon as they got back to their cell, a disdained look spreading across his face.

'Never mind yer get used to it,' Alfie said, dolefully.

'Don't you ever complain?'

Alfie looked at him incredulously, his eyes narrowing, surprised by the remark.

'Listen boy, the first fing yer learn in prison is yer don't complain, unless of course yer wanna finish up on the bomb squad or on some uver equally unpleasant jobs like cleaning the bogs. The screws will take great pleasure in finding nasty jobs for yer to do. So keep yer mouf shut and answer, yes sir, no sir, free bags full sir, when asked or told to do somefing. If yer see someone being beaten up or worse, yer say nuffink, and if yer asked, yer tell em yer eard nuffink and saw nuffink. That way boy, yer'll manage ta survive,' he said, letting the words hang for a moment. 'So eat up boy, I know it tastes like slop, but try and imagine it's the best meal yer ever ad and breakfast tomorrow will be even better. That's how yer survive in this place boy. Let it get yer down and yer struggle to survive,' Alfie said, advisedly, taking another mouthful of his food and chewing on it as though he was really enjoying it.

'Wouldn't be so bad if we had something to wash it down with,' John said, forcing himself to eat what was left on his plate.

'Don't worry the tea bucket'll be around a bit later. In the meantime make yer bed up and get yerself ready, it's almost time to be let out to use the toilets, and let's hope yer can do a crap then. That's what I've trained meself to do,' Alfie said, giving him an expectant look.

'I'll do my best,' John said worriedly, a pensive frown creasing his forehead.

'Let's hope yer do, saves all the messing about.'

As John entered the toilets he was hit by an overpowering smell, a cocktail of urine, stale tobacco and body odour. There were cockroaches and other insects running around in the corners and crevices. Alfie could see the changing expression on his face, the disgust, the horror, the regret.

'Wait till yer slop out in the morning, yer see rats running all over the bleedin' place. But yer get used to it like we all do,' Alfie said, a brief smile crossing his face.

'Did yer manage to knock one out?' Alfie asked, as they made their way back to the cell.

'Yes, as it happens I was dying to go, so you don't have to worry tonight,' John said, shooting an expression of triumph at him, although at the same time feeling rather strange that he was discussing his bowel movements with a complete stranger.

'Fank 'eavens' Alfie said, bringing the conversation back to its basic level. 'And if yer av ta pee in the middle of the night, make sure yer aim for the side of the bucket, that way it don't make so much noise.'

The harsh edge of strain was beginning to show in the lines around John's eyes as he slumped down wearily on his bed.

'Av yer mug ready, tea'll be ere any moment after they've done the 'ead count. Not that I'm planning on going anywhere,' Alfie said, jokingly.

When the tea eventually arrived it didn't surprise John that it was another example of the lack of any regard for hygiene. The tea was in a big steel bucket with no lid and he watched as the trolley was wheeled to the cell door and Alfie eagerly stepped forward, dipped his mug in the bucket and filled it with lukewarm stewed tea. The inmate pushing the tea trolley then offered him a biscuit.

'Don't yer want any tea?' Alfie asked, surprised John seemed to be hesitating.

'I was just wondering how many filthy mugs had been dipped in that bucket before it got to us, particularly as we are the last cell on the top landing,' John said.

Alfie took a sip of his tea and looked at him over the rim of the mug.

'Like I said this aint a bleedin' five star 'otel. If yer don't bleedin' want it, then I'll bleedin' av it. Here give us yer mug,' Alfie said, reaching to grab his mug.

'Sorry, it just takes some getting used to,' John said, holding onto his mug, stepping forward, dipping it into the bucket and taking a biscuit.

The inmate turned the trolley around and the prison officer slammed the cell door shut, inserted the key followed by a series of echoing clicks as the lock turned, securing the cell door.

'That's it for the night. Now yer know why they're called turnkeys or screws as we call em these days,' Alfie said, biting off a piece of the biscuit and chewing on it thoughtfully.

'You wanna listen ta the radio, boy?' he asked, surprising John.

'Have you got a radio?' John asked, without thinking.

'Would I bleedin' ask yer if I adn't?' Alfie said, putting his mug down, then getting to his knees, reaching under the bed, pulling out a portable radio and placing it on the table.

'What yer think of that beauty then?'

'Yeah, looks alright,' John said, wondering what was so special about it.

'All bleedin' right is that all yer got to bleedin' say about it. This is a Roberts Rambler my son, it's the dog's bollocks, the Rolls Royce of radios. You won't see many of these around, especially in this bleedin' place,' Alfie said gruffly as John continued to watch as he reached back under the bed and pulled out a length of electric wire and connected one end of the wire to the radio and turned to John.

'Steady the bleedin' table,' he said, as he clambered onto it, reached up to the neon light fitting, removed the white guard cap, fiddled with the wires, and expertly connected the radio to the power supply.

'There yer are, all courtesy of her Majesty, except she don't bleedin' know about it,' Alfie said with a conspiratorial smile, as he scrambled off the table.

'What do you usually listen to?' John asked.

'I like listening to the oldies, more my kind of music. At least yer can understand the bleedin' words. I mean these days yer can't understand a bleedin' word any of em are singing. That's if yer can call it singing, I mean all this bleedin' pop nonsense, any idiot can do that,' Alfie said disparagingly, switching on the radio, which was already tuned to Radio Two.

'Welcome to the Adrian Love show have I got some real good chilled out classics for you lovely listeners tonight.' The DJ announced.

'There yer are, bleedin' perfect, what better way to spend an evening,' Alfie said, stretching himself out on his bunk with a satisfied grin on his face.

'I could think of some places I'd rather be than here,' John said, reflectively.

'Yeah well, yer bleedin'g well ere and yer better get bleedin' used to it.'

John smiled to himself, knowing Alfie was right and he was going to have to get used to it. The music was soothing and as John lay back on his bed he began to think of Daniel and his mother.

'When can I get to make a phone call? I noticed there are phones at the end of the landing,' John asked, thinking about his son.

'Phone calls? It was only letters allowed when I was first banged up. What yer av to do is go down and see one of the POs and before yer ask, a PO is a senior prison officer, e'll give yer a chit, yer fill it out with five numbers you want ta call, security then check the numbers ta make sure yer aint planning an escape or somefink, it all takes forever by which time yer av got yer canteen money and yer be able to buy yerself a phone card,' Alfie explained. 'Now will yer bleedin'g well stop asking questions and shut up, I want ta listen to the music.'

John placed his hands up behind his head and began to feel himself relax at last. *At least I'm not sharing a cell with a nutter*, he thought as he closed his eyes and listened to the music.

A few days later after John had filled out the forms, he got his canteen money and was able to buy a phone card and couldn't wait to call home. As soon as the cell door was opened for the evening meal he rushed for the phone. He picked up the receiver, eagerly inserted the phone card and listened to the recorded voice message that instructed him to enter his prison number, then the recorded voice instructed him to enter the number he wished to call.

John's hand holding the receiver began to shake as he thought this was the first time he was going to speak to his mother since he'd been sentenced and he was not sure how she was going to react, and then he heard his mother's voice saying.

'Hello, hello.'

But as John went to say hello, he heard another recorded voice announcing,

'The phone call you are about to receive is from an inmate of Her Majesty's Prison, Brixton. Please hang up now if you do not wish to receive this call.'

She took a deep calming breath as she held the receiver to her ear, then she heard a bleep and said.

'Hello.'

'Hi, it's me,' John said, excited at hearing his mother voice.

'So good to hear your voice darling, I can't believe it's going to be nine months before we see you again,' she said, her voice warm, but it was warm tinged with sadness.

'No, it's only going to be four and a half months as long as I don't do anything silly,' he quickly assured her, his voice tentative.

'Four and half months is still a long time for Daniel, what am I going to tell him?' she said and he could hear the tension in her voice.

The question rolled around in his mind.

'Tell Daniel I'm working away and I'll buy him a nice present when I come home,' he said, the words almost bubbling in his throat.

Holding herself together with difficulty she said.

'I will, I just hope he doesn't get to hear the truth from someone. Since it got in the newspapers all the family are talking about it. Fortunately they don't yet know you're in prison but I shudder to think what the reaction will be when they find out.'

He pulled an agonised face and his eyes filled with sadness as he said.

'I can't talk long mum. How's Alex?' he asked, wanting to change the subject.

'Oh, he's doing well, he's still working at the engineering firm and he's met a lovely girl called Samantha.'

'That's great ma, I've got to go because if I don't I won't get any dinner. So I'll call again as soon as I get a chance. I love you mum and tell Daniel I love him too, Bye.'

John quickly replaced the receiver and hurried down the staircase, but was stopped halfway by a prison officer shouting up.

'You're too late Lawson get back to your cell, NOW.'

John turned and trundled wearily back up the staircase, hungry, but pleased he'd spoken to his mother.

'I 'ope it was worf it missing tonight's specialty of greasy sausage and stodgy smashed potatoes, followed by rock hard cake and lumpy custard,' Alfie said, seeing John walk in with his empty plates.'

'I wasn't long on the phone. I even cut it short so as I'd get down in time, it's not bloody fair.'

'Anyone who expects fairness in this place has been seriously misinformed,' Alfie quipped, chewing on a bit of grizzle from the sausage.

'Like I said before, this ain't no 'oliday camp. Anyway, did yer get ta talk ta who yer wanted ta?' Alfie asked, looking at him reassuringly, encouraging him to talk. John gave a thin smile as his face darkened and took a long beat before saying.

'It was great talking to my mother, but when she asked me what to tell my son well I…'

Alfie saw the confusion on his face.

'That's the bleedin' problem. It's not what just 'appens ta yer in 'ere, it's ow the uvvers on the outside deal wiv it. They've got ta carry on trying to liv a normal life, which ain't easy given the circs. But I'm sure she was pleased ta ear from yer.'

John felt his eyes well up thinking of Daniel deserted yet again, wondering how he was going to react when his Nan tells him his dad is going to be working away for a few months more and what if he finds out the truth. He gave an involuntary shiver as the thought went off in his head like an alarm bell and his face clouded over, a haunted expression filling his eyes.

'Yer alright,' Alfie asked.

'Sorry Alfie, it's just that, speaking to her for the first time since…'

'I know, it don't get any easier,' he said, in a matter of fact voice. 'Yer just av ta get used to it. Yer banged up twenty free ours a day, so yer going to av ta toughen it out like I've ad ta, boy.'

24

John's face lightened. 'Yeah, I know, but it's just a bit hard at the moment.'

'Tell yer what I'll put some bleedin' music on as soon as the tea bucket's been round,' Alfie said, trying to cheer him up.

'Yeah, better than listening to the numpties out there,' John said, forcing a smile.

After they had had their tea, John watched as Alfie went through the actions of getting the radio ready.

'Get off yer arse and steady the bleedin' table, you want me ta break me bleedin'g neck?' Alfie said, in his usual gruff manner.

John got to his feet and gripped the table as Alfie clambered on and stretched up to connect the wires. After helping Alfie down, he stretched back on his bunk and raised his hands up behind his head as he listened to the soft music and began to feel some of the tension lifting, slowly coming to the terms that he was in prison for the next four and half months and there was nothing he or anyone else could do about it.

Alfie kept the volume low so as not to attract unnecessary attention and the gentle rhythm combining with the weariness of the day slowly began to overcome John. He reached down and pulled the blankets right up over his head and curled up in the foetal position, the blackness engulfing him. Losing all sense of his surroundings, he felt himself drifting endlessly down a long tunnel, until he found a solid door in front of him. He tried to open it, but it wouldn't open, it was locked. Frightened, he began to panic and hammer at the door and cry out, *'Dad where are you? Come and let me out.'*

But there was no dad, nobody coming to let him out, and then he suddenly heard a voice coming from the other side of the door. *'Dad is that you?'* he anxiously called out.

Then he heard another voice and then the sound of heavy banging on the door. The sound was frightening and he rushed over to the far corner away from the door and curled up, tucking his knees tightly under his chin, frightened his father was angry with him for some reason. *Had he done something terrible to make his dad so angry he wanted break the door down?* he worried as he began to shake in fear as the heavy pounding on the door became louder and louder.

He stared at the door as splinters began to appear in the panelling until finally the door burst open. As the light flooded in through the open door he saw two shadowy figures rushing towards him.

'No, dad please, I haven't done anything, honest,' he cried out. 'Please don't hurt me.'

'Shoosh, it's alright John darling, you're safe now,' he heard a female voice say.

The fear slowly drained from his face as the woman came towards him, leaned over and took hold of him. He felt hands on his shoulders. They felt powerful and they started to shake him and he thought for a moment the woman was angry with him.

He pulled the blanket tighter around him as he heard a man's voice shouting at him.

'What the bleedin' eck's going on? Can't bleedin' sleep wiv yer making all that racket,' Alfie said, bristling with annoyance.

John pulled down the blanket, slowly opened one eye, then the other, blinked several times before he looked up and saw the face staring down at him. He frowned as he shook his head to clear his brain, trying to work out where he was and who it was shouting at him.

'Sorry, I must have been dreaming,' he said, blearily, weariness and fear showing on his face as he realised it was Alfie's face staring down at him.

'Dreaming, more like a bleedin' nightmare if yer ask me. Yer were calling after yer dad not to urt yer. What the 'ell was that all about?'

John looked up at him and sadness filled his eyes as he paused trying to compose himself, his mind racing in a hundred directions, none of them pleasant.

'I think it was the sound of the jangling keys turning in the lock that set me off.'

'Yeah, they can set yer off, they used ta me at the beginning, but after yer bin inside as many times as I av, yer kinda get used to em,' Alfie said, consolingly.

'I was dreaming of hearing my father turning the key in the lock and leaving me alone, locked up in our flat for several days, I was only ten,' he finally managed to say.

'Bleedin' eck, ten years old, yer were only a bleedin' kid, what kind of farver would lock is own bleedin' kid up?'

John felt a moment of chill as he began to remember. He had always worried that the memories would never completely go away; he constantly tried to push what had happened out of his mind, to deny it had ever happened. For as much as he tried to fight it, it continued to lurk at the back of his mind. It was something he was forced to live with, like an incurable cancer growing inside him, becoming harder and harder to bear. The lies, the deceit, the pain and the anguish of being locked up, suddenly combining with the horror of being locked up again had pressed hard down on him.

'It's a long story and it all started when my dad took me and mum from Glasgow in 1969 to find a new life in South Africa,' he said to Alfie.

DURBAN

SOUTH AFRICA

1977

It was a warm evening and the sun dappled across the young boy's face, streaming through the open window as he lay on the bed having just awoken from a deep exhausted sleep. He squinted against the sun's rays as he looked around trying to focus on his surroundings. He was in a bedroom, but the fact he didn't recognise it began to worry him. It was a large bedroom with a dark wood dressing table and mirror set against the window and a large double wardrobe with a tall mirror fixed over one of the doors set against the opposite wall. A floral patterned carpet covered the floor. *Whose bedroom was it, and why was he in it, undressed and tucked into the nice soft clean sheets of a strange bed?* he wondered.

As his mind started to race, desperately trying to find the answer, he lowered his hand to his stomach which was beginning to rumble, telling him he was hungry. *Should he just lay there and wait for whomever to come to the bedroom or get up and try to find someone who could tell him where he was and why,* he wondered.

He decided he had to do something so he swung his feet over the side of the bed and stifled a yawn as he eased himself up onto his feet. He drew in a deep breath as he summoned up courage, his heart drumming in his chest, his legs weak and shaky and made his way to the door. As he slowly opened it he saw a man ushering two children, a boy around his age and a younger girl out to play, then he heard a woman's voice. It sounded a little Scottish and was loud and angry.

John listened as the woman continued shouting.

'You bastard, how could you do this to him. How could you just go off and leave him locked up for days with little food, running off with

28

that woman while your wife is in England with your youngest child caring for her dying father? You disgust me and if you were here, I'd happily slap you.'

Then the voice went silent for moment before he heard the woman say.

'Yes and you had damn well better.' Followed by the loud noise of a telephone receiver being slammed down into its cradle, which made him jump, causing him to quickly shut the door, and retreat back to the bed.

He could feel his heart beating hard in his chest, thoughts spinning around in his head, his mind in turmoil replaying what he'd just heard. *Why was the woman shouting, who was the woman shouting at? Who was she talking to about being locked up? Running off with another woman while his wife was in England, caring for her ailing father? Who was she talking about? Was it him? Was she was talking about him? Was it him that had been locked up? What did it all mean?* he asked himself, his emotions beginning to bubble to the surface, his stomach starting to churn again.

Feeling totally perplexed, unable to understand what was happening, he stared aimlessly around the room until his eyes fell on a box of Easter eggs in the far corner. He leapt off the bed, rushed over, grabbed one of the boxes, ripped it open, pulled out the egg and tore at the wrapping, then sank to his knees ravenously shoving the broken chocolate into his mouth.

'John darling, what are you doing?' the lady asked, surprised, as she walked into the room. John looked up at her, a nervous sheepish look on his chocolate smeared face.

'Sorry, I haven't eaten anything for days and I was hungry,' he mumbled, his mouth stuffed with a large chunk of the Easter egg. There was a brief moment of silence as he stared at the woman and fragments of the nightmare began to flood into his mind, he started to shiver the length of his spine as tears formed in his eyes.

'It's alright John darling, you're safe now,' she said assuring him, anxious to dispel the fear displayed on his face. 'I've run a bath and washed your clothes. By the time you've had a bath and got dressed, I'll have a nice hot meal ready for you.'

'Why am I here?' he asked, his voice tentative, his expression uneasy as his eyes were telling his brain that she was someone he knew.

As he continued to gaze at her, he began to recognise the large oversized glasses she was wearing. She was a short woman just five feet four, dressed in a floral patterned blouse and black trousers. She had dark curly hair, and a round chubby face.

'I'm your Auntie Marion,' she told him, with a benevolent smile.

It's common to address family friends as auntie and uncle in South Africa.

'Auntie!' he exclaimed jubilantly. 'Where's my dad? Was that you I heard on the phone? Who were you shouting at? Was it about me?' The questions just flew out of his mouth so fast he didn't know which question he wanted answered first.

His Auntie looked at him not sure what to say. She could feel the colour rising in her cheeks, a red flush of anger at the thought of what he'd been through.

'Have your bath John darling and we'll talk about it when you've had something to eat,' she said, pulling him to his feet and leading him off to the bathroom.

'Hello John,' Uncle Les greeted him as soon as he entered the kitchen. 'Come and sit down and fill your belly. You must be starving poor lad.'

Uncle Les, in contrast to Auntie Marion, was tall at six feet two. He had slightly bucked teeth which showed when he smiled and a good head of black hair neatly combed and parted to one side. He was wearing a plain, open neck shirt and slacks, his brogue shoes highly polished.

John gave a half smile as he nervously shuffled to the table and sat down.

'Feeling better now you've had a good sleep and a nice bath?' Uncle Les asked, with a broad smile displaying his bucked teeth.

'Yes, thank you uncle,' John answered, in his usual polite manner.

'That's good my lad, maybe you can go out and play with Graham and Lorraine after your meal if you're feeling up to it?'

Marion carried over a plate of sliced ham and two fried eggs and placed it in front of him.

'There, this will make you feel even better,' she said, encouragingly.

John smiled a thank you as he picked up the knife and fork, cut off a small piece of the ham and they both watched anxiously as he began slowly to chew on it. His uncle looked surprised, expecting him to dig into the meal voraciously.

'What's the matter John, are you alright?' he asked, worriedly.

'Sorry Uncle, I ate a whole Easter egg in the bedroom, well most of it anyway,' John explained, shamefully.

'Don't worry about it John darling. After what you've been through I'm not surprised you were starving,' his auntie said, compassionately.

John looked at her guiltily as he forced himself to swallow the piece of ham. 'Where's dad, has something happened to him?' he asked, putting the knife and fork down.

His auntie and uncle exchanged glances both wondering what to tell him.

'You dad will be coming to see you tomorrow,' his auntie finally said.

'Is he alright, has he been in an accident? Has he been shot?'

'Shot?' his uncle exclaimed, and he could see the tears prickling at his eyes. 'Why would he be shot?'

'He's a policeman and policemen get shot and he's been shot at before, he has killed people and they have tried to kill him' John said, fighting to hold back the tears.

'No, nothing like that… it just that…' Auntie Marion hesitated. 'Look he'll explain everything when he sees you tomorrow,' she added consolingly.

The following morning John could not eat breakfast and did not even want to play with Graham and Lorraine. Instead he stood at the widow of the bedroom staring out morosely, as he had been for the last hour, waiting to see his dad's green Volkswagen Beetle draw up. He began to worry whether his father was really going to come or were his Auntie and Uncle hiding the truth of what had really happened to him? A sudden sadness filled him and made him ache as he waited, not daring to take his eyes away from the window. *He is going to come, he won't let me down, he's my hero and he won't desert me, because he loves me as much as I love him,* he kept telling himself over and over again, but the thought became less convincing as the time wore on.

Then suddenly he began to hear the familiar sound of the Beetle engine chugging its way towards the bungalow.

'Dad,' he screamed, elated at seeing the car arriving. He rushed to the door, pulled it open then stopped dead in his tracks, and slammed it shut. *Suppose he doesn't want to see me. Suppose he's mad at me for something I've done?* he pondered, all the uncertainties flooding back as he hurried back over to the window and looked out.

He could see his auntie and uncle come out of the bungalow and approach his dad. His auntie seemed to be waving her arms at him angrily.

John opened the window to try to hear, the voices were muffled, but he managed to pick up some of what was being said.

'You ought to be ashamed, abandoning your son and going off with some floosie, while Josephine, your dear wife is away with your youngest son taking care of her sick father. What were you thinking?' Then he saw her hold her hand up before his dad could answer. 'No, you don't need to answer that. I don't think I want to know the sordid details. What kind of man does that anyway? That's if you can call yourself a man,' she continued to berate his dad.

'I came here to see my son, not to have an argument with you Marion,' he heard his dad say.

'You'd better go and get him,' he heard his auntie say watching her turn to his uncle, who headed back into the bungalow.

'Your dad's here,' his uncle said, as soon as he entered the room.

John stood fixed by the window staring back at his Uncle.

'Is dad angry with me?'

'No of course not, he's come here to see you.'

'But I heard my dad and auntie arguing. Were they arguing about me?'

'No, they were just having a few words, nothing for you to worry about,' his uncle said, wanting to placate him while wondering what he might have heard.

'Come on lad,' he said, crossing to the window and taking hold of his hand. 'Your dad won't wait forever.'

As soon as John got outside and saw his dad standing there, all the troubles seemed to fall from his shoulders as he ran towards him.

His dad was a handsome man, standing five ten. He had a firm muscular body, fair skinned with short wavy, salt-and-pepper coloured hair. He was dressed in his flared jeans with his denim shirt loosely flapping out over the top of the waistband, concealing the Browning 9mm pistol he had strapped to the belt. He spoke with a broad Glaswegian accent. Lex dropped to his knees and scooped his son up into his strong muscular arms.

'I'm sorry son, I'm really sorry,' he said, as he held him tight.

'What are you sorry about dad?'

'It's difficult to explain son,' he began, giving him a peculiar twisted smile. 'You're going to have to stay here for a while with your auntie and uncle until I can book you on a plane to go and see your mum, I will come and join you just as soon as I can.'

'Why can't you come with me?'

'I can't son. I've got work to do and I can't look after you at the same time, so you have to stay here with your auntie and uncle. I will arrange for the plane tickets and I'll come and take you to the airport and I promise I will be with you very soon.'

A few days later John looked out from his window seat as the plane lifted off the runway in Johannesburg and rose high into the sky. It made him think this was a trip he would never forget. As the plane soared higher into the drifting clouds, obliterating his view of the land below, he wondered whether he would ever see his dad again.

BIRKENHEAD

It was a long, lonely journey of over eleven hours for a ten year old boy travelling on his own. As the jumbo jet came out of the clouds and began its approach to Heathrow airport, John looked out the window at the ground below at a cluster of buildings with very little greenery, still not understanding why his dad had not come with him. The plane touched down around lunchtime and his family were there to meet him. His mother had hired a minibus, because his Gran Curtis, Auntie Ruby, Auntie Cath, Auntie Chris, Auntie Rita and several cousins as well his little brother Alex, all wanted to come to the airport to greet him when he arrived.

By the time they had driven all the way back to Birkenhead, just beside Liverpool in the north-west of England, the skies had turned dark and overcast with heavy grey clouds. John got out of the minibus and was immediately struck by the dull drabness of the grey narrow streets. He looked around apprehensively at the rows of dowdy terraced houses squeezed tightly together. It was in complete contrast to what he had been used to; it was a shock to the system as he stared up at the tall chimney stacks jutting out of the grey slated roofs, spewing out an endless trail of black smoke. He was still wearing his light summer clothes and began to shiver as he lowered his eyes to the hard stone slabs that made up the pavements and the greyness of the cobbled streets.

'Come on John, come inside, you look frozen,' his mother said, taking hold of his hand and leading him into the house.

Number 3, Halcyon Road was a late Victorian terraced house. The interior consisted of one large front room with a bay window, containing the best furniture and a colour television set. Considered the *best room* it was kept shut and only used for special occasions. The children were never allowed to go in unless they were given special permission.

In the hallway there was a coin operated electric meter fixed high up on the wall above the front door, which had a fine cotton thread about two feet long hanging down from it. Attached to the end of the thread was a metal bolt that hung rather like a pendulum.

Further along the hallway there was a storage cupboard under the stairs which contained the gas meter and an assortment of shoes, several coats and some cardboard boxes stuffed with all kind of things. At the end of the hallway was the kitchen/ dining room where everybody gathered and ate. There was a sofa, table and chairs, and a few ashtrays scattered around. It was cold and had an unfamiliar smell about it, a mixture of cooked food, stale tobacco and fumes from the gas fire. Upstairs there were three bedrooms, the main front bedroom, a smaller back bedroom and an even smaller box room.

The smallness of the house was so much in contrast to the very modern apartment they had in Durban. It had a large airy living room furnished with top of the range leather furniture and a colour television, a large fully fitted kitchen, and a fully fitted bathroom. There was a long hallway that led off to two good size bedrooms. At the front of the apartment there was a large enclosed veranda and workshop that overlooked the rich green pastures of the area.

Tired and hungry they all sat together, squeezed around the dining room table, and tucked into a meaty stew they called Scouse. It was the same Scottish dish that John's mum often cooked for him back in South Africa where they called it Stovies. As the meal came to an end, John looked around at the cramped table and started to wonder how and where everybody was going to sleep. His mum, as though reading his thoughts suddenly said, addressing everyone.

'Right, since we now have John staying with us, there is going to have to be a change in the sleeping arrangements. I will be sharing the main bedroom with Gran. Auntie Ruby will have the box room and you children will now share the double bed in the back room.'

John's face took on a frown. He'd never had to share a bedroom before, let alone a bed. Back home he had his own bed in his own room. Now suddenly not only was he going to have to share a room, but a bed as well with his auntie's two daughters, Donna aged eight,

Louise aged four as well as Alex his younger brother also aged four. As his mum and Auntie Ruby prepared them for bed, John took out the money he still had hidden in his back pocket.

'Dad told me to give you this when we were at the airport and he even changed it into pounds,' he said, handing her the money that was held together by a big metal paperclip.

'Thank you,' she said, smiling appreciatively at her son, so pleased he was with her.

'Oh, and I have a letter from Auntie Marion to give you. She did tell me it was for you only and nobody else must see it,' he whispered as though part of a secret mission. 'It's in the bottom of my satchel,' he told her.

'Right make sure you go to the toilet, clean your teeth and get to bed and tomorrow you can tell me all about your dad and everything,' she said, giving him a kiss on the cheek.

Sleeping four in a bed was a very strange experience and no matter how he tried to curl up and go to sleep, one of the others would suddenly turn over and disturb him. The room was cold and as the night wore on it got even colder. Not used to a room as cold as this, John began to shiver. As he was on the edge of the bed, he was able to quietly slip out and go looking for something he could put on top of him to keep himself warm. He couldn't find anything in the bedroom and decided to look for something downstairs maybe a large coat, or anything else he could find to put over himself to keep the cold out.

As he slowly crept down the stairs he heard voices coming from the front room. It sounded as though someone was crying, stopping halfway down he could hear more clearly and his heart jumped as he realised it was his mother crying and heard his Auntie Ruby saying.

'That's dreadful, the cheating bastard how could he do this to you?'

'We don't know for sure. It's only what Marion says in the letter,' he heard his mother say.

'Why would she write such a thing if it wasn't true?' he heard Auntie Ruby reply.

What had his dad done that was making his mother cry, he wondered, as he sat down on the step, starting to shiver with nerves as well as the cold.

'She says he told her the affair, if there was one, is over, and he is going to sort everything out when he gets here,' he heard his mum tell Auntie Ruby.

John's heart gave a beat of happiness at what she had said. He could put up with anything now he knew for certain his dad was coming.

As Josephine went to put the letter down on the table, Ruby noticed that there were some words scribbled on the back of the letter and said.

'There is something else written on the back. Have you read it?'

Josephine turned the letter over and read the words.

'NO!' she exclaimed and her body began to shake as if a bolt of heated adrenaline was shooting through her.

Ruby cupped her hands to her face and could feel her heart beginning to beat fast as she looked at the agonised expression on her sister's face.

'Whatever is it?' she asked, almost frightened of the answer.

'It just says. I have just seen the woman. She even had the gall to come to the airport with Lex to see John off.'

The shock of what John was hearing, although not understanding any of it, was making him shiver even more and he had to find something quick to get warm. He spotted his mother's coat hanging up, the one she had been wearing when she had met him, reached up, grabbed hold of it and took it back up to bed with him.

The following morning John was awoken by his mother coming into the bedroom.

'Right John, get dressed. It's the first day of the new term and you are going to be joining Christchurch Primary School. I'm sure you'll be happy there my darling. So hurry up and get ready,' then she spotted her coat as he got out of bed. 'What's my coat doing there?'

'I was so cold I couldn't find anything else,' he said worried she was still upset and was going to get angry with him.

'Sorry darling, I should have realised you're not used to the cold. I'll get an extra blanket or something for you,' she said, giving him a reassuring hug.

His mother looked down at his feet as he hurried along the hallway to the kitchen and shook her head reproachfully.

'You're in England now John, you can't go running around in your bare feet. Go back upstairs and put your socks and shoes on. Then come down and have some breakfast,' she said, with a gentle smile, knowing how he liked to run around in his bare feet at home.

*

School in England was tough at first, there seemed to be a total lack of discipline with bullies running the playgrounds calling him 'white Zulu', as well as other names he had to deal with. It was a sudden change to what he was used to and having to wear shoes only added to his distress.

Several months went by and John never stopped wondering when or if his dad was going to arrive, until one day it all suddenly changed when he came home from school to find his mother waiting for him with a broad happy smile on her face. She crushed him to her and he could feel the happiness vibrating out of her body as she said, 'Your dad is coming to see us, I got the letter today.'

Welling up with emotion, tears began to escape from the corners of his eyes splashing onto the cotton material of his mother's dress, his eyes clouding over as the news of what she was saying began to overwhelm him and his body started to shake.

'When is he coming?' he managed to splutter, trying to control the excitement.

'He's coming in two weeks' time, but the thing is, he's not coming here, we're going to meet him in Scotland. Isn't that wonderful?' she said, giving him a big hug.

'I knew dad would come. I knew he wouldn't let us down,' he said, his eyes shining with happiness. 'When are we going Mum?'

'Just as soon as I can arrange the train tickets.'

SCOTLAND:

THE END OF THE BEGINNING

John was pleased to see his Gran Lawson. He had always been fond of her, and she had always spoiled him with love, especially as he was her first born grandchild. She was sixty now, a tall stocky woman, about five foot nine in height. She had a round friendly chubby face, with a large pair of glasses perched on the end of her nose. Her hair was white and very curly. She was dressed as he'd remembered her, in a flowery blouse with a brown waistcoat and matching brown tweed skirt and heavy brown brogue shoes. Gran had two sofas in the lounge for relatives and visitors to stay, one of which opened up into a bed. John and Alex were to sleep on the sofa bed, while their mother would sleep on the other sofa.

The following morning John eyes brightened as he watched the car draw up. It was a light brown colour, but he couldn't work out the make. But none of that mattered as he and Alex rushed out of the room to the front door and threw themselves into their dad's arms. As John hugged his dad, he looked back and was surprised to see his mother standing back hesitantly the end of the hallway.

'I suppose you had better come into the living room,' gran told his dad with an air of inevitability in her voice.

Lex let go of John and Alex and followed his mother into the living room. John watched as his mother approached his dad noticing that she didn't rush into a hug like he had done, but seemed to give his dad a perfunctory kiss on the cheek.

'When are we going back, dad?' John asked excitedly, as soon as everybody had sat down. 'Are we going back this week? Did you bring me any presents?'

Lex looked puzzled for a moment.

'You know it was his birthday at the weekend?' John's mother, Jose, reminded him with a hint of sarcasm, a look of disdain on her face.

'Of course I know it was his birthday,' he said defensively. 'It's just that with everything that's happening I forgot to bring the presents with me. I will bring them when I come next time,' his dad said, nervously.

'Promise?'

'Promise son, sorry I forgot to bring them,' he added, looking across at his wife beginning to feel uncomfortable, the tension between them so strong that he turned to John and said. 'Why don't you and Alex go out and play while mum and I talk.'

'No dad, I don't want to go out and play. I want to stay here with you,' John protested, clearly upset by the suggestion.

Just then the chiming bells of the ice cream van could be heard coming down the street.

'Come on you two I'll buy you both an ice cream,' Gran volunteered, taking hold of Alex's hand and leading him out with John following.

Lex looked out of the window and smiled as he watched them run out and join the queue of children that had quickly formed. He then crossed over and sat down beside his wife and gently took hold of her hand into his own. 'I'm sorry darling for what happened,' he began nervously. 'It was a silly mistake, but it's over now and I want us to start afresh and all of us to go back to South Africa.'

Jose said nothing, just continued to look into his eyes waiting for him to say more.

'Can you forgive me? I want to put the past behind us,' he said, lightly squeezing her hand as a gesture to convince her he was serious.

The hard composure she had adopted as a curtain to hide her emotions was beginning to crumble.

'Are you serious, that it is really all over with this woman and you'll never do anything like that again?'

'Yes, I even told Marion it was over.'

'Yes, and she told me you had allowed that woman to come to the airport when you packed John off to me,' she said, a sense of foreboding tightening in her chest.

The accusation was so unexpected it caught him by surprise, leaving him speechless not sure how to respond. She turned towards him just long enough for him to see the anguish she was feeling.

'I love you Lex, and if we are going to get back together, you have to be honest with me.'

There was an awkward silence for a moment before he leaned across, put his arms around her and kissed her.

'I love you too, and I never want us to be parted ever again,' he said, passionately, and he could feel little droplets of tears begin to trickle down her face.

'So when do you plan we should go?' she asked, raising her head to look at him, wiping away the tears with the back of her hand.

'The problem is,' he hesitated. 'As you know from the many telephone calls Ma has received from the Durban police, I am urgently needed back as a witness in the trial of the rioters, one of which I shot. They are sending over some papers regarding the trial for me to look at. So that is something else I am going to have to deal with and…'

'You shot someone, is that why they want you back? Are you being accused of murder?' she asked, feeling a stab of fright in the pit of her stomach.

'No of course not, it was all in the line of duty,' he said, without any sense of remorse.

'Do you want to tell the boys?' she said, not wanting to discuss the matter any further.

'What, about the shooting?' he asked, surprised.

'No, you can keep that to yourself. The good news that we're all going back to South Africa?' she said, wiping away more tears, only this time they were happy tears, tears of joy that they were going to be together again.

'Why don't we tell them together?' he suggested, with a warm smile starting to curls his lips.

'We've got some good news for you. We are all going back home to South Africa,' his mum announced as gran walked back in with John and Alex. John leapt into the air with joy and rushed at his father nearly knocking him over.

'When are we going dad, when are we going?'

'Steady on son, don't get too excited. There is a lot of planning to do, so it will take a bit of time. In the meantime you stay here with your mum and gran until I've got everything arranged, then I will come and get you,' his dad explained.

Gran was staring at him, her barriers still up not knowing what had gone on between them, surprised, yet relieved at the apparent happy outcome.

'I've got to go now, but you behave yourself and look after Alex and it won't be long before we'll all be together again.'

It seemed like a long week, John reflected as he walked back briskly from the shops, eager to get to Gran's, hoping as always his dad would be there waiting for him. But he wasn't there. John was in for a shock, a very big shock, something he could never ever have imagined. As he rushed in the door, the smile dropped from his face like a heavy stone, as he heard his mother's voice shouting angrily.

'I can't believe what you're telling me. How could you do this, after all you said?'

As he started to run down the hallway his gran came out of the front room and grabbed hold of him. He looked anxiously into her face. Something was wrong, very wrong; he could see it in her eyes, in her whole expression.

'What's wrong, gran? Why is mum angry?' he asked, nervously.

'Come in the kitchen John, your mum's busy talking on the phone. Come with me and I'll make us a nice cup of tea and you can have a wee biscuit,' she said, guiding him back into the kitchen where his younger brother Alex was already sitting at the table.

'Is she talking to dad?' he asked, still trying to crane his neck to try to listen to what she was saying.

'If that's what you've decided then you better come and get the kids,' he managed to hear his mother say, before he heard the sound of the telephone receiver being slammed down.

The next moment his mum came rushing into the kitchen barely able to contain the sense of anger bubbling up inside her.

'I can't believe it! He's changed his mind, he's going off with that woman,' she said, lines of pain beginning to spread across her face.

John stared at his mother. There was something in her voice he hadn't heard before, something that sounded hard, cold and angry. Before he could say anything his gran grabbed his mother by the arm and propelled her out of the kitchen off to the bedroom. John rushed after them but was stopped in his tracks as the bedroom door was slammed shut in front of him. He took a deep breath to control his emotions as he felt the iron grip of fear constricting his chest. He knelt down and pressed his ear hard against the keyhole and listened to what was being said.

'He's changed his mind. He's going back with her, that, that, that woman, did you know she was here in Scotland?'

'Yes, but I didn't think much to it.'

'Why didn't you tell me?'

'I didn't tell you as she has her family here and I simply assumed, because Lex had told you they had broken up and he wasn't going to be seeing her anymore, that she had come back to stay here permanently. I really wasn't worried about her.'

'I don't know what's happened to make him change his mind. We were all set to go and...I don't know what I'm going to tell the children. Especially John, he dotes on his dad,' she said, shaking her head despairingly.

Tell us what, what is happening? What has he changed his mind about, John was in anguish as he continued to listen.

Gran stared into her daughter in law's face and saw her eyes moisten with emotion and her mouth tremble and said.

'If that's what he has decided then he is no longer a son of mine.'

'Well, you'll be able to tell him that yourself, because he said he is coming round to collect the papers that have arrived about the court case. He seemed more interested in them than he did about anything else.'

'Just as long as he doesn't bring that adulteress woman with him, she will never be allowed to set foot in this house,' Gran said, in an adamant tone.

'I don't think I want to see him. I don't think I can face him. What about the kids? Is he going to say anything to them, explain why he's deserting them for some other woman and leaving us here to fend for ourselves?' she said collapsing onto the bed and burying her head in her hands as the reality of what was happening was beginning to sink in.

John was fighting to control himself with his mind racing with all that he had heard,

Was it true what he was hearing, his dad was not taking them back to South Africa? Was that why his mum was angry? But, dad promised they were all going back.

He tried to reason, but his thoughts were interrupted as the bedroom door sprung open and his gran came out. She looked at

John hurriedly scrambling to his feet, realising he had been listening at the keyhole and a sadness began to fill her as she wondered what to say to him.

'How much did you hear?' she asked, fearful of the answer.

'That dad's not taking us back with him,' he said, his face contorting angrily as he fought back the tears.

Just then his mother came rushing out, her face awash with tears, makeup streaking down her cheeks. She bent down and gathered John and Alex up in her arms.

'Your dad has made some changes to the plans, and...' she began, feeling the pain in her own heart as she looked at them, knowing whatever she said, however she tried to put the words, what she had to tell them would cause terrible hurt.

'He's not taking us with him,' John cut in, before she had a chance to finish the sentence.

'No, he's not taking us back with him,' she sighed, heavily.

John suddenly broke free from her. 'I hate him. I hate him,' he screamed as he ran to the front door, flung it open and rushed out.

His mother went to chase after him, but gran grabbed her arm. 'Let him go, he'll be alright. He's hurting just like you.'

Gran had stood looking out of the front window for a long time before she spotted Lex's car drawing up outside the house and her face turned to anger as she watched him get out and go around to the passenger side, open the door to let a woman step out. 'My Goodness, he's brought that woman with him; well she's not coming in here that's for sure. I won't have her in the house,' she murmured to herself as she rushed out of the room and headed for the front door.

Jose, on hearing the movement, came out of the kitchen with John following behind her.

'Is that him? Has he arrived?' she asked, anxiously.

Gran turned back to look at her, her face stern.

'You stay back, let me deal with this,' she told her, before she opened the door. 'You can keep that adulteress away from this house. I will not allow her under my roof. So tell her to go and sit in the car,' his mother shouted at Lex, as he and the woman approached the house.

'She's coming in with me. I just want to collect the papers and I'll be gone,' he said, as he got closer to the front door.

John suddenly recognised the woman, as someone his dad had

taken him to meet while his mum was in England. He remembered going out to play with her son in a local park in Durban. She was wearing the same kind of clothes she had been wearing then. A flowery blouse with light tan, flared slacks and platform shoes. She was a bit stockier than his mum, with a chunky face, large rimmed glasses and light blonde mousey hair.

As John was reflecting on what the woman was doing there, his mother, the colour rising in her cheeks, a red flush of anger and humiliation spreading over her, suddenly charged forward to attack the woman, but his dad stuck his arm out across the doorway to prevent her getting any closer. As she tried to force her way past Lex, he pushed her back, rather forcibly so that she hit her spine on the side wall, as Alex sat on the floor and began to cry watching the scene unfold.

'You bastard, how dare you bring that trollop here?' she shouted at him as John came rushing forward screaming loudly.

'You leave my mum alone. You are a liar and I hate you,' but his mother held him back before he could get too close to his dad.

The word 'hate' stung Lex and he looked puzzled at John. He had never seen him behave like this before, had not expected this reaction towards him. He could see the hatred in his eyes as he looked at him.

'You see what you've done to him. I never believed you could be this heartless. You disgust me. Go on. Go off with your fancy woman. You deserve each other.'

Lex looked around as people from the neighbouring flats started coming out onto the stairwell to see what the noise was all about.

'Liz, I think you had better go and get back in the car, this is not turning out the way I thought it would,' he said, turning to her.

Gran angrily stepped forward and looked at the neighbours watching the drama unfolding in front of them. This provoked her anger all the more as the family reputation was something she cared about above all and here was her own son, showing her up right in front of them. She knew that they would all soon be gossiping about it to the other neighbours, but it was too late to worry about it now and decided to turn her scorn back on Lex.

'And how did you think it would turn out? Did you think we would all welcome her with open arms? That's your wife in there. The one you married in the sight of God and gave your vows to. Have you no shame that you dare to bring that…that' she said, struggling to get the words out as she watched the woman walking back to the car. '… that adulteress to my house? You stay there. I am not allowing you into the house either. I will get the papers and then you can go,' she said, shutting the door to prevent him from coming in.

Lex stood outside the door and looked back over his shoulder towards the car and gave a shrug, as if to say sorry, but there is nothing he could do about it. His mother opened the door.

'There you are, be on your way and never set foot here again. You're no longer my son. So be off with you,' she said, waving her free hand dismissively as she glanced around at the neighbours who were still intent on watching what was going on, then stepped back inside and slammed the door shut.

She gave an audible gasp of relief as she walked back into the living room where Jose was cradling little Alex in her arms. John was holding her hand and they were all standing looking out of the window with tears streaming down their faces, watching as Lex got back to the car. He opened the door, climbed in, leaned across and gave the woman a kiss on the cheek.

'It's strange how often men go for a woman completely opposite to their wives. I don't know what he's thinking of, you're so much prettier than she is,' gran reflected.

Jose sighed.

'Strange isn't it? I should have seen it coming. He's done this once before.'

Gran looked at her surprised.

'Done it before?' she repeated curiously.

'You remember Ronnie McGregor?'

'Of course, Lex and him grew up together, went to school together, they were inseparable and he even followed him out to South Africa with his wife Mary.'

'Yes, he was best man at our wedding and he used to tell me of some of the things they got up to as kids, you would have thought nothing could separate them, like I thought nothing could separate us, but that's when I first saw the callous side of Lex.'

'How do you mean?' gran asked, taken aback by the remark.

'Ronnie became a 'Born Again Christian' and I liked to listen to some of the things he had to say like, *Unless a man be born again, he cannot enter the kingdom of heaven* but Lex thought it was all a load of rubbish and didn't want anything to do with it.'

'Religion was never his strong point' gran sighed.

'The thing is, Lex became so dismissive of Ronnie that he cut him out of his life, the same way he has done with me. I remember Ronnie's parting words when Lex told him he never wanted to see him again. *Jesus will never desert me and never let me down and if you come to know him He will never let you down either,*' those words have always stuck with me.'

The following week, Jose and the boys headed back down to Birkenhead to see her father in hospital. Sadly Granddad Curtis died a few weeks later on the twentieth of April and the house was suddenly thrown into chaos with Gran Curtis almost losing the will to live after losing her husband. With his mother in tears at the loss of her father, John could only look on in anguish at his gran and mother seemingly crying all the time. A dreadful grief was welling up inside him as he reflected on the thoughts that he had already lost his dad and now his grandad.

Two months of turmoil passed and life seemed chaotic at times. John struggled to settle at school, he missed South Africa, his friends, the sunshine and his father most of all. Every day seemed to drag and there was so much crying going on that he determined to stay strong and never let his mum see him cry.

No more so, when he came home from school one evening to find his mother and Auntie Ruby in tears.

'What's happened?' he asked, upset to see her crying again.

'Your gran died today,' Auntie Ruby said, between sobs.

John stood there shaken by her words and it showed. He was learning to take every day as it came, but as he looked at his mother, he could see her face had darkened and there was such a look of sadness on her face that he felt an overwhelming urge to rush to her. He grabbed her hands and held them tight and looked into her face. 'I'm sorry mum,' he said sadly, not knowing what else to say.

After a while he felt some of the tension lifting from her as she raised her head and looked up at him, wiping away a tear.

'It's alright John darling. Your gran's at peace now with your granddad in heaven, so we have to be brave and carry on.'

Once again Lex came back into her life when she received a letter from her mother-in-law telling her all her belongings has been shipped over in a large trunk to her home in Glasgow.

Life comes down to a few important moments and Lex had unexpectedly started her on a new road. This was to be her important moment and she resolved there was to be no turning back, the only way for her now was forward.

'I've got some good news for you John darling. We are all going back to Scotland.'

'Why?' he asked, looking a little shocked and surprised at the sudden news.

'Because it's going to be better for us darling, we will be able to get our own place and we won't be so crowded. And dad has sent all our belongings to gran, so we have to go up there anyway,' she said, watching his face to see his reaction.

MOTH AND RUST CORRUPT

1977

In the block of flats where gran lived most of the old coal bunkers with big tall doors had been cleaned out and turned into sheds in which to store things. With nowhere else to put it, gran had the trunk stowed in there.

Jose gave a little shriek of horror and felt a stab of pain in her stomach when gran unlocked the shed, for it was the same green trunk that they had used to pack all their belongings when they had set sail for South Africa, and here it was back again with her belongings in it, as though her life had gone full circle, the end of an era.

Jose and gran dragged the trunk out of the shed and hauled it through to the flat with John and Alex helping to push it along the ground from behind. Once they had managed to get the trunk inside the flat, John paced around anxious to see what was inside. The trunk had two large heavy brass hinges each secured with a padlock. Fortunately, Lex had enclosed the keys to the padlocks in the letter he had sent to his mother. Her hands shaking in anticipation, Jose inserted the keys, unlocked the padlocks, lifted the hinges, slowly raised the lid and looked inside. Her eyes narrowed as she stared at the contents for everything was neatly folded.

'He didn't pack this,' she said, shivering inside as she carefully picked up one of her dresses. 'Only a woman would fold a dress like this and we know who that woman was,' she added, with a look of disgust. 'I want to throw all these clothes away and burn them. I can't bear the thought of that woman's hands having been all over my clothes, my underwear. It makes my skin crawl.'

'I know how you must feel. It makes my stomach turn, but you

49

need everything that's in there. They are yours, they belong to you,' gran said, her voice heavy with sadness.

Jose fell to her knees and began to delve deeper into the trunk and feel around for what else was in there.

'Look at these,' she said, her face brimming with anxiety, as she started to pull out the photo frames one after the other and spread them out on the floor. 'These are all the pictures we had, even our wedding pictures,' she said, her eyes brightening for the moment as she picked up one of the frames and her hands began to shake as she gazed at the photo.

It was one of the photos taken at their wedding. It showed her and Lex hugging each other. She was looking out from the picture with big seductive eyes under long lashes and there was an air of vitality and happiness in her smile. It made her think about him as she had known him. The happy times they had spent together. How being with him had felt so right, the way he stood, his hair, his smile, his spirit, his smell, how his skin felt firm under her touch. She held it for a moment longer and then let the frame slip from her hand and drop to the carpet not caring whether it smashed or not, her face riddled with bewilderment and disgust, tears already flooding her eyes as she said.

'I can imagine that horrible woman looking at all these photographs and saying I'm not having any of those here. How could he not want to keep some memories of our lives together?' she asked, looking up at gran. 'Did none of it mean anything to him? Has he no feelings left in him?'

Gran looked sympathetically down at Jose and could see the anguish in her tear-filled eyes and said.

'Most of the time you only ever see the good side of the person you love, but it's moments like this when you see the other side, the real side and we are both now seeing the real side of Lex. You are well rid of him, as I am. He has shamed you and in doing so has shamed me.'

She looked across at John who had picked up one of the picture frames with a photo of him and his dad, the dad he worshipped, dressed in his police uniform teaching him to shoot. As he stared at the photo his hands began to shake and he began to cry, the tears splashing onto the glass of the frame blurring the face of his father. John tried to wipe the tears away but it only succeeded in blurring more of his dad's image. His mother leaned across and could see the changing expression on his face. She looked down at the picture and the blurred image of Lex and it made her wonder was this another omen that she should blur him from her memory.

She reached back in the trunk, pulled out her jewellery box, placed it on the floor in front of her and opened it. She reached in and took out a few of the pieces and examined them.

'I suppose she had a good look at these too. Oh God how I hate that woman,' she cried out, as she let what she was holding slip out of her hands and fall back into the box.

She dug her hands back in the trunk feeling around wondering what else might be in there and felt something hard. She pulled the clothes away that were covering it. A soft smile touched her lips as took hold of it and lifted it out.

'Here John,' she said, holding it up for him to take. 'Remember this?'

John's eyes widened with excitement.

'McBoozer,' he exclaimed as he reached out to take it from her. He loved the musical decanter of an old Scotsman in a kilt that his Grandad Curtis had given him to travel to South Africa with.

Alex jumped up and down crying out excitedly. 'Can I wind it up please?'

'No, you can do that another time, we have to get ready to go to Auntie Betty's where we're going to be spending the night so that your gran can have some peace and quiet,' Jose told him, reluctantly closing the lid of the trunk.

Lurking in the shadows of the back garden two young men watched Jose and the boys leave before sneaking into the close and knocking on Gran's door.

'You two!,' Gran said, surprised on opening the door and seeing her two sons standing there before stepping aside to let them in.

George aged nineteen, the tallest of the four Lawson brothers, at six foot three, moved to the curtains of the front window, his heavy body looking cumbersome in the small confined space of the living room. He was stocky and muscular with a hard face that looked like he was ready to hurt someone, but his mass of curly hair helped to soften the harshness. He had acquired the nickname of Spot. Not because he had spots all over his face, but because he had freckles. George was a petty criminal and was constantly on the run from the police, not able to stay in one place for any length of time.

Dave was twenty one, shorter than George and much leaner with very bushy tight curly hair, but just as villainous and on the run, having escaped arrest one morning at their old house in Tresta Road by climbing naked out the back upstairs window and leaping over the fence into the graveyard as the police broke in the front door. Incredibly he somehow managed to avoid arrest by constantly staying on the move and keeping one step ahead of them.

'How's Jose taking it?' George asked his mother as she came into the room, without risking taking his eyes away from the window.

'Pretty badly, your brother just sent all her possessions back in the trunk with no letter, to say how sorry he was.'

'That's not right. I can't believe Lex behaved the way he has. If he comes back here, I'd like to get my hands on him and let him know how he's disgraced the family,' George said, with a quick glance to his mother before returning his gaze to the window.

She had seen that look on him before, and had learned what it meant to those who were unlucky to be on the receiving end of it.

'I don't think that's likely. I somehow don't think we will see him again. He has gone out of our lives forever and, I, for one am glad,' his mother said, with an air of finality.

George turned and looked at his mother surprised by her words. He was looking at her in a new light, and it showed on his face.

'He's still your son,' he said, his square jaw tightening.

'Not anymore, I disown him,' she said, fervently.

Dave stood up and nodded at his brother, signalling it was time to move on.

'Look, we'd better be off ma. We cannae hang around too long in case, you know...' he trailed off.

'Yes, I know, what do they want you for this time?'

'You don't need to know ma,' he said, dismissively.

'You're in enough trouble as it is and so is George; why can't you try to be more like your brother Alan? At least he is married and settled down. I don't want the pair of you getting into any more trouble than you already are. I'll tell Jose you asked about her,' she said, equally dismissively, not really wanting to know the grizzly details of her son's criminal activities.

'Tell her I'll come by again when I can to see how she is. Tell her not to sit there and let life happen to her. Tell her to go out and find a new life. She's worth more than he'll ever be,' Dave said, turning to hurry out.

Life at Auntie Betty's was good, at least John had his cousin Thomas to play with and Alex was pleased to have his younger cousins to keep him occupied. Cadder Primary was just around the corner and John was enrolled. His first day was to prove interesting as he had never been in a fight before. It was customary for the new boy to be confronted by the 'cock of the school' and John refused to back down. The obligatory fight in the playing field after school cemented him as 'one o the boys' and although no one officially won the fight, John felt he had proved himself. He headed home excited to tell his mum that he made a load of new friends but as he walked into the living room he saw his mum biting her nails and looking worried.

'What's the matter ma?' he asked, nervously.

His mum hesitated, thinking of what to say, how to break the news she knew would upset him.

'Something terrible has happened John,' Uncle Tommy cut in. 'you stay here with Thomas, we have to go to gran's.'

'Why, what's happened to her?' John asked anxiously.

'Gran's fine,' his mother said.

John looked around at all their faces wondering what the terrible thing was that had happened.

'We won't be long,' Uncle Tommy said, as he put on his coat ready to leave with Jose and Betty.

'I want to come with you,' John said, determinedly.

His mother gave a shrug as she looked at her brother in law.

He may as well come he'll only fret if we leave here, now we've told him.'

Gran was already standing by the shed when they got there. The door had been ripped open and was barely hanging on by the one remaining hinge. The lid of the trunk had been forced open and what was left of the contents was strewn all over the ground. Jose rushed to the trunk, fell to her knees and looked inside and her mouth gaped in horror.

'How can people be so heartless? Everything's gone, my clothes, my jewellery, the photos, the toys, everything. Why would somebody want to do this?' she sighed, as she struggled to her feet, her head started to spin and her legs went weak. Luckily Uncle Tommy was standing behind her and managed to catch her before she collapsed to the ground.

'Help me get her inside,' he said to Betty.

Betty took her other arm and they both half carried, half walked her inside.

'Right, don't anybody touch anything. I'm going to phone the police, we may be lucky, they could have left fingerprints,' Uncle Tommy said, once they had got Jose into the living room and settled her into one of the chairs.

'Yes, why don't you do that, while I make us a nice cup of tea,' Gran suggested.

'What have I done to deserve this? I've lost my husband, my dad, my mum and now this. I don't know how much more I can take. I have done nothing wrong and yet I'm being punished for it?' she cried out in anguish.

Gran looked at her with a reflective sadness and lowered her voice to give it an air of reverence as she said,

'The Bible tells us, "Do not lay up for yourselves treasures on earth where moth and rust destroy and where thieves break in and steal, but lay up for yourselves treasures in heaven where neither moth or rust can destroy and where thieves do not break in and steal for where your treasures are, so will your heart be also".'

Jose raised her head, the words seeming to begin to sooth her, lifting some of the guilt she was feeling.

'I know mum, but it's not only the treasures, it's my clothes. I've been walking round in the same clothes since I came back, and now it looks like I'm still going to be walking around in them, as well as John and Alex.'

'I've spoken to the police and they are sending someone round,' Tommy announced, as he came back into the room.

Dave was hiding in the shadows on the other side of the street watching the policeman get into the car and drive off. He waited until it had got to the end of the street and turned the corner before he crossed over the road.

'What was the polis doing here, were they looking for me?' he asked anxiously as soon as he got into the flat.

'No, they were not looking for you or George.'

'So what was that copper doing here, if he wasn't looking for me or George?'

'They found some of Jose's things that had been stolen.'

'Stolen!' Dave exclaimed, the word stolen jarring in his head. 'What's been going on? What the hell's been stolen? Nobody told me anything about it.'

'You remember your feckless brother sent the trunk over with all Jose's possessions. Well, someone broke into the shed, forced the lid off the trunk and took everything,' his mother explained. 'And the policeman you saw was returning what had been found dumped in the midden just a few streets away.'

An angry look began to spread across Dave's face.

'Nobody steals from this family, nobody. But I tell you something, George and I will find out who did it,' he said, his voice thick with anger.

His mother looked at him despairingly knowing what he was thinking.

'No, stay away from it David please, let the police do their job.'

'The polis willnae find out who did it, they're useless. They couldnae find a needle in a haystack if the needle was sticking up their arses.'

'Don't speak to me in that disgusting manner,' she admonished him.

'Dinnae worry ma, we'll get the scumbag that did this, just you wait and see. Nobody steals from the Lawson's,' he said, venomously.

'How are you going to do that Uncle Dave?' John suddenly piped up, having been listening to what was being said.

'Dinnae worry son, we have our ways. We'll get yours and your mother's things back, you wait and see,' Dave said, ruffling John's curly hair.

John didn't have to wait long. Within a couple of days he and his mum were at gran's going through the items the boys had recovered. Jose was pleased to see most of her good clothes and underwear, her winter coat and jewellery was there, as well as John and Alex's clothes.

'How did you get it?' John asked, excitedly looking up at his two uncles.

'I don't think it would help for him to know, and I certainly don't want to know,' he heard his Gran say.

'Let's just say with a little gentle persuasion,' George said, with a knowing smile.

'They were a couple of junkies and I tell you one thing they'll have a lot of trouble using their arms to make a spliff,' Dave said, with a casual arrogance.

John sat there, his eyes glazed looking at his two uncles with a glint of admiration listening intently to what they were saying.

'Yeah and the guy that bought the jewellery won't be fencing anything for a long time and we told him if he does any more fencing we'd nail him to the nearest one,' George said humorously, and it made John smile.

DRUMCHAPEL

1978

Jose walked nervously along the hallway to Betty's front door as she heard the letter box flap open as a brown, official looking, envelope dropped onto the carpet.

'Who's it for?' Betty called out from the kitchen.

'It's for me, it's from the council,' Jose called back.

'What does it say?' Betty asked coming out into the hallway.

Jose tore at the flap of the envelope and opened it. She took out the letter and her hands began to shake as she unfolded it, then her eyes brightened as she read the contents, forcing a smile as she read on.

'We've been allocated a two bedroom flat in Drumchapel,' she exclaimed, a mixture of joy and unease spreading across her face. Jose knew that Drumchapel had just been labelled the worst housing estate in Europe and her favourite comedian Billy Connolly called it *'A desert with windows,'* but at least it would be her own place.

Betty rushed forward and embraced her.

'When do they say you can move in?' she asked excitedly.

'It says, we can take possession immediately.'

'Fantastic, and as its Saturday tomorrow Tommy can drive you over to have a look at it,' Betty suggested.

'That would be lovely, it might be Drumchapel, but at least it will be a place of my own, I can't believe it! A bedroom for John and Alex, they'll be excited about that. I thought it would never happen,' Jose said, putting the letter to her lips and kissing it.

There was a buzz of excitement on Saturday morning as Uncle Tommy loaded them all in the car and set off for Drumchapel. John sat in the back with Alex while his mother sat up front with Uncle Tommy who was driving. John's eyes brightened up as they drove out of Glasgow to see the landscape opening up to large areas of open land with lots of trees and greenery. *'Maybe it's going to be a bit more like South Africa,'* John thought as he gazed out the window.

'This looks like fun I'm going to enjoy playing around in open spaces like that. Just like being back in Africa,' John said, looking happily around the area as they drove onwards pointing out landmarks to Alex.

Uncle Tommy said nothing. The fact that Uncle Tommy didn't say anything didn't worry John as his eyes were scanning the vast open spaces. It just felt so good to be getting away from the overcrowded, built up City. As they got closer to Drumchapel, John saw a massive structure on the top of a hill. From the distance it looked like a prison or maybe a fort.

'What's that up there?' he asked.

'That's Drumchapel. That's where we're heading,' Uncle Tommy said, speaking for the first time.

Doubt was beginning to tug at John's sleeve as they drove up the hill into Drumchapel. Suddenly everything was closing in on him as they passed building after building, all looking exactly the same. Tall square concrete boxes surrounded by more concrete pavements and roads. Uneven roads, with pot holes that tested the suspension to the limits as the car drove over them. If that wasn't enough the streets were littered with all kinds of rubbish, there was graffiti scribbled on almost every wall.

'This is it,' Uncle Tommy announced, as he pulled the car to a stop in Moneymusk Place.

John watched as his mother quickly got out and moved around to the front of the car to look up at the block of flats. He was so horrified at the situation that he felt unable to move. He didn't want to get out of the car, he just wanted the car to turn around and take them back to Glasgow. *Any place has to be better than this, even Glasgow,* he thought, as he sat glued to his seat not wanting to get out of the car.

'Come on John, we're going to go and have a look at the flat,' his mother said, opening the rear door for him to get out.

'It's horrible around here,' John said, sulkily getting out of the car and lifting Alex down onto the pavement.

'Look John, we got the chance of a place of our own and you and

Alex will have your own bedroom. Won't that be nice?'

John looked up at the pebble dashed concrete walls with square holes every so often for windows. Reluctantly he followed his mother and Uncle Tommy, with Alex lagging behind as they entered the block of flats.

'What number is it?' Uncle Tommy asked, as they stood in the concrete hallway, the plastered walls cracked and with pieces breaking away in places. Graffiti was everywhere, not only on the walls, but on the doors, the floor and even on the ceiling. There was an acrid smell of urine mixed with stale cigarette smoke and other smells that were difficult to define, pervading the area; it stung the nostrils.

Jose took the letter from her hand bag and checked the address.

'Number twenty eight,' she told him.

'What floor is it on?' he asked.

'Fourth, it says here,' she told him.

'Right let's go,' Uncle Tommy said, heading for the stairway.

'Isn't there a lift?' Jose asked, surprised he was walking to the stairway.

'No, there are no lifts in any of the buildings here, I'm afraid. They obviously never thought of putting them in,' he said, with a half smile.

Following one another they trundled up the four flights of concrete stairway, graffiti was on every wall. One name which seemed to be appearing more than any other was the name Monkey.

Arriving a little puffed at the front door of number 28, Jose took out the key, slipped it into the keyhole and apprehensively unlocked the door. As they walked in, there was an echo of their shoes on the bare floorboards. Jose gave a gasp as they stepped into the living room. It was completely bare except for a metal bucket by the fireplace. There was a strange smell of damp coal in the air. As Jose looked around the room she see could areas of dampness and mildew in the corners, and it made her shudder.

She quickly moved to look at the other rooms. First the kitchen, which had a few cupboards in reasonable condition fixed to the walls, a metal sink and draining top, but there was no cooker. The floor was covered with some well-worn linoleum. Both bedrooms, as the living room, were completely bare of any furnishings and had the same smell of dampness. Jose walked back into the living room with John following behind her. She was fighting to hold back the tears of desperation.

'I can't live here. This place is disgusting, it's filthy and there's damp everywhere,' she said to Tommy who had remained in the living room.

'Look Jose, I know it looks rough, but I'll help you clean the place up. You'd be surprised what a lick of paint can do. Johnny boy here will help me, won't you son?' John didn't answer, still traumatised, unable to take it all in.

'Look, you don't have to move in straight away and…'

'How can I move in straight away? There's no furniture, no beds and no cooker. How am I expected to find all that?' she asked, despairingly.

'We'll help you find all that. What we need to do first is get the place cleaned up. We'll re-paper the living room and the bedrooms, put some curtains up and then get a cooker and the other bits and pieces,' Tommy said, trying to sound as cheerful as he could.

To show how willing he was he walked over to the far wall and dug a finger into the wallpaper and was amazed when it came away easily in his hand. He was even more amazed when he looked at the damp paper to discover he was holding eight layers of paper.

'My God, they've just kept papering over the paper already on there. That will all have to come off, but by the look of it that won't be too difficult as it's almost falling off already,' he said, throwing the chunk of wallpaper on the floor.

'Look Jose, I promise you we'll make this place fit for a queen, you'll see,' he said, giving her an encouraging hug. 'Now let's get back to Cadder.'

Tommy was as good as his word and set about redecorating the flat. With John helping him, they stripped off all the wallpaper, amazed how easily it came off, revealing how damp the walls had become with no heating. There was a coal fire in the living room, but there was no coal in the grate or as it turned out, in the coal bunker either which was housed in the hall opposite the front door. The only way to help dry out the walls was to open all the windows and let the air circulate. As luck would have it with the windows open they heard the coalman calling out. Jose rushed down to see him.

'We have just moved into number 28. Could I have a bag of coal please?' she asked politely, trying to control the way she was shivering from the cold.

'Are you alright?' he asked, wondering why she was shivering so much.

'We've just moved in and the place is so damp we've had to open all the windows in the hope it will dry out,' she told him.

'Well, once you get the fire going, it'll soon warm up. How many bags do you want?'

'One bag please, that's all I can afford,' she said, with a slight look of embarrassment.

The coalman studied her for brief moment.

'You're gonnae need more than one bag to dry the place out if it's been left empty for a long time. So I tell what I'll do. You pay for one bag and I'll let you have another on credit since you seem a nice person, not like some of the people around here I could mention,' he said, his eyes shining brightly through his blackened face.

'Thank you, that is very kind of you, and I will make sure you are paid when you next come around. '

'Dinnae worry yourself, I'm sure you will. Right, top floor is it?' he asked lifting one of the bags onto his shoulder before climbing the stairs. He poured out the coal into the small bunker in the hallway before heading back down for the other one

'Right John darling, take that bucket and fill it up so that we can get a nice fire going.' his mother said, picking up the bucket and handing it to him. 'That is going to be your job, to fill the bucket every morning before you go to school and when you come home at night.'

Incredibly, the coal fire quickly dried out the rooms and within a few days Tommy was able to re-paper the walls of the living room and the two bedrooms. Once that was done, Tommy used his connections to find three single second hand beds and some bedding, a used cooker with some cooking utensils, some plates, cups, knives and forks. Tommy even managed to blag some curtains and some odd carpets to soften the effect of the bare floorboards.

With all that in place Jose was ready to move in and start a new life.

WHEN HELL FROZE OVER

1979

The winter of 1979 had really set in with a vengeance. It was freezing and there was snow and ice everywhere. The flat became so cold Jose was finding it hard to make ends meet with the extra demand for coal to try to keep the fire burning as well as trying to save some money for the coming Christmas.

Tommy and Betty could see the strain the family was under and how the boys were affected, John was hiding his feelings but Alex was wetting the bed and sleepwalking. They also discovered to their horror that Jose was actually going without food to pay for the coal and to buy her children presents, so they decided to invite her and the children to spend Christmas with them.

John and Alex were excited as it gave them a chance to play with their cousins. Alex was so happy he relaxed and didn't wet the bed at all. The beautiful house was warm and Uncle Tommy, being a baker, was always bringing home lots of lovely cakes and pies. Gran was just up the street too.

Christmas day was the best day ever as John and Alex woke up to be given their presents. John could not believe what his mother had bought him. It was a silver Chopper boy's bike, although second hand, it was still one of the best bikes on the market. Alex was equally excited as he had been given a Scalextric set, which John helped him put together and they and the rest of them spent a lot of the Christmas period racing each other.

The Chopper was John's pride and joy and he rode around on it whenever he got the chance, but like all good things they have to come to an end and before John and Alex realised it Christmas was over and it was time to go back to Drumchapel.

Jose woke up, stretched slowly, scrambled out of bed and ambled across to the window. She wearily pulled the curtains back and looked out. It had snowed heavily in the night and it had covered everything with a thick layer of pure whiteness. Jose sighed deeply, thinking this was the worse winter she could remember. She rubbed her arms as she started to shiver. She hated the cold, even more so since having got used to the moderate climates in Durban. It was so different there, she began to reflect. It would be the middle of summer right now. The sun would be shining and the temperature would be up around twenty eight centigrade and they would probably be sitting out somewhere basking in the sun, looking around at the landscape, the lush green pastures with the abundance of wildlife running freely. The memory brought a tear to her eyes as she continued to stare out at the blinding snow, thinking this was not going to be a good day to have to travel back to Drumchapel. They were going to have to take the bus because Tommy had to go to work at the bakery.

Jose stood at the bus stop in the freezing cold with the heavy suitcase, wriggling her toes in her shoes to keep them from going numb. John was holding tightly onto his Bike and Alex was clutching his big box with the Scalextric set packed in it.

Shortly the bus arrived and Jose mused how uncanny it was that the spirit of Christmas had so quickly evaporated as the bus driver shouted at John.

'Eh, you cannae bring that thing on the bus.'

Jose stared at him in consternation. It was getting colder and they were already freezing. It was a hard silent stare with bleak cold eyes, for she was determined they were going to get on the bus whether he liked or not. She pushed John and the bike forward onto the bus.

'We have been standing here freezing waiting for you and if you think I am going to let my children stand here and freeze for another half hour then you have another thought coming. What do you expect him to do, cycle all the way to Drumchapel? So please show some consideration for other people, thank you,' she said, forcing herself and Alex onto the bus. The driver accepted he was not going to win the argument gave a shrug and allowed them to squeeze in the aisle.

'And a happy New Year to you,' she said, with a heavy sarcasm, as he closed the door and drove off.

The Great Western Road was reasonably clear, but once they drove into Drumchapel and stepped off the bus it was a different scene altogether. The streets and pavements were covered in snow and ice and an artic wind was furiously pounding against the tall buildings. A mass of frozen air was being relentlessly propelled around the gaps between the blocks, splattering particles of ice against the buildings, as the wind whirled and twisted against them.

The cold was seeping into their bones and their faces were beginning to sting as they looked up the hill, realising it was going to be a treacherous climb up to Moneymusk Place. It was, with all of them slipping and sliding on the ice. Jose laddering her stockings and grazing her knee in the process and young Alex having to hang onto John to stop himself sliding.

As they stood at the top of the hill, catching their breath, the freezing air tearing at their lungs, they looked up in bewilderment at the tenement block. It was covered with icicles dripping from every window, from the doorways and from the roof. As they continued to stare up in astonishment they could see that all the windows were boarded up except theirs. Jose felt the hot damp flush of panic and felt her strength drain away.

'What the devil is all this. What the hell has been going on?' she said, hurrying towards the close, but the steps up to the entrance were completely frozen over, almost turning them into a slide and making it impossible to climb up them. The only thing to do was to chip at the ice to get a footing on each step and pull each other up. Reluctantly John chained his beloved chopper to the lamp post with his new combination lock. Being the fittest and strongest he chipped away at the ice with a piece of broken pipe he found amongst the litter strewn around and went to work. Having succeeded in chipping out some steps he scrambled up and then helped pull his mum up and then Alex.

Once inside the block the situation was no better. There was ice everywhere with icicles hanging from the ceiling, giving it an eerie cave like feel. All the neighbours' doors were boarded up. The stairwell and the steps were covered in ice as though water had rushed down them and frozen in an instant to create the perfect slide.

'There's no way we are going to get your bike up those stairs,' his mum sighed. She was worried that someone might steal the case and the bike if it was left there too long.

As they eventually got to the front door of their flat Jose shrieked out in horror as she could see ice protruding from underneath the door. She nervously put the key into the lock, but it wouldn't turn no matter how hard she tried. She then took out her cigarette lighter and used it to heat the key. Once she felt it was really hot she inserted it and tried to turn it, but it still wouldn't budge. It took several attempts at heating the key before it melted the ice enough to free the lock.

Jose pushed at the door, but it was frozen to the frame and it took all three of them all their strength to heave at the door with their shoulders before it started to give way. The ice cracked and there was just enough room for them to squeeze in through the narrow gap. As they stepped over the ice into the living room, a blanket of sadness fell over her as it became clear why the door wouldn't open completely. The lounge was just like a skating rink, the floor completely covered in several inches of ice. She listened to the echoing silence of the flat all around her. It was as though they had just walked into an igloo. She felt her eyes fill with tears. She tried to stop them, but she couldn't. She stood there looking around. All the furniture was covered in ice. The walls and fittings were also covered in a layer of ice. She looked up at the ceiling and there was a big gaping hole just like she had seen in pictures of igloos.

She carefully made her way to the other rooms and saw that they were in exactly the same dreadful state. The beds covered in ice, icicles dripping from the wardrobe. The curtains were frozen, as though they had been caught in a breeze and then time had stood still. The kitchen too looked as though it had been frozen in time. There was no electricity as all the fuses had blown. The eerie silence seemed to go on forever as all three of them stood staring at the devastation as though hypnotised by it.

'We've only been away a week, how could this have happened?' she wondered out loud.

But before she could begin to answer her own question there was a heavy banging on the door.

'My God, it looks like hell's frozen over,' the man gasped, as he squeezed himself through the half open door. Jose spun round at the sound of his voice, but there was no welcoming smile on her face. Instead she glared at him as she asked.

'What the blazes happened here?'

'That is exactly what I've come to ask you,' the man retorted, as he carefully edged his way further into the room.

'Come to ask me? How the blazes would I know? We've only just arrived back. We've all been away for the last week,' she said, her face pale and anxious

'That's why we hadn't boarded your door up like the others,' the man explained.

'Who are you anyway?' she asked, contemptuously.

'I'm from the council. We think it is because you were away with no heating it caused the pipes to freeze and burst with all the water flooding into your flat,' he said, with a hint of accusation.

'You mean to say, all this is my fault because we went away for a week?' she said, outraged.

'Well, if the flat had been heated…,' he said hesitantly. 'I mean we have been experiencing unusually extreme cold weather. The temperature has been well below zero, sometimes as much as twelve degrees below. So perhaps if there had been heating, then maybe…'

'Do you really think one miserable coal fire would have made any difference?' Jose snapped, interrupting him, her eyes coming up and fixing sharply on his face, before pointing angrily up at the ceiling. 'Does that look like burst pipes to you? That looks to me more like a burst tank and knowing the way the council don't give a damn and never have about the state of these flats I would imagine the tank and the pipes were never lagged. So we have a bit of bad weather and this is the result. And before you get all official and try to blame me for the council's shortfalls,' she said her anger rising. 'I would like to know what you intend to do about re-housing us. You don't surely expect us to stay here? Or do you?'

The council man was taken aback by her sudden outburst.

'No, of course not,' he hastened to assure her. 'Everyone from this block has been relocated to temporary accommodation in Summerhill and naturally we have made the same provision for you and your family,' he said, hoping that would pacify her.

'And what about furniture, all of this is totally ruined?' she said, with a sweeping gesture of her hand. 'Even our clothes are ruined.'

'There is some basic furniture there, but we will supply you with anything you need once you're settled in,' the council man explained, forcing a smile to his lips.

Ironically, the area they were moved to was called Summerhill and the flat was identical in every respect to the one they had vacated, with the exception that it was situated on the ground floor. The block of flats inside and out was covered with the usual graffiti and litter was strewn all over the place. It mystified Jose that nobody seemed to care about the state of the area or seemingly wanted to take pride in where they lived. It reminded her of the old adage that says, slums are not built but created by the people who live in them.

The move meant John and Alex had to change schools and John enrolled at Summerhill Secondary School, which meant mixing with a new group of kids who had the bullies just like the other school, all wanting to prove they were tougher than anyone else. This resulted in many of them, to their regret, discovering he was not only a lot tougher than they were, but he was also a Lawson.

Jose was using all her strength to keep strong for John and Alex but she was realising that things had to change. She applied for accommodation with one of the housing associations in Birkenhead, determined one way or another to get out of Drumchapel.

To her delight after a few worrying weeks a large envelope finally dropped through the letterbox. She hastily tore it open and her eyes brightened as she read the contents. The letter was from the Methodist Housing Association informing her she had been allocated a two bedroom house in Birkenhead with immediate occupation, requiring a decision by return as to whether she would like to accept the offer. She didn't need to think twice. As bad as Birkenhead was, she felt it would be a damn sight better than Drumchapel. In fact any place at that moment had to be a damn sight better than Drumchapel.

BREAKING AND ENTERING

1980

Number 29, Hilbre Street was just off Corporation Road in the Dock area of Birkenhead. It was a small, two-up and two-down house, with the front door opening from the street straight into the living room. There was a kitchen-come-dining room at the back, with stairs to a small landing, from which two bedrooms led off. The housing association had built an extension at the back of the house and installed a bathroom and toilet with a gas boiler to heat the water, and an adjoining utility room for laundry. The back yard was concreted over and surrounded with a high brick wall.

The house next door was derelict.

Jose had brought what furniture they had managed to salvage from the winter disaster; a settee, the beds, some carpets and the cooker as well as cooking utensils, plates, and cutlery. Gradually things settled into a daily routine with Jose getting a job in the local Bingo hall to earn a little extra money to supplement the meagre benefits, soon she was able to buy curtains and other necessities to make a home she could live in and be proud of.

John, with his Chopper bike was able to cycle over to meet up with his old friend Flemmo, at least until his bike was stolen. This upset John more than anything. He unfortunately had made the error of thinking they were in a safer and more respectable neighbourhood than Drumchapel. With the high wall surrounding the backyard he didn't feel it was necessary to chain his bike up at night. It was his first awakening to what the area was really like.

John now had to walk the five miles to meet up with Flemmo, who, like him had also become interested in Bruce Lee and Kung Fu fighting and had bought many books on the subject. John was really interested in martial arts and borrowed as many books as he could from Flemmo and avidly studied them. Fascinated by the nunchakas that Bruce Lee made famous in the movie *Enter the Dragon*, he made his own by taking the broom handle and sawing off two lengths. He then went next door to the old derelict outhouse, broke off the metal chain from the cistern and fixed it to the sticks. Now he had his own nunchaka he could practice and practice the moves until he got them right without hurting himself.

His mother, of course, was furious when she got home and found the broom with a much shorter handle. John determined he would steal a new broom handle from the local hardware store as soon as he got the chance.

Jose had got to know Linda Smart, one of the neighbours that lived three doors away. Linda was one of the so called matriarchs of the area, where you went if you needed anything, like a telly, curtains, carpets, clothes; in fact almost anything. Shop lifting was on the increase and most of it mysteriously found its way to Linda.

Linda had a sister Rita, was known as Nellie, a brother Michael, known as Midgee and Phil, who some reason didn't have a nickname. Phil was gingered haired and rather skinny, always in and out of Borstal for thieving and other misdemeanours. He had only recently come out of Borstal and while kicking a ball around with John outside the houses Phil suddenly said to him.

'You see that factory over there?'

'You mean the tea factory?' John asked, curiously as it was across the other side of the road.

'No you divvie, look over the top of it to the roof over there.'

John rose up on his toes and craned his neck to be able to see the roof on the other side of the tea factory.

'Yes I can see it, what about it?'

'It's a car repair garage and it's loaded with tools – and it's got a safe as well and I'm thinking of doing it over. Do you want in on it?' Phil asked, holding his gaze steadily.

John thought hard for a moment thinking what he could do with the money. He'd had his beloved Chopper stolen and wanted to get another one, and he also wanted to buy more books on Kung Fu as well as get some more training gear to wear.

'Yeah, I'm game. I'll have a go,' he said, cheerfully.

'Good we'll do it this Sunday afternoon when the place is shut and there's no one around.'

On the Sunday afternoon John met up with Phil, who was carrying a good length of rope, a strip of metal and some holdall bags, but he was surprised to see David Robinson, one of the other local boys, that he didn't like, standing alongside Phil.

'What's he doing here?' John asked, in an irritant tone.

'We need the three of us on this job, so no messing, just let's get on with it and earn ourselves some dosh,' Phil said, moving off across the road.

They climbed over the concrete fence of the tea factory then scrambled up onto the fence the other side. Phil tied the rope to the concrete post before he leapt across onto the roof of the garage. John and Dave followed and they all moved across the roof to the skylight. Phil used the strip of metal to lever the skylight open, lowered the rope down through the opening and they all climbed down. Fortunately the garage had a mezzanine containing the offices some twenty feet above the ground floor, so they only had about eight feet to drop. Phil looked over the balcony and said.

'You two get down there and grab as many tools as you can. Look for the expensive ones and don't waste time with the crap, while I see what I can find here. Okay?'

Dave and John had to be careful, adjusting their eyes to the dark as they made their way down the steps to the ground floor. There was an abundance of tools for them to choose; power tools, grinders, spray guns and expensive sets of spanners. They quickly grabbed as many of the power tools as they could and carried them back up to the mezzanine. Having got used to the dark they went down again and gathered some of the grinders and sets of spanners. Dave then climbed back up the rope onto the roof as John bundled as many tools as he could into the holdall and tied it to the rope so that Dave could haul it up. Just then they heard Phil say excitedly.

'I've found the safe. I want to see if we can haul it up.' But what he didn't know was that the safe had a pressure mat and as he stepped close to it, it triggered the alarm.

'Crap! Let's get the hell out of here,' Phil exclaimed, beginning to panic, urging John to clamber up the rope. Once they were back on the roof they hauled the rope up and grabbed the holdalls. Back in their own street they took the bounty to the derelict house and hid it in the upstairs backroom. John was surprised to see beer bottles, cans and pages of porn magazines as well as human excrement littering the floors. It made John wonder what kind of people were using the place.

'We'll leave it here for a few days, just in case the bizzies come looking around, then we'll sell the stuff,' Phil said.

'What's the bizzies?' John asked, not having heard the expression before.

'The police, the pigs,' Phil explained.

John began to feel guilty about what he'd just done, wondering what his mother would say if the police came around and she found out. He hated lying to his mother, particularly as she was working hard at the Bingo hall even on a Sunday. Also he knew she didn't like the idea of him mixing with Phil, knowing the things he'd been up to.

In the back of his mind John always remembered what Uncle George had told him when they were sitting by the canal in Cadder. Don't ever tell your mum what you're up to. Don't cause her any aggravation. She's been through enough as it is. Always tell her everything's okay, just stay under the radar.

John had learned some time ago that some things were worth being afraid of, and some things were not. The things he had done before had never made him this fearful and he continued to fear for several days that there was going to be a knock at the door and a policeman would be standing there wanting to question him about the break in.

Phil eased his worries a few days later when he told him it was now time to move the stuff and he'd already got some buyers. The three of them went to the derelict house, careful not to tread into any of the mess as they gathered up the holdalls and set off to sell the goods. Phil was as good as his word and he managed to sell the lot for one hundred and twenty pounds.

'Here's twenty quid each,' Phil said, handing them each the money.

'I thought it was going to be a three way split,' John protested, expecting a lot more from the proceeds.

'No, you've got a lot to learn kid. I'm the boss and it was my idea. I planned it all and you get what you're given,' Phil told him, in no uncertain terms.

John gave him a half smile of acquiescence, at least he'd got twenty quid, which was more than he'd ever earned from any other caper.

Now he could buy his own Kung Fu books and take the bus to Flemmo instead of the long five mile walk.

Maybe life in Birkenhead was not going to be so bad after all he began to think as he made his way back home with the twenty pounds in his pocket. His face broke into a broad smile thinking he could even buy that second hand stereo record player for his mother that he'd had his eye on for a long time. It made him feel good he could do something to please his mother. Yes he felt he could be happy in Birkenhead, he told himself as he quickened his step.

THE NEIGHBOUR FROM HELL

1981

Winter was coming to an end. Spring was approaching. The trees were beginning to bud, the birds were slowly returning, the daffodils were starting to flower, the heavy dark clouds were lifting and the skies were becoming brighter. It made everybody begin to feel happier and there seemed to be a new found energy as people had a purposeful spring in their step.

It was a quiet Saturday evening. Jose was working at the Bingo hall and John and Alex were at home playing the tennis game on John's latest Sinclair ZX 81 Spectrum computer he'd been given for Christmas. They were enjoying themselves and the two of them were becoming very good at the game. Alex was improving all the time and the games were getting harder with John having to fight for every point. The only noise in the house was the boys cheering when they won a point.

Out of the blue they heard a heavy banging on the front door. Alex looked up nervously at John as the banging became more frantic.

'Don't open it. It could be that nasty man again,' Alex said, and John could see the fear in his eyes.

'Please let us in. Please hurry!!' the voice called out from the other side of the door.

'That sounds like Mary Holloran,' John said, leaping up from the table, rushing to the door and quickly opening it.

Mary and her four children rushed in exactly as they had done on Boxing Day when Peter, her husband had smashed up their house in one of his drunken states.

'Close the door, close the door, the bastard's out there. He's been on another bender,' she screamed, ushering the children into the safety of the room.

John just managed to slam the front door shut as Peter reached it and started banging his fists as hard as he could while shouting out.

'Come out you bitch, else I'm going to break this bloody door down.'

Peter continued to hammer away with his fists and then raised his foot and violently kicked out at the door making it shake in its frame.

'Get in the back room,' John said to everyone as he realised any moment the front door could give in with the incredible force Peter was using.

As soon as everybody got into the back room, John shut the door and got the others to help move the kitchen table up against it. Peter was in such a rage that it didn't take him long to kick the front door in. Once inside he charged at the dining room door with his shoulder, but the door held with the table wedged against it.

'This door won't stop me,' he yelled out. 'Get my wife and kids out here NOW and tell that Scottish tart I'll get her as well, so open the door NOW!!!' he screamed, starting to look around for something to break the door down with. He picked up the nearest chair and smashed it against the door, but it was a frail second hand one and it shattered into pieces after a couple of heavy blows.

He tossed the back of the broken chair he was holding across the room and began to pound on the door with his fists. The interior doors were not as solid as the main door and he was starting to punch holes in it. This was making the two youngest children Katie and Michael scream and Alex was beginning to shake in fear. Peter junior and his eldest sister Mary were frantically trying to drag the twin tub washing machine from the laundry room to support the table. Mary, already suffering a black eye, was now becoming hysterical as Peter smashed a hole through the door with his fist, trying to grab at anything.

'We've got to do something, or he's going to break this door down,' Mary said, screaming with terror.

John looked around looking for a weapon. If only he had his nunchakus he could really do something with them but they were up in his bedroom. He looked around anxiously for something else he could use. He was running out of time as Peter smashed another larger hole in the door and thrust his hand in to feel for the lock or whatever he thought was still holding it closed.

Just then John spotted the screwdriver he had been using to fix a mirror for his mother. Picking it up he rushed over and stabbed it into the back of Peter's groping hand. He heard him scream in pain and quickly withdrew his hand, but it only seemed to make him angrier as he thrust his fist in again. John stabbed the hand again as hard as he could and saw the point of the screwdriver penetrate into the flesh on the back of Peter's hand. The scream was much louder this time and there was a splash of blood on the door as Peter pulled his hand out.

'You Scottish tart, I'm going to make you pay for this, you just wait and see,' Peter screamed at the top of his voice thinking it was Jose who had stabbed his hand.

Hearing him calling his mother a *Scottish tart* sent a shock wave through John and his temper rose, the fear dropping away from him.

'No one calls my mother a Scottish tart,' he raged, as he started to drag the table away from the door, finding incredible strength from the adrenaline that was building up in him. He flung the door open expecting Peter to be standing there but he had gone. John rushed out into the street and saw him stumbling off holding his injured hand.

'Hey you bastard, I'm going to kill you,' John yelled at him, his face distorted in rage. Peter turned and looked at John rushing at him still thrusting the screwdriver out in front of him. He managed to knock it out of John's hand and grinned at him.

'You stupid little dickhead, you think a scrawny teenager like you can hurt me? You go back and tell that stupid tart you've got as a mother I'm going to get her. No woman messes with me, especially a jock tart like her,' he said, with a contemptuous scowl on his face.

John could feel his heart beating hard in his chest at the words. His jaw tightened as he gritted his teeth, his cheeks flaring an angry red as he felt another bolt of adrenaline shooting through him. Instinctively he turned sideways and lashed out with a powerful side kick which caught Peter completely by surprise and sent him sprawling backwards, landing heavily on the hard surface of the pavement. He lay there dazed looking up at John trying to work out in his alcohol fused brain what had just happened. He was a strong man and he managed to get to his feet without much difficulty and swung a vicious punch at John which, had it connected, would almost certainly have taken his head off.

But John was too quick for him and dropped beneath the punch, spinning around and delivering a perfect leg sweep taking Peter's feet from right under him. Peter was back on the ground staring up at John, his face crumpling in pain, bewilderment and fear as he sobered up fast trying to work out what his next move should be. But the decision was made for him as he heard the distant sounds of a police siren approaching. John watched as Peter scrambled to his feet and ran off in the opposite direction of the imminent arrival of the cops.

As John waited for the police to arrive, he bent down and picked up the screwdriver. It still had blood on it and there were splashes of blood on his shirt.

'Drop that weapon,' the police officer shouted as soon as he got out of the car.

John looked at him surprised, still clutching the screwdriver.

'I said, drop the weapon,' the police officer repeated.

'Look you don't understand. You should be going after...' John started to explain.

'I won't ask you again,' the police officer persisted, reaching for his truncheon.

John did as he was told and let the screwdriver drop to the ground.

'Now what have you been up to lad?' the police officer asked, in a not too friendly manner.

'Me? It's that bastard Peter Holloran who's just run off you should be after,' John said, angrily.

'There's no need for that language lad. Just tell me what you were doing with that screwdriver?' the police officer said, already convincing himself John was the trouble maker in all this.

'Defending myself, from the drunken bastard that ran off,' John retorted, unsure of the implications.

'I told you once to watch your language, else you'll find yourself in trouble lad,' the police officer warned him.

'In trouble, have you any idea what we've been through? If you lot had turned up when he kicked off on Boxing Day and smashed their house up then maybe none of this would have happened,' John said, and there was a firmness of anger and a sense of injustice in his voice.

Just then Mary came out of the house followed by the children.

'Aren't you going after him?' she asked the police officer.

'After who Madam?' he asked, brusquely.

'My husband, the cause of all this,' she said, indicating the broken front door.'

'That's what I tried to tell him, but he didn't take any notice. More interested in what I was doing with a screwdriver,' John said, resentment brimming in his voice.

Ignoring John, the police officer turned his attention to Mary.

'Perhaps you will be good enough to tell me what happened?' he said, gratuitously.

'My husband came home in one of his violent drunken rages, punched me in the face and shoved little Peter hard against the wall. I knew I had to get myself and the children out of the house and away from him before he attacked us again. I rushed to my friend's house with the children for protection, but as you can see he's kicked the front door in and done some damage to the door inside and if it hadn't been for the bravery of this young man I don't know what would have happened to us. So I suggest you leave him alone and go and look for my husband; lock him up and throw away the key,' she said, with as much venom as she could muster.

'Difficult to catch him now, he could have gone anywhere,' the police officer said, with little enthusiasm.

'Why don't you try the Piggy, in Victoria Street, he's probably there getting pissed again,' John told him.

The policeman looked at John irritated.

'What's the piggy?' he asked.

'Everybody knows, it's the bloody Victoria Vaults, except you lot of course.'

'I told you to watch your language, lad,' the officer admonished him as he turned his attention back to Mary. 'So the man's your husband?'

'Yes, unfortunately.'

'Then this looks like a domestic, so there is not a lot I can do about. I'll take a few notes and…'

'Domestic, what are you talking about? That bastard kicked our front door in for starters,' John said, his voice rising in anger and disbelief and what the officer was saying.

'If I hear another word out of you, I shall put you in the car and take you down to the station. So keep your mouth shut,' the police officer said curtly, as he turned and walked over to the door, took out the note book and pencil from his breast pocket and started to make notes.

'Right, I shall report this matter and I advise you to ring the council or housing association and have them secure the property,' he said, replacing the note book and pen to his breast pocket.

'So that's it, you're going to let him get away with it?' John asked, ominously.

The police officer's face flushed indignantly as he stared at John.

'You've got a big mouth for a young lad and I advise you to keep it shut and as for you Mrs Holloran, I suggest you take out an injunction against your husband,' the police officer said caustically, as he walked off to his car, got in and drove off.

Police, what good are they, bloody useless, a waste of time. Like my uncles said, don't trust the police. If you want anything done, then do it yourself. I really wish they were here now, he thought as he watched the police car drive off.

Walking home from the Bingo Hall that night Jose reflected that whilst she had still not managed to get over Lex walking out on her and the children, she had managed to create a life of sorts for John and Alex and felt content that she had brought a sense of normality back into their lives. She was determined that whatever the circumstances she would make sure the children would be loved and cared for despite not having a father. It made her feel good and she quickened her step, anxious to see her boys.

But her steps came to an abrupt stop as she turned the corner into Hilbre Street and saw the state of the front door. A dreadful grief welled up inside her. She could feel the colour rising in her cheeks, a red flush of anxiety and anger. Her thoughts began to race as she rushed to the house, pushed at the damaged door which swung open freely. As it opened, it creaked and leaned at an odd angle, the top hinge having been wrenched from the door frame. On hearing the noise, John charged out of the back room holding the screwdriver and was relieved to see his mum as Mary pushed past him.

'Thank goodness you weren't here, Jose, Peter tried to kill us. He'd gone berserk, smashed the front door in and would have got to us in the back room if it hadn't been for John here,' Mary said, stepping towards to Jose.

Jose let Mary embrace her, keeping her arms limp at her side, her eyes checking the room, still unable to take it all in. The house that she had so lovingly worked hard to make into a home was now a wreck. Her head was spinning and she was beginning to tremble. Mary could feel her body trembling.

'We'll help get the place straightened,' Mary said, but she knew as she said it, the words were empty as it was going to take a bit more than straightening up.

'You should have seen our John 'Kung Fu' that Peter up the street ma, it was wicked' Alex piped up in awe of what his brother had done.

Jose looked at John.

'And what were you going to with that, try and kill someone?' she demanded, pointing at the screwdriver he was still holding in his hand.

'Yes, if it was him again,' John retorted, his eyes blazing defiantly.

'And what good do you think that would do? Isn't there enough trouble without my son going around wanting to kill someone with a screwdriver?' she said, angrily.

'He deserves to die for what that bastard did and....'

'Don't you dare swear or I'll wash your mouth out with carbolic soap,' she screamed at him, her voice quivering in anger.

John began to feel a sense of injustice at the harshness of his mother's words and it showed on his face as he dropped the screwdriver to the floor. She looked at him in silence, this was someone she loved, someone she cared for and was now lashing out at him as though it was his fault all this had happened.

'I'm sorry John darling. It's all too much of a shock to come home to all this,' she said, collapsing down into the nearest chair.

'I'll make you a nice cup of tea,' Mary offered, going off to the kitchen.

Jose looked up and smiled a thank you, the harsh edge of strain beginning to show on her face.

'And I thought we would have a safer and happier life here, but it's no different from any of the other places. I don't know how much more I can take of this. Just look at the place after all my hard work. It's just not fair,' she said, shaking her head in despair.

'We'll be alright mum, we'll soon get this house cleaned up, you'll see,' John said, as he knelt by her taking hold of her hands. His mother looked into his eyes, a little of the tension eased as she said.

'You're a good boy John, and I'm sorry I shouted at you.'

John smiled back.

'It's alright ma. It's Mary and her children we have to worry about.'

He said it with such a quiet conviction that she suddenly felt proud of him.

'Yes, you're right, she must be feeling awful.'

Just then Mary came back into the living room with a cup of tea.

'Here you are Jose, have a drink of this and you'll feel better.'

It always amazed John how people seemed to think that a simple cup of tea was the cure for everything.

'Have the police been called?' she asked after taking a sip of the tea.

'Yes, but I didn't get a chance to phone them until after John had chased him off,' Mary explained.

'So what happened when they arrived?'

'As soon as I mentioned Peter's name it was just another domestic as far as they were concerned, so they weren't really going to do anything about it,' John said, with a scoff.

'Have you phoned the housing association,' Jose asked, her nerves steadying, beginning to think about the practical things that would need doing.

'No, I thought they wouldn't believe me if I rang them.'

'In that case perhaps I'd better do it,' Jose offered, finishing her tea. 'They have a number for emergencies somewhere on the file,' she added getting to her feet.

THE NORTH END

1982–1986

Jose hurried home from work, bristling with excitement, feeling happier than she'd ever felt for a long time unable to contain herself with the news she had just been given. Mike Jeffries, the general manager for the Bingo company where Jose worked, had told her he was moving and as a consequence the house he was renting in Thorneycroft Street was available and he would happily recommend her as a tenant if she was interested.

Number 1, Thorneycroft Street was a much larger house with a large living room that had a bay window, a dining room, and a separate kitchen in the extension. Upstairs it had three bedrooms, a large one at the front, a good sized one at the back and a smaller box room, together with an upstairs bathroom.

After the move, life quickly settled down again and continued as normal until John learned his Uncle Dave had been involved in a motor cycle accident, had suffered serious brain damage and was in a coma. John wanted to rush to London to go and see his uncle, but neither he nor his mother had the money to pay for the fare. Lack of money was something that was to harden his attitude, particularly now that he had finished his sixth form at school. He'd obtained a City and Guilds in Technical Engineering and it was time to go out and start looking for a job.

In his last two years at school John had at least made one good friend in Jamie Lowe, who joined the school in the fourth year after his dad had tragically committed suicide a few months earlier. John noticed how introverted he was, tending to keep himself to himself, appearing not to want to mix with the other lads; a situation John had learned from experience always attracted the bullies. It hadn't been long before they started on Jamie, calling him 'ballhead' and other nasty names. John had become increasingly concerned about the continuing bullying of Jamie and his unwillingness to challenge them, especially as Jamie was a talented amateur boxer, so he had decided he should intervene on his behalf and it cemented their friendship.

Job hunting was tough going. Even with his City and Guilds, he failed to find a decent job in an area where the odds seemed to be constantly stacked against him. He was at the mercy of mass unemployment, and hated having to go to the dole office and be looked down upon as though he was an idle scrounger, by people who thought they were cleverer than him, more successful and stronger than him. The only good news was that Uncle Dave had come out of his coma and regained consciousness, but was suffering badly from memory loss.

Eventually John managed to get himself a job as a bartender in the St James's night club, nicknamed 'The Jimmy's.' It was a rough kind of club owned by the Demetrious family and was situated down by the ferry terminal. There was always trouble there and they needed the services of heavy bouncers to keep order and remove the trouble makers.

John's baptism of fire was to come sooner than he expected, not that he was expecting to be on the receiving end of trouble because he was just a barman and the bouncers were there to take care of that. But on one particular night he had been assigned to what was called the VIP bar where a few of the better off preferred to sit quietly and drink. It was early evening and he was on his own with only one customer, who had slumped into a chair having had far too much to drink, and seemed to be asleep. John feeling a little concerned for him came around from the bar and gently shook him awake as he quietly said.

'Mate you can't go to sleep here, would you like me to call you a...'

John didn't get a chance to finish the sentence as the man sprang to his feet and tried to head butt him. Luckily John saw it coming and managed to raise his arm and catch the man on the cheek with his elbow, enough to send him flying over onto his back. To John's amazement the man sprang to his feet and came charging at him again. John swiftly sidestepped sending the man crashing over a low table and delivered a side kick hard in the chest. But the man just got back up on his feet and glared at John, blood starting to run down the side of his face where it had been cut by the sharp edge of the table.

The man grinned as he came at John again managing to grab him by the arms. A silly mistake to do to someone who knows Martial Arts because it gave John the perfect opportunity to force the man's arms wide open, exposing the whole of his body as an easy target. John then kneed him hard in the groin causing the man to buckle up and with the man's head lowered, elbowed him hard on the side of the temple which should have laid him out for good. Extraordinarily the man got back on his feet and said in a venomous tone.

'Is that all you've got mate?'

John stood poised, staring at the man, amazed he was not only still standing but somehow had an incredible ability to absorb such punishment and still want to fight.

'I'm going to kill you,' the man screamed, as he charged at John.

John neatly stepped back and delivered a perfectly timed roundhouse kick to the man's head, telescoping him to the floor with a heavy thud. At that moment the bouncers, who had been alerted and came rushing in, leapt on the man and held him down until they could get a firm grip on him. The man was struggling violently and screaming, more like an animal than a human.

'I'm going to get all you bastards, and kill the lot of ya.'

It took the combined efforts of three bouncers to control the man as they wrestled him to his feet. John followed as they managed to drag him bodily out of the bar. As they got to the main door, one of the bouncers named Paul punched the man in the stomach.

'Get the hell out of here and never come back or you'll get more of this,' he said, cracking the man over the head expecting him to go down, but the man didn't. He just turned his head and said.

'Is that all you can do? Well I tell you what, I'm coming back to do you all in.'

The remark threw Paul into rage and he grabbed the man by the throat and began to throttle him. Big Vic the head doorman quickly pulled him off.

'Just throw the idiot out,' one of the other bouncers said.

After they had thrown the man out onto the street and watched him walk away as though nothing had happened, they turned their attention to John.

'You seemed to have handled yourself well kiddo, I saw that roundhouse kick as we came running in,' Vic said, appreciatively.

'I still can't believe he was able to walk out with all the punishment I gave him and the whack on the head he got from you lot,' John said.

'He was obviously high on speedballs,' Vic said.

'Speedballs, what are they?' John asked.

'Speedballs are a mix of heroin and cocaine. They can make you feel and look fatigued, but they can also make you violent, snap at the slightest thing and as you found out, you feel don't seem to feel any pain and there is nothing anyone can do can hurt you. You could have hit him with a brick and he wouldn't have felt it, but I tell you one thing, when he wakes up tomorrow, he is going to feel it and need an ambulance,' Vic said, with a chuckle.

'You seem pretty well able to handle yourself. Have you done any training?' Paul asked.

'Yes, I practice Kung Fu and Karate, mostly self-taught though,' John told him, with an air of pride.

'You should think about becoming a bouncer, how old are you?' Vic cut in.

'I'm nineteen, well almost twenty, any jobs going here?' John asked.

'Not at the moment, but we'll let you know if one comes up and if you try for a job somewhere else, you can always get them to call me for a reference,' Vic offered.

'Thanks, I may take you up on that, you never know,' John said, pleased with the thought as he strolled back to the bar.

John continued working at the bar wishing he could be one of the bouncers. He was unhappy to learn that due to his accident Uncle Dave's criminal records had flashed up that he was a wanted man, and as a result as soon as he was well enough, he was arrested and carted off to prison. This had also upset Uncle George and he had decided to go back to Scotland. John felt a compelling urge to go and visit Uncle George and find out what was happening with Uncle Dave and how long he was going to be in prison.

With his mother's blessing he took the train to Glasgow. Uncle George met him at the station and took him to the house he was renting and put him up in the spare room. John was really surprised to find that Uncle George had appeared to have given up criminality and started a picture framing business he called Cairnlandia. The pictures were made using all kinds of light metal materials in a way that had never been done before. To John's further surprise Uncle George asked him to come and work for him helping to make the pictures and sell them.

Unfortunately the concept was so unique, nobody had seen anything like it in Glasgow and didn't seem to take to this modern form of art – the business failed before it had a chance to get off the ground. Dismayed at the failure and with no job prospects, together with the unhappy knowledge Uncle Dave was going to be spending twelve months in prison, John decided to go back to Birkenhead and Uncle George headed back to London after giving John a metallic picture of a snow leopard as a keepsake before he left.

WIGAN

1986

'How do you fancy a trip to Wigan at the weekend?' Jamie his friend suggested, as they met up for a drink in the local pub.

'Sounds great, I've heard there are loads of nightclubs down there and some tasty birds,' John enthused.

'Then Wigan here we come. The birds better watch out and if we don't manage to pull, then we'll sleep in the park and head home the next day,' Jamie said, raising his glass.

When they arrived in Wigan they headed for King Street which was well known for its clubs and nightlife. They decided on a club called 'Scotts' and it was there that something was to happen that would change John's life forever.

Jamie and John sat down at a table and scanned the dimly lit club trying to pick out the most likely girls to pull, John noticed two girls sitting on their own. One had flaming-red hair, her face animated and eyes sparkling brightly as she talked with her friend.

'How about those two over there?' John suggested, indicating the two girls. 'I bag the one with the red hair,' he asserted as they moved across to ask them for a dance.

As John got close to the girl with the red hair, his eyes instinctively travelled over her body starting at her legs, moving swiftly to her hips and waist before finally settling on her well-formed breasts. Lifting his eyes to meet hers, she smiled back, pleased with the appreciative look on his face. She was about five feet four and had long flaming-red hair encasing the pale skin of her lightly freckled face then falling in soft waves down over her shoulders. Her large sparkling blue eyes shone with mischief. Her makeup was smooth, not overdone. Her nails painted a gentle red.

She had long shapely legs which were emphasised by the short black leather mini skirt she was wearing. She was also displaying a fair amount of cleavage with the low cut white blouse enhancing her ample bosom. She had on knee length black socks that matched the colour of her shoes. She told him her name was Jackie and her friend's name was Louise. To John's delight they seemed to hit it off straight away.

Jamie was immediately taken by Louise. She was equally voluptuous, about the same height as Jackie, but had short brown curly hair, brown eyes and large pouting lips. She was wearing a short skirt with a jumper that moulded to the curves of her upper body with her cleavage prominently on display. It was a long jumper which draped down over the skirt and made it look like she wasn't wearing a skirt at all. On her feet she wore black high heel boots which covered the lower part of her long shapely legs. As the evening came to an end, John was still with Jackie and Jamie still with Louise, all of them wondering what was going to happen next. John and Jamie knew what they would like to happen, but were too shy to suggest anything. But, the situation was answered for them as Jackie surprised them by saying:

'You two aren't thinking of driving all the way back to Birkenhead tonight are you?'

John and Jamie exchanged glances, 'No we were going to look for somewhere to stay, but I guess we've left a bit late. Do you happen to know of anywhere we can crash out for the night?' Jamie asked, awkwardly.

Jackie and Louise exchanged glances.

'The only thing I can suggest is, you come back with us,' Jackie said, with broad inviting smile.

John and Jackie ended up sleeping together, sleeping being the operative word as they were both too drunk to attempt anything as vigorous as making love.

Jamie and Louise made up a bed for themselves on the living room floor, but judging by the loud grunts and groans emanating from the room it didn't sound as though they were doing much sleeping!

The following morning refreshed by a good night's sleep, John's and Jackie's bodies responded and they made love. It was an exhilarating experience for John because Jackie was less inhibited and led the way.

John had had several girlfriends, but never gone all the way with any of them, this was his first time. John had often wondered what it would be like to be in bed with a naked woman and make love, but he never imagined it would be anything like this. None of the girls he had been with were anything like Jackie. She was eight years older than him, insatiable and experienced and she revelled in teaching him the arts of love making.

When John got up in the morning ready to leave he was surprised to discover Jackir had two children, Stephen aged three and Craig aged five. As he gradually got to know them on his regular visits he began to take to them because like him they appeared not to have a father, at least not one taking any interest or caring about them. In fact there were two fathers.

At the same time John was beginning to feel desperately unhappy at home, things were becoming difficult with his mum. They were beginning to tip toe around each other like strangers. Alex was beginning to get on his nerves to the point he had given up his room to him and moved into the box room and the whole situation was becoming unbearable. He began to feel he had to get away, become a little more independent and get a place of his own. He was working and could afford it and there was something else tugging at his heart. He was falling in love with Jackie or at least with the idea of falling in love.

There was an uneasy silence after he told his mother he was moving in with Jackie and a chill swept over her as she thought over what he had just told her.

'Do you really know what you're doing?' she asked, regarding him with a look of displeasure.

'Yes mum I do, I need to get away. I'm twenty now and we are beginning to get on each other's nerves and it upsets me that we argue. I'm sure it upsets you too,' he said, falling to his knees and taking hold of her hands.

She pulled her hands away and buried her head in them. Choking back all of the hurt of the last few years she said.

'I know it's not been easy for either of us, but I want you to think hard about what you're planning to do. How well do you know this girl? You tell me she has two young children. Do you really want to take on that responsibility at your age?' she said, lowering her hands, her face bare and hurt.

'They're good kids and they don't have a father either,' John said, instantly feeling the smile freeze on his face realising the impact of what he had just said.

'Sorry mum, I didn't mean it that way,' he said, taking hold of her hands again and gently squeezing them.

'I know you didn't son, but I want you to think carefully about everything. I'm not ready to be a grandmother and you're not ready to be a father,' she advised him wearily.

'Don't worry ma, I'm not planning to raise a family yet,' he assured her.

'Are you planning to get married?' she asked, the thought sending a shock wave through her body.

'I don't know we haven't talked about it,' he said, feeling a slight trembling in her hands.

'Do you love her?' she asked.

'I think so,' John said, hesitantly.

Her eyes came up and fixed on his face.

'I want you to promise me one thing. If you do get married, you stay married and you never behave like your father. At least promise me that,' she said, and he could see the unhappiness in her eyes as she stared into his.

This was something he didn't expect her to say and the thought of his dad deserting her cut deep into him.

'I'll never do that and I'll never desert you. I will always be there for you,' he said, almost choking on the words. 'I won't be that far away and I will come and see you and Alex as often as I can,' he added, as he let go of her hands and got to his feet.

A blanket of sadness fell over her as she watched him walk out of the room wondering whether this was another turning point in both their lives.

Jamie had broken up with Louise and as a result his friendship with John was drifting apart. John moved in with Jackie, who was renting a house on the Worsely Hall Estate, a pretty rough area with all the usual troubles, petty crimes, drugs, gang fights, a general disregard for other people's property and the police. It saddened John, but he had committed himself and was determined to make a go of things.

Now he had the responsibility of Jackie and her two children, John had to find himself a job and he decided he would try to get a job as a bouncer, remembering what Vic had said to him at The Jimmy's.

He walked along King Street enquiring at the various clubs with little success. He went into Scotts, the club where he had met Jackie, they didn't have any vacancies, but told him there was a club called Gigolos in the basement at the back of their building that was looking for a bouncer.

Elated John made his way there. It seemed a little seedier than the other clubs, but John needed a job and here was one. He asked around and was eventually approached by the manager who introduced himself as Anthony. John was a little shocked at first as Anthony looked a little like George Formby in appearance. He was very slim and had mousy hair greased straight back, by his manner and the garish clothes he wore with the pink silk hanky sticking out of his breast pocket, he was obviously gay, which seemed rather incongruous in a tough seedy nightclub.

'So where have you worked before?' Anthony asked, looking him over from head to foot which made John feel a little uncomfortable.

'I haven't, but I know I can do the job, I do a lot of Kung Fu and Karate, I worked in a club in Birkenhead and had to deal with a few awkward customers and Vic one of the bouncers there, said I should think about becoming one myself, so here I am.'

'I see,' Anthony said, still giving him the once over.

'Look, I tell you what, how about you give me a month's trial and if in the end I don't measure up, then fair enough. How's that?'

'That seems fair enough. What's your name?'

'John Lawson.'

'Okay, John Lawson, when can you start?'

'As soon as you like.'

'In that case you can start tomorrow night, which will give one of the boys a break. The pay is fifty pounds a night, cash, and you're responsible for your own tax and other things.'

'Sounds fine,' John readily agreed.

'Right then, you better come and meet the other boys you'll be working with,' Anthony said, walking off with a fluffy wave of his hands.

'This is John Lawson our new man and this is Dave, Billy, Graham and Steve,' Anthony said, gesturing to each one in turn.

'Hi, good to meet you,' John said, offering his hand with a welcoming smile.

They each shook his hand.

'John will be starting tomorrow, so one of you can have the night off at last,' Anthony said, as he turned and sauntered off.

'Bleedin' poof,' Dave scowled, watching Anthony walk off.

John said nothing, but noticed that Dave stood out from the others. Though he was smartly dressed, he looked every bit a thug, he was very muscular, his head was shaven and he had tattoos on his neck.

On his first night, John was in for a big surprise at the way the bouncers conducted themselves, particularly Dave who behaved exactly like the thug he was. There was a man and woman sitting opposite each other having a loud argument about something and the woman suddenly slapped the man across the face. Dave immediately reacted. John watched as he stormed over and punched the woman in the face knocking her unconscious to the floor. The man protested and Dave swung a left hook and sent him sprawling to the floor. A young couple, a few seats away started to protest and they got the same treatment. John was aghast that within the space of a minute four people were laying on the floor in a state of unconsciousness. The other two bouncers Billy and Graham who had just stood watching the action, stepped in to help Dave haul them to their feet and thrown them out.

'Bloody hell, Dave's a bit quick with his fists,' John remarked, surprised by his actions.

'Yeah, we call him the removal man,' Billy said.

'The removal man?' John queried, with a puzzled look.

'Yeah, he removes people,' Graham chirped in, jokingly.

This kind of senseless violence immediately began to worry John and he resolved to try to show them there was a better way of dealing with trouble makers. If John spotted any trouble coming his way, he would approach the culprits and warn them that if they didn't calm down they could get seriously hurt. It usually did the trick as long as he could keep Dave away.

In the end, John became so worried by Dave's love of violence that he spoke to Anthony about his behaviour, saying men who beat up women are scum, they're not men, they're just bullies, warning him that one day, Dave is going to go over the top and he'll have a dead body on his hands and the police to deal with.

As John reported for work the following night, Dave came charging out of the office, his face purple with rage as he deliberately bumped in John. John wondered what happened as he watched him storm off down the road not bothering to look back. Realising something was wrong, John's natural instincts clicked in and he rushed in to Anthony's office. His instincts were right, Anthony was lying flat on his back his face covered in blood.

'What the hell happened?' John asked, helping Anthony to his feet.

'I told him I couldn't take any more of his violent behaviour and it had to stop or I'd fire him. He told me I could shove the job up my poofy arse and then smashed me in the face. I think he's broken my nose,' Anthony said, flamboyantly taking out his bright pink hanky from his breast pocket and gently putting it to his bloody nose, before collapsing into his chair.

'I think you had better go to the hospital, it does look nasty and yes I think he could have broken your nose the way that lunatic punches,' John said, in an effort to comfort him.

'Yes, I think you're right. It bloody well hurts. I can tell you that much and look at the state of me hanky, I'll never get the blood out of it,' he said. 'Can you go and get me some ice and serviettes from the bar please? I can't stop the bleeding with this.'

'Okay and I'll phone for an ambulance while I'm at it,' John told him.

'Okay, but just say I tripped over and fell on my face. I don't want the police sniffing around here, okay?' Anthony pleaded.

'No problem, I'll tell them exactly what you said.'

'By the way, I'm going to need you more than ever. You've proved yourself and you can now consider yourself a permanent member of the team,' Anthony said, holding the pink silk hanky under his nose to catch the blood.

John allowed himself to smile, pleased with what Anthony had just told him and pleased Dave would not be around anymore, as he rushed off to get the ice and serviettes and phone for an ambulance.

John had now been living with Jackie and working at the club for three months when she told him there was a house on Severn Drive, around the corner from her mum's house on the Norley Hall Estate she had been offered which was much bigger than the one they had. Norley Hall was just as rough as the Worsely Hall Estate, but as Jackie pointed out, it was a much nicer and bigger house.

John hired a Ford Transit van and gradually moved the furniture across, but he couldn't manage to get it all in. He'd only hired the van for the day, so once they had unloaded everything, it had to be returned. That still left a few more things to be collected from the old house such as the fridge freezer. It was only about a mile away, so John decided to borrow a trolley and wheel it across himself. The children were at their gran's house so Jackie came with him to help in any way she could.

It didn't take long to walk there, but it took much longer coming back wheeling the trolley laden down with the heavy fridge. As they got to the house, John almost let go of the handles as Jackie screamed. The front door was gaping open.

'You did lock the door, didn't you?' John asked, as he gently lowered the trolley.

'Of course I bloody did,' Jackie scowled, as they both rushed inside.

They had been burgled. The telly, the video recorder, the Hoover, the stereo and his precious picture of the snow leopard had all gone. John and Jackie were crest fallen, it wasn't a good start to their new home and John was furious that someone would do this, someone local, someone who had been watching them move the stuff in and waiting for the chance.

John had a code, you can rob a bank, steal from a factory, but you don't steal from your family or your neighbours and it made him angry. He knew there was very little chance of getting the stuff back, but he was determined he would find out who had done it and punish them.

John managed to get hold of a telly pretty quickly, but what gnawed at him was the loss of the picture, not because it had any monetary value, but because Uncle George had given it to him and it was the only one of its kind.

Setting off for work one evening just as it was beginning to get dark, he strolled happily along, wondering what sort of night it was going to be at the club. As he continued he passed a house that had the lights on, but had not closed the curtains. John suddenly stopped dead in his tracks. He took a few steps back and peered in through the window, blinking his eyes in disbelief as he stared at the picture hanging on the wall at the back of the lounge. It was his picture of the snow leopard. His face filled with anger as he stormed to the door and with one furious kick, the locks caved in and the door burst open. He charged in just as a man nervously poked his head out of the lounge door.

'Where did you get that picture?' John screamed, as he barged into the lounge where the man's wife and two children were sitting staring at him in fear. 'That's my picture and I want it back,' John continued to scream at the man.

'I bought that in good faith. How do I know it's yours?'

John rushed over and pulled it off the wall and turned it over to show him the back.

'You see that?' John said, jabbing angrily at the little sticker with his thumb. 'That my uncle's company and he gave me this picture. It's the only one of its kind. Do you want me to call the police?'

'No, please just take it and leave us alone,' the man pleaded.

'Where did you get it from?' John demanded.

'I bought it off a guy called Banny Wharley down the pub,' the man told him.

'And where does this scumbag Banny Wharley live?' John persisted angrily.

'On Serven Drive on the Norley Estate, number 303 I think.'

'Bloody hell,' John exclaimed. Banny Wharley was his next door neighbour.

'Look, I'm sorry I burst in on you like that, but I hope you understand that Banny, believe it or not is my neighbour who bloody stole it from my house the night we moved in and he is going to pay heavily for it,' he added, his anger rising.

'Yes, I understand, but please can you go now,' the man pleaded, becoming even more nervous at seeing the twisted anger on John's face.

'Good evening Madam, sorry to have disturbed you,' John said, forcing his twisted face into a smile, as he turned and walked out, clutching the picture.

To be told the scumbag who had burgled his place and sold off the stuff, including his beloved picture, was actually his next door neighbour made John feel angrier than he'd ever been and he was determined he would teach this Banny a lesson he would never forget. He started to ask around about him and was shocked to discover he was a real heavy, well into drugs and anything else that he could make money from. He had his own little gang which meant he was not a man to confront face on. John thought about what Uncle George had told him. *Lay low, keep your head down, stay in the shadows, be patient, wait for the right moment which will come, then strike and when you do make sure you do it well and it can't be traced back to you.'*

John decided to heed Uncle George's advice and wait until he could get this bastard Banny Wharley somewhere on his own. Having him next door it was a little easier to keep an eye on him and watch his movements. John soon became aware that Banny had the habit of going out into the back garden to roll a joint and smoke it. One night he waited patiently for Banny to walk into the garden and start to roll a joint. John slipped on his big black coat, took out the balaclava he had in one of the pockets and pulled it over his head. He grabbed the piece of two by four he had prepared and quietly slipped out of the back gate of his garden into the alleyway and took the few steps to the next gate, kicked it open and before Banny, already in the first stages of a drug haze, could do anything John whacked him in the face as hard as he could.

Banny went down and stayed down. John enraged gave him a few good kicks in the ribs into the bargain, which was not like him, as his Martial Arts training had taught him never to kick a man when he's down. John made his way back to his house, pleased he had got his revenge for what Banny had done, particularly as they were never going to see any of the stuff he'd stolen back – except of course for the picture.

'What the hell you been up to?' Jackie asked, as she saw John pulling off the balaclava as he walked in through the back door.

He inwardly cursed himself for not remembering to have taken it off before he came back in, but decided to tell Jackie the truth.

'I found out who stole our stuff. It's that bastard next door and I've just given him a bloody good hiding.'

Jackie felt panic growing inside her.

'Bloody hell, do you know who he is? He runs most of this estate. Do you imagine for one moment, he's going to let you get away with this? How could you be so stupid? I've got two kids to worry about in case you've forgotten.'

'Don't worry; he didn't know it was me, that's why I wore the balaclava. I have a simple rule, anyone who messes with me or my kind does so at their own risk,' John said, becoming upset that she seemed to be angry with him.

'So what was the point of beating him up if you didn't want him to know it was you?' Jackie asked, looking at him quizzically.

'I just felt he needed a good hiding for what he'd done to us. I know there's no chance of us ever getting the stuff back, but people who steal off their neighbours are scum, and he got what he deserved.'

'That won't stop him stealing, everyone knows he's a thief and a junkie,' Jackie said, with a hint of agitation.

'Yes, he obviously is, but I don't think we'll have any trouble from him,' John said, wanting to assure her.

'I just hope you're right,' Jackie said, and he could see the fear creeping into her face.

The next day as John and Jackie were coming out of the house, they saw Banny coming out of his front door. He looked a mess, his face was all bruised, a black eye, cut lip and he appeared not to be walking too easily.

'What happened to you?' John could not resist asking.

Jackie felt a stab of fright in the pit of her stomach that John had dared to confront Banny after what she could clearly see he had done to him.

'A group of thugs jumped me. Bastards, they were five of them and they had baseball bats, but I managed to fight them off,' he said, bullishly.

'When did this happen?' John asked, struggling to maintain a concerned look.

'Last night.'

'You should have called me. I would have come and helped,' John told him.

'No, I can take care of myself. As I said, I beat them off and I don't think they'll dare to come around here again. Nobody messes with me and gets away with it,' Banny expanded boastfully.

'Well, I think you're a real tough guy. I wouldn't want to mess with you,' John said, now struggling to hold back from laughing.

'You take care of yourself Banny and call me if you ever need any help' John offered as took Jackie's hand and walked off.

'I can take care of my own problems,' Banny called out, as he hobbled off in the opposite direction clutching his bruised ribs.

John's face broadened into a big grin as he looked at Jackie.

'Five men, what a dickhead.'

On one of his evenings off, Jackie had invited one her friends, Linda and her boyfriend Jimmy to dinner. Unbeknown to John, Jimmy was a notorious burglar and took John aside while the girls busied themselves with the washing up and said to him. 'You game for earning a bit of extra money?'

'Sure, I'm always game for earning a bit of extra money. What have you got in mind?' John asked, enthusiastically.

'There's this working man's club. It's loaded with fruit and cigarette machines. So we break in, crack open the fruit machines, take all the cash, smash open the cigarette machines, take the money and the fags and none of it can be traced to us. It's ripe for the taking,' Jimmy explained.

'Sounds interesting, when are you planning on doing it?'

'Saturday night's the best time, it's bingo night which means the club is busier and the machines will be full of cash. I've checked the place out and I know where the burglar alarm box is and we can get in at the back through a kitchen window. So if you're up for it?'

'Yes, I'm up for it,' John said, the idea beginning to excite him.

'Good, bring a few pairs of strong socks with you, they're great to stash the pound coins in, and a nice heavy hammer if you've got one,' Jimmy advised him.

'Yeah, I've got a hammer,' John assured him.

On Saturday night Jimmy climbed up onto the flat roof of the club and went straight for the alarm box, knocking it off the wall with a couple of heavy blows with the crowbar he was carrying. Unfortunately what he didn't know was the alarm being torn from the wall in the way it had would alert the police and the caretaker.

It was easy levering the kitchen window open with the crowbar so that they were able to scramble in. The main hall of the club had a small stage at one end where the acts would perform and where the bingo caller sat. At the other end was a long bar stretching the width of the hall. All the chairs were still laid out facing the stage from the evening's bingo session. Jimmy and John weaved their way through the maze of chairs to the fruit machines and immediately set about breaking into them, taking out the coins and stuffing them into the socks. Having emptied the fruit machines, they started on the cigarettes machines, doing the same with the money. They then removed the packs of cigarettes throwing them into a sack Jimmy had brought with him. It looked like it was all going easier than expected until they heard a commotion coming from the front of the building.

'What's that?' John asked apprehensively.

'Probably nothing, but better go and have a look,' Jimmy told John.

John moved cautiously through the swing doors to the entrance hall, crept silently to the main front door and peeked out through a crack in the curtains. He was horrified to see a police car with a constable standing there looking at the door. Then another police car arrived, the driver got out and approached the other policeman.

'The caretaker will be here any minute he's got the keys, so we may as well wait. It could be just a faulty alarm,' he heard one of the policemen say.

John rushed back to Jimmy.

'It's the bizzies, they're right outside, but we've got a few minutes as I heard them say they're waiting for the caretaker.'

'In that case they'll be coming in through the front, so let's stack some of these chairs up against the swing doors so they're jammed shut while we leg it out through the back fire exit. By the time they manage to force the doors open we'll be well gone. Grab a chair,' Jimmy said.

They just managed to wedge enough chairs against the doors as they heard the voice of what sounded like the caretaker saying with no sense of urgency in his voice.

'Bloody alarms, they can be a damn nuisance sometimes. Can't see any sign of a break in.'

Then they heard the keys turning in the door as they gathered up their stuff and quickly weaved their way through the chairs to the back fire exit. They waited until they heard the police and caretaker struggling with the chairs before they pushed down on the fire exit bar and flung the heavy door open. It was then they heard a thud and groan as a police officer, who had reached the exit, slumped to the ground with a bleeding nose having been hit by the force of the opening door. John and Jimmy ran fast as they could and managed to scale a wall at the bottom of the car park.

'That's what I call a good night's work,' Jimmy said, laughing his head off as they made good their escape.

'Can I call you dad?' Craig asked, looking beseechingly up at John.

John dropped the football out of shock. He liked Craig and had sympathy with him, because while Steven still had contact with his dad and would go off for weekends with him, Craig's dad had left his mother the moment he discovered she was pregnant.

'Can I?' Craig asked again, still looking up at John with warmth and expectation and there was a gentle smile playing around his mouth.

John knew better than anyone what it was like to have a dad and to hate him because he wasn't with him and yet still love him. He'd cried many buckets over his dad, the bastard. Feeling guilty because he hated him and yet hating himself because he still had feelings for him. And here was this boy, who also didn't have a dad asking him to call him dad, to be his dad.

'Of course you can,' John said, guessing that Craig even at his age must be struggling to understand his situation. 'Of course you can call me dad,' he said, as he walked towards him and swept him up in his arms.

'You're crying dad,' Craig said, using the word for the first time, wiping away a tear with his little finger.

'No, I just got something in my eye,' John said, brushing Craig's hand away and lowering him back to the ground in an attempt to hide his emotions.

Later that day when John was sitting at the table having dinner before going off to work, his mind kept drifting off. He was hardly eating his meal, rather pushing it around the plate than shoving it in his mouth.

'What's the matter?' Jackie asked, lowering her fork to the plate as she looked across the table at him.

'You alright, dad?' Craig piped in.

Jackie swung her look to Craig surprised he'd used the word dad, but pleased at the same time.

'Did you tell him he could call you dad?' she asked, switching her look back to John.

'Jackie, I guess with Craig calling me dad it has made me determined to find my dad. I need to know what went wrong, why he abandoned us,' John said, with a lost look on his face.

'Why don't you try and track him down through the police station he worked at?' Jackie suggested.

HELLO DAD

1986

It took about a month to track down his dad and John was surprised when he offered to pay for his ticket to South Africa.

The walk through Johannesburg airport brought back many memories and there was a sadness in his eye as he remembered himself as a ten year old clutching tightly to his satchel and being led by an air stewardess in the opposite direction he was now walking. Unfortunately for John, the Rugby World Cup was on that very weekend in Durban, where his father lived, and as all flights from Jo'burg to Durban were already booked the only way of getting to Durban was by taking the overnight milk train.

It was 7.30 in the morning when the train finally pulled into Durban Station, John eager and excited to see his dad, got off the train and hurried to the exit, but like Johannesburg station and every other station there were separate entrances and exits for whites and blacks. John in his eagerness took the wrong exit and walked out through the blacks exit. Without realising what he had done, he looked around anxiously for his dad, but could not see him anywhere.

After sometime standing looking around in every direction, he became increasing aware of the same odd stares he was getting from the blacks. It eventually dawned on him he was standing in the wrong place and he picked up his case and hurried off back the way he had come from the platform and frantically looked around for the whites only exit. As he spotted the sign he saw his dad hurrying towards him not looking particularly pleased.

'Where the devil have you been? We've had people searching the train for you.'

He looked at his dad's angry face as Liz and Tom quickly caught up with him. It was not the welcome he had hoped for. His dad was dressed as John remembered in his denim shirt, jeans and black boots. Liz looked just like he vaguely remembered her, the same mousy hair, the same large framed glasses, wearing a flowered patterned blouse with a light brown cardigan and black skirt and black shoes. Tom was also dressed casually in a denim shirt and jeans and had changed quite a bit having grown older like John.

'Sorry, I came out the wrong exit,' John said, sheepishly.

'Yeah, well that's just what the Kaffers want, to see whites mixing with them. We've got enough trouble with what's going on as it is, what with free Mandela and all that malarkey. So watch your step, where you go and who you talk to,' his father said, the tightness on his face beginning to relax as he surprisingly stepped forward, wrapped his arms around John's shoulders and embraced him.

'My, you have grown up,' his dad said, holding him out at arm's length to get a better look at him. 'You look strong and fit, you've got nice broad shoulders just like a rugby player,' his dad said, appreciatively.

'I used to play rugby for the school' John said, feeling a little embarrassed as he sensed Liz and Tom standing watching him.

Liz stepped forward and gave him a fleeting kiss on the cheek, her lips barely brushing the skin of his face.

'Nice to see you John,' she said, her voice void of any real emotion.

Tom shook John's hand.

'Good to see you John. I've been really looking forward to you coming,' he said, and John felt the first bit of warmth in any of their voices.

'Good to see you too Tom,' John said, shaking his hand firmly.

'Right, let's get you out of here' his dad said, leading the way.

John picked up his case and as he began to follow him, his dad stopped and looked around.

'Is that all you brought with you, one little suitcase?'

'The other one was stolen at Johannesburg Station when I put it down to check the timetable board. It had all my clothes in it,' John explained, feeling stupid at having to admit his carelessness.

'Yes well, that's what the Kaffers do, they'll steal anything if it's not nailed down or chained to a wall,' his dad said maliciously, turning back and strolling off not caring whether some of the blacks standing around watching could hear what he said.

It was a fifteen mile trip to Umhlanga Rocks and there seemed to be a nervous tension and very little said on the car journey to their home. John sat quietly in the back of the car with Tom, staring out the window taking in the scenery. Lex explained he had joined the Umhlanga Rocks protection service a few years earlier which effectively acted as the local police force and he had been allocated a large bungalow on Fairview Drive. It was situated in one of the more affluent areas of Umhlanga Rocks with beautiful tree lined wide avenues, everywhere looking bright, clean, and respectable. The bungalow had a wide drive with a slight slope down to a large garage, wide enough for two cars. To the side of the drive was a concrete pathway that led to the front door and just off to the right of the path was a very large tree. On the left side of the bungalow stood a large brick outhouse that the servants would have lived in at one time.

'I'll make us a nice cup of tea,' Liz announced, making straight for the kitchen as soon they had stepped into the huge living room.

John was amazed at the size of it and he could see the doorway to what looked like a very large well fitted kitchen. Lex watched her go and turned to John 'I think you should know, Liz and I got married so she is now Mrs Lawson.'

'So when did you get married?' John asked surprised, his chest seizing and his throat gagging tight as he choked on the words Mrs Lawson. Although he knew they were divorced, there would still be only one Mrs Lawson as far as he was concerned and that was his mother.

'And Tom has also changed his name to Lawson. I hope you two are going to get on well together,' his dad added, ignoring the hurt he could see beginning to appear on John's face.

'Yeah, I'll show you around and we'll have some fun together. Looking forward to it,' Tom said, with a broad grinning smile.

'Good, but first things first, I've managed to fix you up with a job and...'

'A job!!' John exclaimed.

'Yes, a job, you'll need to earn your keep while you're here.'

'Earn my keep?' John exclaimed again, aghast at what his dad was telling him.

'You have to pay something towards you board and lodging,' Liz said, as she came back into the room carrying a tray of mugs and a plate of biscuits.

'It's a video rental shop and I've arranged for the boss to see you tomorrow morning and if he likes you, as I'm sure he will, then you can start straight away and everybody will be happy,' his dad said, grabbing one of the mugs and holding it up in a toasting gesture. 'Good to have you here son.' It was the first time his dad had called him son since he had arrived and he was not sure what to make of it.

'Glad to be here, dad,' John reciprocated.

'Right I'll show you to your room,' his dad said.

John followed him along the passageway which led to the bedrooms at the back of the bungalow. There were three. The main bedroom was spacious and richly furnished. The second bedroom was smaller but still spacious and well furnished, and the third room was a much smaller box room, but again well furnished.

'This is your room, son' his dad said, indicating the middle room, which pleased John, he was not going to have to sleep in the much smaller box room.

'The bathroom is back here,' he said, leading him out of the room.

The bathroom was equally spacious and sumptuous in its fittings, everything was clean and sparkling, the towels neatly folded in a perfect line on the shiny chrome towel rails. Looking out of the window John could see a massive landscaped garden and there was a big white Alsatian running around.

'Is that your dog?'

'That's Rolf, he's there to keep intruders out. He can stop a Kaffer dead in his tracks, but he's quite friendly once he gets to know you. You and Tom can take him for walks down to the beach,' his dad said, seeing him looking out of the window.

'Just make sure you keep the bathroom clean, otherwise you'll have Liz on your back, she hates mess and untidiness,' his dad warned him.

Untidiness and mess, what does she think she caused when she broke up the marriage, wasn't that messy and untidy? John thought as he followed his father back into the living room.

'I have prepared you a bite to eat. You look exhausted and I suggest you get some rest as we're going to be taking you out to dinner tonight at the Sands Hotel,' Liz said with aplomb, as she breezed into the room to join them.

'No, he's alright, I want him to come over to my room first, then he came have a rest,' Tom cut in, with what looked like a mischievous smile.

'Fine, if that's what you want to do,' his dad said, rather dismissively. 'I've got to pop to the station to check on a couple of things, so I will see you all a bit later,' he added, giving Liz a kiss on the cheek before making his way out.

John moved across to the window and watched as his dad walked to the garage, raised up the big double door, stepped inside and moments later reversed out driving the police car.

'Come on then,' Tom said, dragging him away from the window.

'Where's your room then?' John asked, following him.

'My room is the outhouse. I've had it converted, it's rather comfortable and allows me to get away from mum and dad,' Tom told him.

The fact Tom was now calling his father 'dad' jarred on John and he had to check himself to hide any appearance of resentment as Tom was being very friendly towards him.

'Well, this is it,' Tom said, with a wide sweep of his hands. 'I can shut myself away here and do what I like.

'Looks great,' John said, slumping down on the bed and looking around at the place. It just had the one big room with a small bathroom and a small kitchen off to one end.

'What was this place used for, before you converted it?'

'It was used to house the servants, that was in the days when whoever owned the place before could afford to have servants; although I guess they didn't pay them much, if they paid them at all,' Tom explained, 'but we do have a black maid, her name is Edith, 'one-eyed-Edith' I call her, because she's only got one eye,' Tom said, making a joke of it. 'It must be her day off as I haven't seen her around. We also have a gardener, he's black too.'

John looked at Tom, a frown beginning to crease his forehead.

'I don't understand, we're supposed not to mix with blacks yet here you and I guess other white people have them working for them.'

'Yeah, well it's cheap labour and perfectly alright as long as they know their place and don't cause trouble, dad always says. Anyway, I'm sorry what happened about you and your mum. I was only a kid at the time and really didn't understand what was going on.'

'Me neither, I was just a kid too, but I do remember coming over to play with you one time, which was the first time I met your mum.'

'Yeah, I remember that, I think we had some fun together and look at us now, step brothers, who would have believed that, back then?' Tom said, with an affectionate smile.

'Yes, who would have believed that,' John said, and felt a moment of guilt, thinking he was betraying his mother by saying that.

'Hey, I don't know about you, but I need to smoke some Dagha,' Tom said, going off into the kitchen.

'Dagha, what's that?'

'Weed, blow, man.'

'You mean drugs?'

'You bet, the best in the world, Durban poison,' Tom said, coming back out of the kitchen with something wrapped up tightly in newspaper.

'What's Durban poison?'

'What's the matter, don't you do drugs back home?'

'No, I've never touched the stuff.'

'You don't know what you're missing. Here have a whiff of this,' Tom invited, unwrapping the newspaper and offering it up to John's nose.

'Phew, it stinks,' John exclaimed, jerking his head away.

'Yeah man, but when you smoke it, its pure lekker.'

'What's lekker?'

'Lekker, cool man, real cool.'

'What does your... I mean our dad, think about you smoking that stuff?' John asked, as he watched with interest as Tom began to prepare a smoke, by rubbing the Dagha in the palm of his hand, to separate the stalks and seeds from the leaves, before rolling a joint.

'That's the beauty of this place, he never comes in here, so he has no idea. I've even got my own stuff growing behind the shed. Here come and have a look,' Tom said, moving over to the rear window. 'If you look down you can just see them. It started by accident. As you just saw, you have to rub the Dagha to separate the seeds and the stalks before you can roll a joint and I just throw the seeds out the window and to my surprise they started growing and now I've got my own stash. They're not ready yet, they have to grow taller and the leaves have to take on a certain hue before they're ready,' Tom explained.

'But surely your dad must know about that?'

'No, he has no idea boet, like most of the police they can never see what's right under their noses,' Tom said, a big smile stretching his face as he went back to preparing his smoke.

'But what about if they walked in now?' John asked, amazed at the risk he was taking.

'Then I guess I would be in trouble,' Tom said, continuing what he was doing.

'I guess we both would, and hey that's the second time you called me boat' John said curiously.

'Ha ha, not boat, its boet, b- o- e- t, its Afrikaans for brother,' Tom laughed.

After a good night's sleep, John awoke bright and cheerful, climbed out of his comfortable bed, crossed over to the window and looked out at the clear blue sky. It made him feel good and he wondered what the day was going to bring.

'I see you're up at last,' his dad said, popping his head around the door. John could see he was already dressed in his police uniform, a gun strapped to his hip. 'Liz has gone to work and the bathrooms free so get yourself ready. Edith will make you some breakfast and I'll run you down to the video shop,' he told him.

'Okay, I'll be as quick as I can,' John said, setting off for the bathroom.

The drive to Glenashley, where Video Venture, the video rental shop was located proved interesting as Lex drove him in the police car and the memories came flooding back of when his dad used to drive him around in the police car as a kid. Tom had also decided to come for the ride to keep John company and both of them were having fun asking what all the controls did. Lex explaining that this one switches on the flashing lights, this one switches on the siren, and this one switches on the speaker if you want address a crowd or warn someone and that is the radio switch to speak to HQ.

'You said Liz had gone to work, what does she do?' John asked, curious to know.

'She works at the Sands Hotel on the beach front where we had dinner last night. She's one of the managers, she's in charge of the laundry, wardrobe etc,' Lex explained.

So that's why she was greeted so regally last night when we arrived for dinner, John thought.

'Good morning Officer Lawson,' the owner greeted Lex as they entered the video shop.

'Good morning Clive, this is my son John, who I mentioned is over from England for a short while and looking for a job to earn his keep,' Lex said, by way of introduction.

'Know anything about the video rental business?' Clive asked, offering his hand to shake at the same time.

'The thing is, they get all the videos released in England before we get them here, so John can tell you the ones that have been really successful and the ones that haven't. Can't you John?' Lex said, turning to John for confirmation.

'Yes, I suppose so,' John conceded.

'That would be very useful. We get offered packages from the distributors and are never sure which will sell the best,' Clive said, appreciatively. 'Can you start straight away?'

That was something John didn't expect.

'I only arrived yesterday and Tom here has promised to show me around for the day.'

'Okay, tomorrow will be fine. Can you be here at nine o'clock?'

'Sure, I will be here at nine o'clock on the dot,' John assured him.

'He's a bright boy and I know he won't let you down. Good to see you Clive,' Lex said, giving him a strong handshake.

John spent the rest of the day walking around the town with Tom, finishing up with them playing around on the golden sandy beaches of Umhlanga Rocks. They were late getting back home and Liz had already set the table and the evening meal was ready to serve.

'Hurry and get cleaned up otherwise the dinner will be spoiled,' she said, annoyance beginning to sound in her voice.

John had to admit Liz was a good cook and the meal was enjoyable. Afterwards while everybody began to relax and Liz started to clear away the dishes John felt it was the right moment turned to his dad and said.

'I've got some questions I want to ask you.'

Lex was a little surprised at the firmer tone to his voice which he had not heard before.

'Do you want to talk here at the table or do you want to talk privately just the two of us?'

'I'm happy to talk here, openly,' John told him.

Lex could see the determination on John's face and it began to worry him.

'I think perhaps we ought to go into the other room and talk quietly,' Lex suggested.

'No, sit and talk here,' Liz insisted, as she came back into the room. 'We don't have any secrets around here, do we darling?' she added, looking pointedly at Lex.

Her sudden interference and the thought she just wanted to hear everything that was going to be said, really irked John and he said.

'No, I would like to talk to you alone.'

'Okay, let's go and talk in the living room,' Lex agreed, and John watched as Liz turned and walked off in a huff.

'So okay, what do you want to ask?' Lex said, a little irritably as he plonked himself down in one of the plush leather armchairs.

'I want to know why you didn't stay in touch. Why you didn't write or phone? Why you never ever sent me or Alex birthday cards, let alone send any presents? Not that we were ever without presents, mum made sure of that. But it would have been nice to have received something from you.'

'Liz, thought it was for the best.'

'The best for who?' John retorted, angrily.

'For everyone. It was difficult resettling back here, sorting out everything with Liz and Tom. Before you realise it a month flies by and then a year and then another year has passed and then you start to think I should have written. I should have phoned. But then you start to worry because you've haven't been in touch and that it's too late and if you do, what sort of reception are you going to get? So in the end you're too nervous to do anything, so you don't do anything.'

'It's never too late. Tell me honestly would you have ever contacted any of us, if I hadn't had contacted you?'

'To be honest, no I probably wouldn't have, but I'm glad you did,' Lex said, offering up a smile.

'So as far as you were concerned, we were part of the past and that was it?'

'We can't live in the past John, we all have to move forward and...'

'Like you, you mean? Dump one woman so you can move forward to the next is that it?'

'It wasn't like that?'

'Then how was it, did you ever love mum?'

'Yes, I did, but it's as easy to fall out of love as it is to fall in love. We were young when your mum and I got married. We were both around about your age and it all seemed so romantic and we decided to start a new life here in South Africa and...'

'What I remember of those early days was that we were happy and you used to teach me all sorts of things. I've still got the photograph of you teaching me to shoot. I don't think you realised how much I worshipped you. You could no wrong in my eyes and you seemed so happy with mum.

'I was, we were, but things change and…'

'Changed when you met Liz, I still remember you taking me to meet her and then sending me off to play with Tom. Tom remembers it too. So it was already going on, you and Liz while mum was back in England?'

'Yes, it was just one of those things that happens. You can't explain it. Maybe one day it will happen to you and then perhaps you'll understand,' his dad said.

'I've already met someone and we are together, but the difference is, I'm not deserting a wife and kids to be with her,' John said, with an air of derision, his eyes hard as he stared at his dad.

The inference made his dad wince and shift uncomfortably in his chair.

'That's a bit hard John. I thought now that you've grown up you would understand.'

'I understand, but it doesn't mean I accept it, or it takes the hurt away. You have no idea how shocked and devastated mum was. The shame she felt at being tossed aside and left to fend for herself with two small children, and all we ever got from you was the trunk with all our belongings in it. Have you any idea what that felt like? It was like the final nail in the coffin,' the tension was building up in his voice. 'The end of everything and that was the last contact we had with you until I had the urge to phone you because I felt I needed some answers,' he said, his voice hard, cold and determined and it made Lex feel uneasy.

'And how do you feel now, have you got the answers you were looking for?' his dad asked, hoping this would be the end of the conversation.

'You know Alex hates you. He didn't even want to speak to you on the phone let alone come out with me. I bet you don't even remember when Alex was ten years old, he wrote to you in all his innocence to find out if you were alright, and what was your response? You criticised his handwriting even addressing him as Alexander, not Alex or son and that was the one and only time he heard from you and he's never got over it. As a result of that, Mum's had a lot of trouble with him, he was traumatised by everything, couldn't sleep, wetting the bed, not understanding why he didn't have a father to tuck into bed and say goodnight to him anymore.'

'And what about you, do you hate me?'

'I love you and I hate you. I love you when I think of all the good times we had together and the beautiful country you'd taken us to. But I hate you when I think about the dirty overcrowded concrete jungle you dumped us in and didn't give a damn that we had nowhere to live and if it hadn't been for mum and your family, we would have been out on the streets with only the clothes we stood up in. My mother did not deserve any of that, she loved you and amazingly in a strange way I believe she still does. And what amazes me is, that in the short time I've been here, you have never asked about her once. Not really interested in how she has managed to cope through the years bringing up the two of us all on her own with no financial support from you whatsoever.'

'Look John, all I can say is I'm sorry and yes you're right I should have handled things better and I truly wish I had, but it's in the past and we can't go back. I'm glad we've had this conversation and I'm glad you're here and I would like us to get on together while you're here,' his father said, getting up from the chair. 'Do you fancy a beer? I sure as hell do.'

'Yes, I could do with one too,' John said, following him out, feeling a bit better that he had said what he had wanted to say.

John lay in bed that night, unable to sleep feeling unhappy about the conversation he had had with his dad thinking it hadn't resolved anything. He started to feel guilty about his mother, wondering what she must be thinking about him being here, and he was also starting to miss Jackie too. He decided he would leave just as soon as he could get enough money together for the return ticket. Ironically, it was the video shop that was to provide the very means of making extra money, but even if he was successful, which he felt confident he would be, it was still going to take around three months to make enough money for the return fare.

The following day when John got home from work Liz was in the kitchen preparing dinner.

'Jackie called and wants you to call her back urgently,' she said, with a slight disdained look.

'Can I use the house phone?'

'Sure go ahead, only don't be on it too long,' Liz said, cautioning him.

John rushed in, went straight to the phone, picked up the receiver, dialled Jackie's number with the international code and waited for it to be answered. Lex arrived home from work just as John was talking on the phone and stood back listening in the hallway wondering who he could be talking to. John's face broke into a smile as soon as he heard her voice.

'Hi, it's me,' he said, which was a bit silly really as she recognised his voice immediately.

'Hi me,' Jackie said back.

'How are you?' John asked nervously, worried because she had asked him to call back urgently.

'I'm pregnant,' Jackie informed him.

'You're pregnant!' Lex heard John exclaim, causing a wry smile to spread across his face as he watched John begin to shuffle uneasily.

'How far?' John asked.

'I've missed my second period so I must be nearly two months,' Jackie told him.

'Two months,' John repeated. 'Then I'm going to have to get back as soon as I can. The problem is I'm having to work for a bit longer to be able to get the money to buy my return ticket and...'

'You mean to say your loving dad that you were so anxious to see only paid for a bloody single ticket. Bloody hell, if I had known that I'd never have let you go. You idiot, who the hell flies anywhere around the world, without making sure they have a return ticket?' Jackie ranted at him.

'Yeah, I know stupid of me. Anyway, I will soon have the money and will get back just as soon as I can darling, I promise. How are you, being sick and all that?'

'A little, but it's not too bad. I hope you're going to be a much better father than the others,' she chided, good naturedly.

'Don't worry he will have all the love I can give him.'

'How do you know it's going to be a boy?'

'Girl or boy, you forget I know what it's like not to have a father,' his dad heard him say, indignation showing on his face.

'So Jackie's pregnant,' his dad said, more a statement than a question, after John had replaced the receiver and turned towards him.

'Yes, and that's changed everything. I'm going to have to get back as soon as I can.'

'How do you know she's pregnant? She could just be saying that to get you back. I heard you say she was two months. In which case if that is true, she could have told you before you left,' his dad said, with a doubtful expression.

John looked at his father's dubious face and sensed a coldness he had felt many times before, a coldness that seemed to say *'if there's a problem in your life then walk away from it.'*

'No, I have no intention of doing what you did and what the other fathers have done. This is my child and it's going to get all the love I never had from you.'

'You can stay here and live with us if you want,' his dad offered.

The offer surprised John, for it was the first time his dad had showed any sign of wanting to have John live with him.

'You mean you would like me to stay here and live with you?'

'Yes I would. Does that surprise you?'

'Yes it does surprise me, but it comes too late and in any event I couldn't desert mum like you did. It would break her heart.'

'Yes, I guess you're right, but I'm still glad you came.'

'Yes, sorry I snapped. I'm glad I came too,' John said, embracing his dad.

'So, all I've got to do now is wait until I've saved up enough money for the ticket,' John said, thinking, *any decent father would say, of course you've got to get back and don't worry I'll give you the money for the air fare,'* but he knew now his dad was never going to do that and he would have to sweat it out and pay for his own fare.

Over dinner John asked whether his dad was still in touch with Auntie Marion and Uncle Les. Lex told him they hadn't been in touch for a very long time, but he did know they still lived in the same place and he had their address and phone number in one of his old phone books.

John spent a lovely weekend with Auntie Marion and Uncle Les, but it was something they told him that had really shocked him and brought back some harrowing memories. That was something he was going to have to confront his dad with, but was not quite sure when or how to go about it.

When John got back home, Liz told him Jackie had called and wanted him to call her urgently. As it appeared urgent they allowed him to use the phone, and Jackie told him she had lost the baby. She sounded distraught and begged him to come back. John wanted to tell her he would be back very soon, but he knew Liz and Lex were probably listening so kept a check on his emotions, although if they had been watching his face, they would have guessed something was wrong as he listened and then lowered his voice and whispered. 'I'm sorry, I'll be home as soon as soon as I can.'

The next morning John decided following the terrible news of Jackie losing the baby he was going to tell his dad the time had come for him to leave. The house was empty so it would have to wait till after work. He set off to catch the bus. He had fiddled enough money for the air fare so there wasn't any reason to stay any longer and it made him smile.

The smile dropped from his face as he saw the police car, his dad's car, parked right outside the shop. He took a deep breath before entering, guessing the game was up and he'd probably be leaving quicker than he had planned and it would be his dad telling him, not him telling his dad. Bracing himself he entered the shop and saw his dad standing there with the owner.

'Hi dad, what you doing here?' John asked, pretending surprise, although his gut was telling him he had a good idea why his dad was there, just by the look on his face.

'What the hell have you been up to?' his dad shouted at him.

'What do you mean up to?' John asked, trying to maintain a look of innocence.

'Don't come the innocent with me. You're a thief. They've told me hundreds, maybe even thousands of Rands have gone missing since you've been working here. Customers have been complaining they've paid their fees but there doesn't seem to be any record of them paying. They want you out of this shop and I want you out of the country. I've managed to persuade them not to press any charges, and if you were anyone else you'd be arrested. Now get out and wait for me in the car,'

There was an uneasy silence as they drove back in the car until his dad turned and said.

'You've brought shame on the family.'

John didn't turn to meet his gaze, but just stared straight ahead, feeling for the moment better to say nothing.

'And after all I've done for you,' his dad added.

'Done for me?' John snapped, turning his head to glare at his father. 'You've done nothing for me or for my mother or for Alex. How dare you say that? You're so mean and tight you couldn't even buy me a return ticket. Why do you think I fiddled the money? It was the only way I was going to be able to pay for a ticket back home.'

'We did all we could to make you welcome.'

'Make me welcome? The first thing you told me when I got here was that I was going to have to get a job to pay for my keep. What kind of welcome was that? How do you think that felt?' John's temper was beginning to rise at the coldness of his dad's concern for his own reputation.

'Liz is always making me feel as though I don't fit in, as though I should be beholden to her for everything.'

'And she's been proved right hasn't she?'

'You know what, I had decided I was going to tell you tonight I'd had enough and was going to leave and…'

'That's of course after you'd robbed the shop of enough money to pay for the fare.'

'Yes, what other way was there? You certainly weren't going to come forward with the money. I don't know what you thought I was going to do, stay here forever?'

'I did hope at one time that you might like the idea of settling down here with us.'

'So is that why you only bought a single ticket?'

'Look, we can argue over things all day. When we get back, I want you to pack and get the hell out of my house and out of my life,' his dad, with an air of finality.

'Out of your life?' John reacted angrily, his eyes sparkling with hostility. 'We've been out of your life for the past ten years. I wanted to come and see you to try to get some answers. You didn't care then and you don't care now. And don't blame it all on Liz. She wasn't responsible for locking me in the apartment and leaving me there for days while you ran off somewhere. I was only a kid then, but of course I now know where that somewhere was that you were running to.'

Lex braked hard and stopped the car and turned his head to John.

'And you've carried that with you all these years?'

'No, as a matter of fact, for some reason I had washed it from my memory and it was Auntie Marion who reminded me and said how they had had to break the door down to rescue me. What kind of father does that to a ten year old? I was there for days without food.'

Lex turned his head away and stared out of the windscreen as though looking for an answer, the heaviness of guilt pressing in on him. John looked across at him. The way his jaw had tightened and the way he was gritting his teeth told him he had struck a chord, touched a nerve that had brought back the memory to his dad.

'Well, aren't you going to say something?' John said when the silence had stretched out longer than expected.

Lex slowly turned his head to look at John.

'I'm sorry,' he began his voice tentative, his expression uneasy. 'I didn't mean to leave you that long. It was just that…'

'Liz was more important, Auntie Marion told me you had gone off with Liz,' John cut in, watching him frown, desperately searching for some way to explain, but whatever his dad said, he knew it could never excuse what he did.

The tension was broken when a voice on the police radio requested Lex to go to the assistance of another police officer dealing with a road traffic incident.

'Sorry I have to go. You'll have to walk the rest of the way. I expect you gone when I get home,' his dad told him.

'Where do you expect me to go?'

'I don't care where you go; Liz just wants you out of the house.'

John got out the car as quickly as he could and it sped off as soon as he closed the door. He watched the car accelerate away at speed, the tyres screeching, dark puffs of smoke emitting from the exhaust. It reminded him of the last time he had watched his dad drive away from his gran's, the dark puffs of smoke emitting from the exhaust, vaporising and mixing with the early evening mist, beginning to shroud the car, as though it was driving into the abyss. He remembered feeling then he may never see his father again. This time as he stared at the car as it turned the corner he knew he would never see his father again.

The journey to the airport was eerie, almost a replay of the last time he had driven with them, except his dad wasn't there this time.

'Have you spoken to your dad, since you had the row last week, to say goodbye to him?' Marion asked, breaking the silence, except for the quiet music coming from the car radio.

'No. There's no point. I've said all I want to say to him.'

'It's sad it should have ended in this manner, after coming all this way to see him,' Auntie Marion said, with a reflected sigh.

'I came hoping we could become friends again, but the way he is and her of course, it stood no chance from the beginning. It was silly of me to think we ever could be friends,' John said, with a sense of remorse. 'He's made his life and I've now got to get back and carry on with mine.'

Suddenly the music stopped as a news announcer broke into the programme. 'News has just come of a serious incident on the freeway leading from Umhlanga Rocks,' the announcer began. 'Protection Service Officer Lawson having stopped a driver for a traffic violation on the M4 was seriously injured when another speeding car crashed into the police car on the hard shoulder hurling Officer Lawson into the air. According to reports the driver causing the crash got out of the car wielding a gun in a desperate attempt to flee the scene, he was then shot and killed by Officer Lawson as he lay injured. The freeway has now been closed as the police continue their investigation. We will bring you further news when we have it,' the announcer ended.

'Do you want to go back?' Uncle Les asked, slowing down ready to turn the car around.

'No, he won't thank me for it and it won't help the situation. It would probably only make matters worse, if that's possible. He's a big man and can look after himself. He's made it clear he doesn't need me, so let's just carry on to the airport,' John said, finding himself once again having to struggle with his emotions.

BORN AND BETRAYED

1987

Jackie gave birth to Daniel on the fourth of August 1987 in the labour ward of Billinge Hospital in Wigan. John was there at the birth and watched anxiously as the baby was delivered. As the umbilical cord was cut, his chest swelled as he heard the first little cries of his son beginning to exercise his lungs. He felt proud as the nurse gave the baby for him to hold after he had been cleaned and wrapped in a soft blanket.

'I'll never leave you son, I'll never leave you,' he said, before looking across at Jackie with the nurses fussing around her. 'Thank you, my darling, for giving me such a wonderful and healthy boy. He's got your red hair alright.'

Soon they were back home and life went on as normal with John working as hard as ever and Jackie looking after Daniel. But Jackie had a restless spirit and began to miss going out to the clubs. She felt it was alright for John, working at the club most nights as a bouncer, but she resented being left at home taking care of the baby, so decided to take the baby with her and go and visit some of her friends.

This pleased John as he understood it was not much fun being on your own for most of the day and he encouraged her to go out more. It didn't bother him when she told him one of her friends had asked if she could babysit her child as the friend and her husband had been invited out to a party. Jackie told John they would probably be late coming back, so would it be alright if she stayed over. John not wanting her to be travelling anywhere at night readily agreed and re-arranged his shift at the club so he could stay at home and look after the baby. He gave Jackie some money to buy herself some cider, her favourite drink and walked with her to the bus stop, kissed her goodbye and hurried back home carrying Daniel in his strong arms.

Other friends of Jackie it appeared also wanted her to babysit for them, and it started to become a regular occurrence, particularly at weekends. John didn't mind as it seemed to brighten Jackie and she was more cheerful around the house. It also gave him the opportunity to take Daniel to see his mother who by now absolutely idolised her grandchild and loved every moment she spent with him.

It seemed an idyllic situation until one Sunday when Jackie was later than usual coming home and John was beginning to get a little worried. Stephen and Craig had gone off to play football with their friends and John needed to get some food for Daniel. While wheeling Daniel along to the shops in his new pram he bumped into Diane, one of Jackie's friends and politely asked how she was doing.

'Fine, I see she left you to look after the baby again,' Diane replied.

'Well, you know how it is with Jackie off babysitting for Debra and…'

'Debra?' Diane exclaimed, raising her eyebrows in surprise.

'Yes, she's been babysitting for her. Why what's the problem, why are you so surprised? She's been doing it for them several times now'

Diane looked away from his face, her eyes troubled as she struggled trying to decide what to say and then a wry smile twisted her face as she said.

'You're a decent guy John and here you are running around with the baby while your wife is…,' her voice starting to trail off as she continued to struggle with her conscience as to whether to tell him or not.

'While my wife is doing what?' John asked, suspicious of the expression on Diane's face.

'She doesn't deserve you,' she began, as a look of sympathy spread across her face 'She hasn't been babysitting. She met up with this guy Michael and she's been staying at his place and…' she hesitated, seeing the way John was beginning to stiffen.

He was stunned by her words. His heart beginning to beat hard in his chest as his eyes took on a murderous look.

'I have to go. Can you please do me a favour and look after Daniel?' Diane looked at him hesitantly.

'I don't know John, I don't think I can…'

'Look I'm going to have to sort this out and I don't want Daniel to…'

'Okay, but don't be too long. I'm sorry I should have kept my mouth shut,' she said, her eyes full of pain and her mouth beginning to tremble ominously.

'No, you did the right thing and I'm glad I know. Someone only makes a fool of me once. I promise I will be back to pick up my boy, because he is everything to me and I will never leave him,' John said, spinning around and running as fast he could along the pavement.

Oh God, what have I done? Diane sighed, as she took hold of the pram and headed off in the opposite direction looking for the nearest phone box.

As Jackie unlocked the door and breezily walked in calling out.

'John darling I'm home,' she heard the phone ringing.

She waited to see if John would appear from somewhere and pick up the receiver, but he didn't and the phone kept ringing. She waited a little longer thinking maybe he was in the garden, but there was no sound of the back door opening and the phone continued ringing. She decided she had better answer it and rushed over and picked up the receiver.

'Hello,' she said, then her face changed and her legs went weak as she listened.

'Bloody hell! You stupid cow,' was all she could say before slamming down the receiver. In a panic she rushed to the front door, flicked the latch up, then rushed upstairs, charged into the bedroom and threw herself down on the bed. She buried her head in her hands as she began to cry uncontrollably, sobbing. *What am I going to do?* She raised her head and looked into the dressing table mirror as though looking for an answer, but all she could see was her tear stained face with fear written all over it. The answer she wasn't looking for came from John's voice shouting above his heavy hammering on the front door.

I've been such a fool and he's going to kill me, she said to her reflection as though she already knew that was the only answer there could be. As the hammering became incessant, Jackie got to her feet and moved to the window, slowly opened it and looked down at John still hammering away at the door.

'Stop it,' she shouted down.

John looked up, his face bristling with anger. 'Come and open this door NOW!!!' he screamed up at her.

119

'No, you need to calm down first and then we can talk. I don't know what you've heard, but it isn't true, the truth is I…'

'I know what the truth is, I know what you've been up to, you've been sleeping with some guy called Michael If you don't come down and open this door I'll kick it in,' John shouted up.

Jackie knew that whatever she said was not going to stop John from doing whatever he was going to do. She slammed the window shut, frantically dragged a small chest of drawers over to the bedroom door and wedged it under the handle, then threw herself back on the bed and buried her head in the quilt in an attempt to blot out the sound of John kicking the door. In the jealous rage he was in, it didn't take John long to kick the door in. He flew up the stairs two at a time and charged at the bedroom door, but it didn't open. Supercharged with fury it only took a couple of heavy charges for the chest of drawers to shift and the door to open. Jackie screamed as John threw himself on top of her and grabbed her by the collar, she could see the naked hatred in his eyes as he raised his fist ready to smash it into her face.

'You cheating bitch,' he screamed at her.

But something stopped him. It was like a powerful force clutching at his wrist restraining him as a voice in his head repeated, *'men who beat up women are scum,'* At the same time he felt some of the tension lifting as calmness washed over him as he unclenched his fist and lowered his arm to his side. Slowly he got off her and the bed and stood staring down at the petrified Jackie.

'You know what you've done?' he growled at her, and she could feel the weight of his anger. 'I could have killed you and you need to thank whatever it was that stopped me. You make me feel ashamed that I came so close to almost killing you. You have ruined what I thought was a happy marriage. I loved you, I loved your kids and above all I love Daniel, the boy we made together. I always thought it was the fault of the other fathers that had deserted Stephen and Craig, but after this I'm not so sure,' he said, and saw her wince at the shame of it. 'If you're wondering where Daniel is, he is with Diane, I will collect him and bring him back with me when I collect my things. I hope you're pleased with what you've done and Michael whoever he is, is welcome to you, for our marriage is over,' he added, as he turned and stormed out, leaving her straightening her blouse where he had gripped her, shuddering at the thought of how close he had come to doing her serious harm.

John decided to call Uncle George and tell him what had happened.

'It's better to have got the hell out of it than to have been stuck with her forever,' Uncle George said, with quiet conviction. 'Why don't you get your arse down here, Uncle Dave and I will sort you out and...'

'Uncle Dave, is he out then?' John said, excitedly.

'Oh yes he's out, and we've got some good things going, so just get yourself here and we'll look after you,' Uncle George told him.

SOHO, SEX AND SCAMS

1988

The 80s was turning out to be a golden era with the Marquee Club on Wardour Street which had witnessed the early performances of rising stars like David Bowie, the Rolling Stones, Led Zeppelin and countless others, gradually earning itself the reputation of being the most important venue of its kind in Europe.

Gay bars were starting to multiply in and around Old Compton Street, but it was the oldest profession in the world that benefitted most from the 'enlightenment.' There was no longer the stigma attached to prostitution that there had been, and the gangsters quickly set up shop knowing there was big money to be made from the sex industry. It was an industry turning over millions of pounds, most of which was unaccountable and could be used to finance drugs and other criminal activities.

John was picked up from Euston Station by Uncle George in his big shiny Range Rover and as they drove along Euston Road John watched in horror as Uncle George brought his knees up to hold the steering wheel so that he could keep driving while he reached in his pockets for some hash and rolled a spliff.

'Hold the bloody wheel,' he shouted across at John as the car started to veer a little.

'Nice motor,' John said nervously as he reached over, gripped the steering wheel and straightened the course of the car.

'Sure is, cost a few bob these. Anyway great to see you son, you'll be pleased to have got away from all that shit up there. This is where it all happens, where all the money is, and we've got some good jobs lined up for you,' George said, pushing the cigar lighter in to heat it up.

'Where's Uncle Dave?' John asked, watching him pull the lighter out and put it to the end of his spliff.

'Oh he's busy sorting out some problem or other with one of the clubs we're involved in. You'll meet him later and Uncle Tony.'

'Uncle Tony, who's he?' John asked, surprised.

'Well, when your Uncle Dave was banged up, he met with this Maltese guy Tony who was doing time for tax evasion amongst other things. Although connected to the Maltese Mafia, Tony isn't a violent man nor is he physically strong, so some of the hard nutters in the prison wanting to make a name for themselves would try to pick on him. One night while he was sitting in his cell, one of the inmates charged in wielding a knife wanting to slash Tony. Well you know what you're Uncle Dave can be like, he leapt to his feet, drew a knife he had concealed on him and slashed the guy's face before he knew what had happened. Tony never forgot what Dave had done and told him when he got out there would be a job waiting for him. Tony explained about all the sex clubs, hostess bars and peep shows he was running and Dave, being the smartarse he is, told him he didn't want a job, he wanted a partnership and Tony, surprisingly, agreed.'

'So what sort of job are you thinking for me,' John asked, a little worried at the mention of sex clubs.

'You'll be working the kiosk at the live shows.'

'Live shows, what are they?'

'Dinnae worry we'll show you when we get there.'

They made their way through the busy streets of the West End along Shaftesbury Avenue, turning left past the fire station into Newport Street and parking the car in the NCP car park. As they came out of the car park, in front of them was Gerrard Street and John was amazed to see the glittering display of colours and the mass of tourists and Chinese people moving around. John gazed admiringly at the colourful Chinese arch, magnificently decorated with tall pillars painted in red, the arch itself decorated with intrinsic designs and Chinese calligraphy and the roof covered with coloured tiles.

'This is called China Town there's some great restaurants here. You ever had Chinese food?' Uncle George asked as they walked along.

'Yeah, we used to get a takeaway now and then.'

'Nah, I mean real Chinese food. I'll take you one night. You're in for a treat,' his uncle said, as they crossed back over Shaftesbury

Avenue and walked up Greek Street. Entering Old Compton Street John could see Ed's Diner ahead of him. As they turned right the road divided with Old Compton Street going off to the left and Moor Street going off to the right, creating an island of the buildings in between the two streets.

'You see those buildings behind Ed's Diner? Well, Uncle Tony and your Uncle Dave own them. Oh, make sure you always call him Uncle Tony, because the only one who gets to call him Tony is your Uncle Dave, as they're partners, okay?'

'What, they own all of them?' John asked, stopping in his tracks to stare up at them.

'Aye, all of them. Come on Uncle Dave will be waiting for us.'

John followed his uncle along until they came to a doorway that had a large illuminated neon sign above it with the words

PEEP SHOW

As they entered John saw there was a small kiosk with a man sitting in it giving change in pound coins to a customer, who then moved across to what appeared to be a series of booths, opened the door, slipped inside and closed it behind him.

'I'll explain all that to you in good time,' Uncle George said, as he worked the combination lock to a door. 'This is where it all happens,' he said as he opened the door and ushered John up the stairs. 'Go on up, right to the top,' he said, making sure to secure the door before he followed John up.

'This is my flat,' Uncle George told him, unlocking the door. It was a nice well furnished, spacious flat with a good view over the area.

"We've got a nice little flat for you on the next floor down,' he said, handing him a key. 'Come on, let's go down and have a look, you can put you stuff in and then we'll go down and meet Uncle Dave.'

There was a row of single bedsits that had originally been used by prostitutes, but were now being used by those who worked for the organisation. They were well equipped with comfortable beds, carpeted floor and a television. In the passage way there was a shower unit and a washing machine. On the next floor down was Uncle Dave's office, large and impressive with an adjoining luxury bathroom with a sauna. Uncle George led him down a small flight of steps into the gymnasium.

'You'll be able to keep yourself fit in here,' Uncle George said, with a sweeping gesture of his hands.

'I'm going to love this, just what I've always dreamed of,' John said, taking in the surroundings.

The gymnasium was expensively furnished with all types of weight training equipment; punch bags, boxing gear, and hanging from the walls around the gymnasium were swords, spears, body armour, protective headgear and nunchakus.

Just then Uncle Dave walked in, his huge afro haircut making John do a double take.

'Hey John, you made it alright?'

'Uncle Dave!' John exclaimed, excited at seeing him.

'Glad you got rid of that stupid lassie. You're with us now. Keep your nose clean and you'll do alright. I'll catch up with you later as I'm off to buy a roller,' Uncle Dave said, chirpily.

'A roller, what's that for?' John asked.

'It's not for anything, it's a car. The best there is, a Rolls Royce Silver Spirit.'

'Right, let's go for drink and I'll explain everything to you,' Uncle George said, as soon as Dave had left.

Uncle George took John to the Admiral Duncan, a pub that was increasingly being frequented by the gay community and it began to unnerve John to see the pub full of men with no females around, some of the men seeming to be standing very close to each other in an intimate way. Uncle George bought a couple of pints of beer and then found a table to sit down at.

'They're all poofs, dinnae worry about them,' his uncle said, noticing John looking around curiously. 'Anyway, we run the peep shows around here and…'

'What are peep shows?'

'You saw one when we arrived. They are a series of booths that have a shuttered window. Men go into the booths, put a pound coin in the slot, the shutter goes up and they can ogle at a girl dressed in a skimpy leotard costume doing provocative poses on one of those exercise bikes. After a few minutes the shutter comes down and if they want to keep on watching they have to insert another pound. Most of the punters finish up spending ten or twenty pounds at a time, so it's a real money maker, but the big money is in the hostess bars we run. I'll show you those later after we have had something to eat, let's go across to the Compton, the food is good there,' his uncle explained.

The Compton was a much larger pub also frequented by the gay community and the customers were a little more overt in their behaviour. As John looked around he could see one couple were sitting embracing and kissing while another man was sitting with his partner on his lap stroking his thigh.

'Oh no, come on uncle, let's go somewhere else, I'm not used to any of this, It's kind of weird,' John said, turning to leave.

Uncle George grabbed his arm and pulled him back.

'Relax, you're in London now, where anything goes. You just have to get used to it. We're going to have a beer and something to eat. So go and order two beers and two bangers and mash,' his uncle told him, slipping him some money.

'What you looking at?' he heard his uncle shout at someone as he crossed to a table. John found himself having to control his temper as the barman tickled the palm of his outstretched hand as he handed him the change.

It was beginning to get dark as they came out of the pub and Soho at night became a very different place. There were still crowds of people on the streets. The neon signs of the strip clubs and peep shows stood out in the darkening night amongst the hustlers, the toms, the pimps, the transvestites, drag queens, and prostitutes. So much flesh on offer, both in the pictures displayed in the windows of the porn shops and in real life on the pavements.

'This is Wardour Street, once the domain of the British film industry, all the major film companies had offices here at one time, but not many of them are left now. Anyway, just along the street on the left is another good pub, the Intrepid Fox and right at the top is Oxford Street, you've heard of Oxford Street?' his uncle explained as they stood on the corner of Old Compton Street.

'Yes, of course.'

'Well, that's where all the famous stores are, Selfridges, John Lewis, Debenhams and the rest, and the other way,' he said turning round, 'is Lower Wardour Street, which leads into Gerrard Street, which is the other end of China Town you saw earlier. So if you ever get lost, remember these land marks and you'll always be able to find your way back.'

They crossed over and stood on the corner of Wardour Street and Brewer Street.

'Along there is Madame JoJo's where all the trannies hang out and that's the famous Raymond's Revue bar and you will find a lot of sex shops down that alley. Now we own this building here,' his uncle said, pointing up at the tall building right on the corner where they were standing. 'It used to be called the Round House, apparently the Rolling Stones once played here, but we now call it the Erotica, and the other building in Moor Street where you're going to be living and working we call the Phoenix. You got it, this one is the Erotica and the other the Phoenix, okay? They used the Erotica in the Bob Hoskin film, *Mona Lisa* and your Uncle Dave got a nice bung for the privilege.'

'So what is it used for now?'

'Didn't you notice the sign up there?' his uncle said, indicating a neon sign with the words LIVE SHOW blazing out.

'What are live shows, are they sex shows?'

'They used to be but the Council clamped down on all that and now they're just fake sex shows. There's no real sex, just fake blow jobs.'

'Fake blows jobs, what does that mean exactly?'

'You dinnae need to worry about that now. We only use the ground floor and the basement. We have the peep show on the ground floor and the hostess bar in the basement. The other floors are all empty flats, twelve in all which we've got plans for. Anyway, this is where you're going to be working too. Come on I'll show you inside,' his uncle said, leading him through the side door.

Inside was a kiosk, very much like the one he saw when he first arrived.

'Now, your job will be to sit in the kiosk and take the money. The charge is two pounds and you issue them with a ticket and tell them that gives them entry into the club. This is Adam by the way who you'll be working with,' his uncle told him, indicating the man sitting in the kiosk.

'Hi Adam,' John said, offering his hand, which Adam took with a firm grip and gave it a strong shake. Adam had a kind of Gothic appearance with his long black hair swept back and tied tightly into a pony tail. He was wearing a long black coat and black boots. There were also some other heavy guys standing around who acknowledged George with a certain amount of deference as he walked in.

The basement club was dark and dingy, with a few spotlights

shining on the small low tables which were arranged in a semicircle in front of which was a bed. On each of the tables was a menu in a black plastic holder listing the various beers and cocktails available, together with the prices, which were not easy to read in the dim light. At one end there was a bar that looked authentic enough, with optics for the various spirits and other exotic looking bottles for the cocktails. Several girls, dressed enticingly in sexy underwear, stockings and suspenders and basques, were sitting at the bar waiting for the next lot of punters to walk in.

'Let me explain how it works,' his uncle said, taking him quietly to one side. 'The punter buys his entry ticket, comes down into the club and stands for a moment adjusting his eyes to the dark. He looks around sees the bed, so he thinks it's all genuine and there is going to be a live sex show. The punter sits down at one of the tables and one of the hostesses will approach him and ask if he would like a drink. The punter usually says no, as they've only come to see the live sex show, but the hostess tells them they have to buy a drink or leave, as that's the rules of the club which are clearly printed on a small sign at the entrance to the club and also printed on the back of the ticket. The punter, not bothering to have read anything, only interested in one thing doesn't want to leave for the sake of buying a drink, so usually orders a pint of larger, which if he had bothered to read the menu he would have seen costs twelve pounds. All drinks are non-alcoholic of course, as we don't have an alcohol licence.'

'What about the optics with all the spirits like gin, vodka, etc?'

'The bottles are genuine, but the contents are fake. The gin and Vodka are filled with water. The drinks are not actually served from the bar. They are prepared in the backroom in case the punter gets suspicious and are brought out on a nice looking silver tray. Once the hostess has served the drink, the punter usually asks when the show is going to start. The hostess will tell him they are just waiting for a few more customers and then the show will begin. In the meantime she will ask, putting on her practised seductive voice, if he would like her to sit with him. Most think she is just being friendly and say yes why not? She then asks the punter if he would like to buy her a drink. The punter readily agrees noticing the sexy way she is dressed with her boobs threatening to burst out at any moment. She naturally orders the most expensive cocktail on the menu. Right let's go and sit down pretending we're punters so you can see what actually happens,' his uncle suggested, looking around and seeing the tables filling up.

As soon as they had sat down a man appeared and began to walk around the tables.

'That's Martin, he's one of the Maltese gang, we call him the showman. He's someone you'll have to get to know once you've started working here,' his uncle told him.

They both watched as one of the scantily clad girls climbed onto the bed and spread herself out in a provocative manner, while the other hostesses quickly presented their punters with their bills.

'How the blazes do you work this out, I only had a pint of bloody lager,' John heard one of the punters complain to the hostess. 'Did you not read the menu sir?' she asked, politely, although John could see a few of the heavies alerted to what was going on, ready to move in.

'Look sir, you've had your fun, and about to see the live show and now you have to pay like everyone else,' the heavy said, as he came across with enough aggression to start to worry the man.

The punter hesitated for a moment then said

'I will call the police and I bet they won't be pleased when they find out what kind of clip joint this is.'

'Okay, if that's what you want sir, but what do you think your wife will say when you get hauled off to court and she finds out you've been watching a live show and flirting with a sexy young female,' the heavy bluffed, noticing his wedding ring, knowing full well there was no way they would ever contemplate calling the police.

'I hope you're studying all this,' Uncle George whispered to John.

'Just remember where you are,' the heavy reminded him, 'you're in the middle of Soho and we don't take kindly to people who don't pay their bills. So if I was you, I would pay up and save yourself a lot of trouble,' the heavy advised. There was no attempt to hide the threat of what could happen if he still refused to pay.

'You watch what happens now. Once the first the first one pays, it has a domino effect and rest of them usually cough up without too much trouble,' Uncle George explained.

John watched in amazement as the hostesses moved around the punters collecting hundreds of pounds one after the other.

'Is it always this easy?'

'Not always son, that's where the fear factor comes in useful.'

Once the final bill had been collected, Martin in a flamboyant theatrical manner began to rouse the expectation of what all the punters have been patiently waiting for.

'Right we're going to do the live show now. This beautiful girl wants me and I'm going to give it to her, right gents?' Martin called out clapping his hands above his head, as he continued to pace around the floor.

'Yeah go on let's see you give it to her,' one of the punters called out, obviously well inebriated before he came into the club.

'Don't you worry sir, I will,' Martin called back. 'One of the hostesses will come around with a box and the more money you tip us, the more I will perform, but no coins just nice folding notes if you please,' Martin added, as he watched the girl move around the tables collecting the money.

When he felt they had collected all the money they were going to get he climbed up onto the bed. He stood up with his back to the tables and the girl got down on her knees in front of him. She then raised her hands and unzipped his trousers and began to move her head backwards and forwards simulating the sex act. In fact she was just moving her head against his belly button while both of them made appropriate noises as though they were building to a climax. After a while Martin would cry out in ecstasy as though reaching an orgasm. Then zipped himself up and turned to the punters and said.

'That's it gentlemen, the show's over!!!'

'This is the point when the punters realise they've been well and truly ripped off and storm out angry and embarrassed that they've been conned. You'll then notice the heavies moving in just in case any of the punters still want to make a complaint. So now you can see how the system works. You will always get one or two awkward ones, but they always pay up in the end. Sometimes we have to rough a few up, but usually the threat is enough,' his uncle explained as he got to his feet. 'You start here in the kiosk upstairs tomorrow, it's a five hour shift and you get paid fifty quid in your hand per shift. You can always do two shifts a day in you feel up to it. We'll see how you go and then maybe move you up to possible bar manager, where you get to keep ten per cent of the take. We reckon to be making between two to five grand a shift,' his uncle explained cheerfully.

'Sounds great, look forward to tomorrow,' John said, eagerly.

'Right, I'll take you back to your room so you can sort yourself out and get a good night's rest ready for tomorrow,' his uncle suggested as they made their way out of the club.

John lay on his bed thinking about what had happened to him since his return from South Africa. It had been hard, harder than he had expected, Jackie's betrayal hitting him the hardest. But now with his two uncles he began to realise how naive he had been and promised himself he would never allow himself to be that innocent again. His only anguish was having to leave without Daniel. He promised himself he would visit him regularly to assure him he was not being abandoned, that he still had a father who loved him and that one day they would be together again.

THE MALTESE MAFIA

John was suddenly awoken by the heavy banging on the door and the voice of Uncle George shouting.

'Come on, get yourself out of bed, you can't lie there all day, there's work to be done.'

John rubbed his eyes and stretched himself as he heard his uncle banging on the next door calling out. 'Come on Martin, time to get up.'

John got out of bed, went to the widow and looked out over Moor Street and smiled to himself, not quite believing he was in the big city, the streets already alive with people hurrying in all directions. He looked to his left and could see Cambridge Circus with the mass of traffic. It was an exhilarating feeling as he moved his eyes to the side of the Palace Theatre and took in the big signs advertising *Les Miserables*. At that moment his uncle walked in and saw John standing at the window looking out.

'Quite a sight isn't it? I remember when I first arrived I found it difficult to take it all in, but you'll soon get used to it son. Get yourself washed and I'll take you for some breakfast before you start for work.'

The aroma of roasting coffee beans emanating from the coffee shop on Wardour Street opposite the end of Old Compton Street was permeating the air.

'I love that smell, it helps to soothe the brain and reverse the effects of the night before,' his uncle said, enthusiastically breathing in the aroma. 'It really gets the juices going, sets you up for the day. We're going to Café Bruno just up the road, they do a great breakfast,' he added, as they crossed over the road and walked up to the café on the opposite corner to the Intrepid Fox.

'Right, go up and order two full English and coffee, okay,' his uncle said, handing John a twenty pound note.

While John was up at the counter ordering the food, Martin and Andy came into the cafe and joined George at the table.

'Make that two more,' he called out to John.

'So who's the new kid?' Martin asked, looking across at John standing with his back to him at the counter.

'He's family, his name's John. You'll both be working with him and I want you to look after him and teach him the ropes. He's got a lot to learn but he's a quick learner and he's pretty handy with his fists, been doing a bit of Kung Fu and Karate.'

Just then John returned with four cups of coffee on a tray. Uncle George waited for him to hand the cups around and sit down before he said.

'This here is Martin, he's got the flat next to you. We call him the showman. You remember you saw him doing his bit yesterday.'

'Yes, I remember. Hi Martin,' John said, offering his hand, which Martin took and shook welcomingly.

'And this is Andy, Uncle Tony's nephew and the son of one of Soho's most celebrated prostitutes. He is also the general manager, taking care of the day to day running of the operation. Andy has one of the bigger flats on the floor below me.'

Andy seemed unusually proud that his mother was a prostitute nodding his head in acknowledgement. He had light olive skin and was quite handsome, clean shaven with jet black hair he had the appearance of a rather young Mel Gibson.

'Right, after breakfast I'm going to introduce you some of Uncle Tony's guys you'll be working with. It's important you know who and what they are,' Uncle George told him, as he tucked heartily into his breakfast.

'This is Bullets, this is Fingers and this is Diamonds,' his uncle said, introducing the three men as soon as they arrived at the hostess club and saw them gathered there. John studied them and almost laughed as they looked as though they had just stepped out of a Warner Brothers gangster movie. They were all in their forties, stocky built, of average height, wearing pin stripe suits, spats on their shoes and sporting trilby hats, looking every bit like stereotypical Mafia mobsters.

'This is John. He's family and has come to join us. He'll be starting in the kiosk of the hostess bar to begin with and we'll see how he gets on,' his uncle told them.

'Good to know you John,' Bullets said, in his heavy Maltese accent. 'I sure we will be bumping into each other all over da place. Keep your nose clean and I sure you do alright,' Bullets added, shaking his hand.

'Yeah, good to know you, John,' the other two joined, each shaking his hand, before turning and walking off.

John waited until they had left, before he turned to his uncle and said.

'Are they for real?'

'You'd better believe it. They are connected to the Maltese Mafia and I'm telling you, you don't want to mess with them. The Maltese Mafia virtually runs Soho. Tony's the boss man and they are his lieutenants and they zealously guard their territory, not letting any other mobs moves in. There's a rumour that Bullet's dad chopped the head off of one gang leader who had tried to muscle in on the area in the sixties. Whether it's true or not, I don't know, but I'm sure as hell they're capable of it. They even drove the Kray Twins out when they tried to move in. So always be careful what you say to them. Dave is their boss, because of his partnership agreement with Tony, but it would only take one stupid act to unbalance things.'

'But how did they get names – Bullets, Fingers, and Diamonds?'

The question made his uncle smile.

'Well, Bullets apparently gets his name from having been shot several times. He even wears the bullets taken from his body on a chain around his neck like a lucky charm. Fingers, well, he is reputed to be a brilliant card shark and you should see him shuffle a pack of cards, he can do things with one that would blow your mind. Diamonds, well he just likes diamonds. Don't know whether you noticed but he was wearing a good size diamond in his ear. Just remember those guys have an assortment of weapons and they aren't afraid to use them.'

'So am I starting in the kiosk?' John asked, anxious to get to work.

'Yes, but first you're going to run an important errand for us. I am going to give you a bag which I want you to guard with your life and I mean with your life. You'll be carrying twelve grand in cash. Now you get a taxi and tell him to take you to the Café Bascillico in Covent

Garden. Order yourself a coffee and wait there until you get a phone call and…'

'I don't understand where is the…'

'You don't need to understand, you just need to listen and do as I say. The owner will come over and tell you there is someone on the phone for you. That someone will tell you what to do next, Okay?'

'Okay.'

'Right, we'll pop back to the office, pick up the money and off you go.'

John stood on the corner of Greek Street and Old Compton Street and hailed the first taxi he saw approaching with the For Hire sign lit up.

'Where to John?' the taxi driver casually asked.

It seems everybody knows Uncle George and Uncle Dave, he even knows my name, John thought as he said.

'Do you know the Café Bascillico in Covent Garden?'

'You bet,' the taxi driver said, waiting for John to open the door and get in.

John watched excitedly as the taxi turned left into Shaftesbury Avenue, crossed over Cambridge Circus, turned right into Earlham Street and stopped at the corner with Neal Street.

'There you are John, Cafe Bascillico,' the taxi driver said, pointing to a rather run down cafe the other side of the street.

'How much is that?' John asked.

'£5.60 on the clock.'

John handed him one of the ten pounds notes Uncle George had given him and waited for the change.

The taxi driver handed him the change, irritation beginning to show on his face that he hadn't been offered a tip.

'Do all the taxi drivers know my uncles?' John asked, pocketing the change.

'Your uncles, who the hell are they?'

'The Lawsons,' John said, proudly.

'Never bleedin' heard of them, but I tell you one thing. I won't forget you. The last of the big spenders,' the taxi driver said, driving off.

The Gaggia machine hissed and the steam drifted across the café as John sat nervously looking around while he sipped his coffee, wondering when the phone call would come and what he was going to be told what to do next.

He had finished his coffee and was trying to decide whether to order another when he heard the pay phone fixed to the wall at the far end of the cafe start ringing. He was wondering whether he should go and answer it when the owner came around from behind the counter, snatched up the receiver, listened for a brief moment, looked across at John and called out.

'Your name John?'

'Yes,' John answered.

'This call's for you.'

John rushed over, and took the receiver from him.

'Hello' he said hesitantly.

He listened to a gruff cockney voice telling him to take a taxi to the Cell Block Cafe in Wandsworth, The phone went dead before he had a chance to repeat the instructions to make sure he understood them.

John hailed a taxi and watched the smile break out on the cab driver's face when he told him where he wanted to go. As the taxi turned away from the river into Trinity Road, then right into Heathfield Road John was surprised to see a massive structure with a large sign that read:

HMP PRISON WANDSWORTH

John looked across at the Wandsworth Prison sign as the taxi drove past, thinking *that's one place I'd hate to be in.*

The taxi finally pulled up and John smiled as he looked up at the sign CELL BLOCK CAFE painted above the doorway. As he entered he looked around not sure what to expect. Seated at the back were two rather elderly gentlemen. One of them raised a finger beckoning him over and John moved across towards them, firmly holding onto the bag with the money in it. Without saying anything the other man pointed to the floor. At first John wasn't sure what he was indicating, then realised he wanted him to place the bag on the floor, which he did and waited again for them to say something. They said nothing, just stared up at him. John waited, still not sure what to do or say.

'Now bugger off,' one of them finally said.

John did as he was told and hurried out as quickly as he could.

'Did you give them the money?' Uncle George asked when John walked back into the office.

'Yeah, I did. They're a couple of strange guys, must be in their late sixties I reckon, quite aggressive, didn't say hello, just indicated for me to put the bag down on the floor and then told me to bugger off.'

'They're the Smiths. We rent some of the buildings from them and that's the rent money you took to them. I should have told you before you went the reason they wouldn't take the money off you is because they don't know who's watching them. Could be the police, taxman, they don't even touch it. Someone else will come and pick up the bag. Make sure you remember that next time as you'll likely to be doing the run from now on. You don't talk to anybody about it okay?'

'Sure Uncle George.'

Just then they both looked up as Tony strolled into the office.

'Hi George, how's it all going?' he asked casually.

'Fine Uncle Tony, everything's going just fine,' George assured him. 'This is my nephew John, he's come to work for us.'

John felt Tony's eyes giving him the once over. Tony was casually dressed in a smart pair of jeans and a tennis type short sleeve shirt with a collar and smart casual slip on shoes. He was wearing an expensive watch on his left wrist and an equally expensive solid gold bracelet on his right. He was clean shaven and had dark hair. John reckoned he was aged around fifty.

'Good to meet you John. You'll see me around from time to time. Keep your nose clean and do as your uncle tells you and you can do well for yourself,' Tony said as he turned and walked back out the office without saying another word.

'So that's Uncle Tony. He's alright, but he doesn't suffer fools gladly so always be on your toes when you see him around. If he likes you then you can do well, but if he doesn't, then you're out on your ear. Okay?' His uncle explained, turning his head as Nicola, one of the peep show girls walked in, wearing a skimpy leotard.

'Alright if I use the shower and sauna?' she asked, already starting to remove the leotard as she breezed past.

John's eyes instinctively followed her, almost popping out of his head as she stepped out of the leotard without bothering to close the door. She saw John looking at her, turned to face him and gave him a friendly smile before disappearing further into the room. Uncle George followed John's eyes and guessed what he was thinking. He waited until he was sure Nicola couldn't hear what was being said.

'You don't mess on your own doorstep. You don't mix with the girls. They're off limits, it only leads to trouble. We pay them for what they do and that's as far as it goes. You fancy a bit you go outside of where you work and find it. Okay?'

'Okay Uncle, I understand.'

'Make sure you do. The temptation is there and a lot of the girls will happily offer it if they think it will give them some advantage over the others. But that's where the trouble starts. So keep it in your trousers as far as they are concerned. Right, you're going to do the late shift tonight, six to around eleven thirty over at the Erotica in Wardour Street where I took you yesterday. All you've got to do is sit in the kiosk and issue the two quid tickets. If any of the punters come up complaining you didn't tell them they had to buy a drink you point to the sign on the wall and just say, *'didn't you read that sign sir, when you came in?'* Tell them it's also printed on the back of the ticket, they don't bother to look at that either. Don't worry they can't get at you. They'll have a good moan and amble off. If any of them look like giving you trouble, you let them see you use the intercom and call for security, that's usually enough to scare them off,' his uncle explained.

John settled himself into the kiosk and was surprised at the number of punters happily paying their two pounds to see what they thought was going to be a live sex show. It wasn't long though before he experienced his first complaining customer, who came up the stairs and shouted angrily at him.

'This whole thing's a bloody con. You didn't tell me I had to buy a drink.'

'It states it clearly on that sign, sir,' John told him politely, indicating the sign 'and it is also printed on the back of your ticket, sir.'

The man studied the sign for a brief moment, then huffed and stormed out.

As the night wore on John got more and more used to the punters coming up to the kiosk and moaning, realising they had been conned, and he became more skilful in how to answer without them resorting to threats. Apart from the occasional confrontations, the job was boring and John overcame it by looking out through the open doors that gave him a good view all along Old Compton Street with the pavements bustling with all kinds of life. Gay couples, walking along holding hands as they made their way to the Admiral Duncan or the Compton.

Transvestites making their way to Madame JoJo's, prostitutes walking up and down trying to attract a customer. It amused John to watch the girls walk off with a man and be back on the beat just fifteen or twenty minutes later. It was a scene that was constantly changing.

Suddenly John's image of the street became blurred as a tall man moved in front of the kiosk blocking his view. He said in a rather refined voice.

'This is an absolute scam. There was no live sex show, just a fully clothed man and a female pretending to have sex. It's a total disgrace. Do you realise I'm a solicitor and I've a good mind to call the police and...'

'In that case sir,' John said, interrupting him. 'You will have seen the sign outside that said live show before you came and...'

'Exactly live sex show, which is what I expected to see.'

'No sir, it says live show, not live sex show and you as a solicitor would know the difference. So if you feel you want to call the police do so, but I wonder what your colleagues and family will think that you came here expecting to see a live sex show?' John said, his voice gentle and polite, but there was no mistaking the threat that lay behind it.

The man stared at John for a moment longer considering his options until he realised he had none, turned and walked out saying.

'You haven't heard the last of this.'

John allowed himself a smile, thinking it takes all sorts and that the solicitor would probably be in court tomorrow prosecuting some poor bugger for indecent exposure.

At the end of day Andy appeared and handed John fifty pounds, his pay for the night. He felt pleased as he walked back to his flat with the money in his pocket, knowing he was going to be earning that amount every shift, a hundred pounds per day if he wanted to do two.

He lay in his bed feeling euphoric that he was now earning good money and living rent free in a nice little flat in the centre of London. It was perfect and he couldn't believe his luck, but then his thoughts turned to Daniel and how he had abandoned him and he decided he would have a word with Uncle George to see if he could have a weekend off sometime to go visit him, his mother and Alex.

John continued to learn how the business worked, moving around the hostess bar and the peep shows. He also got to know the girls and was surprised to discover most of them who worked the peep shows and hostess bars were actually students who were simply doing it to pay for their education and student fees. Others were single mothers having to support themselves and their child after the husbands had walked out on them. To them it was an easy way of earning good money without prostituting themselves.

There were of course the strippers who went from club to club, took their clothes off, put them back on, moved down the road to the next club and took them off all over again. The little side streets where there were red lights shining out from the windows was a sign indicating there was a prostitute available offering her services. It always amused John to watch a man enter the building, then watch as the red light was switched off and the curtains drawn. Ten minutes or so later the curtains would be drawn back and the red light would be switched back on again.

John was also amazed to find out when talking with Andy during one of his breaks that not only was his mother a prostitute, but his girlfriend was one too and he was quite proud of it. He emphasised she was not a common prostitute, but a high class one.

'What's the difference between a high class one and the others?' John asked, bemused.

'A high class pro is at the top of her game only dealing with the rich and the famous, visiting them in the most expensive hotels, or occasionally going to their palatial homes. They earn two to three grand a time. My fiancée has made enough to buy herself a nice house and...'

'She's your fiancée?' John asked, startled.

'Sure, and she plans to pack it in when we get married. The other pros are a bit down the line. They work from their own homes or through an escort agency, some have little flats around the area with red lights in the windows. After that it's usually on the streets with a pimp taking care of them as well as taking their earning off them,' Andy explained.

'I'm learning all the time,' John reflected.

'What you've got to watch out for are the touts.'

'The touts?'

'Yeah, they're the rip off merchants that hang around outside the hostess club.'

'Yeah, I wondered about them and what they were doing?'

'They try to sell tickets to the live show and...'

'But how can they sell tickets to our show? We're the only one who can do that.'

'Yes that's what the stupid punter finds out when he walks in and presents his ticket which he's probably paid a fiver for.'

'So what do I say if one of these walks in?'

'Just say sorry mate you've been conned, but you can come in, the entrance fee is only two quid and that makes them feel at least we're genuine.'

'Until of course…'

'Yeah, well that's the way the game is played. Another thing you'll see going on is what's called the key scam. The touts will approach someone they suspect of looking for a pro and say to him, "*You see that pretty girl standing over there? Well that's my girl but she can't be seen to be openly soliciting. So if you want a good time, and I can promise she'll give it to you, you pay me twenty quid. I'll give her the nod and give you this key to her flat which is number 26 Berwick Street. You wait to give her time to get there, then you let yourself in and she'll be waiting for you.*" The punter will usually say, "*how do I know she'll be there?*" The tout looks at the punter indignantly and says, "*do you think I would give you the key to her apartment if she wasn't?,*" which is usually enough for the punter to part with their money. Of course the key is fake and doesn't fit any doors anywhere. By the time the punter discovers this, the tout and the girl are long gone. Some of the girls work the scheme on their own.'

'It just shows how easy it is to get ripped off,' John said, with a shake of his head.

'Thank heavens for that otherwise we would soon be out of business,' Andy said, with a knowing grin. 'Anyway enough of this idle chat. You'd better get back to work as they'll still keep coming. There are thousands out there ready to be parted with their money. So let's get to it,' Andy said, getting to his feet.

Ironically, it wasn't long after what Andy had told him about the touts that he spotted one hanging around just outside the entrance. He rushed out, grabbed the tout by the scruff of the neck, pulled him inside and set about him with some hefty blows to the head and body while saying to him.

'If I ever see you hanging around here again, I'll break every bone in your cheating body.'

The tout struggled to his feet, his face swollen and bloodied, clutching his stomach as he stumbled to the entrance and staggered out. When Uncle George and Uncle Dave got to hear about it they gave him a two hundred pound bonus.

John's reputation that he could handle himself and wasn't afraid to dish it out when necessary was spreading and the hostesses would often call him down at collecting time when they feared things were getting a little out of hand. John didn't have to resort to violence as he now exuded an aura of fear which was enough to scare the punters into paying. Pleased with the way John was handling himself, his uncles agreed he could have the weekend off to go and visit Daniel and his mother.

When the weekend came, Uncle George surprised him, by saying.

'You really want to rub it in and show Jackie what she's lost? Then take the Range Rover and show her how well you're doing,' he said, tossing John the keys.

'Thanks Uncle George.'

'Buy yourself a new suit and make sure you take plenty of cash with you. Let her see it so she realises what a stupid selfish bitch she's been. Here's another bonus. You've done well since you've been here and you deserve it,' his uncle said, handing him another two hundred pounds.

John jumped at the chance and couldn't wait for the moment he pulled up outside the house to see Jackie's reaction to the big car and him dressed in his smart new suit with an expensive watch strapped to his wrist.

'I've come to collect my son, so hand him over Jackie,' John demanded, handing her a hundred pounds.

'Wow!! Thanks John,' Jackie exclaimed surprised at his generosity as she happily handed Daniel over.

'I'll drop Daniel off on Monday. By the way that money is to pay your bills and not to be flittered away on yourself or your fancy man,' John told her as he took hold of Daniel ready to leave.

JOHN GETS HIS COLLAR FELT

'I've got other plans for you now,' his uncle said, as they made their way back to his office. 'I'm opening another hostess bar and I want you to run it for me. How do you fancy that?'

'You mean it's going to be your own hostess bar?'

'Yes. I've rented the basement in the Phoenix from Uncle Tony. It's not as large as the Erotica but it can still be a good earner. You will be in charge, taking care of security and making sure everything runs smoothly. You'll obviously be earning more money plus a percentage of the takings and Martin will be the showman, Okay?'

'Okay, thanks uncle, I'll enjoy doing that.'

'But, first you're going to have to help me paint the place up and make it look nice.'

A week later the hostess bar was open for business. The walls and ceiling were painted black. Six tables were set in a semicircle around a bed on which the live shows would be performed. There was a small illuminated decorative bar at one end, opposite the entrance, so that the punters could see it when they entered. Also the latest in close circuit cameras were installed for extra security. There were four hostesses, a barman and a man in the kiosk taking the entrance fee, with John taking care of security.

Everything was working well and John could not have been happier until one evening a German punter started getting very argumentative at the size of the bill and was refusing to pay. He was becoming very aggressive as he got up from the table and started threaten the hostesses. John kept a careful watch from a distance by the door, ready to move in if the situation got any worse. The man had a big Olympus camera over his shoulder which he slipped off and then gripped by the straps letting it swing low ready to use as a weapon. John's reaction was swift and he moved forward ready to protect the girls, fearing the man might hit them with it. Suddenly, without warning, the man swung the camera at John, catching him on the side of the head causing a four inch gash, the long focus lens snapping off and the camera smashing into pieces in the process. With blood starting to pour from the wound and running down his neck, spilling onto his white T shirt, John stared at the man in his controlled manner and said.

'You shouldn't have done that.'

The man stared at John in disbelief that he was still standing and hadn't gone down from the impact. John measured the man and suddenly turned and gave him a side kick, propelling him backwards with such force that he ended up embedded in the plaster board wall with his legs dangling out. The hostesses then joined in taking off their stilettos and hitting the man with them. Unfortunately one of the other punters had called the police and they had responded quickly.

'So what's going on?' the police officer asked, taking in the scene and looking at John's blood soaked T-shirt.

'This man was getting very aggressive towards the girls and as security I stepped in to protect them. He smashed me over the head with his camera,' John explained.

'Did you do this sir?' the police officer asked, turning to the man.

'Yes I did,' he admitted in his broken English.

The police officer immediately put a restraining hand on the man's arm and proceeded to caution him as he marched him out. Two other police officers turned up and the first officer told them to bring everyone else to the station to give witness statements.

At West End Central Police Station John and the girls gave their statements and were then taken to the canteen and offered tea or coffee. John's head was still bleeding and he was still wearing the blood soaked T shirt which prompted other police officers and staff to ask what had happened to him. It was then that things took a sudden turn as John was asked to go back to the interview room.

'Your name Lawson?' the police officer asked, sombrely.

'Yes, I already told you that. It's in my statement,' John said, surprised at the need to confirm his name.

'Right. Wait there,' the police officer said, getting up from the desk and leaving the room.

John sat idly tapping his fingers on the desk wondering why they wanted to talk to him again. He looked up as he noticed someone looking at him through the square glass in the door. A face unbeknown to him, but a face he would learn to recognise in time, for it was the face of Inspector Ronald Atwell.

The police officer quickly returned, resumed his seat and looked hard at John as he said.

'John Lawson you are under arrest. You are being charged with threatening behaviour.'

'Charging me? He was the one that attacked me and I've got the wound to prove it.'

'No, you intimidated him, threatened him with his life and he felt the only way to defend himself was to use whatever he had to hand, which happened to be the camera after you had hit him.

'No. It was me who was forced to defend myself. It's all on tape from the security cameras, you can check it for yourselves,' John said, glad that Uncle George had thought to install the cameras.

'Yes, we checked the tapes, but they're all blank. That's the trouble when you install the cheap crap; they never seem to work properly, particularly when you need to rely on them. I'd ask for your money back from whoever supplied you with that heap of junk,' the police officer said in a derisory tone.

Having been formally charged John was put into a cell and left there to his own devices until around one o'clock in the morning when two police officers came to take him to Middlesex Hospital to have the wound seen to. John allowed himself to smile as the nurse started to berate the two police officers for not bringing the patient for treatment as soon as the incident had occurred. The wound was cleaned and he needed five stitches, after which he was taken back to the station. By now it was three o'clock in the morning and he was informed he was being released on bail to report to the police station in four weeks' time.

This situation worried Uncle George. He was particularly concerned that the name Lawson was being bandied about by the police and suggested that John take a break and go and visit his family until he had to report back to the police. His uncle told him he could have the use of the mobile phone as they would need to stay in touch in case of emergencies.

'This is a Nokia Mobira Cityman. It's at the cutting edge of technology which means we can call each other from anywhere. They're bloody expensive but much better than the brick and...'

'The brick?'

'Yeah, that's what they call the Motorola, because it's bleeding heavy, shaped like a brick, weighing over two and half pounds, whereas this one is much lighter. Take care of it because you have to go on a waiting list to get one of these and every scheming sod out there is after one. If they see one lying around they'll pinch it, or even rob you if they see you walking round with it,' his uncle said, handing him the phone.

Deciding to travel first class, John waited until the train was nearing Wigan and used the Nokia to phone Jackie. He smiled broadly as he heard her voice loud and clear as she said hello.

'It's me, I reckon I shall be with you in the next half hour,' he told her.

'Where are you now?' Jackie asked.

'I'm on the train,' he said, imagining what her reaction would be.

'Don't be daft, trains don't have telephones,' she said with an air of disbelief.

'I'm calling you on my mobile phone from the train. You can call me back on it, but you'd better not as the calls are more expensive,' he told her, liking the way he had said more expensive. Then he heard her say

'That's your dad, he's talking on one of those new-fangled phones they say you can use anywhere,' and it made him smile again.

He couldn't resist calling her again from the taxi. When he'd finished the driver looked over his shoulder and said.

'I've heard about those things, are they any good?'

'Well, you've just heard me talking on it that ought to tell you something,' John said boastfully.

As soon as he got out of the taxi Daniel came rushing out of the house to greet him.

'Daddy, daddy,' he cried out, bristling with excitement.

Daniel was now two years old and John's heart swelled with pride at how his son was growing up. He looked him up and down and was concerned to see that his clothes looked a little shabby. He decided he would buy him some new ones when they got to Birkenhead.

'Last time you came in a flashy car, this time you come with a flashy phone. So what's it all about?' Jackie asked as he carried Daniel back into the house.

'It's not about anything. The car is in for repairs, so I took the train up,' he told her, not wanting to explain about the car or anything else for that matter.

'Where are Craig and Stephen' John asked, secretly relieved when Jackie told him they were visiting their Nan's. It was difficult and emotional for John to see the boys, especially as Craig would give him a sad look as he left with Daniel. *Poor lads,* John thought as he looked around the living room.

'Did you use the money I gave you to clear the bills?'

'Yes. But as soon as you get rid of one bill, another one pops up and when you've struggled to pay that, another appears out of nowhere,' Jackie said sullenly.

'So what do you owe now?'

'Two hundred.'

'How do you manage to chalk that up?'

'You forget I have three children to clothe and feed as well as myself and another on the way, so it's difficult to make the money stretch at the best of times,' she said wearily.

'Another on the way?' John retorted angrily. 'I suppose it's that Michael.'

'Yes it is. But he did a runner as soon as he found out I was pregnant,' Jackie said, with a hapless shrug of her shoulders.

John dug his hand into the inside pocket of his jacket pulled a wad of fifty pound notes, counted off five.

'Right, here's two fifty. That gives you fifty to spend on you and the kids,' he said handing her the money.

'Thank you, I can breathe again,' she said, clutching the money to her face.

'Right now we've got that sorted out I'm going to take Daniel for a bit longer as I've got some time off if that's okay with you?'

'Fine by me, it'll give me one less to worry about for a while,' she said a wry smile twisting her face.

It was a look that made John decide things would have to change.

'I'll phone for a taxi and Daniel and I will be on our way,' John said, taking the mobile phone out his bag and punching in the local taxi service number from the card the driver had given him. Jackie and Daniel looked on, their eyes alive with curiosity as he waited for it to be answered.

'It's on its way,' he said with a smile, looking at the wonderment on their faces.

His mother was waiting at the door as soon as she saw the taxi draw up in Thorneycroft Street and was delighted when Daniel got out and rushed into her arms.

'Hello my precious darling,' she said, scooping him up into her arms and giving him a huge kiss.

'We've got him for as long as we like. I'm going to be staying here for a few weeks, my uncles have given me some time off to spend with you and Daniel,' John said following them into the house.

'So where did you phone me from? It certainly wasn't from a phone box?' she asked putting the kettle on to make some tea.

'From this.' John said, taking the mobile out of his bag and showing it to her. 'With this I can call you from anywhere.'

'I suppose that's another one of those expensive gadgets your uncles can afford through their ill-gotten gains,' his mother said disparagingly.

'At least they're looking after me. I'm earning more money than I could up here. Look at Flemmo slogging his guts out at the Vauxhall car factory for a measly hundred and fifty a week. I earn more than that in a day,' he said, in a defensive tone as he sat down at the table. As his mother brought the cups over she noticed the scar on the side of John's head.

'You been fighting again?' she asked. He could see the concern etched on her face.

'No, it was just a silly accident. I tripped and banged my head that's all. Nothing to worry about.'

'I worry all the time, you getting mixed up in their sordid businesses.'

'Look, I'm only involved in the peep shows where the girls are fully dressed in leotards. I just sit in the kiosk and give out change.'

'And they pay you all that money for just doing that?'

'I also do some other little jobs for them.'

'That's what worries me. They will gradually draw you in until you get into real trouble.'

148

'No, they're not doing anything illegal, so there's nothing for you to worry about,' John lied, not daring to tell her he was already under arrest having been charged with a serious offence.

IMMORAL AND INDECENT

John arrived back at Euston Station and headed straight to Soho and was surprised when he walked into Uncle Dave's office to find his uncles sitting with a rather overweight man with an equally fat face and a bulging stomach sitting there.

'This is Cecil Watkins who takes care of all our legal problems,' Uncle Dave announced by way of introduction.

'Hello sir,' John said offering his hand.

'You will be pleased to know all charges have been dropped,' Cecil Watkins informed him with a beaming smile and a nod of his head as he shook his hand.

John noticed he had a mop of unruly hair and as he shook it flakes of dandruff flew out in all directions falling down over the shoulders of his crumpled dark blue pin striped suit.

'We leave such matters in the hands of our trusted solicitor here. It was through his skilled negotiations that all charges were dropped.'

'You see,' Cecil Watkins cut in. 'there is a way of dealing with these matters that in the end benefits everyone. To pursue this case the police would have had to keep the German tourist here paying for his stay until the case was heard, or pay to bring him back. Either way would be expensive. Particularly when I argued it would take time to gather all the evidence, which meant the case would have to wait until such times as my client, you, had fully recovered from the injuries he sustained in the unwarranted attack, plus the fact we would also commence proceedings against the German tourist for GBH. So in the end it was agreed to drop all charges.'

Uncle George waited until Cecil had gone before he turned to John.

150

'Now do you know of any of your mates up North who would be interested in working as front men?' his uncle asked.

'Front men, what are they?'

'Front men are people we pay to front the businesses. They don't have to do anything and they get paid well for it. You see your Uncle Dave and Uncle Tony on paper have nothing to do with the ownership or running of the businesses. So if there is a raid they can't be touched,' his uncle explained.

'So the front man takes the rap?'

'Not necessarily because we usually get a tip off when the raid is going to take place. So front man A by then has sold the business to front man B which means the police have to start all over again and then front man B sells the business to front man C and so on. Fingers is the front man at the moment with Bullets ready to take over and then Diamonds.'

'Very clever! I've got so much to learn. Unfortunately I can't think of anyone I would feel safe in recommending,' John said pensively.

'Yes well better to be sure than sorry. Anyway Uncle Dave has decided to shove two fingers up the Council and the girls in the peep shows are now going to be completely nude, which means it will draw in more punters. We still won't do anything about the live shows as we know for sure the council will come down on us like a ton of bricks.'

'But won't the Council come down on us with the peep shows?'

'We don't know but Cecil Watkins has worked out the difference between something being considered immoral and something being considered indecent. If we ran a real live sex show he reckons that would be considered immoral and would be a police matter and lead to prosecution, but the girls posing naked he reckons would be considered indecent and simply a Council matter. So, we're going to rebuild the booths with one way mirrors that the punter can only see through when he has inserted his pound coin. The girl will be on a bed on a raised platform doing a slow strip until she is completely naked. The idea of that, of course, is for the punter to keep putting his money in eager to see her get completely naked. There will be two booths to each bed and the timer mechanism will allow the punter thirty seconds to watch the girl in action. The beauty of this is there is no rip off, the punter gets what he pays for and we reckon we will triple our turnover as we will be operating eighteen hours a day, seven days a week. There will be fourteen booths with seven girls performing, which means we're going need twenty one girls working the three shifts at the Erotica. There will be twelve booths here in the Phoenix, with six girls working at one time, meaning we will need eighteen girls to work the shifts.'

'Fantastic. You've really worked this out. I'm impressed.'

'So you should be, your uncle is one smart cookie and never misses a trick. So starting later tonight after we've closed for business we're going to knock the booths down and rebuild them in the new style and with the new coin mechanism, most of which has already been prefabricated ready to be assembled. Rob and Lyndsey, Fingers, Bullets, Diamonds, Andy and Martin are coming to help so we should be up and running by the morning,' Uncle George told him.

It was a hard day's night and the team worked tirelessly to get everything completed in time. The booths had been painted black and the viewing windows fitted with the new coin mechanism. The platforms were in place with the beds angled correctly to give each booth a good view of the performing girl, so that by the morning they were ready and open for business.

Word quickly spread that the girls in the peep shows were now posing completely naked and business increased to the extent that there was a continuous flow of punters from the moment the booths opened at nine in the morning. It never ceased to amaze John that it wasn't just the dirty old man in the mac that frequented the booths, but businessmen in their smart suits carrying their brief cases who would come to the kiosk, change their ten or twenty pound notes for pound coins, go into the booths, have the coins ready in one hand to be able to continuingly feed the coin slot, while they unzipped themselves with the other hand. John would see the same well attired businessmen come back again later in the day, probably on their way home from work, making him often wonder what their home sex life must be like, or whether they had a sex life at all. He also imagined the poor naive wife fussing over her husband when he got home, concerned at how tired and exhausted he looked.

One of the most unpleasant jobs for whoever was running the kiosk was to have to go into the booths and clean the disgusting mess off the walls and the floors as well as the piles of discarded tissues. The other task was to have to crawl under the platforms to replace the plastic buckets before they overflowed with the pounds coins that were constantly dropping down into them. With the money coming in so fast it was becoming impossible to count it by hand so Uncle Dave had decided to buy a counting machine to do the job more efficiently.

With the popularity of the nude peep shows spreading it wasn't long before the Council got wind of what was going on and decided it must put a stop to what they considered was such an outrageous affront to its policy. Armed with workers and a pickup truck, the Council made their first raid at the Phoenix very soon after they had opened for business, wanting to make a public show of what they were doing. The Council official burst in.

'We are from Westminster City Council. This is a raid and you have three minutes to vacate the premises,' the official announced in a loud voice, thrusting a formal notice he tore from his clipboard to Adam who was manning the kiosk.

'What's all this then?' Adam asked feigning innocence.

'The Council have deemed your activities to be of an indecent nature and therefore, as you can see from the formal notification, we are closing you down,' the official informed him in his pompous manner.

As soon as the Council workers entered armed with sledge hammers the girls ran out onto the street, some in various stages of undress, clutching their clothes to hide their modesty, much to the delight of passers-by. The Council official then gave the go ahead for the workers to set about smashing the booths apart and to carry the broken sections out to the pickup truck. Uncle George immediately called Cecil Watkins to come and deal with the matter.

'Don't do anything to stop them, let them get on with it,' he cautioned. 'This is purely a Council matter and once they have confiscated the material and think they have destroyed your ability to commit any further acts of indecency, they'll walk away and you can simply start up again,' he said brushing the fine dust from his shoulders that had mixed with the dandruff falling from his hair.

'How can we start up again? They've closed us down,' John exclaimed, looking around the room that was now just and empty shell.

Uncle George looked at him with a wry smile.

'No they haven't. We knew this was likely to happen, so we've had everything prefabricated like we did last time, which means we're going to be busy rebuilding the booths and we'll be up and running in no time.'

'But, they'll just close us down again,' John said, still confused at what his uncle was saying.

'Legally they can't do anything like this again for at least the next six weeks as they have to apply for a warrant to smash up our stuff. So we can carry on running the business as usual until that time comes. By then we will have raked in another hundred grand from this one alone and then we simply rebuild it again and so on until the Council get fed up with it. We're not going to let the bastards beat us, there's too much money at stake, so we're all going to have roll our sleeves up and get the booths up and running,' his uncle said seemingly unperturbed by the whole incident.

After another hard night the peep show was back up and running, the raid not seeming to have scared off the punters. Ironically, the Council's action seemed to have had the opposite effect adding to the notoriety of the girls posing stark naked simply resulting in attracting more and more punters.

John would sometimes watch from the back of the booths with amusement at the antics of some of the weirdos who came into the peepshows. The way they would check their appearance in the one way glass that acted as a mirror before they inserted their coins always made him laugh. There was one regular punter John used to watch with fascination who, for some inexplicable reason, would take out a tooth pick and pick his teeth of any bits of food that were stuck from the meal he's just had before he unzipped his trousers. Thankfully John was only able to see them from the chest up.

But the punter that fascinated him most was a very short man who, every time he visited the peep show, brought a milk crate with him. The staff had nicknamed him 'milk crate Eddie' as he would take the crate into the booth, place it down on the floor and stand on it so that he was able to look through the one way glass without having to raise himself up on his toes to see the girls, therefore removing the risk of falling over at the critical moment. It began to make John wonder whether there was anything else that could shock him about what men and women found and did to satisfy their sexual desires.

With everything running smoothly with the peep shows, Uncle George decided to promote John to bar manager of the hostess bar with the responsibility of running the place.

'I want you to take over as bar manager of the Erotica hostess bar. You'll be under Andy's supervision to begin with but you'll be effectively in control, particularly as far as security is concerned, keeping the girls in check, making sure they get the maximum number of punters in and get the maximum amount of money out of them, as well as dealing with any trouble makers that refuse to pay.

'That's great Uncle, but I promised Daniel and my mum I would be home every fortnight to see them,' John said, with a despairing tone.

'Aye son, as long as you keep bringing in the business then that's okay with me,' Uncle George said, happy to assure him.

Things settled down in the business and everything was running well. The money continued to pour in. Lindsey and Rob were running the porn shops and had set up a sophisticated duplicating plant with the latest equipment in the garage of one of the houses they rented, churning out hundreds of VHS tapes a day. His uncles had also decided to rent out the vacant flats to prostitutes who advertised their wares on cards pasted in all the telephone boxes around the area. All in all it seemed the sordid side of Soho was doing all it could to meet an ever increasing demand from visitors to the area, as well as tourists eager to explore the darker side of London.

John settled comfortably into his new role as the bar manager of the hostess bar, earning the nickname 'Sergeant' from the girls, because of his strict rules that they arrived on time, kept themselves clean, dressed neat and tidily and kept the place clean. He also introduced a new working scheme for the girls that would benefit them and the business. Instead of being paid a hundred pounds per shift they would in future have to pay the company fifty pounds to work there, but would be paid ten per cent of the bill they were responsible for, meaning they could finish up earning a lot more than a hundred pounds, with the club benefitting at the same time.

Apart from the occasional difficult punter things seemed to run relatively smoothly until one punter started to get awkward over the size of his bill. Fortunately he didn't get violent but just kept complaining he was being ripped off and wasn't going to pay. After some 'gentle persuasion' he reluctantly paid. John breathed a sigh of relief as the man stormed out threatening he would complain to the police.

At that precise moment Inspector Atwell happened to be doing his rounds. The disgruntled punter spotted him and rushed over and told him what had happened. It was music to Inspector Atwell's ears and he assured the man he would immediately investigate the matter. The punter, not wanting to be directly involved in case he would be called as a witness or have his name in the newspapers, was happy to leave it to the Inspector. Bracing himself, pushing his shoulders back, Inspector Atwell entered the hostess bar which fortunately was still empty with only the girls clearing the tables ready for the next lot of punters.

'Can I help you officer?' John said, hurrying towards him as soon as he saw him walk in, guessing the punter had complained.

'That rather depends,' Inspector Atwell said, sourly.

'On what?' John asked his face hard as he stared back at him.

'I know who you are.'

'So do I,' John retorted mockingly.

'You're Lawson aren't you? I never forget a face,' Atwell said, his eyes fixed on him his expression serious. 'We had you in once before for beating up some innocent tourist and I've just had a complaint from another man who stated you had threatened him with violence unless he paid you some extortionate sum of money. So what do you have to say about that?'

'Have you got a search warrant to enter these premises?' John asked his expression implacable.

Atwell seemed taken aback by the question.

'I am investigating a complaint I have received and I don't need a warrant.'

'A complaint from whom?'

'One of your customers has complained you ripped him off and threatened him when he refused to pay.'

'And who is this man. I don't see him with you?'

'He left me to deal with the complaint, which is why I'm here.'

'Well, we don't know of any trouble, all our customers seem to enjoy their visits and go away happy.'

'That's not what I've heard.'

'Well, you know what they say about rumours?'

'No, do enlighten me?'

'A rumour is like a character who wears a garment full of painted tongues.'

'Quite the philosopher all of a sudden aren't we? Those fancy words won't save you.'

'Look Inspector, you're beginning to bore me. You have no real evidence except a complaint from someone who couldn't even bother to come back with you and you have no other witnesses. Nobody has seen anything untoward here, so I suggest you leave as you are on private property.'

'I'll leave when I'm good and ready. I've not finished my investigation into the complaint,' Atwell insisted.

'A complaint from a disgruntled punter who thought he was going to see a live sex show which you, Inspector, know only too well we are not licensed to do,' John said, giving him an indulgent smile.

'But that's what he expected and said he paid for.'

'That's the trouble Inspector there are a lot of these dirty old men who would do better going home to their wives and asking them to put on a show. He's only complained because he's probably spent all his wages and got nothing to give to the missus when he gets home. He'll probably make up some excuse he was robbed.'

'He was robbed. By you!' Atwell retorted, angrily.

'Like I said, where is your evidence? Now if you don't mind I've got a lot to do and you're delaying me. Let me escort you to the door,' John said, giving him a little shove on the shoulder.

'Take your hands off me or I'll have you for assault,' Atwell, remonstrated.

'Once again you would need witnesses and I can't see anyone here who would state I assaulted you. So be sensible Inspector and leave,' John advised, giving him another shove towards the door.

Atwell's face showed his resentment as he turned and walked to the door with John following closely behind. As they got to the street, Atwell suddenly spun round and grabbed John by the scruff of the neck, shoving him hard against the wall.

'You're on my territory now, you bastard and I'm going to have you,' he screamed, the veins beginning to stand out on his neck, spittle flying out between his gritted teeth, splashing onto John's face. 'You think you lowlifes can get the better of me? Well you've got another think coming. I've dealt with people like you all my life and you think the law doesn't apply to you? Well you're about to find out it does,' he continued screaming, beginning to bang John's head against the wall.

'Help!' John cried out to anyone who could hear. 'I'm being assaulted. I'm not offering any resistance,' he added raising his hands in the air.

The cry was heard by someone passing by, who watched what was happening and approached the Inspector.

'Excuse me officer, but I don't think there is any need for that. The person is clearly not offering any resistance and...'

Atwell turned to look at the man without relaxing his grip on John.

'I would ask you to mind your own business sir. This is a police matter and I am dealing with it.'

'That maybe so but I don't care for the way you appear to be dealing with it,' the man said, taking a cigarette packet out of his pocket and tearing off the lid. He then took out a pen and wrote his name and phone number on the lid. 'Here take this if you need a witness. My name and phone number is on there,' the man said, trying to hand it to John as the Inspector tried to snatch it from him. Luckily John got a hold on it and shoved it in his pocket. As the man walked off Atwell took out his two way radio and called for backup. Within a few minutes two squad cars arrived and John was bundled into one of the cars and driven off to West End Central Police Station. He was ushered into one of the interview rooms by Atwell and a police constable with Atwell screaming,

'I'm going to throw the book at you Lawson! Assaulting a senior police officer and using threatening behaviour against a member of the public,' he said before he stormed out, leaving John sitting there pondering maybe he should have had handled things differently.

'You appear to be in a bit of trouble,' the constable said, looking at John's troubled face. 'The inspector seems in a right old mood and he's not nice to be around when he's like that, I can tell you,' he added.

'Yeah well, I would like to see the duty sergeant as I wish to make a complaint that it was the Inspector who actually assaulted me, not the other way around and I have evidence to prove it,' John told him.

'You got evidence to prove it?' the constable asked, surprised.

'Yes. I have a witness so get the desk sergeant please.'

The constable turned on his heels and left the room leaving John feeling a lot better.

'Right, empty your pockets Lawson,' Atwell ordered, as he burst back into the room.

John did as he was ordered and placed the contents of his pockets, including the torn off lid of the cigarette packet, down on the bare table. Atwell immediately snatched it up, tore it apart and tossed into the waste bin on the floor in the corner of the room.

'So where is your evidence now Lawson?' he said, with a malevolent grin before storming back out and being replaced by the constable.

'I still wish to pursue my complaint constable so will you please take me to the duty sergeant or get him to come here.'

'Well you'll be seeing him in a minute as you're going to be charged,' the constable replied as he led John back to the front desk.

'You are being charged with assaulting a police officer and demanding money with menace. You do not have to say anything but it may harm your defence if you do not mention when questioned something which you later rely on in Court. Anything you do say may be given in evidence. Do you understand?'

John said nothing as he looked back hard at the sergeant.

'Do you understand?' the sergeant repeated.

'I understand you have refused to listen to my complaint. I was the one that was assaulted by the officer making the charges and you have even allowed him to destroy the evidence that would prove my case.'

There was an uneasy silence as the duty sergeant looked at him, his face darkening a little as he said.

'And where did the officer destroy this evidence you say you had?'

'In the interview room just a few minutes ago. He tore it up and threw it in the waste basket,' John replied.

'I see,' the duty sergeant said, not sure what to do next 'well, I suppose we had better go and have a look, but if you're playing games then you will be in a lot more trouble making serious accusations against a senior police officer,' he warned him as he came out from behind his desk and walked off towards the interview room. The duty sergeant lifted the waste basket off the floor and placed it on the table.

'What exactly are we looking for?' he asked, and he began to scrummage through it.

'A torn lid of a cigarette packet,' John told him.

The duty sergeant looked at John with disdain.

'A torn lid of a cigarette packet?' he said, convinced he really was playing games.

'It has the name and phone number of the witness, which is why the Inspector tore it up,' John explained.

'I've warned you about making wild accusations.'

'When you find it, you will see I'm telling the truth.'

'Is this what you're on about?' the duty sergeant asked, holding up a piece of the torn lid with part of a word or name scribbled on it.

'Yes and if you find the other pieces then you'll have the name and the contact number of the witness, like I said.'

The duty sergeant found a few more bits, laid them flat on the table and started to try to piece them together. As he shuffled the pieces around a name began to take shape.

'Right, you sit there,' the duty sergeant said, irritation creeping into his voice as he gathered up the pieces and left the room.

A feeling of relief swept over John as he looked across at the constable and said.

'I bet that Inspector's going to be even worse to be around after this.'

The constable said nothing.

Just then the duty sergeant walked back in the room and there was an indulgent smile on his face as he said.

'It has been decided not to proceed with the charges against you, but to issue you with a warning that should we receive any further complaints of you demanding money with menace then you could be in serious trouble, so count yourself lucky,' the duty sergeant told him. 'Get him out of here,' he instructed the constable.

JAMACIAN YARDIES MUSCLE IN

John was surprised when Uncle George called him to the office and asked. 'How good are you with a gun?'

John stared curiously back at his uncle. 'Dad taught me to shoot,' the thought stirring his childhood memories. 'So I guess I'm pretty good, why?' he asked, his attention sharpened.

'Good because some of the drug gangs are moving in trying to take over our territory and it's frightening the punters away. So we're going to have to deal with them, because if we don't, the prostitutes will move out and we will be left with a lot of empty flats and no income. You will need to have a weapon.' Uncle George explained.

'I see,' John said, a worried look spreading across his face. 'I don't know uncle, what if I get caught with it? That Inspector is out to get me.'

'No, you don't need to carry it all the time. We will keep it locked up here, until you need it. Any special gun you like?'

'A Browning 9mm, that's what dad trained me on.'

The Browning 9mm single action semiautomatic is one of the most popular handguns used by the military and police forces all over the world.

'No problem. As it happens my man has a Browning for sale,' his uncle said. 'If you are ever called on to bring 'your little friend' you know what to bring. Okay?'

'Okay, I understand,' John acknowledged.

John carried on as bar manager of the hostess club as well as doing the regular deliveries to the Smith family when a few days later he got a call from Andy to go to the sex shop in Berwick Street straight away. Waiting for him was not only Andy but also his Uncles Dave and George, Martin, Bullets, Fingers, Diamonds, Lindsey and Rob as well as some of the Maltese heavies.

'Right as you all know we have some prostitute flats directly across the road and that's where we're having serious trouble with the Yardies. They're now starting to operate in this bloody street and they are scaring the punters to the extent the girls did hardly any business last night. So we are going to have to sort them out, teach them a lesson, this is our territory and they are not to encroach on it,' his Uncle George said.

'What have you got in mind?' John asked.

'A few cracks over their heads should do it,' Andy suggested.

'Have you any idea who we're dealing with. The power these people wield is phenomenal. They're notorious for their involvement in gun crime and drug trafficking; marijuana and crack. They are moving in all over the place trying to take control of the drug trade. They consider themselves different and superior to us white criminals because they are ruthless and not afraid to kill anyone who gets in their way. The killings are worn as a badge of honour telling others they are not to be messed with. They use machetes, Uzis or the Ingran Mach10. Everyone knows this and most of the other gangs won't go up against them,' Uncle Dave explained, like some kind of expert on gang culture.

'So how do we handle it? We're going to have to one way or the other or they will take over,' Uncle George said.

'But an all-out assault would turn into bloodshed if, as you say, they have all those weapons. The place would soon be swarming with police,' John said.

'So what else do you suggest we do?' Andy asked.

'We could try talking to them, show them some respect, because I've learned that's one thing that's important to them is respect. Show them respect and explain that we don't want to stop what they're doing; we're not into drugs and have no wish to take over their business. We just want them to find another place to conduct their trade,' John suggested.

'And you think they'll listen to us?' Uncle Dave asked, a little bemused at the idea.

'It's worth a try and if it doesn't work then we will have to quickly think of something else,' Uncle George said.

'Right, we'll try your idea John, if you're willing to take the risk and go and talk to them,' Uncle Dave said, a little reluctantly.

'Yes, I'm happy to have a go but give me a few days to suss them out and come up with a plan,' John said, putting on a brave face.

'Fine, but come up with it fast and if you do decide to go and talk to them I think you ought to take your friend with you, just in case,' Uncle George advised.

John decided to use one of the empty flats above the sex shop in Berwick Street to observe how the Yardies operated. It gradually became clear there was one central man, the man with the drugs, who was the actual supplier and had lookouts and runners around the area touting for new customers as well as the regulars. The customer would be escorted to the central man by one of the runners who would then produce sachets from his mouth or from the pockets of his jeans and hand them over in exchange for money. He was tall with a mass of dreadlocks. His face was marked with a scar that ran from his temple across his right eye to the tip of his nose, giving him an intimidating appearance. He was displaying a fair amount of gold with a heavy bracelet on his right wrist; a gold watch strapped to his left, a heavy gold chain around his neck and a mouthful of gold teeth.

While studying the way the system was operating, John noticed another man standing in the doorway on the other side of the street, closely watching everything that was taking place. This man was dressed more plainly that the others. His dreadlocks were tied back more neatly; he wasn't displaying any gold and was obviously keeping a low profile. John noticed that before any of the drugs were handed over by the central man he looked across at the man standing in the shadows for a nod of approval. It became apparent to John he had to be the top man and it was him he was going to have to talk to if he was going to achieve anything.

Once he had sussed the Yardies out, John went back to his uncles and explained what he proposed to do. With their agreement to the plan they met with the others in the Intrepid Fox to put the plan into action.

Heading through the alleyway leading to Berwick Street, the group held back as John tapped the Browning he had tucked into the front of his waistband, concealed under his buttoned coat. Confidently he made his way towards the main man and was immediately surrounded by the look outs.

'Wha you want English man?' one of the look outs demanded, his manner threatening, his wide eyes glinting dangerously.

'I want to speak to this man,' John replied, his own eyes hard as he stared back into his.

'Why you wan speak to me white boy?' the main man asked.

'I would like to speak to you about a business arrangement,' John told him.

'Don't dis me man. Wha kind of business arrangement, wha you got that would interest me, white boy?'

'My family own most of the buildings in this street and the girls that work in them.'

'You mean you wan sell me the business?'

'No, like I said, I want to come to a business arrangement that could be very lucrative for both of us,' John persisted.

'Business arrangement is it? Very lucrative is it, how lucrative?'

'That's what I would like to discuss. But, it would not be sensible to discuss it here on the street. Would you care to come to my office where we can talk more privately,' John suggested.

'White boy wannna talk business, so Denzil you take care of tings till I be back,' he told one of look outs.

'Sure ting, Winston,' Denzil acknowledged.

'If I not be back soon you all come looking for me, okay?'

'Sure,' Denzil acknowledged again.

John took him to one of the flats above the shops along Berwick Street that was in the process of being refurbished for renting out to another prostitute. All that was in the room was a small table and two chairs. John opened the door and Winston followed him in. Once in the room John casually unbuttoned his coat and purposely let it flap open so that Winston could see the gun tucked into his waistband.

The smile froze on Winston's face as he stepped back reaching for the door handle with one hand while reaching with the other for the handle of a machete he had tucked in his waistband. There was a tense stand-off with neither knowing what to do next. John could feel his heart pounding that everything was about to go wrong. The silence went on a bit too long and the situation grew awkward.

'Blood clot man, you gonna shoot me?' Winston finally said, drawing out the machete, the look of fear turning into a long hard silent stare, his bleak cold eyes unblinking.

John met his stare then looked at the machete with the light from the window glinting menacingly off the long steel blade, the edge razor sharp and wondered whether he was really going to have to shoot him or could he still take the risk and stick to his plan. He knew he could shoot him well before he had half raised the machete, but if he shot him, he also knew all hell would break loose and there would be killings on a massive scale. His uncles and the others would be defenceless against them down on the street as they were only pretending a show of force and were not actually carrying any weapons.

'I don't like being dissed with a gun. I'm outta here. So go ahead bumbaclaat shoot me in back and my bredren will find you, rape you in front of your family and then cut your head off,' Winston said, turning to leave.

John knew from what he had read about the Yardies that the threat was very real and now had to make the biggest decision of his life… If he wasn't going to shoot him then he going to have to show respect by disarming his gun and laying it down on the table, knowing at that point he would be defenceless against an angry Yardie wielding a machete that could chop a limb off or sever his head with a single blow.

'Wait,' John called out as Winston stood gripping the machete, 'if I was going to shoot you you'd be dead by now.' He carefully removed the gun from his waistband, with the thumb and finger of his right hand, then gripped the butt with his left hand, raised it and pressed the clip releasing the magazine that dropped into his other open hand. He then pulled back the slide and ejected the bullet from the chamber and placed the gun, magazine and bullet on the small table with the butt facing him so that if necessary, he could quickly grab it with one hand and the magazine with the other and reload within seconds.

'That could be the most stupid ting you do, English man,' Winston said, still uncertain waiting to see what John was going to do next.

'I've done that to show respect so that we can talk sensibly without any threats and…'

'Okay so you don't wanna dis me man, so wha this lucrative deal youz offering, English man? You wan in on the action? We don't deal with whites,' Winston said, the fear disappearing as suddenly as it had come, recovering his confidence, tucking the machete back into his waist band and pulling out one of the chairs to sit on.

'This is how it is,' John began. 'My family and the Maltese Mafia own these buildings and the girls that work in them and what you're doing is beginning to interfere with our business and that is starting to upset the bosses.'

'How wha we do interfere in your business?'

'We've been watching you. You've got your guys hanging around outside here and that's frightening away our customers because it makes them scared to venture into the street. We don't want to interfere in your business, we're not into drugs, and we have no intention of in the future. So here's the lucrative part I was offering. If you move your activities further up the street away from our business, then you won't have to pay a heavy price, a very heavy price.'

'Are you treatening me English man?'

'Let me put it this way. We are also involved with the Smith family and...' John paused as he saw a flick of recognition flash across his face. 'So you know who else you could be dealing with. So quite simply if you don't move, you'll be taken out...shot. If you think you're the only ones carrying weapons and willing to kill, then you're misjudging us white gangs. If you want an all-out war then keep operating where you are and you will get it. But, like I said, it will be much more lucrative for you to move.'

'So if we move up the street, there be no problem?'

'No problem, you can deal, do what you like. I told you we're not interested in drugs.'

'Tell me someting English man. Would you have shot me if I had given you trouble?'

'You better believe it, I sure as hell would have,' John said, and he could see the fear creep back into Winston's eyes hoping he could not read the fear in his own eyes.

'Okay English man, everyting cool, you show respec, so we move. I don't wan no trouble,' Winston said, getting to his feet and moving to the door.

John picked up his Browning, quickly replaced the magazine, slipped the loose bullet into his pocket and followed Winston out, breathing a silent gasp of relief. As they walked out of the building Uncles George and Dave, Martin, Andy, Bullets, Fingers, Diamonds, Lyndsey, Dave and a few of the Maltese heavies as planned emerged from the alleyway and lined up on the opposite side of the street as a show of formidable force.

'Winston, whag wan' Denzil shouted across at him.

'Nuttin' ah gwan bredren, all is cool.' Winston assured him.

'You see that lot standing there? Well that's how close you came. They're all armed and would have taken out the lot of you if you had given us any trouble.' John said, coldly.

Winston, felt a stab of fright in the pit of his stomach as he looked at the line of men standing on the opposite pavement, their arms tucked under their coats as though they were holding onto weapons.

'Respec English man,' Winston said, gesturing towards his uncles and the Maltese Mafia.

'Respect to you, Rasta man. By the way I'm Scottish not English. Remember make sure you keep to your end of the street, because you know what the consequences will be if you don't,' John whispered, before he crossed over to join Uncle George and the others.

Uncle George slapped John on the shoulder as they made their way back through the alleyway to the Intrepid Fox for a well-earned pint.

'I didn't think it was going to be that easy,' Uncle Dave said, as soon as they got to the private room on the first floor.

All the fear of the moment seemed to flood up in John's throat almost choking him as he thought about the incredible risk he had taken and how close he had come to making the wrong decision. Uncle George read the look on John's face.

'It took some guts to do what you did and you pulled it off without a shot being fired. Here son,' he said, handing him a thick wad of notes, 'you just saved the business,' he added. 'You took a great risk John and we're proud of you so what would you like to drink?'

John's reputation grew after shaking down the Yardies in the way he had without it breaking out into a turf war and everything continued on as normal until Uncle George called him to the office.

'You were warned but you seemed to have taken no notice of what I said,' Uncle George said, his manner brusque, his voice devoid of any emotion.

John stared at his uncle trying to work out what he had done, that he had been warned not to do.

'Dinnae look so innocent. You've been having it off with Nicola, one of the girls from the peep shows and I warned you not to get involved with any of the girls. I know it's difficult with beautiful naked girls running around all over the place offering it on a plate, but it only leads to trouble. You start to favour them, relax with them and tell them things about what goes on here. And if they get nicked they'll grass you up without another thought if it's going to get them off the hook. So, if you can't keep it in your trousers, make sure I don't find out, because nephew or not I'll damn well fire you. Understood?' his uncle warned him.

The problem for John was it didn't stop there because he was not only sleeping with Nicola, but with three beautiful Czechoslovakian girls from the hostess bar at the same time, although neither of them knew about the other two. As always with triangular affairs, the inevitable happens when one finds about the other and the infighting starts, with the three girls falling out with each other and finally walking out of the hostess bar. This really infuriated his uncles who were so angry that the business had lost three of its most beautiful girls that in spite of his heroism with the Yardies he was ordered to pack his things and head off back to Birkenhead for a month to cool his ardour.

John felt pleased to be back in Birkenhead and was doubly pleased when Jackie agreed to let him keep Daniel for a whole month as she had now had her baby and had got involved with yet another man. He was finding it increasingly hard to let Daniel go back to Jackie and noticed how much his son cried when it came time to hand him over. It made him even more determined to see a solicitor and apply for custody.

Having found a good solicitor the application for John to be granted full custody of Daniel was filed together with the divorce proceedings and a plan was put in place for social services to visit both parents' homes and prepare a report for the court.

THE LOVE OF MONEY

1988

'Good to have you back son. I hope you've learned your lesson, no messing on the doorstep, okay?'

'Okay uncle, it will never happen again I promise.'

'We're closing down the video sex shops,' Uncle George said, after John had told him all about the social services visiting and his conversation with his solicitor.

'Why are you closing them, they were doing alright weren't they?' John asked surprised.

'Nah, there's too many of them opening up and the competition is hotting up. They're all starting to set up their own duplicating machines so by the time we've paid the rent, Lindsey and Rob and the guys doing the duplicating, it's not worth the aggro. We're going to put up a big sign saying all videos ten quid to get rid of them and then close the shops,' his uncle explained.

John helped put the signs up and to everyone's amazement the shops were invaded and they sold out the entire stock of videos within a few hours. Lyndsey had to rush back to the garage and gather up the rest of the stock to meet the demand. By accident the whole idea of getting rid of the stock had turned into a roaring success, so much so, that it forced some of the other sex shops to close down as they couldn't compete at that level. Uncle George and Uncle Dave decided to snap up the shops that were closing down and stuck the same closing down sign on the windows and sales continued to go through the roof, selling thousands of videos a week.

As John walked back to the office one day with the takings from the hostess bar he was surprised to see a security van used to transfer large sums of money parked outside the building. As he approached the door to Uncle Dave's office, Uncle George came out and stopped him. 'Have you any idea what a million pounds looks like son?' he asked with a big brimming smile.

'How do you mean looks like?' John asked, bemused.

'Just imagine a million pounds in twenty pound notes, have you any idea how big a pile that would be?' Uncle George asked, the smile stretching his face.

'I can't even begin to imagine.'

'Right, close your eyes and don't open them until I tell you, okay?' his uncle told him.

John clamped his eyes shut; his uncle took his hand and guided him into Uncle Dave's office.

'Okay, you can open them,' his uncle informed him.

John opened his eyes and they bulged as he stared at the pile of twenty pound notes stacked in neat piles on the table.

'What do you think of that, son?' Uncle Dave asked, with a sweeping gesture of his arms. 'There's exactly one million pounds there.'

'I've never seen so much money,' John mumbled, almost unable to speak for the enormity of what he was staring at.

'There are fifty thousand twenty pounds notes weighing 54.5 kilos,' his uncle explained. 'Don't you think it's an amazing sight? Take a good look at it John because you'll never ever see anything like that again for the rest of your life.'

'What are you going to do with it?' John couldn't help himself wondering, thinking how worried he got carrying around twenty grand in a carrier bag to the Smith.

'Do with it? I'm not going to do anything with it. I just wanted to see what a million pounds actually looked like in cash. It's going straight back to the bank with these guys,' his uncle said, indicating the two security guards standing quietly in the back of the room dressed in black protective clothing and wearing helmets.

'This whole exercise has cost me twelve grand but it's been worth every penny. Okay guys, you can take it away now,' he said to the security guards before turning his attention back to John. 'If you can't visualise what a million pounds looks like then you'll never make a million. If you have no money, you have no power, so keep that image in your head and who knows, maybe one day.'

That image of a million pounds laid out on the table embedded itself in John's mind and he couldn't shake it off. It was like a carrot dangling in front of his eyes that he could never reach, but it gave him a determination to work harder, be harder and make as much money as he could from the punters.The love of money was now going to be his motivation which meant he was going to stamp even harder on any punter who refused to pay.

The test of this came unexpectedly one afternoon, when a young American walked into the bar. He was quite tall, around six feet three. He had long dark hair and was wearing a long black leather coat.

'Hey man, when's the show start?' he asked, his voice loud as he moved swiftly towards the bar where John was standing.

'One of the hostesses will attend to you sir, if you care to take a seat at one of the tables,' John politely informed him.

As it happened John had an American hostess working that night. Her name was Linzy and she had long blonde hair with extensions. She was tall, just under six feet, with long shapely legs encased in stockings held up by suspenders attached to a basque that pushed up her boobs to display an ample amount of cleavage. John thought she would be perfect for a fellow American and told her to take his order.

'What would you like to drink sir?' she asked demurely, accentuating her American accent as she approached his table.

'No, I don't want a drink; I just want to see the show. What time does it start?'

'I'm afraid you have to buy a drink sir.'

'I just told you, I don't want a drink, I just want to see the show,' he persisted.

'Didn't you see the sign on the door as you entered sir, and it is also printed on the back of your ticket that all customers must buy a drink, what would you like, beer, spirits, or a cocktail?'

'Ah damn it, just give me a coke,' he said, irritation beginning to sound in his voice which didn't go unnoticed by John.

A few minutes later Linzy returned carrying a glass of coke on a shiny silver tray. She bent over and placed the glass of coke down on the table giving him a good view of her ample bosom.

'You're obviously American the same as me. Would you like me to join you sir?'

'Yeah sure, why not,' he said, with a gesture of his hand for her to sit down.

'Are you going to be a gentleman and buy a lady a drink?' she asked, in her demure manner.

'Sure, what would you like?' he asked, already beginning to assume she was on the game and was going to make a proposition once she had a drink.

Linzy picked up the menu and pretended to peruse it as one of the other scantily clad hostesses came over with a note pad to take the order.

'I'll have a sex on the beach,' she ordered.

'Sex on the beach, what kind of drink is that?' he asked.

'Oh it's our nickname for a tequila sunrise, it just sounds sexier' she explained with a pout of her lips.

'I must remember that,' he said, as he felt a little stirring in his loins.

The American was becoming impatient as he watched the bar gradually fill with punters which the other hostesses quickly served with their drinks and then sat down with them.

'When is the damn show going to start?' he demanded.

'Any minute now sir. Just as soon as everyone has paid their bill, the show will start,' she explained as one of the hostesses approached and placed the bill down on the table in front of him.

The American instinctively reached into his pocket as he picked up the bill with the other hand and his eyes almost popped out of his head as he screamed.

'A hundred and six pounds, how the hell do you make that out I only had a damn coke.'

'Please sir, keep your voice down and I will explain.' Linzy said, picking up the menu. 'The charges are all here,' she began, pointing to the items. 'You had a coke that as you can see is twelve pounds, the cocktail you bought me is forty four pounds and the hostess fee for sitting with you is fifty pounds which in all makes a total of one hundred and six pounds.'

'This is outrageous.' he screamed leaping to his feet and throwing the tray across the room alerting John to what was happening. He pushed Linzy away and she fell backwards over the table and then he shoved the other hostess out of the way as he charged his way to the exit.

There were two exits and entrances to the bar and John had learned from experience that most people in a hurry to leave always seemed to go for the exit they came in from. A bad mistake for the American because John, already angry that he had manhandled the two girls, came swiftly out from behind the bar and waited for him to get close enough to give him his trademark side kick full in the chest. This sent the American flying into one of the tables, causing it to collapse and sending him telescoping to the floor.

Whilst he laid there dazed John came over, grabbed him by the collar, his eyes blazing with fury as he dragged him across to the bar and slammed his head hard down on the counter.

'I don't like men who manhandle women. I can have you for assault. Now are you going to pay your bill or do I have to get really rough?' John said.

John saw his face crumple in pain.

'Look, I'm sorry man, I panicked. I was just so surprised at the bill. I didn't expect it to be so high. I haven't got that kind of money on me,' he pleaded.

The other punters, watching in horror as to what was going on, quickly paid and fled out of the other exit.

'So what have you got?' John asked, still holding him ready to bang his head on the bar again.

'I've only have thirty of your English pounds.'

'So what else do you have?'

'I have American Express traveller's cheques.'

'That will do nicely,' John said with a smile, releasing his grip but ready to grab him if he tried to make a run for it.

The American didn't. He just looked nervously at John as he slipped his hand into the inside pocket of his long leather coat and drew out a book of travellers cheques, opened it up and tore off four cheques each to the value of fifty dollars.

'I think another one for the damage you caused and the hurt to the lady's feelings,' John said, taking hold of the four cheques and holding his hand out for another one, while checking to see if they were signed.

'Just sign these buddy and then you can go and enjoy the rest of the day,' John said, with an air of sarcasm.

The American quickly signed the cheques and then made a hasty retreat.

'Well, you sorted him out good and proper,' Linzy said, as she came over to the bar.

'Stupid Yank, thought he could get one over on me. No one does that, people mess with me at their own risk. Are you alright?' he asked Linzy, worried she might have got hurt.

'Yes. I'm okay, just laddered my stockings that's all. I always have a spare pair as they often get laddered with the gropers,' she said.

'He finally paid, so you'll get your percentage, in fact you'll do even better as I squeezed another fifty dollars out of him,' John told her with an air of pride. 'Right move your arses and get the place straightened up ready for the next lot,' he told them.

'Yes Sergeant,' the girls mockingly saluted as they set about up righting the tables and clearing away the mess.

'Lawson!!' Inspector Atwell called out loudly and everybody stopped what they were doing and looked up as he entered the bar followed by several policemen coming in from both entrances.

'He described you well,' Atwell said, as he approached the bar where John was standing. You're in real trouble this time and I'm going to throw the book at you,' he added, a look of angry triumph spreading across his face. 'I've got a real live witness this time, that is as alive as he could be after the beating you gave him. And he is going to give a full detailed statement as soon as the hospital has treated his injuries. I'm arresting you on a charge of demanding money with menace, assault, causing grievous bodily harm and robbery. You do not have to say anything but it may harm your defence if you do not mention when questioned something which you later rely on in Court. Anything you do say may be given in evidence. Do you understand?'

John nodded he understood.

'Cuff him,' he ordered two of the policemen.

The two policemen grabbed John's arms and tried to force them behind his back, but he resisted clamping his arms tight to his side.

'Don't try to force my arms back behind my back, let go and....'

'Resisting arrest, that's another charge I can add that to the book,' Atwell cut in, enjoying the moment.

'What I was trying to say, if they just let go of my arms I will voluntarily place them behind my back so they can cuff me.'

'Then do it,' Atwell shouted at him.

The two policemen cuffed John and escorted him out of the bar.

'Right, all you ladies will be required to come to the station to give statements, so if you have some decent clothing to cover yourselves, I suggest you get them quickly, otherwise you will be taken as you are,' Atwell informed the girls, with an air of contempt.

*

John looked up relieved as Cecil Watkins finally walked into the interview room at West End Central Police Station.

'Sorry couldn't get here any earlier,' Cecil said, as he sat down at the table across from John. 'This one is not going to be so easy. I've just been talking with them and it looks as though Inspector Atwell is determined you get a prison sentence. As you have no criminal record and this is your first offence I have managed to get you bailed. But there are conditions. You must not work or frequent any of the bars, peepshows, sex shops in the whole area of Soho. If you do you will be immediately arrested and bail withdrawn. It can take anything up to twelve months before the case comes to trial. I will do all I can to try to delay the case so hopefully I can make it run over the twelve months period which means the case will have run out of time and will have to be dropped. Don't hold your hopes too high though because Atwell is out to get you, and the American you allegedly assaulted is willing to come back and give evidence. It looks like Atwell is going for a charge of robbery which could carry a custodial sentence of up to five years. The thing to do now is go back to Birkenhead, lay low and above all stay out of trouble,' Cecil advised him.

'Cecil has told us about the bail conditions,' Uncle George said, as soon as John got back to the office.

Guilt was hammering at his conscience, his face pinched with regret as he said.

'I'm sorry it happened but you know what some of the punters are like? And that Inspector Atwell had been gunning for me. He must have been lurking around the area just waiting for something to happen.'

'I suppose it was bound to happen sooner or later. I know you thought you were doing the right thing, but unfortunately it means you're finished here, we can't employ you. You're still family, but you're now a liability and too much of a risk to be seen around us. Uncle Tony, as you can guess, is not happy at all. So we're packing you off to back to Birkenhead and you must stay there until your trial comes up and we see what the outcome is. I have to say, Cecil doesn't feel very confident about it, but we will just have to wait and see. If there is anyway the case can be dropped, you can be sure Cecil will find it,' his uncle said, reaching into his pocket and pulling out a thick wad of notes.

'Here's two grand to keep you going and make sure you stay out of trouble. We don't want the Lawson name dragged all over the press.'

'No I'm going to concentrate on getting custody of Daniel and settling down with him which will keep me busy.' John said, wanting to assure his uncle he intended to behave himself and stay out of trouble.

'I'm glad to hear it,' his uncle said, getting to his feet and embracing John. 'Give our love to Jose and Alex and make sure you take care of them.'

'I will,' John promised, breaking from the embrace, turning and leaving the office.

As John walked back along Old Compton Street to collect his belongings, he took one last look back at the Phoenix and then around at the bars beginning to fill with the early evening crowd realising he may never walk along the street again or feel the atmosphere, the energy, the vitality, the buzz that was so unlike anywhere else he knew.

TRIALS AND TRIBULATIONS

1989

'We're here, because you're going to be meeting your barrister Mr John Stanford QC who will be handling your defence in court,' Cecil explained.

'But I thought you would be defending me,' John said, somewhat surprised.

'No, the trial is being held in the Crown Court and this is how it works. You instruct the firm, and we instruct the barrister to conduct your defence in court. They're the ones that wear the wigs. So the purpose of this meeting is to go through everything so the barrister can prepare your defence,' Cecil explained.

Just then a junior clerk appeared and announced.

'Mr Stanford is ready to see you now.'

They both got to their feet and followed the junior clerk into the inner office.

'Ah, Cecil, good to see you,' John Stanford greeted him, getting to his feet and offering his hand.

John Stanford was tall, just over six feet, with short dark wavy hair. He had a handsome unblemished intelligent face that emitted an aura of confidence. His skin was soft but the handshake was firm.

'So,' he began as he gestured for them to sit down, 'we have a difficult case. The charge is now robbery; they have dropped the other charges of extortion, demanding money with menace, causing grievous bodily harm etc.' the barrister said, pausing to pick a paper from his desk and waving it at John. 'The police are really out to get you and the Crown is paying for the witness' flight from America and his hotel expenses to attend the trial. This is the basis of his statement in which he states, he walked into the bar expecting to see a live sex show, not realising it was a rip off joint. He got upset when he was presented with a bill for one hundred and six pounds for a glass of coke. He claims he never attacked the hostesses, rather he claims they attacked him and as he tried to leave you came from behind the bar and did a double footed drop kick catching him full in the chest. You then dragged him to the bar and threatened him with a gun or a knife. He also states he wasn't sure which because he couldn't see it, but felt something being pressed against his head and was in fear of his life thinking you were going to kill him,' the barrister put the paper down and looked across at John. 'The problem with him stating he was in fear of his life because he thought you had a knife or a gun was the reason he paid the money, which the prosecution will argue is the same as actually having a gun or a knife in the eyes of the law. They, of course, have the traveller's cheques he says he was forced to sign, even claiming his signature is shaky due to his nervousness. The good news is the medical report when he went to the hospital for treatment shows no signs of broken ribs or any injury to his chest. The witness has clearly been briefed as to what to put in his statement and it does look serious and I have to say you could be looking at five years if the jury believe his account of what happened,' the barrister advised him.

'Well, first of all, if I had done a doubled footed drop kick I would not have landed straight back on my feet, it's a physical impossibility and another thing I don't carry weapons. I've never had a knife or a gun anywhere on me or on the premises. And what about him attacking the two girls, that should prove how aggressive he was and...'

The barrister held up his hand to silence him.

'Yes, the two hostesses. I have been trying to contact them but they seemed to have disappeared and no one seems able to find them. And you've had no luck in trying to find them have you?' he asked, turning to look at Cecil.

'No I'm afraid I haven't. They just seemed to have disappeared off the face of the earth,' Cecil said.

'Yes, that's a shame. Anyway the defence I am going to put forward is that the witness lives in Hollywood Boulevard where there are an abundance of strip clubs and hostess bars so he therefore can't claim he didn't know exactly what he was walking into. He was disappointed there wasn't a plethora of sex on display and that he attacked you as he tried to leave without paying, knowing full well what the kind of charges were levied in these kind of places. That is an offence in itself. It's not the best defence I could have wished for, but the fact you do not have a criminal record will hold you in good stead. Let's just hope we have a sympathetic jury and a lenient judge if the case goes against you.' The barrister said judiciously, getting to his feet indicating the meeting was over.

'How do think that went?' Cecil asked as they walked along Chancery lane.

'Not as good as I'd hoped. You sure he's the best?'

'The best there is, you'd be surprised the people he's got off for me,' Cecil said with a wry smile.

'It's a pity about the girls. Their evidence would have made my case stronger. I can't understand why they wouldn't want to come and give evidence on my behalf after all I did for them.'

Cecil stopped and turned to face John.

'They didn't simply disappear, they were paid to disappear and…'

'Paid! You mean the police paid them to disappear?'

'No, we did.'

Every pulse in his body started to speed up as he looked at Cecil in sheer disbelief.

'Are you telling me my uncles paid the girls to disappear?'

'Yes. Your uncles could not allow the girls to give evidence because the prosecution would have made mincemeat of them, making them reveal things about the organisation which would not only have done you damage but would have caused immense damage to your uncles. We had to make them disappear because even if we hadn't called them as witnesses the prosecution would have made them compellable witnesses and…'

'What's a compellable witness?'

'A compellable witness is someone who can lawfully be required to give evidence even if they have refused to and you can imagine what the prosecution would do with them. The proverbial shit would truly have hit the fan. So we had no choice but to make them disappear before any notices were served on them.' Cecil explained.

'I'll never understand the law,' John sighed.

'You don't have to, that's what I'm paid for.'

'Will my uncles be coming to the court?'

'No, they can't be seen to have any association with you or the case. So, I suggest you go straight back home and the next time I will see you is with the barrister at Southwark Crown Court. Come prepared you might go to prison. In the meantime make sure you keep out of trouble,' he added as he turned to wave down a taxi.

Birkenhead seemed boring compared to Soho but John was enjoying all the time he now had with Daniel especially as it had been several months since Jackie had been in touch. To his delight the date for the custody hearing was set and John attended with Mr Angilvy his solicitor and Jackie was there with her solicitor. The hearing was held in the judge's chambers at the family court in a rather relaxed informal manner, John and his solicitor sitting one side of the long table, Jackie with her solicitor sitting opposite. The judge dressed in his black gown sat at the head of the table with a clerk sitting to his left ready to make a record of the proceedings.

'This hearing is to determine what is in the best interests of the child,' the Judge began to formally address both parents.

'I have studied the reports presented by the social services that have visited both of the parent's homes and they make interesting reading. It is unusual, very unusual, for the father wanting to be granted full custody of the child and that has made me look hard into the case.'

John lowered his head and looked at his solicitor thinking, *that's it I've lost.*

'However,' the judge continued which raised John's hopes, 'the report shows Mr Lawson has a genuine love for the child and his wellbeing. The child appears to be happy and it his wish to stay with his father. The house was found to be clean and well maintained and Mr Lawson does have the support of his mother in taking care of the child which assures me the child would well looked after. Whereas, the former Mrs Lawson has four other children from four different fathers as well as being pregnant with a fifth child from yet another different father and, according to the report, is already finding the situation difficult to cope with. Whilst I appreciate the problems she is experiencing through financial difficulties or otherwise, the report also states concern for the condition of the house which was not found to be as clean as one would expect where children are concerned. The social services also state concern that the children's behaviour was a little disturbing. It is therefore my judgement, after considering all the evidence presented to me, that the interest of the child, Daniel Lee Lawson would be best served by the father being granted full custody and…'

'No, you can't do that, he's my son and I won't give him up,' Jackie screamed at the judge, leaping to her feet. 'I carried him for nine months, I nursed and breast fed him, clothed and took care of him. What more can a mother be expected to do for her child as well as taking care of two others and another one the way?' she added before she was quickly being restrained by her solicitor.

The judge looked at her sternly.

'Madam, if you do not resume your seat and remain silent I will have you removed from the court room.'

'In granting full custody to the father,' the judge continued after Jackie had resumed her seat, 'you will of course have full non-residential access and visiting rights to the child, which I hope can be mutually agreed between the two of you without further recourse to this court. I'm sure your solicitor will advise you of those rights.'

'Rights, what rights? You're taken my kid away from me after all I've done for him. What's he ever done for the kid except come and visit him occasionally? You ask him that, before you make such harsh judgements,' she shouted at the judge.

'I was there for him right from the beginning until you went off and…'

'This court is adjourned,' the judge announced silencing John as he got to his feet and left the chamber followed by the clerk.

Jackie started to bang the table screaming out.

'It's not fair, it's not fair, I don't deserve this,' before collapsing back into her chair and bursting into tears.

John looked at Jackie a cloud of concern narrowing his eyes.

'I'm sorry to see you distressed like this. I didn't do this to hurt or punish you or for revenge. I did it purely out of interest for Daniel.'

'It's alright, I'm sure we can sort something out so you will be able to see him and take him out whenever you like,' the solicitor cut in, trying to console her.

'Of course she can see Daniel whenever she wants. I have no intention of making it difficult for her,' John said compassionately and he lent across the table.

'There you are it won't be so bad. You're not going to be stopped from seeing your son,' the solicitor assured her. 'I will make formal arrangement with the other party's solicitor,' looking across at John's solicitor for a nod of agreement, which he got.

John was over the moon with the judgment and so was his mother. John had spent all the money his uncle had given him mainly on the solicitor, but felt it was money well spent because he had got his divorce and he had Daniel. John happily agreed with the formal arrangements that were put in place for Jackie to see Daniel but after the second visit she made no further effort to see him. It seemed she had just walked away from everything in the same way his father had done.

With all this unpleasantness now over, John knew he had to do something to get himself out of the situation, to raise himself above the rest, to make a better life for himself and Daniel. That determination took a severe knock when a letter arrived informing him, his trial was set to take place in London in nine months time. *How could I have been so selfish, so reckless, so stupid'* he cursed himself, *but I won't go to prison, my uncles have got the best lawyer there is and they pay him a lot of money to have cases like this dropped.* But still the thought that he might go to prison rose like bile in his throat.

BUSTER AND A PAT OF BUTTER

John was sad to say goodbye to Alfie as he had taught him a lot during their short stay together, but was a little upset that Alfie appeared to be rather casual about his going, but quickly realised it was just Alfie's way of not showing any sign of emotion, in case it was taken as a weakness as he cheerfully chirped.

'Don't worry boy, Wandsworth will be a doddle compared to the Ritz here, just remember, keep yer ead down.'

As John sat in the confines of the sweat box he reflected on the times he'd driven past the prison on his way to deliver the cash to the Smith family and the irony of vowing he would never end up in a place like that. But here he was about to enter the gates as a prisoner.

John was led along with the other prisoners towards their various cells. The prison officer took a delight in guiding the prisoners along E wing where the execution chamber was situated. He opened the door so that the inmates could see inside. There was a huge beam from which hung three chain adjusting blocks, with a noose hanging from the centre one. In the centre of the floor was the nine foot by five foot trapdoor with the operating lever to the side.

'Down below is the pit where the condemned man drops and it has a gate to the yard where the body is taken out. The system is regularly tested every six months because the death penalty is still in force for treason, piracy with violence, or mutiny in the armed forces. So as long as none of you fit into that category then you won't be falling into that trap,' he chuckled, laughing at his own pun. 'There've been some interesting people hanged here. William Joyce, better known as

Lord Haw Haw was hung here. There was a double execution when Edward Smith and Joseph Brown were both stood on the gallows together, John George Haigh, the acid bath murderer, Timothy Evans and John Christie. Francis Forsyth was only eighteen when he was hanged in 1960, and the last executions to take place was Henryk Niemasz on the September 18th 1961,' the prison officer told them, showing off his gruesome knowledge.

John was then guided to the middle cell on the top landing of D wing but there wasn't a friendly old face like Alfie installed there. It was the face of a scruffy con, obviously a junkie by the look of him. The cell had the acrid smell of urine, excrement and stale tobacco, which seemed to delight the prison officer as he shoved John in and relocked the cell door.John looked around. The cell was dirty, paint peeling off the walls, cockroaches crawling around in the corners, the floor splattered with cigarette stubs and ash and, to his horror he could see as well as smell the excrement in the bucket.

'Welcome to my Peter,' the scruffy con said with a sweep of his hand.

'Peter? Who or what the hell's that?' John asked, looking at the dishevelled state of his new cell mate, his grubby shirt, creased jeans and stained boots caked in dirt.

'What's the matter with you? They're known here as Peters. You know Peter Pan...Can. So you're in the can, right, what you in for then?' his cell mate asked, slouched back on his bunk not bothering to sit up.

John took an instant dislike to him and realised he would have to put some fear into him if he was to get some order and cleanliness into the cell.

'Robbery with violence,' John said wanting to make it sound heavy. He could see it had the desired effect as he saw him wince.

'So what are you in for?' John asked, abrasively.

'Breaking into a few homes and that,' he said casually as though it was no big deal.

John looked at his cell mate's dirty unwashed state with contempt, determined he would he would frighten him into cleaning up the cell.

'What's your name?' John asked.

'Michael, what's yours?' he replied offering his hand, the nails filthy and long.

'John,' he replied not wishing to shake his hand. 'And I tell one thing Michael, you're going to clean your act up or there's going to be trouble and if you ever shit in that bucket again…'

'You're joking aren't you? Where else can you shit when you're locked up for the night?'

'You get some newspaper or one of your old socks, crap in or on that and toss it out the window or better still learn to control your bowels so you can crap in the toilets before lock up. That way the cell won't stink like it does now. Because I tell you, if you ever shit in that bucket again, I'll make you eat it, understand? I'm not prepared to live in a shit hole, which is what this cell is right now,' John told him, his anger rising to the surface ready to smack him one if he made the wrong remark.

Michael didn't, but it made him sit up, swing his legs off the bunk and look at John who was much bigger and stronger than he was and knew he would be no match for him.

'You know who's across the landing?' Michael said, wanting desperately to change the subject.

'No, how the hell would I know? I've just arrived you idiot.'

Michael winced at the word idiot, but did nothing.

'James Hussey,' he said, with great aplomb.

'James Hussey, who's he?'

'None other than one of the Great Train Robbers.'

'But they've all been released ages ago except for Ronnie Biggs who's still in Brazil,' John said, looking at Michael as though he was mad.

'Oh, he's here alright. He was only out a few months and now he's doing a seven stretch for cocaine smuggling. You know he was the one that bashed the train driver Jack Mills over the head with an iron bar?' Michael said with a strange sense of admiration.

'More fool him if he's stupid enough to get himself banged up again.' John said not showing much interest.

'You not interested in going to the movie on Wednesday afternoon then?' Michael asked, offhandedly.

'What movie's that?' John asked surprised.

'This'll make you laugh talking about Hussey; they're only going to be showing Buster.'

'You mean the Phil Collins movie about Buster Edwards and the great train robbery?'

'Yeah, it's our turn to see it on Wednesday.'

'How do you mean our turn?'

'Each wing sees the movie on a different day because they won't let more than a hundred and fifty assemble at one time. They show the movies in the gym and you can't get more than that in there when they got the screen and the projector set up,' Michael explained.

'That should prove interesting what with him across the landing,' John said, ruefully.

Just then they heard the sound of the keys being inserted and turned in the lock and the cell door opening.

'Right, move yourselves it's meal time. Come on move yourselves,' the prison officer barked at them.

They both grabbed their plates and hurried out the cell, John having determined he was going to keep his nose clean and not do anything to antagonise the prison officers, particularly as they seemed to be more strict and aggressive than they were at Pentonville or Brixton.

The food was laid out on a line of trolleys on the Ones with an inmate standing behind each trolley serving the inmates as they queued with a dollop of potatoes, a dollop of some kind of meat, a dollop of soggy vegetables as they progressed along the line. Then they would be served the dessert, whatever it was that day. With all that piled onto their trays, the inmates would move to the end where there was a trolley with a pile of sliced bread being served by another inmate who was busy talking to the inmate dispensing the pats of butter and it was here that John was to have his first serious confrontation.

As he stood waiting to be served his pat of butter the inmate, a big black guy, was continuing to talk to the inmate serving the jam, taking no notice of John standing there with the line building up behind him. John waited a little longer then picked up the pallet knife and helped himself, but as he moved on the inmate called out.

'What do ya tink you're doing man. That's my job.'

'Oh shut up you dickhead,' John said as he moved on to the big urn to fill his mug with tea.

'No man talks to me like that, I'm going to do you English man,' he shouted at John.

'You and who else?' John said, stopping and turning around to go back to face him, but was stopped by one of the prison officers stepping in and blocking his path. 'None of that, you've got your food, now get back to your cell before you cause trouble.'

Sitting in the cell trying to eat his meal with the stink permeating around him, he looked across at Michael shovelling the food down as fast as he could as though it was his last meal. *It would be if I had my way.* John thought as he pushed his food around the plate.

'What was all that about with the black guy?' Michael asked, swallowing the last fork full of food from his plate.

'Oh, nothing really the dickhead got upset over a pat of butter.'

'Yeah, but I heard him threaten you.'

'So what, all talk to impress his mates.'

'Yeah, but that's just the point. The fact that he said it openly means he is going to have to do something otherwise he'll lose face.'

'So let him lose face, who cares?'

'No I don't think you understand. There was a case where one of the inmates made a threat to a guy who had bad mouthed him and later that night the inmate that had bad mouthed him was rushed to hospital with a deep gash down the whole side of his face. If he hadn't carried out his threat then he would have been picked on and been at the mercy of the others as someone with a big mouth but no guts. So watch your back because that guy will as sure as hell come after you,' Michael warned him.

'So what do I do? Just sit and wait for it to happen?'

'No, you look as though you could stand up to him, so try to get him first.'

'I'm only in here for nine months, which means I'll only do four and a half, so I don't want to get into any fights.'

'You haven't got much choice, he's going to come after you whether you like it or not. He won't give a shit how long you got to serve. He's probably a lifer, so it won't make much difference to him either way.'

'Then I'm going to have to think of something to get myself out of this,' John said, puffing up his shoulders to hide his fear.

Every day during the exercise period John would walk around with Michael and see the black man strolling with his mates continually pointing a finger at him.

'You see, he's marked you, which means he's going to have to do you soon,' Michael warned him.

When he got back to his cell John began to feel nervous. *Strange how trouble comes looking for you without you going looking for it, all caused by an idiot just wanting to show off how big a man he is.* John had not expected that reaction towards him over a silly thing like a pat of butter. The last thing he wanted or needed was a fight. He simply wanted to keep his nose clean, do his time and earn his remission.

The usual boring routine continued and John was relieved when Wednesday afternoon came and they were all ushered down to the gym to watch the movie. The chairs were lined out in rows and the inmates were told not to talk to the row in front of them or the row behind them. All the prisoners were keen to see the film and watched in silence until one of the inmates shouted out pointing his finger at the screen.

'That's him, that's Buster Edwards.

The film was showing the sequence where the real Buster Edwards is seen arriving at the airport in Mexico walking with Phil Collins's wife Jill.

'Whose stupid idea was it to show them this film?' John sitting on the end of the row heard one of the senior prison officers say to his colleague.

'I think the Governor thought it would be a good example to show them crime doesn't pay,' his colleague said.

'Well, seeing the way Buster's lorded it up is hardly an example of crime not paying. I wouldn't have minded some of that myself,' the senior prison officer said.

The inmates remained quiet through the rest of the film until the end, and as the credits rolled, the inmates began a slow hand clap and started to chant 'JIMMY!! JIMMY!!' applauding James Hussey sitting in the audience with them, something the authorities had obviously overlooked.

'Shit, I thought this was a bad idea, and now we're going to have trouble. Let's just hope we can keep it under control,' the senior prison officer said getting worried as the clapping and the shouting got faster and louder.

The other prison officers also started to get nervous that the situation was going to get out of control and they would have a riot on their hands. They looked towards the senior prison officer not sure what he wanted them to do with some of them already drawing their batons. The senior prison officer started shouting trying to make himself heard above the noise for everyone to quieten down, but to no avail as James Hussey stood up, took a bow and a great cheer went up reverberating around the gym as he raised his hand and waved, acknowledging the cheers. It was a euphoric expression of defiance in a united protest against authority.

As the prison officers began to move around the gym, some of them drawing their batons, the inmates quietened down and began to get to their feet ready to be moved back to their cells, all of them with big grins spread across their faces. None of the inmates were surprised when they went down the following day for their lunch time meal to hear some of the inmates from the other wings were moaning because further showings of the movie have been cancelled. John smiled to himself at the stupidity of whoever had organised the showing of the film without realising the affect it would have, particularly with one of the train robbers sitting in the audience.

As he got to the end of the line to collect his bread, the butter guy was standing waiting to serve him.

'I'm still going to do you man, that's for sure,' he said as he threw the pat of butter at John's plate so that it splattered onto his shirt.

'Yeah well, what are you going to do, smother me in butter and give me a massage?' John said, contemptuously, as he wiped the little splash of butter off his shirt.

'No man, I'm going to cut you. You remember your face while you can, because it ain't going to look the same when I cut up your bloodclaat,' the guy said, venomously.

'You don't scare me butter boy. Carry on serving your little pats of butter but be careful you don't strain yourself,' John retorted with heavy sarcasm.

After John had eaten his lunch he felt the nervousness building up inside him and could feel the hot damp flush of panic beginning to grip his chest, combined with the stench of the smoky cell it was making his stomach churn. He was feeling the need to crap but the thought of doing it in the cell was making him feel worse. The more his stomach protested the more urgent it became. He knew there would be one hell of a stink if he had to do it in the bucket and it would go going against everything he said to Michael about using the bucket.

'I need a crap,' he said out loud without thinking.

'So use the bloody bucket, I don't mind. But don't bloody moan at me afterwards.'

John got up and pushed the bell.

'What you doing that for?' Michael asked, looking up surprised.

'Because there's no way I'm using the bucket and neither are you,' John told him, gently rubbing his stomach as the need to go intensified.

Very quickly a prison officer appeared.

'What is it?' he asked gruffly.

'Sorry Boss, but my stomach's upset and I need to go to the toilet and I don't like the idea of having to do it in the bucket, as it won't be very pleasant. Is there any way you can let me go to the toilet? I would really appreciate that Boss' John asked, in his most polite manner.

'Alright Lawson. Just this once but don't make a habit of it. I'll leave the cell on the latch and I want to hear it slam shut as soon as you get back. Don't take too long that I have to come looking for you, Okay?' the prison officer said opening the cell door and letting him out.

The prison officer watched John hurry along the landing to the toilets as he made way down to the next landing to deal with another inmate on his buzzer. To John's surprise when he got to the latrines all the cubicle doors were wide open and there was an inmate down on his knees cleaning out one of the toilet bowls. As John moved closer he recognised it was the butter guy who had threatened him. He couldn't believe his luck! The guy was obviously on cleaning duties, singing away to himself.

There was stillness about John as he assessed whether to seize the opportunity and strike first. If he did, he would have to strike fast and strike hard. He wanted to sort this out once and for all. Acting on pure adrenaline, a grim look on his face, John crept up behind him, raised his leg and brought his boot down hard on the back of the guy's head. His face pounded into the bowl smashing his face and teeth, cracking the toilet, blood splashing everywhere, rendering him unconscious. John then pulled the chain.

'Maybe that'll flush some of the stupid arrogance out of you,' John said, as he turned and hurried out, not risking staying there a moment longer as the need to use the toilet had somehow evaporated with the excitement.

'I'm done Boss,' he called out as he got back to the cell and slammed the door shut.

'You feel better now?' Michael asked, seeing the smile on his face.

'Yeah, I feel a lot better.'

That night John hardly slept, worried, not knowing whether he had killed the guy and if at any moment he would hear the heavy footsteps approaching the cell to collect him and haul him to accuse him of murder. He thought about the execution chamber he'd seen and a shudder went up his spine as wondered whether the death penalty still existed for killing a prisoner. If they traced it to him he knew he would end up serving a lot more than nine months.

Ironically, as John got ready to go down to breakfast, the prison officer unlocking the cell door surprised him by saying.

'After breakfast, pack your stuff Lawson, you're being moved.'

'Where to this time, Boss'?

'You're going to Stanford Hill on the Isle of Sheppey. It's an open prison.'

'Brilliant, glad to be getting out of this bloody awful place,' John said, gathering up his plates and mug.

'Watch your mouth Lawson,' the prison officer warned him.

'Sorry Boss.'

'You're lucky to be moving, there's going to be a clamp down, someone was beat up in the toilets yesterday and the Governor is pissed off about it as whoever did it smashed up one of the toilets.

After breakfast, John got his stuff together and waited for the prison officer to come and collect him.

'Boss, can I make a quick phone call and let my mum know I'm moving, before we go down to reception?'

'Alright Lawson, you've got five minutes, then make you way down to the PO's office on the Ones while I gather up the others that are moving with you.'

John walked to the end of the landing, picked up the receiver, inserted his card and followed the usual procedures and waited until he heard his mother saying hello.

'Mum, I haven't got long, just to tell you the good news that I am being moved to an open prison and I'll have loads of time to talk to you and Daniel once I'm settled there.'

'Oh, son, so good to hear from you, that's good news, you must have been behaving yourself to be moved there,' she said, fighting back the tears.

'Only had a bit of trouble going to the toilet,' John said, not able to resist the joke.

'Must be the prison food.'

'Yeah, I think it had something to do with the butter.'

'So when are you moving?'

'Just getting ready now.'

'Have a quick word with Daniel, he's standing right here' she said, and he could hear her saying. 'It's your daddy,' as she pressed the receiver to Daniel's ear.

'Daddy, daddy, when are you coming home?' Daniel cried excitedly. John's chest tightened, full of emotion at the sound of his son's voice. He wanted to say *I'll be home tomorrow*, but he didn't know when he'd be home. Daniel was waiting for him to say something.

'I don't know son, but it won't be too long now.'

'How many sleeps dad?'

'Dad's got to work a bit longer, but it won't be too many sleeps before I'm back home. You be a good boy for your Nan while I'm away. Can you put your Nan back on quickly?' John said as he heard the prison officer shout up.

'Come on Lawson, time to move.'

'Sorry I have to go. I'll phone you when I get to the open prison. I love you mum and take care of yourself, bye.'

As John replaced the receiver his shoulders slumped. He was missing Daniel terribly but he still had two and half months to do.

TAKING THE LAW INTO HIS OWN HANDS

1989

As John got off the train at Liverpool's Lime Street Station he was pleased to see his mother and Daniel waiting at the barriers to meet him.

'Daddy, daddy,' Daniel cried out, bristling with excitement, happiness shining on his face at seeing his dad and rushed into his arms.

'Good to see you son,' John said holding Daniel tightly to him. 'I've got you a nice present.'

'What is it dad?' Daniel asked his eyes wide with anticipation.

'Wait until we get home, then you can have it. How are you ma?' John asked, turning to his mother and giving her a light kiss on the cheek.

'I'm fine John darling, let's get the train and get home, it's been a bit cold waiting around for you.

'No, we're taking a taxi,' John insisted.

'Do you know how much that'll cost?' his mother protested.

'It's alright ma, I can afford it,' he said, leading them off to the taxi rank.

'So how long are you planning on staying?' his mother asked, as they travelled through the Mersey tunnel.

'I'm not planning on going anywhere. I'm back here for good.'

'I'm pleased to hear it. At least you won't be mixing with those unsavoury people anymore, the first thing you're going to have to do is look for a job.'

'I know ma, you don't have to worry about that. I will go straight down to the job centre tomorrow. What about Jackie, has she been in touch?'

193

'Not a word, it would seem she has lost all interest.'

'Does she know about me being away?'

'Not that I'm aware of, there's been nothing from her or her solicitor so I guess she doesn't know. Let's keep our fingers crossed and hope it stays that way,' his mother said, the sunlight temporarily blinding them as the taxi emerged from the tunnel into Birkenhead.

John was pleased to see Alex but noticed he did not seem to be too happy, not chatting away as usual about how he was doing at work.

'What's the matter our kid?' John asked, walking into his bedroom where Alex was sat on the edge of the bed looking morosely into space.

'You know that girl I met while you were inside?'

'Yeah, Samantha isn't it?'

'Yeah well Sam…she's up the duff and I haven't even told ma yet.'

'You'll have to man up our kid and tell her before its too late and the baby arrives.'

'Yeah I will, but that's not the only problem. The foreman's got it in for me at work,' he said looking up and John could see the sadness in his eyes.

'It seems all of a sudden I can't do anything right. He tells me to do one thing and then comes back and asks why I'm doing that instead of something else.'

'Can't you complain to the bosses, I'm sure they'd sort him out?'

'No, I don't want to cause any trouble, because I don't want to lose my job especially now with a baby on the way.'

'Okay bruv, I understand. But just don't let the bastard walk all over you.'

'No, it pisses me off, but I can handle it, like you've had to do for the last four and half months. At least you managed to stay out of trouble. I always had visions that one day some prisoner would say something to upset you and you'd smash his face in.'

'Actually someone did say something to upset me in Wandsworth.'

'So what happened?'

'It's a long story, I had a row with the butter man and…'

'The butter man?'

'Yeah, he served the pats of butter out at meal times. The knobhead ignored me so I helped myself and he got upset and threatened to do me. In prison if you threaten to do something in front of the other prisoners then you have to do it, because if you don't then you're finished.'

'So he tried to beat you up?'

'No, I got him first and smashed his head in the toilet. Fortunately no one knew I had done it and before an investigation was started I was moved to Stanford Hill.'

'I fear for anyone that crosses you,' Alex said, looking at his brother in admiration.

'I have a simple rule, people mess with me at their own risk, bruv.'

'Yeah, I certainly believe that. So what are you going to do now?'

'Go and look for a job like everyone else, I guess.'

'That's not going to be easy, there's little work around here.'

'Yeah, I know, but I'll find something don't you worry, bruv.'

The dole office was exactly the same. They still had bouncers on the door and the seating was still bolted down. Depression washed over him as looked at the same mismatch of people sitting around waiting their turn in quiet desperation. When his turn came he hurried to the counter with the reinforced glass and explained the situation.

'So does that mean you're on probation?' she asked, ponderously.

'No it means I'm on parole,' he quickly corrected her unsure of the implication.

'What's the difference?'

'The difference is I'm a free man and don't have to report to anyone,' John explained, sounding a little irritated.

'I see. Well we have all your details on record and as you are a single parent, we'll reinstate your benefits as from today. It will of course help if you start looking for work to get yourself off benefits.'

'I will start on it right away,' he said as the feeling that he wanted to smash his fist through the toughened glass swelled up in him.

Surprisingly, after only having been back a week a letter arrived from the Methodist Housing Association informing him he had been allocated a two bedroom end of terrace house on Elm Street. It was well positioned, right next to the shops and the market and Birkenhead town centre. The problem was John had no furniture and even with what was left of the £2,000 he was not going to get everything he needed.

Around the corner from his new house, on Hemingford Street was the Charles Thompson Mission church and to his luck John heard they had second hand furniture available. As he approached the entrance to the building he looked up at an overhanging sign and studied the words displayed on it which read:

*'It is appointed unto men to die once
and after this the judgement.'*

John shrugged, not sure what to make of it. Once inside the large
hall he looked around at a scraggly group of men and women lining
up and being served a hot meal by a small group of smartly dressed
women. A friendly looking man in his early fifties came out of the
kitchen area and noticed John standing there.

'Hello, I'm Rob Jeffs the Pastor here, what can I do for you?' he
said a beaming smile spreading spread across his face.

'I was just passing and was wondering whether you might know of
anywhere I can buy some cheap furniture. You see, I've just come out
of prison and I'm a single dad. The Methodist Housing association
has given me a house and my son and I have moved into number
2 Elm Street but have very little furniture,' John explained, playing
heavily on the situation.

'Oh that's just on the corner, we must see what we can do to help
you,' the pastor said, his smile broadening. 'That is what the mission
is here for,' he added as he led John to a door at the back of the hall,
opened it and ushered him inside.

'Will any of this be of use to you?' the pastor asked, indicating the
stack of second hand furniture piled high to the ceiling.

'Where do you get all this from?' John asked amazed at how much
was there.

'We do house clearances. We dispose of the rubbish and hold onto
the good stuff. So choose what you need and we'll arrange to get it
to you.'

'Thank you, but first how much is it going to cost me?'

'My dear boy, there is no charge, these are God's gifts to those in
need,' the pastor said, with a benevolent sweep of his arms.

John had another stroke of luck when he was offered his old job
back as a barman in Jimmys. It was only for the weekends and wasn't
exactly what he wanted as he still had the urge to be on the door
as a bouncer, but it was a job and that's what he needed. John was
also making regular visits to Flemmo who was still having difficulty
getting over the death of his father. He was now living alone in the
house as his mother had re-married and moved out of the family
home.

It was on one of his visits that Flemmo's sister Lynn walked in.

She was just as beautiful as he had remembered her even though he had not seen her for over seven years. He had always admired her lovely blonde hair and her beautiful light green eyes. She was dressed casually, nothing flashy, but it still showed off her firm shapely figure. John had always had a crush on Lynn ever since they were school kids but back then fourteen year old girls were not interested in fourteen year old boys. Lynn had brought her son with her to John's disappointment.

'So you're married now and have a son?' John remarked.

'Was. This is Michael, he's four,' she said, taking hold of her son's hand.

'What do you mean was?' John asked, picking up on it.

'Michael is Phil's son, you remember the guitar player in the Beatles tribute band? Well anyway after we split up I got married to a guy called David but we're divorced now thank goodness. David's a bodybuilder but he started on steroids and as the steroid intake increased so did his anger – he became violent and impossible to live with, I was afraid for our safety, me and Michael, I had to get out. We'd only been married a year,' she said, her voice quavering.

'Same as me, I was only married for a year, I have a son too, his name's Daniel and he's also four.' I found out she was having an affair while I was at home looking after the baby. 'Who fancies a drink?' Flemmo suggested as he went off to the kitchen to get some glasses.

'You know I used to fancy you,' John told her as soon as Flemmo had left the room.

'I know you did,' she said, coyly

'Maybe things have changed.'

'Maybe,' she said, shyly.

'We're both single, what would you say, if I was to ask you out?'

The question caught her by surprise although she guessed she should have expected it.

'You won't know unless you ask,' she said with a coyness that made her eyes sparkle.

John did ask her. They began to date and their relationship began to grow to the point Lynn moved in with John.

Flemmo's mother Kath wasn't happy about it as she had always looked on John as a bad boy. Flemmo himself was not sure how he felt about the arrangement, but didn't want to fall out with John or his sister, so said nothing and kept his thoughts to himself. Daniel and Michael got on well and enjoyed playing together, but Lynn was becoming unhappy at the lonely weekends with John working at Jimmy's and coming home in the early hours of the morning, sleeping all day too tired to take them out anywhere.

In the midst of all this, John got some good news from the Methodist Housing Association, who wanted to know if John would be interested in an exchange for a more modern three bedroom house in Wood Close. Both John and Lynn were excited about having a larger house so that the boys could have a room each and happily agreed to the transfer.

John continued working weekends at the club and everything seemed fine until he was awoken by Lynn early on a Saturday morning, shaking him out of a deep sleep to tell him his mum had just phoned to say the house had been burgled in the night and she needed to speak to him.

It was enough of a shock to jolt John into his senses and leap out of bed. 'I must get round there,' he said, grabbing his clothes and hurriedly putting them on.

'So what the hell happened?' he asked his mother as soon as she opened the door.

'We never heard them, we were all asleep,' she explained as she led him off to the kitchen and immediately put the kettle on.

'So that's how whoever did it got in,' John said, as he looked across at the broken window of the back door. 'So what did they take?'

'The television and video recorder, some of my jewellery and Alex's pay packet, which he had left on the mantelpiece, they even took Daniel's leather jacket and a pair of his trainers,' his mother told him, her voice trembling, her hands shaking, the mugs clanging together as she set them down on the table. 'I've called the police.'

'Huh, that won't do any good, I've got a good idea it might be one of the local druggies around here, they'll steal anything to get a fix ,even that little shit Lee across the road could have done it.'

'Don't talk like that, the Henrys are a nice family and I'm friends with them,' his mother said, regarding him with a look of disfavour.

'Yeah, but their son's gone off the rails and is a real druggie, breaking into places and they don't know what to do with him. If it wasn't him, I bet he knows who did so I'll have a quiet word with him.'

'Yeah well, we all know what having a quiet word means,' Alex said, coming into the kitchen.

'So what do you suggest bruv?'

'I told you, I get on very well with the Henrys and I don't want any trouble with them over their wayward son. Let the police handle it,' his mother said, her face pale and anxious as she poured the boiling water into the teapot.

'The police won't do anything about it, they're all too busy policing law abiding citizens to have any time to bother with the criminals.'

'Don't worry ma, John will sort it out, but I would like to get my wages back, I work bloody hard for it,' Alex cut in.

'Watch your language, you know I don't like either of you swearing,' his mother chastised him.

'I'm going to have a look outside to see if they left any clues,' John said, getting up from the table.

'Don't you want any tea, now I've made it?' his mother asked.

'I'll have some when I get back,' John said, hurrying out.

It was while he was looking around that he spotted Lee coming out of his house and scamper off down the street. John waited until Lee passed the bus station on Laird Street and turned into one of the narrow alleyways and chased after him.

Catching up with him was easy and John grabbed him by the scruff of the neck and pulled him round to his face. 'You broke into my mother's house last night, didn't you, you little toe rag?'

Lee stared into John's angry eyes and it made the hairs on the back of his neck rise. 'No, I didn't, honest.'

'Honest, everything that comes out your drugged filled mouth is a lie. So tell me what you've done with the stuff, or...'

'I didn't do it honest. I swear on my mother's life,' Lee squealed, his body beginning to shake with fear as John squeezed his throat.

'You'd swear on anything, but I tell you this, if I don't find out by tomorrow who did this, I'm coming after you and Lee, if I have to make you disappear then so be it,' John said, relaxing his grip on Lee's throat before punching him in the stomach.

It was later that evening his mother received a phone call from the local police station to tell her that someone had phoned in giving the name of a possible suspect and they were looking into it. But that wasn't good enough for John and he decided to go and visit the police station to find out more.

The local police station on Laird Street was very small with the proverbial blue phone box standing outside for people to be able to phone the police when the station was closed. Inside was equally small with a police sergeant sitting at a desk behind the counter. 'What can I do for you sir?' the sergeant asked, getting up and moving to the counter.

'You 'phoned my mother, Mrs Lawson, earlier to tell her you had been given the name of a suspect who could have carried out the burglary and I wondered whether you had progressed any further with it?' John informed him.

The sergeant looked thoughtfully at John and smiled indulgently as he said. 'We get a lot of people phoning in with names, some do it for revenge, others do it for mischief, so we can't just run off and arrest every name that's given to us, even though in this case it's a name well known to us,' he said, as he crossed back to the desk, picked up a file, brought it over to the counter and opened it up.

'I wonder if you could give me the name as I have a sneaking feeling I know who might have 'phoned you,' John said, pleadingly.

'I'm afraid I can't do that sir,' the sergeant said, closing the file, 'but if you will excuse me I must go to the toilet,' he said, a wry smile twisting his face as he walked over to the door. 'I trust you won't be tempted to look in the file while I'm away,' the sergeant said, turning round as he got to the door.

John smiled taking the hint and looked at the closed file on the counter, flipped it round, opened it and quickly scanned the pages. His smile broadened as he read the name Michael Atherton and the smile stretched as he read the address, 21 Tees Street, one of the River Streets in the North End.

He managed to close the file and quickly flip it back round, just as the sergeant came back into the room. 'That's better, if there is any further information forthcoming, we will of course let you know,' he said, picking up the file.

'Thank you sergeant, you've been most helpful,' John said, appreciatively.

'One more thing, if I happen to hear about a certain individual in the River Streets having an unfortunate accident, it won't have had anything to do with you, will it Mr Lawson?' the sergeant said, with a wry grin.

'No sergeant, absolutely not,' John replied, matching his grin. *At least there are some good cops*, John thought as he walked out of the station.

As John prepared himself, putting on his crisp clean white shirt, black trousers and shiny black shoes for his night's stint at The Jimmys, he pondered on what to do about Michael Atherton.

The urge to sort him out played on his mind all through the night's shift at the club. By the time his shift was finished the desire for revenge was so overwhelming that he decided he couldn't wait any longer.

John went straight home, quietly let himself in so as not to wake anyone and crept silently out to the backyard shed to dig out the truncheon he had bought that afternoon at Mac's Second Hand Shop.

The truncheon was sixty years old, made of solid wood, about fourteen inches long and still had the leather strap handle attached

By 6.30 that morning he had made up his mind to go straight round to Tees Street and confront Michael Atherton. He slipped on his black leather jacket slid the truncheon up his left sleeve and quietly left the house.

As John got to the address, he was relieved to see there were no one about and all the curtains of the neighbouring houses were closed. With adrenaline already coursing through his veins John started hammering on the door. 'Michael Atherton, open this door now,' he shouted out.

After a few bangs, a top window opened and a man's head poked out. He looked a mess, his puffy, pale anaemic face, dirty and unwashed, his hair long and scraggy. He guessed it was Michael Atherton gazing down at him and before John could say a word his head ducked back in and the window slammed shut as John heard him shout out. 'It's the bizzies.'

John allowed himself to smile realising the way he was dressed made him look a bit like a policeman.

'Open this door now or we'll be forced to break in,' John said, putting on a formal voice.

He listened as he heard footsteps hurrying down the stairs then heard the chain being slipped on and waited for the door to be opened. Slowly the door opened as far as the chain would allow. 'Open the door,' John demanded, as a face peered out through the gap.

'Where's you search warrant?' the face asked.

'Here,' John said, raising his foot and kicking it hard against the door, snapping the chain that held the door which swung open and trapped them man against the wall.

At that moment a woman came down the stairs screaming. 'You can't do that.'

'Stay out of this, it's this scumbag I've come to see,' he told her, closing the door behind him, grabbing Atherton by the scruff of the neck he dragged him across the room. As Atherton struggled to get to his feet John drew the truncheon and whacked him over the head, sending him reeling over the back of the sofa.

'You can't do that, that's police brutality,' the woman screamed at John.

John turned to look at her and shoved her down into the armchair waving the truncheon in her face. 'I don't like hitting women, but if you don't shut that mouth of yours I might be forced to. I'm no copper and this scumbag broke into my mother's house and stole her stuff.'

'It wasn't me,' Michael pleaded, his eyes narrowed, his mouth gaping to reveal a row of chipped yellow teeth as he made another attempt to get to his feet.

John raised the truncheon threateningly as he looked around the room and spotted Daniel's jacket dumped on one of the chairs.

'So it wasn't you,' John said, his anger rising as walked over, picked the jacket up and waved it at Michael. 'You lying bastard, this is my son's jacket. I know because I bought it for him. So where is the rest of the stuff?'

'I sold it,' he said and John could see the fear creeping into his face.

'What about the wage packet you stole, that was my brother's money that he worked bloody hard for. I don't care how you do it, but I want everything you stole returned to my mother's house by tomorrow night and if it isn't there, I will come back and I promise you, you'll wish you had never come anywhere near us,' John said, breaking his nose with a thud, splattering the truncheon with blood 'You have until tomorrow night to get everything back, okay?' John said with clenched teeth as he grabbed Daniel's jacket and stormed out.

John went round to his mother's on the Monday evening as Michael Atherton returned her television and video recorder, Alex's wages and the other items he had stolen.

'How did you manage that?' his mother asked, rhetorically already guessing what the answer would be.

'Let's just say, he was full of remorse and wanted to make amends,' John said, with a sheepish grin.

'How did you get to be so devious? I remember how your uncles talked like that when they caught the person who had stolen the stuff from the trunk,' his mother said, ruefully.

'The one thing my uncles taught me was not to rely on the law, if you want any justice, you have to go out and get it for yourself,' John said, his face twisted in a savage grin of triumph.

By now the paperwork had now been completed so that John and Lynn could move into the new larger house as part of the exchange. It made Lynn happy as she busied herself putting her personal touches to the rooms to make them more homely. Both Daniel and Michael were attending the Priory Primary School so everything was settling down into a nice comfortable routine.

John saw an ad for taxi drivers and thought that at least it would be a bit more exciting, but was told that he needed to get a full medical certificate before he could be granted a licence.

'Why do you need that for?' John asked one of the cabbies as he came out the office.

'They need to know, your heart's okay so you won't suddenly faint while you're driving and you've got good vision so you can see where you're going, but don't worry,' the cabby told him. 'Go and see this doctor, bung him forty quid and he'll give you a clean bill of health,' the cabbie added, handing John a piece of paper with the name and address of the doctor.

True to the cabby's word, as soon as John had slipped over the forty pounds, the doctor started filling in the form without attempting any physical examination. 'Any criminal convictions?' the doctor asked without looking up from the form.

'None,' John lied and watched as the doctor completed the form, scribbled his signature and handed it to John saying. 'There you are, that will satisfy the council's licencing department.'

'Thanks doc,' John said, as he got to his feet and left the room, not believing it was that easy to get a full medical certificate.

John packed in his job at The Jimmys and leased a Ford Mondeo and the radio from the Taxi firm and was allowed to keep anything left over after he paid for the fuel. He chose to work nights as the takings were better, especially at the weekends.

On one particular Friday night Lynn had been invited to a girl's night out with some friends to celebrate one of the girl's birthdays so John had arranged to pick her up from the Fishermans Wharf club in Seacombe up at the end of his shift.

Lynn seemed very upset when John arrived.

'What's wrong, what's happened?' he asked, showing concern.

'It's David my ex, he's in there and he came over grabbed hold of me and insisted I dance with him. I tried to pull away, but he's a strong man and he had hold of my wrists which really hurt. I was scared so had one dance with him and thought that was it, but he kept coming over. The girls and other people tried to stop him, but he wasn't having any of it and tried to grab me again so we all left and I've been waiting in the manager's office for you to come and collect me,' she explained, tearfully a mixture of relief and guilt sweeping over her.

'Why the hell, didn't you call the office and let me know. I would have come straight away.' John said, looking at the red marks on her wrists which inflamed his anger.

'You were working and I didn't want you to lose any money by packing up early.'

'Is he still in there?'

'Yes.'

'Right you wait in the car, I won't be a moment,' John told her, a surge of rage coursing through his body as he charged past the bouncers.

David was standing at the bar with a group of men downing a drink when he saw John enter. He casually placed the glass on the bar, turned to face him, puffing himself up in the way body builders have a habit of doing.

John in his anger charged at him, kicking him full in the chest propelling him backwards crashing into some tables and chairs scattering the people sitting there with drinks spilling everywhere. John stepped over to where he was lying looking up at him, his eyes wide with disbelief at what had just happened trying to decide whether to get to his feet and fight back.

But John made the decision for him with two heavy punches to the face. Putting any thought of a fight out of his mind as he slumped into a near state of unconsciousness.

'If you ever speak to or touch Lynn again I'll kill you,' John told him, as every pulse in his body seemed to speed up.

Lynn looked up anxiously as John came out and got back in the car. 'What did you say to him?' she asked, relieved there were no tell tale marks on his face that they had been fighting.

'Oh, I just simply told him in no uncertain terms that if he ever touched you again I would kill him,' John said, the anger inside him beginning to subside.

There were no further incidents until one night he was called to an address to pick up a passenger from Harrowby Road in Birkenhead. As he knocked on the door to tell them the taxi was there, a smartly dressed, but decidedly angry looking man came storming out of the front door charging straight at John.

John swiftly side stepped him and opened the rear door for him to get in. 'Where to?' John asked as he settled back in the driver's seat.

"The Queens Arms pub in Oxton Village and don't take any crafty detours, right?' the man said, gruffly.

John didn't like the remark, but said nothing, as he watched the man's brooding face carefully through the rear view mirror as he set off.

'You alright mate?' John asked, being a little concerned by the man's demeanour.

'Fine, as long as keep your mouth shut and mind your own damn business,' the man snapped in a gruff manner.

A tiny spark of anger flared up in John and it took all of his self control not to stop the car, drag the man out and give him a good thumping, but instead he put his foot down and speeded up, wanting to get to the destination as quick as he could to get rid of the moron.

The man remained silent for the rest of the journey.

'Right stop here,' he shouted as they approached the pub in Storeton Road.

'That'll be five pounds please,' John said, as he turned around to face the man.

'You're getting nothing. I don't like you or this poxy car,' the man said, opening the rear door and getting out.

'Hey dickhead you owe me for the fare,' John called out hurrying after him.

The man stopped and turned to face John as he said. 'I'm not paying you anything, so just get back in the car and piss off,' the man said, aggressively.

'You owe me the fare and I want it,' John told him, desperately trying to control his temper.

'I told you I'm not paying you, so what are you going to do about it?' the man said aggressively, moving threateningly towards John.

If only the man had known, that what he was saying was like a red rag to a bull to John and the flare of temper that had been festering inside him rose to the surface and he gave the man a side kick in the chest sending him reeling into some bushes, but as he turned to go back to the car, the man had scrambled to his feet and called out. 'Is that best you can do, dickhead.'

John stopped to check himself, it was only a few pounds and certainly not worth risking getting into trouble over, so continued back to the car, but as he did so he felt the man charging after him repeating. 'I said is that the best you can do, dickhead?'

Whatever control John was still trying to hold over himself snapped and as the man got close, John gave him a roundhouse kick to the head and the man went down like a ton of bricks, unconscious before he hit the pavement.

'No mate, that's the best I can do,' John said, as he turned and walked back to the car.

'Do you realise the uncle of the man you attacked last night sits on the licencing committee and…'

'Hang on, it was him who attacked me and refused to pay the fare,' John cut in, annoyed at what he was hearing as he sat facing the owner of the taxi company the following morning.

'Yeah I know that lad's trouble but the rule is whatever the provocation you never get out the car.'

'You mean, if any customer refuses to pay, you just sit there and take it?' John said, glaring at the owner is disbelief.

'What you don't do is get out the car and knock someone unconscious. You're lucky the uncle has decided not to report the matter to the police,' the owner told him.

'Yeah well, that doesn't surprise me, the way his nephew was behaving, a right dickhead he was.'

'That's as maybe, but the fact of the matter is, you left him lying unconscious on the pavement. So you're fired and your licence is revoked,' the owner told him, stretching out his hand for John to hand over his ID badge.

BOARDROOM SCUFFLE

1993

John was helping Lynn move some furniture around in their new house when his mother phoned in the middle of the afternoon asking him to come round as something had happened to Alex. When he got to his mother's house, he found Alex sitting slumped in one of the armchairs and immediately felt something was wrong, very wrong.

'What's the matter our kid, why aren't you at work?' John asked, a cloud of concern tightening the lines of his face.

'Work...they've...sacked...me,' Alex stuttered, exasperation hardening his words as he struggled to get them out, the hurt was there in his voice, in his eyes, in his whole expression.

John could see the hurt. 'How do you mean, they've sacked you? You only had two weeks to go before you completed your five year apprenticeship.'

'I think that's why they sacked me. All those years of hard work wasted. I think I was set up,' he said, clasping his hands tightly together to prevent any sign of shaking.

'Set up, how do you mean?'

'I was given the job of cutting a quantity of metal bars to a length of a hundred and forty millimetres which I did. Then the foreman appeared and accused me of cutting them to the wrong length saying he had told me to cut them to a length of a hundred and forty four millimetres. I told him he had stood there and watched me set the machine at a hundred and forty millimetres before signing the job off to me. He denied it of course and reported it to the bosses, who summoned me to the office, told me I had been negligent and had cost the company money as the steel bars were all the wrong length and would have to be redone and with that told me I was sacked.' Alex explained.

'Where were the union in all this?'

'If you want to become a member of a union you have to inform the management and they would probably sack you before you joined. With so much unemployment the bosses seem to be able to do what they like. And it's not only me, there are other apprentices I know who have been sacked before they've completed their apprenticeship, so the company wouldn't then have to pay them full rates.'

'The bastards, I'm going to go and have a word with them. They can't be allowed to get away with this,' John said, as a surge of outrage coursed through his body.

No,' his mother called out, her frown deepening. 'There's nothing you can do about it, these companies can do what they like. What do you think you're going to do?'

'I don't know, but I'm sure as hell going to do something. I'm not letting them get away with this.'

'No please Bruv, you'll only make matters worse,' Alex pleaded.

'How worse can it get? You've been sacked by a load of scumbags and…'

'Sam and I have split for good this time and now I've got to go through all the crap you went through to see my son Jamie, where am I going to get the money to pay for that now?'

'Well, we could all see that coming, but this is different and I'm not having it,' John said, the urge to go ahead and do what he had to do and damn the consequences had become overwhelming as he stormed out before either of them could stop him.

Amazingly, fuelled by so much aggression, no one attempted to stop him as he charged through the factory demanding to know where the MD's offices were.

Finding it, he charged in causing the secretary to almost jump out of her chair. 'Excuse me!! Excuse me!! You can't go in there, there's a meeting going on. Are they expecting you? Do you have an appointment,' the words flying out of her mouth, as she sprang to her feet to try to block him as he made for the inner door.

'If I was you I would shut that trap of yours and sit down,' John snapped at her.

She looked into his angry eyes and it was enough for her to step aside and watch helplessly as he kicked the inner door open with such force that it almost swung off its hinges.

The five directors were sitting around the boardroom table and all looked up surprised at the noise of the banging door.

'What the devil is this?' one of the board members exclaimed in horror.

John stood there glaring at them, his body almost filling the door frame. 'Which one of you bastards sacked my brother?' he shouted across the room.

'Just a minute, we don't know who you are and how you managed to get in here, but I suggest you turn round and go back out, before we call the police,' one of the directors said, in a quiet controlled manner.

'I'm not going anywhere, until I get a few answers,' John said, standing his ground. 'My brother Alex Lawson, left school early forsaking his exams to work for you and has been working here serving his apprenticeship for the last five years and he had only two weeks to go to get his qualifications and you lot sack him because of what some evil twisted minded foreman accused him of. Where is the bully boy now? Go get him and bring him up here now and see what he has to say for himself.'

'The director sitting at the far end of the table spoke up saying. 'I don't know where he is, but if your brother is anything like you, then I suspect he deserved to be sacked.'

The words smacked John in the face and he became incandescent with anger. He raised his foot up and kicked the edge of the desk with such force that it shot backwards pinning the man and his chair against the far wall. 'My brother's a good man. He left school early to take up the apprenticeship, missing out on his final exams. He put his life and soul into this factory. He's worked hard for you, never took a day off with illness, even eating his lunch at the machines and often working late to finish a job, without receiving any extra pay because he was an apprentice and he cared, and you lot used him as cheap labour. If my brother does not receive his time served papers in the next two weeks which would be the completion of his apprenticeship, then I will come back and burn the bloody factory down with you lot in it.'

'You can't make threats like that,' one of the other directors said, as he struggled to push the table away to try to free his trapped colleague. 'I can have you arrested.'

John reached over grabbing the man by his tie and dragging him across the table as he spat out the words. 'Go on then, why don't you? But I tell you the newspapers would love a story like this, exploitation of cheap labour and all that, so if I was you, I would just do the decent thing and there'll be no more trouble,' John said, as he stormed out.

'There you are, as you can see I didn't need an appointment,' he said, to the still bemused secretary as he rushed past her.

It was about two weeks later that Alex received his qualifying certificates together with two weeks back pay.

After being sacked from the taxi company John decided to take up an offer of a job from the brother of the owner of The Jimmys, delivering frozen products to the fish and chip shops around the area, but soon became suffocated by the tedium of being a delivery driver. He couldn't let go of his dreams and it was tearing him apart, it wasn't long before he jacked in the delivery job and started looking for something else a little more challenging and exciting.

His frustration culminated when his relationship with Lynn became so strained that they decided it would be better if they were to split up. It was mutual and there was no bitterness between them as Lynn moved out and left John to get on with his own life.

ALONG CAME JENNY

1995

Thorneycroft Street was becoming increasingly run down so Jose was excited when the housing associating informed her that she could move in to a new ground floor flat opposite Birkenhead Library.

John had his own house taking care of Daniel, while Alex had made things up with Samantha so everything seemed fine, but as the months went by alone in the flat Jose was succumbing to a sense of hopelessness often crying with tears of bitterness for all that had happened and was still happening. The past was finally catching up with her and cracks were beginning to appear in her tough exterior. The sense of loneliness left her feeling lethargic and emotionally exhausted. She sensed her life was falling apart, frightened she would not be able to make it through the next month, the next week, even the rest of the day. The bouts of depression were increasing and as a consequence she began to drink more to ease her worries, but that did nothing to solve the problems. Even taking a larger dose of sleeping pills only delayed the anxieties until the morning when they were back again in force, pounding her troubled mind to the point she began to hope that she would fall asleep and never wake up.

John's unsettled life was adding to her anxieties and the bouts of depression were becoming so overwhelming that suicidal thoughts began to play in her mind. One day in despair she cried out to the heavens 'God if you are up there, if you are real then you better show up because I have had enough of this life.' Emotionally exhausted and in floods of tears Jose fell asleep on the sofa.

When you're asleep you're at a subconscious level and vulnerable to your surroundings. As Jose slept she heard the gentle sound of

211

tapping which roused her into a near conscious state, she thought it might be a sign from God and a happy smile began to form on her face as she wondered, *Can God speak to us, is that God speaking to me, telling me he is here to prove he had heard her prayers.'*

The tapping became louder although she was not yet consciously awake enough to know where the tapping was coming from.

'It's the gasman,' she heard a voice suddenly shout out.

The smile dropped heavily and her eyes opened wide as she listened to the voice calling out again. 'It's the gasman, is anybody there?'

'How silly of me, that just proves there is no God, it's just the gasman come to fix the meter, that's all I need,' she muttered to herself as she levered herself up to the sitting position and swung her legs round to let her feet rest on the carpeted floor.

'Thank goodness I'm still dressed,' she sighed as she heaved herself off the sofa, crossed to the door and let him in.

'Sorry I feel asleep on the sofa,' she said, becoming worried about her the appearance as he followed her in carrying his bag of tools.

'Don't worry, you're the first customer on my list and I start very early, my name's Mike Haynes,' he said offering his free hand, the other hand still holding on to the tool bag.

'Are you alright?' he asked, looking into her troubled face. 'I can come back later if you prefer,' he offered.

'No, it's alright, well it isn't really, it's just that everything is getting on top of me and I don't know which way to turn.'

'I know the feeling, I've been there myself but I learned that no one can store up immunity from disaster or tragedy. All any of us can control is how we respond when tough times come. We often convince ourselves that we cannot change, that we cannot overcome the circumstances of our lives. That is simply not true. When you feel life is falling apart it could actually be falling together. Learn from yesterday, live for today, hope for tomorrow. I've been through some rough times in my life and it was then that I prayed to Jesus and He helped me overcome my circumstances and I surrendered my life to Christ. As well as working for the gas board I am also a church pastor now and have started a small church meeting in the Tranmere Rovers supporters club. You are welcome to come, in fact my wife and I and a few friends are meeting at my house tomorrow night if you would like to come,' he invited.

After he had gone Jose thought hard on what he had said, she was not interested so much in the religious side of things but her need of love and friendship was overwhelming.

The following night Jose braved her anxieties and went to the house in Prenton and nervously knocked on the door. A woman opened it and greeted Jose warmly as though expecting her and introduced herself as Angie, Mike's wife.

Jose went to a few more meetings at their home before one Sunday she decided to attend the church meeting in the supporters club

It was at one of the meetings listening to Mike preach about how God will never desert or let his people down, where her mind drew back to South Africa. She remembered Lex's scoffing at his childhood friend Ronnie McGregorr thinking he had gone mad when he told him he was a Born Again Christian. As she continued to listen it reminded her of how Ronnie used to talk. She listened passionately to Mike preaching and in that moment she broke down as a feeling of calm washed over her, without really knowing what she was doing fell to her knees and prayed, inviting Jesus into her life. The change in Jose was as remarkable as night is to day and at first John and Alex thought their mum had gone mad with all this talk of religion and they began to worry that she was caught up in some sort of cult.

John was living in his new house in Wood Close but was still restless, missing the stimulation that Soho had given him, the excitement, the challenges, the dangers, the cosmopolitan atmosphere and the money. He tried to push the feelings to the back of his mind, but they kept coming back to haunt him. It was like a cancer growing inside him, yearning for more excitement, making it harder to bear. It was like a deep underlying vacuum sucking at his brain, like some kind of drug he had no fix for. At least he had a job interview to look forward to the following week. Lynn, the manager at Bon Marche in Birkenhead was impressed with John and offered him the job as full time store detective explain that they had a huge problem with stock loss. The job was just what John needed and he caught a shoplifter on his first day, a local junkie and notorious shoplifter named Siobhan Clark. Sure, it was exciting catching thieves but it never came close to the excitement he found in Soho. John's reputation grew and this attracted the attention of Colin Crowley whose sister Sue owned the hardware shop Contraband situated in the basement store beneath Bon Marche. Colin was a single dad of two boys, Alan and Paul whose mum had walked out on them a few years earlier. Colin had a mop of wavy blond hair and piercing blue eyes and a wicked sense of humour but unlike John, he was not very physical. One day John was chasing a shoplifter up Grange Road when Colin came around the corner and somehow managed to trip himself and the thief up accidently landing on the guy and pinning him to the ground before John dragged them both to their feet.

'Thanks Colin, I think this guy would have outrun me if you hadn't jumped in.'

'Oh its ok mate, anytime,' replied Colin sheepishly.

'Tell you what, you fancy grabbing a beer after work? I owe you one' said John appreciatively.

'Hey lads, I'll buy you both a drink now if you let me off,' butted in the bedraggled looking shoplifter.

'Just give me the bag of clothes you stole and get lost,' replied John feeling amused at the situation, knowing that Colin had fallen over the guy in the first place.

Colin and John became good friends and would often go out for a pint with the other workers from his sister's shop. It wasn't long before Sue the owner asked John if he would come and work for her as their store detective was on long term sick leave. John made sure Bon Marche was covered by getting his brother Alex to take over his job. Alex was delighted, especially after being out of work after the drama at Breck Jig and Tool.

Several months went by and John and Colin became good friends but the strain of normal life and being a single parent was stressing John out.

'What I think you need is a break, a good relaxing holiday. I was thinking of taking my boys to Butlins Holiday Camp in Wales, why don't you and Daniel come too?' Colin suggested as they sat having a drink in the Charing Cross pub in Grange Road West.

'That sounds like a good idea, I certainly need to get away from this damn place for a while, let's do it,' John said, getting enthused about the idea.

Butlins Pwllheli holiday camp in North Wales had all the ingredients for a fun packed couple of weeks for the kids. It had a fun fair, indoor and outdoor swimming pools, a ballroom, a boating lake, tennis courts, a sports field, table tennis and snooker tables, an amusement arcade, a theatre, shops, and a miniature railway, as well as the famous redcoats to make sure everyone enjoyed themselves.

It was there that John chanced to meet Jenny who was also holidaying there with her four year old daughter Siobhan. Jenny was petite with mousy blonde hair and an innocent looking face, wide eyes, a slender figure, an intoxicating smile and a soft lilting Scottish accent. Jenny came from Musselburgh, known as the Honest Toun, just outside of Edinburgh.

John was surprised when Jenny told him she worked as a bus driver; he could not imagine her sitting behind the wheel of a double decker bus. He was already smitten with her, her attractiveness went deeper than the curves of her body and a romance quickly blossomed with the result that within a short time, Jenny and her daughter moved from Scotland into Wood Close with John.

It seemed the perfect arrangement and John was contented, continuing to work as a store detective and Jenny having given up driving buses got herself a job as a bar maid in the Crown pub in Argyle Street. John seemed to have got his life in order, nothing could upset the contentment he was feeling having taken Colin's advice about staying away from trouble.

But that feeling of happiness was to be marred on 19th July 1995 when his mother turned up unexpectedly at Contraband in a very distressed state to tell to John that his Gran Lawson had suddenly died. It was such a shock to his system that he went weak at the knees and had to sit down, for he loved his gran so much and could never ever think of her dying.

'Why, what happened? She was so fit. I remember her doing high kicks the last time I was there,' John said, emotions beginning to swell up inside him.

'If it's any comfort son, she didn't suffer, she died peacefully in her sleep,' his mother said, comfortingly.

'It's still not fair mum, she was such a good person, why do bad things happen to good people?'

'Your gran would have told you not to cry for her, she's been called home by God. I remember her telling me once, "I never worry about dying, I only worry about living." Come on son, be strong because we have to go upstairs to Bon Marche and break the sad news to Alex,' his mother said, giving him a comforting hug.

John travelled to Scotland with his mother and Alex to attend the funeral, where there were a multitude of aunties, uncles, cousins and friends, for Mrs Kathleen (Kit) Lawson was well respected. John was pleased to see his uncles George and Dave had made the effort to come all the way up from London to be there as well as Uncle Allen, Auntie Karen and Auntie Deborah. All gran's children were present except for his dad. John was sad at the thought that his dad was so emotionally cold that he did not make the effort to attend his own mother's funeral. It was a cold August morning when the funeral took place at the Cadder Crematorium and gran's ashes were scattered in the Garden of Remembrance.

Back in Birkenhead the following week, John was driving along Shrewsbury Road past the Williamson Art Gallery in Birkenhead, with Jenny, Daniel and Siobhan when a speeding car came out of a side street and smashed into them and fracturing John's spine. The driver was arrested and charged and as a consequence John was awarded £10,000 in compensation. The money came in useful but it was soon spent on a new kitchen and a custom built Kawasaki Hard Tailed Chopper motorcycle – which didn't please Jenny one little bit.

NICKS NIGHTCLUB

1996

Sadly after having been back at work at Contraband a few weeks he was told by Sue the owner that the store detective he had been standing in for was now ready to return from sick leave and she would regretfully have to let him go. John was now looking for a new Job and waiting for the phone to ring regarding several applications he had filled in.

With having walked out of Bon Marche and lost his job at Contraband, Jenny suggested John might like to come and work with her at the pub as they happened to be short of a barman. On the face of it, it seemed a good idea as he could also learn the tricks of the trade so that they could get a pub of their own one day. But, John's inability to draw a curtain over the past, particularly after his beloved gran had died and re-connecting with Uncle George, heightened the urge to be back in London that had been niggling at the back of his mind. He craved excitement and felt life was passing him by.

The call came surprisingly from his brother Alex who was now working as a bouncer with his mate Darren Powell at a club called Nick's in Oldham. The club which had been converted from an old cinema had a reputation for being a local for drug dealers and general trouble makers, but that wasn't going to worry John because he felt it would give him the excitement he sought. John met up with the head doorman, who was immediately impressed and offered him the job. John with his experience at the hostess bars soon displayed his abilities at handling difficult customers, it wasn't long before the manager of Nick's offered him the top job as head doorman.

John's first test of his supervisory skills came when he spotted a couple who appeared to be out of it with too much drink. The man was collapsed on the floor, propped up against the wall, having passed out and fallen off his chair, while the female, a rather large lady was slumped over the bar. John asked two of the bouncers to go and escort them off the premises. What John didn't realise was the couple were on speed balls. As one of the bouncers, Tony, bent over the man to help him up, the woman leapt to her feet, grabbed a pint glass from the bar and shoved it in his face, almost severing his upper lip and gashing other parts of his mouth. Tony screamed for help while trying to hold the loose flesh together. Alex, Darren and Andy came to the rescue and managed to manoeuvre the man to the entrance and get him out onto the street while Tony made his way to the manager's office to get the first aid kit.

John with two other bouncers tried to tackle the woman, but she seemed to have the strength of ten men and started punching and biting the two of them as they tried to get her to the entrance. It took yet another two bouncers to drag her to the top of the stairs that led to the entrance. Resisting all the way she held onto the rails gripping them tightly as she kicked out with her feet. One of the bouncers punched her in the face as she tried to bite his nose off, sending her tumbling down the flight of stairs, but she just sprang to her feet and carried on the fight.

'I don't believe it, I've just punched her hard in the face which should have knocked her clean out, but look at her, she doesn't seem to have felt a thing,' Darren said, in astonishment.

'I reckon they must be on speedballs, they don't feel anything, you can hit them as hard as you like, but it won't hurt them. The first time I experienced it was when I was at The Jimmys in Birkenhead and. It was incredible, the more I kept hitting him the more he kept coming back,' John told him, as they finally managed to get her out onto the pavement. The man now began to struggle violently too and as Alex stepped forward to help control him, the man kicked out violently, catching Alex full in the shin and snapping the bone just below the knee. The pair ran off as John and the other bouncers rushed to help Alex who had collapsed to the ground in pain.

An ambulance quickly arrived to tend to Alex and Tony, followed shortly by the police who, with John's help immediately set about going looking for the couple. Driving around the area in the police van, it wasn't long before they spotted the pair hurrying along the pavement. The man saw them and ran off at a fast pace. John leapt out along with one of the police officers and chased after him while the other police officer set off after the woman. The man was running incredibly fast, so much so, that the police officer couldn't keep up the pace in the heavy uniform he was wearing, but the fact this man had broken his brother's leg spurred John on and he eventually caught up with him. With a flying rugby tackle he brought him down and John laid into him with heavy punches, but even then he continued to struggle. Fortunately the police officer managed to catch up and together they cuffed the man and hauled him into the van.

As they drove back to collect the woman they were surprised to see the other police officer lying on the ground, his uniform in tatters, his tie ripped off, all the buttons torn from his shirt, his helmet tossed across the pavement and the woman climbing into a taxi. The police officer driving the van quickly blocked the taxi in and all the police officers hauled her out of the taxi and eventually cuffed her and shoved her screaming into the van.

John discovered that the man was well known to the police as a big time drug dealer and was on bail for attempted murder. Allegedly he had had a row with another drug dealer and had thrown the man over the third floor balcony of a block of flats where the man was hiding out. Alex was taken to hospital where his broken bones were pinned together which, the doctors explained, were likely to remain in his leg for the rest of his life.

The following evening John and the others left the club earlier than usual having, managed to get the last few straggling customers out by 2.30am, and because of the events of the previous night the team decided not to stay and have the usual staff drink. They crossed over the road to the Kwik Fit garage where they parked their cars, to avoid them being damaged by disgruntled or drunken customers. As John and the others got in their cars they saw a small convoy of 4x4 jeeps draw up outside the club and watched in horror to see a group of men leap out, wearing balaclavas and carrying shotguns. They stormed the main door of the club expecting everyone to still be inside and began battering on it, but it was a heavy door and locked firmly. Realising it was closed and everybody had gone home, they retreated back to their cars and sped off, not knowing their intended targets were just across the road sitting in their cars holding their breaths.

'Someone up there must be looking after us lads,' John said, to

Darren, Andy and Paul who were sitting in the car with him breathing a sigh of relief, aware of what would have happened if they had still been in the club. Even more so as seconds later, with lights blazing and sirens sounding, half a dozen police cars flashed past in pursuit of the gangsters after the town centre CCTV team had seen the gang on camera and alerted the police.

'Let's get out of here while we still can,' John said, nervously as he put the car in gear and sped off in the opposite direction.

With Alex still in hospital and the ever increasing danger from the local drug dealers the team at Nick's was reinforced with two new guys, Jason Davies, an ex British paratrooper known as Jay or 'animal' to his many friends' and Rico' an ex South African special forces soldier and professional wrestler. With John in charge, the team had a formidable reputation and word soon spread that Nicks night club was not a place to cause trouble.

About a month later, as the dealer's case was about to come to court a deal was offered by of his associates. They offered to pay five grand to John and the other bouncers and compensation money to Alex for his broken leg if in return they would agree not to press charges. The deal was struck and the case never came to trial.

PRIME SUSPECT

It's strange how life can imitate itself and this had come about when Jez, another doorman, suggested they take up some weapons training. There was an ever increasing violence on the doors with some of the gangs turning up armed to the teeth. Jez told John of an ex-SAS guy he knew who had permission to use the army firing range at Altcar on the outskirts of Liverpool and regularly trained bodyguards.

John with the skills he had been taught by his father was keen to learn more and Jez arranged for them to meet 'Mack,' who because of his SAS connections would not reveal his full name. Jez arranged to meet Mack at his house in Knotty Ash in Liverpool and the first thing that struck John when he met Mack was how much he resembled Sean Connery with his trimmed white beard, bald head and dark eyebrows.

'You know you don't half look like…'

'Sean Connery, yeah I've been told many times, but that's where the resemblance ends, I can shoot a lot better than he ever can.'

'Good to meet you,' John said, stretching out his hand. 'My name's John Lawson.'

'I'm Mack, good to meet you,' Mack responded, taking the proffered hand and shaking it, his grip strong and hard almost crushing John's fingers. What also struck John was the aura that exuded from the man even though he guessed he must be well into his sixties.

'Mack what?' John asked, impressed by the man.

'Mack is all you need to know. It's a long time since I was in the forces but there could still be some nasty people out to get me. I know Jez, but I don't know you, but he has vouched for you and that

221

is good enough for me, so let's just leave it at that, you're John, I'm Mack,' he said firmly, but with a smile.

'Fine by me,' John said in acceptance.

'I do basic bodyguard and firearm training, how to handle a weapon, how to strip it down, clean it and put it back together again. How to draw and fire from the hip and walk in correct formation with your principle. Teach you about firing arcs so you don't end up shooting each other instead of the attackers and some basic CQB – that's short for Close Quarter Combat. So if you're up for it, we'll meet here tomorrow and I'll take you to the Army firing range where we'll start with the basics, okay?'

Four weeks later after an intensive training session, Mack suddenly said to them. 'You two interested in doing a bit of filming?'

'What kind of filming,' John asked.

'Occasionally one of the television companies will get in touch with me, when they want people who are experienced at handling weapons to do some authentic weapon scenes. The stunt co-ordinator liaises with me about what he's looking for. In this case it's for a production called 'Prime Suspect' starring Helen Mirren, it's going to be shot around a disused railway station in Manchester. You'll be considered as extras with action, so you'll be paid ninety pounds a day and you'll be on the production for three days. So what do you think, you up for it?' Mack asked, guessing what the answer would be.

'Sounds great, I'm up for it,' John eagerly agreed.

'Me too,' Jez offered excitedly. 'What exactly are we going to be doing?'

'Well the stunt director has asked if I can supply three guys, so I'm one short, but as far as I know you will be acting as armed police wearing all the protective gear, you'll be armed with real live rifles and hand guns that have been modified to fire a pellet that looks like a real bullet,' Mack explained.

'So what are we going to be shooting at?' Jez asked.

'You shoot the bad guy when he raises his gun to shoot Helen Mirren.'

'One of our team, Jay, was in the paras, I'm sure he would be up for it too,' John offered as a suggestion.

'Sounds good, I was in the paras myself before joining the two-

two's, so get your friend to meet us at the location and I can have a quick chat with him,' Mack told him.

On the day as John, Jez, Jay and the others walked around the disused railway station in Manchester that was being used for the filming, waiting for their moment to come.

'They think we're real police,' Jay said, as crowds began to gather wondering what was happening with so many armed police present.

Hang on a minute, I want to try something,' Jez said, as he moved towards the crowd.

'Right you people move back to a safer distance,' Jez instructed them.

John and Jay were impressed at the way the crowd obeyed him without question. 'Just shows what effect a uniform can have on people,' John said, reflectively.

'What's happening?' one of the crowd called out.

'I'm afraid I'm not at liberty to tell you,' Jez replied, hurrying away.

The moment came when John was positioned on the railway track with three men placed in supportive positions behind him. Jez and his team were positioned in one of the old ticket offices.

'Right, the scene is this,' Philip Davis the director began to explain. 'You will be down there on the track with your sniper rifle. Open your bipod and support your weapon on the platform edge, taking aim at the target. When the signal is given, you open fire, then jump up onto the platform and rush forward directly towards the camera, weapons still at the ready, Okay?'

'Sure,' John acknowledged as did two others with him.

The others in the ticket office will do the same, fire their weapons and then rush forward at the same time as you, got that?'

'Sure, no problem,' John said, with an element of arrogance.

'I'm told you are experts with these weapons,' Philip said, looking at John who had been issued with a sniper rifle, 'so be careful where you point them, as you can see the crew are wearing protective glasses just in case of an accident, I'm told those pellets burst into flames as they blast out,' Philip advised them.

'Just one thing, sir,' John spoke up. 'This sniper rifle has a bipod attached, in ordinary circumstances the sniper would stay in position and let the others run forward.'

'Well this is television and it looks more dramatic if you're running with it,' Philip Davies said, more interested in the overall picture than mere detail.

The moment came, the cameras were lined up the scene was set, John positioned himself, his feet firmly planted, the sniper rifle lined up ready to fire, tensed, just waiting for the director to give the cue by dropping his arm.

Philip dropped his arm and everyone opened fire, the volley of shots reverberating around the station and as John made his move to leap up onto the platform, he unfortunately caught his foot on the edge and fell backwards onto the track, nearly crushing the men behind him.

'CUT,' Philip screamed. 'I thought you guys were supposed to be good at this. You only had to jump up onto the bloody platform and run,' Philip said, scornfully.

'I told you, you wouldn't normally run with a fixed bipod, but don't worry, I won't mess up next time,' John promised, feeling a bit miffed with himself for screwing up.

The scene was re-set, the rifles reloaded, everybody set in their first positions ready for the cameras to roll.

The director lowered his arm, everyone opened fire, the volley of shots reverberating once again around the area as John made his move, swiftly leaping up onto the platform and making a perfect run past the cameras.

'CUT...Well done lads, we got it that time. Looked great, you guys sure know you're stuff,' Philip said, a satisfied smile spreading across his face.

Riding on the success of that, Mack got a call from 'Sianel Pedwar Cymru', ('Channel Four Wales') who were producing a cop drama series called A41. The sequence they were required to take part in was where a group of terrorists armed with weapons and explosives had taken hostages and were holed up in a café, threatening to blow the place up if anyone approached. Dressed again as armed police, John and his team were required to drive up in the police car, get out, grab their weapons and surround the café. John was given the special action of taking out a MP4 sub machine gun, inserting the magazine and pulling back the safety catch, the cameras moving in close to capture the action.

Having completed their sequence they were held in position as the big moment came to blow up the café. The set by now was surrounded by fire engines, ambulances, first aid personnel, health and safety officials, explosives experts, real policemen; so much so, it was impossible to work out who were extras and who were not. Once again John noticed how the bystanders watching from a distance reacted to him and Jez as they approached them still dressed as policemen.

The explosion was spectacular with the café being totally raised to the ground.

'I know a few buildings in Birkenhead I'd like to do that to,' Jez said, staring at the smouldering remains.

'Yeah and I know a few buildings in Drumchapel I'd like to do that as well,' John said reflectively, thinking about the ugly, tall, square concrete boxes called homes they once lived in.

He and the team earned a hundred pounds each for the day's work which pleased everybody.

Mack was very pleased with the work that was coming in from the television companies but told John and Jez that he was moving abroad in a few weeks and was unlikely to return. However there was one more filming job to do before he left. Christopher Eccleston was to play the lead role in the controversial drama documentary called 'Hillsborough.' This time the team were to play normal police officers with no weapons and Mack was asked to find more extras to make up numbers. John asked Jay if he was interested and he roped in a couple of real police officers he knew. Together they all travelled to the football ground that had been set up to look like the real Hillsborough stadium and got kitted out in police uniforms before taking their places in the stadium. The show attracted a huge audience, especially from the people of Merseyside who had been affected by the tragedy in which 96 Liverpool fans had lost their lives. In one scene there was a close up of John's face, the day after the show was aired, he was picking up Daniel from school when several of the parents asked him if he was on telly last night.

It was strange that during this time Jenny, unbeknown to John, had applied to be a contestant in the television game show 'Wheel Of Fortune' She was informed that all applicants had been chosen, but they would like to invite her to an audition at the Adelphi Hotel in Liverpool to take part in another show called 'Blankety Blank' being hosted by the female impersonator Paul O'Grady's character Lilly Savage.

Jenny persuaded John to come with her and he finished up being auditioned as well, to their surprise he was selected to be one of the contestants to take part in the Christmas Special edition, to go out on Boxing Day.

The show was to be recorded in November in London at the BBC Television Centre and the BBC arranged for Jenny and John to stay at the Sherlock Holmes Hotel in Baker Street. Jenny was very excited sitting in the audience as one of her favourite singers, Ronan Keating, was appearing on the show. John did well and won through to the head to head final, winning a digital camera and the famous Blankety Blank cheque book and pen. After the show they met up with Uncle George and his girlfriend Yasmin to see 'Mamma Mia' at the Prince Edward theatre in Soho before heading back to Merseyside. It was John's first time back in Soho for a couple of years and the yearning to be back there was surfacing in the back of his mind once more.

SHOTGUN AND MARRIAGE

1997

As uncertainty continued to plague John, he was surprised when Jay contacted him with an interesting proposition to earn big money. Jay knew John didn't like anything about drugs or the people that dealt in them and explained he was having a problem with an ex-bouncer who had the nickname Pedro because he looked Spanish.

Jay explained Pedro was a drug dealer and had a vile reputation for inflicting pain and torture on those who dared to cross him. Jay had not crossed him, but they had a few choice words in the pub they both frequented one night when Pedro was showing off, flashing his money around letting everyone know how rich and successful he was. When Jay told him to shut up and flash his filthy money somewhere else, Pedro with his small gang of followers threatened him. There were too many for Jay to take on so he made a hasty retreat, swearing to himself he would extract his revenge for being made to look a fool.

'So what have you got in mind?' John asked, not sure that he wanted to get involved in a revenge attack unless there was a financial reward.

Jay explained, he'd been doing a bit of surveillance on Pedro and knew where and when he bought his drugs.

'He stocks up on a Thursday so the best time to hit him would be on Wednesday when he's ready with the cash to stock up again on the Thursday. He'll be holding thousands in his house and that's what I plan we do, break in and take the lot and anything else we can find that's worth money. So, you interested?' Jay asked. He really didn't have to ask, he could see the answer in John's face.

'It's going to take three of us, know anyone who might be interested?' Jay asked.

227

'Yes I think I know someone,' John told him.

John and Darren drove up to Kirkham to meet Jay and were surprised to see Jay sitting there with a sawn off shotgun laid out on the table, unloading the pellets from the cartridges.

'What are you doing that for?' John asked, curiously.

'It's an old trick I learned in the army. If you want to really shock someone, but don't want to kill them, you take out the bearings and refill the cartridges with rock salt, reseal the top with wax and it will give off the same blast, pelting them with the rock salt, enough to knock them off their feet and hurt them, but not kill them,' Jay explained.

'The plan is, we go to his house in the early hours of the morning and bang on the door as though we're the police. I've already done a recce and his house is at the end of a country lane, it's detached so nobody will hear us. I've also worked out where we can park the car and approach his house through a hedge at the rear. I've also done a test on the police response time, I made a fake call the other night and I reckon we've a good eight minutes to do the job and get clear away if anyone did call the police,' he outlined, watching for their reactions.

They were now acting on pure adrenaline, the heightened awareness made John feel more aggressive than ever. He had a grim look on his face, he knew the risk he was taking and what the consequences would be if it went wrong, but it was a chance he had to take. Chances like this don't come along very often and the reward was going to be worth the risk, he needed to prove to Jenny he could still bring in the money and take care of them.

Pedro was awakened by heavy banging on the door and wondered what lunatic would dare wake him up at this time of the morning. His second thought was it had to be the police, but that didn't worry him so much, he could take care of them as he usually did, bung them a few grand and they'd happily piss off reporting they had found nothing. As the banging persisted, he cursed as he hurried down the stairs to the front door, slipping the chain on, before cautiously opening the door and peeping out. The first thing he saw was the tip of the barrel of a sawn off shotgun and tried to slam the door shut.

But Jay was ready and jammed the crow bar between the frame and the door so that he couldn't shut it, causing Pedro to panic and run back up the stairs. John and Darren put their shoulders to the door and the chain quickly gave way under their pressure. All three chased up the stairs after him, but Pedro had managed to get into the bedroom and drag the double bed over and wedge it against the door.

With the three of them heaving at the door it wasn't long before they managed to force the bed back far enough to be able to squeeze through. Pedro was standing there wielding a machete while his wife was screaming her head off.

Jay was in no mood to argue and blasted him with the shotgun, propelling him back about three feet before crashing to the floor. His wife became hysterical screaming they had killed him. Jay grabbed her by the throat and shoved her hard against the wall telling her to shut up or she'd get the same. She stopped screaming and slumped to the floor sobbing her heart out.

'Right let's get the bastard downstairs,' Jay told John and Darren who grabbed hold of Pedro as he slowly began to recover.

'I'll have you bastards killed. Do you know who I am? You'll regret this. No one does this and gets away with it,' Pedro shouted, gasping to get his breath back from the blast as they dragged him into the kitchen and plonked him down on one of the chairs.

'Shut it,' Jay told him as he whacked him over the head with the butt of the shotgun, blood now covering his head where his hair used to be. 'Tie him up,' he told Darren. 'And see what you can find in the drawer,' he said to John, indicating the cutlery drawer.

While Darren tied the still protesting Pedro to the chair, John searched the drawer and found a long sharp heavy carving knife. 'You're going to tell us where the money is?' John said, as he carried the knife over and menacingly put the point of the blade to Pedro's throat.

Pedro stared him out as a show of bravado.

'Maybe another blast of that shotgun might help persuade him,' John suggested turning to Jay.

Jay smiled as he re-cocked the shotgun and placed it between Pedro's legs and pushed it up to his crotch. 'I'm telling you now, you're going to lose your crown jewels if you don't tell us where the money is.'

'In there. In there,' Pedro screamed, nodding his head towards one of the kitchen cupboards.

John crossed to the cupboard, opened the door and saw a big Quality Street tin, pulled it out and opened it. The tin was crammed full of money.

'Right keep an eye on him while I have a look around to see what else I can find,' Jay told them as he moved off to the other room.

'Who are you bastards?' Pedro persisted as he struggled to free himself.

'Keep it shut and lay down on the floor,' John told him as he and Darren pulled him to feet, but to their surprise he had more strength than they had realised and he had managed to break the cable ties they had used to bind his hands and made a dash to get away, barging past Jay as he came back in carrying a stash of drugs he'd found.

Pedro was now behaving like a raging bull feeling he was fighting for his life and was showing incredible strength for his size.

John moving swiftly managed to get a strangle hold around Pedro's neck and had to keep the pressure on to restrain him from kicking out, squeezing his neck until he passed out.

'Who the hell are you?' Pedro asked again as he slowly regained consciousness.

Jay put the shotgun to his head as he said. 'We're a rival drug gang and you've been encroaching on our territory, so you've got three days to pack up and move. If you don't and we have to come back, then we'll kill you and the missus,' Jay told him, giving him another whack over the head for good measure.

'Right lads, let's get the hell out of here,' Jay said, gathering up the Quality Street tin containing the money.

John's reward was two and a half grand. *Not bad for a night's work, Jenny will be pleased with me when I show her how much I've earned*, he thought as he happily made his way home.

The money came in useful as John and Jenny had been living together for just over a year and both felt it was time to tie the knot, they set the date for the 11th June 1997. Jenny wanted a romantic wedding and they decided to get married in the Dominican Republic at a resort called Playa Dorada in Puerto Plata. John's mother agreed to look after Daniel and Siobhan so that they could arrange a two week package holiday, Dominican Republic's regulations stated they would have to be resident in the country for a full week before the marriage ceremony could take place.

John wanted to be traditional and wear the full regalia of a Scotsman. He chose to wear a kilt of the Bonnie Prince Charlie Tartan, with sporran, thick black woollen jacket and black waistcoat underneath as well as the traditional *Sgian-dubh* tucked into white woollen socks. On his feet he wore traditional black brogues.

Jenny looked radiant, her hair was set with ringlets and a sparkling tiara. She was wearing a long white silk dress that moulded beautifully with the slim curves of her body. In her hands she was holding a beautiful bouquet made up of the tropical flowers the Dominican Republic. After the ceremony they posed for photographs on the sun drenched beach with everyone taking pictures, even people passing by stopped, more interested in taking pictures of a man dressed in some kind of skirt than they were of the bride. John and Jenny were then treated to a ride around the resort in a pony trap specially decorated with colourful flowers and yellow and white balloons.

When they got back to the hotel, they found the staff had filled the room with a beautiful array of colourful flowers that exuded an exotic bouquet of fragrances around the room. Back home, his mother arranged a reception party at the Conservative Club in Birkenhead, which was attended by all the family and friends, even Uncle George made it, to John's delight.

It was a few weeks later that Jenny announced she was pregnant, much to the delight of John and the rest of the family. John was jubilant and felt things couldn't be better, he was married and his beautiful wife was pregnant with their first child. He was still grieving over the loss of his gran, but felt nothing else could go wrong.

JOHN MEETS THE WARRIOR

Mick Powell had always loved motorcycles and decided to leave Leisure Security, the company John and the other bouncers were working for and started a Biker gang on the Wirral called the Nomads with his right hand man Martin. They found premises in the New Ferry area and rented a building to turn into a clubhouse. Keen to have John as a member they quickly initiated him into the Nomads.

Mick and Martin also set up a new security company with Mike Ahearne, who, as 'The Warrior' had been one of the stars of the television show 'Gladiators,' and Gary Sandland, a World champion kick boxer. They called the security company 'Ahearne and Sandland' and put a team together to parachute them into various nightclubs where local bouncers were unable to handle things any longer. The task was to get the club back under control, establish a new team of bouncers, then move on to the next trouble spot.

John and Alex, who had now fully recovered from his broken leg, as well as the other bouncers from Nicks were keen to join the new company, particularly as Mike Ahearne's celebrity status, would be able to open doors to lucrative contracts. Mike enjoyed the highlife that fame was giving him, liked the lavish life style, liked gambling and loved the ladies, but it came at a price and he soon found himself in financial difficulty; he was keen to get involved in the security business as another source of income, accepting at some point his television career as a gladiator would come to an end At the time was sharing an apartment with Elmore Davies, one of Merseyside's high ranking police officers, who was later discovered to have been selling information on other drug dealers operating in Merseyside to the notorious drug baron Curtis Warren, who at the time was serving a long prison sentence in Holland. Mike Ahearne had other connections with various policemen in the Merseyside force and arranged for some of them in their off duty time to train John and the other bouncers on various restraint techniques, and how to deal with awkward and violent customers within the law.

The first job John and the team were sent to was a nightclub called Northern Lights in Blackburn, which was now being managed by Jason Donavan, who had been moved from Nick's in Oldham because of the trouble there. To his shock he discovered the trouble was even worse in Blackburn where Adam one of the doormen had been badly beaten, his arm broken, in a fight with a gang of drug dealers when he refused to let them in. Northern Lights was close to Blackburn Rovers Football Club and there was always a strong police presence in the road opposite the club on match days. The club had a steep flight of steps that led up to the entrance and was on two levels, the first level as you entered was like a balcony with tables and chairs and a large bar, below was a large dance floor that had stairs leading down from the balcony.

The first punch up was on one particular Sunday evening when a group of Asians had booked the club for a Bhangra. An upbeat type of popular music associated with Punjabi culture developed in Britain in the 1980s by immigrants from the Punjab region of India and Pakistan. The Indian community and the Pakistani community did not get on well together and although it was admission by ticket only there was fear trouble could break out at any time. Inevitably fights began to break out as arguments flared over which music the DJs should be playing, more Indian or more Pakistani. As the arguments became intensive so did the fighting, to the extent it spread beyond the dance floor to the balcony, finally spilling out into the street and the car park until the police were called to break it up.

The following week, the gang of drug dealers about fourteen of them who had callously beaten Adam and broken his arm, decided to visit the club to test the new security. This was the moment John and the team had been waiting for and he told the two bouncers on the door to be polite and let them in so as not arouse any suspicion.

The gang thinking their fearful reputation was the reason they were being treated with respect made their way to their usual spot at the back of the dance floor by the rear emergency exit just behind the DJ's desk. At this point John telephoned Adam to get to the club so he could identify the gang for sure and point out the one that had broken his arm. Once the gang had settled and were confidently boozing away, John decided it was the moment to strike. He instructed the other bouncers to move down to the dance floor and cautiously manoeuvre themselves into a position where they could move in when John gave the signal.

'Excuse me sir, I'd like to have a quick word with you,' John said, tapping the shoulder of the guy Adam had pointed out as the gang leader, which was the signal for the rest of the bouncers to move in.

Before any of the gang could do anything, John and his team set about beating them viciously with their truncheons and knuckle dusters, finally opening the emergency exit and driving them out into the yard where they continued to beat them senseless.

John grabbed hold of the leader. 'I believe you like breaking arms,' he told him, exuding an aura fear as he hauled him to his feet.

The gang leader stared at John, terror written all over his bloodied face. 'I don't know what you mean,' he said, pretending innocence.

'You broke the arm of one of the doorman that worked here and the reason you've got a hiding is to remind you that we don't take kindly to people like you doing things like that to one of us. We're going to break your arm so that you can feel what it's like,' John hissed through gritted teeth.

The gang leader said nothing, pinning his arms to his side as he continued to stare, beginning to shiver in fear.

'That's the trouble with scum like you, you're willing to dish it out, but when it comes to taking it, that's another matter, you're a quivering wreck,' John said, dragging him across to some wooden crates and stretching his right arm over the gap between the crates. He then turned to Adam and said. 'Do you want to do the honours mate?'

'Too right mate,' Adam said zealously, his eyes glinting dangerously, barely able to contain the thirst for revenge as he grabbed hold of one of the stainless steel bar stools.

'This is going to hurt and serve as a reminder that if you and your mates ever attack one of our doormen again, we'll come and break more than your arms, okay?' John told him, his eyes hard as he looked at him before Adam brought the steel bar stool crashing down on the man's arm with such force he could hear the bone snap above the gang leader's screams.

*

Everything was going well at home, John was happy with the news Jenny's pregnancy was progressing well. She was now three months, having discovered to their delight they had conceived the baby while on their honeymoon.

Through Mick Powell association with Mike Ahearne, the company was becoming well known in nightclub circles, gaining a reputation as the team to call on when a club was experiencing trouble. Mick was very pleased with the way John was handling things as head doorman and doubled his salary so that he was now earning thirty pounds an hour. John had put a good strong team together consisting of Jay, Andy, Jez, Darren and Phil all from Birkenhead and his brother Alex and they all had their salaries doubled too. Rico had left to pursue his wrestling career in Mexico.

Aware that violence in nightclubs was increasing, it was becoming necessary in certain night clubs for John and his team to have to wear protective armour like shin pads, elbow pads and bullet proof vest as well as arming themselves with collapsible truncheons and knuckledusters. There was trouble of some kind at every nightclub they were called in to help, but one particular nightclub, Sacha's, situated in the basement of the Britannia Hotel on Tibb Street in Manchester's Piccadilly was having real problems with gangs from Moss Side and Cheatham Hill who were storming into the club, refusing to pay and helping themselves to drinks and whatever else they could lay their hands on and then storming back out before any of the doorman could do anything to stop them.

On their first night there, John was put to the test as one of the local gangsters attempted to storm in without paying. John blocked his way and told him he wasn't going to allow him in. The gangster, a black man with short dreadlocks, in his mid twenties, sporting a heavy gold chain around his neck and wearing a red baseball cap turned the wrong way round. He immediately threatened John with all kinds of violence if he didn't step out of the way and let him in.

John showing no sign of fear slapped him hard across the face, with what they called in Manchester, 'a bitch slap' and his face coloured where he had been struck as he tumbled backwards and fell to the ground. John then grabbed hold of him by the scruff of the neck dragged him a through a puddle, then pulled him to his feet and sent him on his way with a solid kick up the backside.

'You're crazy, you shouldn't have done that, you have no idea what you're up against and I don't want to be around when he comes back with his mates, they'll kill the lot of you; I'm out of here,' Rob, one of the temporary doorman who had stood watching what John had done, said, as he came back into the reception.

With his attention sharpened by the remark, John walked around the club to check everything was alright, finally making his way to the VIP entrance at the rear of the club where only the hotel guest were allowed entry.

Satisfied everything was okay and he could relax a little, he decided to phone Jenny to see how she was, but as he turned to face the door he was surprised to see the gangster back with the rest of his mob, his face twisted into a grin of savage triumph. 'So what are you going to do now, slap me like a bitch again?' he challenged, his cheeks still flaring an angry colour.

John flipped the mobile back in his pocket as he looked around at the mob and it was quite clear they were tooled up, the weapons bulging just inside their coats.

'Like I told you before, I'm not letting you in, so do one and find somewhere else that will let the likes of you in,' John said, defiantly, thinking about how he had confronted the Yardies in Soho.

'Listen to him, he thinks he's ten men, you got a death wish or summit?' the gang leader asked.

'No, but some of you might have, because you may get me, but I tell you what, a few of you bastards will go down with me, so if you want to, bring it on,' John challenged, maintaining his defiance as he reached into his jacket as though reaching for a gun.

'No, it's okay mate, like you say, we can find somewhere else,' the gang leader said, as they turned and began to move off.

The tension dropped like a heavy weight from his body, replaced by a feeling of exhilaration as he watched them walk off, not quite believing his bluff had worked and he had scared them off so easily.

But, as he turned to go back inside, the smile dropped from his face as he saw Mick Powell standing there with a stocky bald white man who was surrounded by a group of black men.

'This is Brian Phillips, who shall we say is well connected in the Salford area running most of the business around here, and this is his team,' Mick said, indicating his crew of black guys. 'With the reputation this place has, I just thought you might need a little back up, so I rang me old mucker here and asked if he wouldn't mind helping out,' Mick added, his mouth set in a wry smile.

'So that's why they turned turtle and ran off and there was me thinking I had scared them off,' John said, resignedly as he stared at Brian Phillips.

Brian Phillips stood five feet ten inches tall. A thick set, hard looking man in his late thirties, his head was completely shaved, he had an intelligent face, his eyes dark and serious and he had a slightly predominant nose. He was wearing a black mid length heavy leather coat.

'Listen, you were great kiddo. It took a lot of balls to take them on, but you're in Manchester now, it's different here, the gangs go around proper tooled up and you had better watch your back because you showed up the leader and made him lose face and I'm telling you now kiddo, you'd have taken a bullet if we had we not been around,' Brian said, and a flash of panic came over John at the thought and he hoped they hadn't seen it.

Carl Ince, an ex-boxer who operated a company called Elite Security that ran a lot of the doors in the Preston area such as Tokyo Joes, was running short of man power and called on his old pal Mick Powell for help at a little club that had opened up in Main Sprite Weind just off Church Street called Cheeky Monkeys. The club was mainly frequented by students just out for a good time, but was now beginning to be targeted by gangs of drug dealers moving in from Manchester, as well as by local gangs who didn't like the idea of outsiders moving in on their territory.

The club was owned by an Italian family who also owned a restaurant on the opposite side of the narrow street, who were not experienced at running a night club and did not know how to deal with the developing situation and desperately needed help. Mick Powell gave the task to John, who made up the team with Alex, Jay, Michael, Darren, Jez, Phil and Michael.

There was only the one entrance to the club from the narrow street, which led directly into the reception area where customers paid their entrance fees at a kiosk, before going up a short narrow flight of stairs and through the swing doors into the club itself. The club was divided into two reasonably sized rooms. One room contained the bar, while the other was equipped as a disco with a DJ booth, flashing lights and smoke machines. The room also had an emergency fire exit at the back which led out onto the street.

John had placed his men strategically around the club so as to be able to spot trouble as soon as it broke out, but the disco created a problem, painted jet black with its flashing lights and smoke machine reducing visibility to a bare minimum making trouble harder to spot.

The first night went off relatively peaceful except for some drunk with a knife, who was quickly dealt with and bodily removed from the dance floor before he could do any harm. It was the second night that John and his team were to be tested to the limit. All seemed to be going well until the swing doors suddenly burst open with Alex, Jez, Phil and Darren dragging out two black guys. John and Jay obligingly opened the front door to allow them to throw them out onto the street.

'What the hell were they up to?' John asked, after he shut the door.

'We caught them selling drugs,' Alex told him.

'Good that'll teach them not to come back,' John said, as the warning light in reception began flashing, a signal from the DJ that there was trouble brewing.

'Damn, what's the trouble now? You boys had better go and look while I bolt the doors here,' he told the others.

After securing the doors, John and Jay hurried through the swing doors to the bar room where they burst upon a very strange situation.

The tables and chairs had been knocked over and scattered to one side. Innocent customers scared and not knowing what to do, had pressed themselves together against one of the walls trying to keep out of the way of trouble that was threatening to break out at any moment.

Alex, Michael, Andy, Darren, Jez, and Phil were standing in a line now facing a group of fifteen black guys raring for a fight, egging the bouncers on wanting them to make the first move.

John looked around at the crazy situation thinking it was almost like the gun fight at the OK Corral, but in the same instant he stepped forward, reaching into the pouch he had strapped to the belt of his trousers and pulling out collapsible nunchaka's which telescoped out with a metallic whoosh.

John began swinging it around in his practiced style, the metal tips making a swishing sound as they spun through the air.

Some of the gang started to throw bottles as John advanced on them. Dodging the bottles he caught the guy nearest to him with a whack to the head who buckled as John whacked the next guy across the knees, sweeping his legs from under him.

As John expertly swirled the nunchaka's around his body he screamed out challengingly. 'Come on then, who wants it next?'

The gang decided they didn't want any of it, turned and rushed out through the emergency exit.

John looked down at the two dazed guys with their bloodied heads trying get to their feet. 'Throw these two out and lock the emergency exit,' John told them, as he realised it had been opened by someone from the inside who had let the gang in, including the two blacks they had just thrown out. 'I don't think we'll see any of them around here again,' he said, folding the nunchaka's and replacing them back in the pouch.

To John's surprise as he walked back into the reception, and looked out through the small square reinforced glass window in the solid wood door, he saw the whole group gathering menacingly in the street, some of them talking on their mobiles.

'So what do we do now?' Alex asked, a cloud of concern darkening his eyes.

This was the scary part John decided. 'I'm going to tell them to piss off and not to come back,' he said as he unbolted the door, stepped out and walked straight across to face them.

They all went silent, even those on their mobiles stopped talking as John said. 'I don't know who you lot think you are, but let me tell you who we are. We're used to dealing with dickheads like you, all full of it when you're together, but on your own you're nothing and no match for any of us. You lot are from Manchester and should know better, we're with Brian Phillips, and if you don't know who he is, then you'd better get on your phones and find out, before you get seriously hurt.'

There was a moment's hesitation before the group exchanged several glances deciding it was better to leave and quietly shuffled off.

The news of the Manchester drug gang being thrown out of the club by some Scousers spread wide, but there was one gang that didn't like the idea of Scousers coming into their territory and telling them what club they could go into and what club they couldn't. So the gang hatched a plan to gradually filter into Cheeky Monkeys one by one, bringing their girlfriends along so as not to arouse suspicion and quietly mingle with the students and other customers.

It was now about 12.30 and the plan was working with the gang gathering together ready to cause trouble, run the Scousers out of town and take over the club so that they would be free to sell their drugs without interference. Some of them were already high on a form of Temazepam, a prescription drug that can be crushed and used as a substitute for heroin. The gang hyped up and fuelled with alcohol, were waiting for the sign for something to happen. The trigger was Jez walking up and politely said to one of them. 'Do you mind taking your glass off the dance floor?'

The man ignored Jez and carried on dancing.

'I said, would you mind taking your glass off the floor?' Jez repeated more firmly.

The man stopped dancing, turned and glared at Jez. 'Why don't you Scousers just piss off back to Liverpool and leave us alone. We don't like you and don't want you around here,' he said, scathingly, his face showing his resentment.

'We're not Scousers, we're from Birkenhead and you still need to take that glass off the dance floor.'

'Birkenhead, Liverpool, you're all the same to us and like I said, why don't just piss off back to wherever it is,' the man said, carrying on dancing.

'In that case I have no choice but to ask you to leave, and if you refuse then you will be forcibly assisted off the premises,' Jez told him, doing his best to keep his calm.

'You and who else?' the man said, as his mates began to gather around him.

Jez pressed the alarm button on his walkie-talkie and in no time John and the others joined him and quickly set about the gang, who in their drugged and boozed up state were no match for John and his team.

Having bundled them out the fire exit without too much trouble and secured the doors, things returned to normal with the music starting up again and customers coming back onto the dance floor.

As John returned to the reception he noticed a lot of the girls hurrying out and guessed they must have come in with members of the gang, which was confirmed as he noticed them joining up with the gang who were gathering in the street outside the front of the club.

'John, take a look at this, they're still hanging around, what do you think they're up to now?' Jay asked, as he came to join him.

'I think they were just waiting for their girlfriends to come out,' John said, watching them closely through the small reinforced glass window in the door as he instinctively bolted it.

'What any woman sees in the likes of them is a mystery to me,' Jay remarked airily.

As John was about to turn his back and move off, he heard one gang call out. 'Hey, doesn't the eye-tie who owns the club, own that restaurant as well?'

'Yeah, you're right. Why don't we all go in there and help ourselves to few bevvies?' another of the gang members suggested.

'Yeah, but it closed,' one of the gang said.

'Well, we better go and open it,' another of the gang shouted.

John watched horrified as they began to shuffle towards the restaurant, realising he had to do something and something fast, he quickly unbolted the door, stepped out and yelled at the top of his voice. 'Don't you lot go anywhere near there.'

The gang stopped and turned as the leader said. 'And who's going to stop us, you lot of lousy Scousers, we're on the streets now, our territory, so if you want a fight bring it on.'

By then the rest of the team had joined John and were standing shoulder to shoulder with him. 'What do think lads, shall we go for it?' he asked.

'Yeah, let's show the bastards we don't like being called Scousers,' Alex said, giving his brother a pat on the shoulder.

As they moved forward they pulled the brass knuckle dusters out of their pockets and slipped them on and began to lay into the gang, the girls scurried off to get as far away as possible to avoid being caught up in the fighting.

It wasn't long before the combined skills of the team, even with the odds stacked two to one against them took their toll, with bodies beginning to litter the ground.

Jay, who was a gymnast and into Aikido, had simply picked up one of the gang members and tossed him into the air, the body flying over John's head before it landed with a deep thud onto the concrete pavements on the opposite side of the street. Jez had wrestled one of the gang to the ground and was now straddled over him pounding him in the head. Phil and Darren, standing side by side, took on three of the gang, with Darren flattening the tallest of them with one powerful punch to the jaw, knocking him clean out,

241

his head bouncing off the pavement as he landed with a thud.

Phil laid into the other two, catching one of them with a heavy knee to the groin instantly crippling the man, before turning on the other guy and delivering a deadly left hook to the side of the head causing a deep gash with blood spurting out everywhere.

One of the remaining gang members still on his feet, picked up a beer bottle that had been left lying around, smashed the end off and came charging at John, just as Jay had come to his side. Without exchanging a word they let the man come at them, then at the last moment John lowered his body and leg swept the man, who was flung into the air, giving Jay the perfect chance to catch him with an elbow in the face, his lips exploding and his teeth bursting out of his mouth, he was unconscious before he'd even hit the ground.

The street was now like a battle scene with bodies lying everywhere. There was only one member of the gang still standing and fighting back against Alex who was pounding into him, finishing him off with his trade mark head butt, the man's face becoming a bloodied mess, almost unrecognisable as he too slumped to the ground.

John looked around at the motionless bodies littering the blood stained pavements realising they had really gone overboard and could now be in serious trouble. 'Right lads, quickly turn them over and put them into the recovery position, we don't want any of this scum dying on us,' John said, without compassion.

'As soon as we've made them comfortable, get back inside, get rid of your weapons, knuckle dusters, truncheons, shin pads, and put them in a bin bag with any of your clothes that are blood stained or ripped. Then hide the lot in the bottle skip in the back yard. Wash your hands and faces of any blood stains and change into your spare shirts so you look pristine when the bizzies arrive, you can bet your arse they will,' John informed everyone.

As John predicted, the ambulances arrived, quickly followed by the police, heralded by the heavy banging on the front door.

'What the hell's been going on here,' a chief inspector in uniform demanded, forcing himself inside as soon as John had opened the door, followed by several of his constables.

'Been going on where?' John asked, feigning innocence.

The officer raised his eyes to the ceiling in exasperation then lowered them and fixed sharply on John's face as he said. 'Don't try fooling with me. Does it look like I've got mug stamped across my forehead son? I want to know what's been going here,' he said, jabbing his finger in John's face.

'What do you think's been going on? It's a club and there's been dancing and drinking like any other licensed club,' John said, continuing to feign innocence.

'I don't mean in here you idiot. I mean out there in the street where the paramedics are treating some seriously injured people,' the chief inspector shouted at him, his face twisting in anger.

'Why has there been a car accident?' John asked whimsically, knowing it was a useless thing to say; he could see it in the officer's face.

'Accident, my arse, that lot out there have taken a terrible beating and I want to know what you lot have to do with it.'

'Look officer, there was someone in here earlier trying to push drugs, bu, we don't stand for any of that nonsense in this club and we escorted him from the premises through the emergency fire exit, keeping everything peaceful just the way it should be,' John explained, doing his best to keep his expression composed.

The officer was amazed at his words and frowned in annoyance. 'Oh, really,' he said, his voice heavy with scepticism. 'If you think I believe all that crap, then you're the one with mug written across your forehead, make no mistake, I'll get to the bottom of this. I'm going to inspect you and your team, so get them out here now,' he demanded. 'And if any of you have any cuts, bruises, or blood stains, then I'll nick the lot of you,' the chief inspector added, with a twisted grin of triumph.

'No problem,' John said, watching the grin slip from the officer's face not having expected him to agree so readily.

All the team were lined up and the chief inspector examined them one by one, looking at their hands for any tell tale marks on the knuckles for signs of swelling or bruising from punching, then examined their clothing for any rips or bloodstains.

Desperation was beginning to show on the officer's face as he got to Andy, the last in the line without having found a single blemish on any of them. 'I don't know what's been going on, but I tell you this, when those guys wake up in the Royal Preston, you can be sure of one thing, I'll be the first face they see and I'll interview every single one of them and then I'll be coming back to nick the lot of you,' he said, as he turned in frustration, looking like a man worn out by defeat, ready to give up and leave, but was stopped in his tracks as John and the team burst out laughing.

'And what's so funny about that?' the officer asked, the anger back in his voice.

'Sorry officer, it's just that you never told us they were unconscious,' John said, doing his best to suppress his laughter.

'Yes well, you'll all be laughing the other side of your faces when I get to the bottom of this,' the officer said, a scowl crossing his face as he headed for the door and walked out.

'What a dickhead,' John exclaimed, as they all breathed a sigh of relief.

'I didn't realise we'd knocked so many of the bastards out,' Darren said, with a mischievous grin.

'Yeah, well for your sake, let's just hope they don't remember a thing when they wake up,' John said, adding a serious tone.

'Shouldn't have been so stupid as to try to take us on anyway, should they our kid?' Alex said, patting his brother on the back.

'Right let's round the few stragglers up and get them out of here and then I think we all deserve a bloody good drink,' John said, as he led them back to the bar.

The chief inspector's frustration was further compounded, when visiting the hospital after the gang members had regained consciousness, only to discover not one of them could remember a thing about what had happened – thanks to Tamazepan.

AN EXPLOSIVE REVELATION

1998

After John and his team's success at routing the trouble makers from Cheeky Monkeys, Mick was ready with another club that had similar problems.

JFK'S was an American themed nightclub, named after the American president John F Kennedy, situated on Washway Road in Sale, Manchester. It had been converted from the Pyramid cinema, given that name because of its Egyptian themed frontage. The converted cinema was set well back from the main road with a large pavement area in front. The interior, which still retained the Egyptian theme with large mouldings and finishes, consisted of the ground floor being the main area of activity with a large dance floor and long bar at the far end, behind which were the kitchens. The second floor had a balcony and rooms reserved for private parties and special occasions. The stairway from the reception area to the second floor was sealed off by a metal gate.

Mick told them it was going to be hard work to restore order as the club was having a lot of trouble with gangs running riot. They had had a drive by shooting with one of the gangs trying to kill a doorman with an Uzi submachine gun. The front door was still riddled with the bullet holes. Not quite sure what they were in for, John and his team of Alex, Jay, Darren, Jez, Phil, Andy and Mike Ahearne who had won the contract, together with Mick Powell, set off in two cars for Sale.

John was surprised when they arrived to see doormen working as normal and before he could say anything Mick spoke up.

'You and the others wait here, because the first thing I have to do is go in and tell them their services will no longer be required.'

'I would have thought that would have all been done, before we got here,' John said, as he and Mike Ahearne watched Mick walk into the club.

'Billy McIntosh, the manager of the club thought it best to wait until Mick was here and let him take care of things, knowing he had the back up if any of the doormen were going to make trouble,' Mike explained.

'Makes sense, I suppose, although I can't imagine anyone of them wanting to have a go at Mick.'

'No, Mick's got a unique way of dealing with these situations. It won't be the first time he's had to sack someone,' Mike said, with a hint of admiration.

'Yeah, he's certainly not the sort of person you want to get on the wrong side of,' John agreed, approvingly.

Just then a few of the doormen came out shouting obscenities and slamming the doors behind them as they stormed off, passing the cars and giving the V sign.

'They don't seem too happy do they?'

'Should have done their job properly in the first place,' Mike said, disparagingly.

At that moment Mick appeared in the doorway and beckoned them to get out of the cars and come into the club. Alarms started ringing as John and the others entered the club; they had set off the metal detectors with the knuckle dusters and other weaponry they were carrying.

'Just shows you can't walk in here carrying, although the gangs have been doing it without the doormen making any effort to stop them, which is something we will have to stop. Mick told them, as soon as they were all gathered in the reception area. 'Firstly, this is Billy McIntosh the manager, who you will be working closely with,' Mick said, introducing him.

'Hi guys, hope you're gonnae bring some order back to this place, cause it's got completely out of hand and it's driving the customers away,' Billy told them with in his broad Glaswegian accent.

'Right, this is the situation lads, I've decided to keep these two guys on, Damon and Tony, because they know most of the trouble makers and will be able to point them out before they're let in. Most of them causing the problems come from Cheatham Hill and the Racecourse estate,' Mick explained, introducing the two regular doormen.

John studied the two men, firstly Damon who was a handsome looking black guy dressed smartly, about six feet four in height then, Tony, who was short by comparison at only five six, but very stocky and looked as though he could take care of himself. The club opened with the new team in place and word got round that 'Warrior' Mike Ahearne was in attendance, everybody wanted to be photographed with him – particularly the ladies. Alex who was manning the metal detectors noticed a very attractive girl eager to have a photograph taken with Mike Ahearne.

As she stepped away Alex cheekily said to her. 'Aren't I good enough to be photographed with then?' She looked at him quizzically, her piercing blue eyes glinting. She had short blonde hair and was wearing a black top, black slacks with matching black high heel shoes. She was also sporting a lovely golden tan having just come back from Ibiza. She told him her name was Vicci and happily agreed to be photographed with him. It was love at first sight and from the moment he stood with her posing for the picture, he had the intense feeling she was the woman he wanted in his life. She was beautiful and everything he could ever hope for in a woman. As soon as the picture was taken Alex couldn't wait to ask her out and to his delight she agreed, soon they were dating on a regular basis.

John decided to have Damon and Tony on the main door with him so they could spot the troubles makers as they arrived, but they said nothing as three big black limousines with blacked out windows pulled up outside.

'Do you know who this lot are?' John asked, beginning to worry something big was about to kick off.

'Don't recognise any of them,' Damon said, watching closely as a number of black men emerged from the cars and began carefully scanning the area.

'Better get the rest of the boys, this looks like it's going to be heavy stuff,' John said, tapping the nunchaka's he had tucked in the pouch strapped to his trouser belt. He watched one of the men go to the middle limousine, open the rear door, and then broke into a smile of relief as he saw Brian Philips step out.

'Alrite kiddo, how you doing?' Brian greeted John as he walked into the club, closely guarded by four of his men.

'Fine, relieved to see it was you getting out of the car,' John said, with a hint of nervousness.

'I 'eard the firm that employs the doormen we sacked are a bit upset and are planning a bit of retribution, so thought I would come and show support,' Brian explained with a wink, tapping the gun hidden under his coat.

'Well, I don't think they'd be stupid enough to try something if they know you are here,' John said, pleased at the news.

'No, I don't think so either, because one of their sidekicks has already been on his moby telling them the situation, but if there is, you call me, kiddo?' Brian said, as he turned and walked back out with his men closely following him.

'Bloody hell mate, I didn't know you guys were involved with Brian Philips, I mean he's someone you don't mess with, not if you value your life,' Damon said, clearly impressed with the way Brian had spoken so pally with John.

'I'm bloody glad we decided to stay with you,' Tony said, with a sigh of relief.

'I told you we're well connected,' John said, pleased Damon and Tony were impressed, for he knew now, they would both have a greater respect for him.

The rest of the night passed without trouble, but it was on the second night John was to face his first confrontation as he stood in reception watching a heavy built black guy with short dreadlocks, walking purposefully towards the entrance.

'That's James, he's banned,' Damon told him.

'What for?'

'He smashed a bottle over a girl's head.'

'Why did he do that?'

'He asked her for a dance and she refused which to him was showing disrespect. He's skitso and hadn't taken his medication. He comes from the Racecourse Estate,' Damon told him and John could sense an element of fear in his voice.

'Okay, I'll take care of it,' John said, moving swiftly out onto the pavement to confront him, not wanting to wait until he walked into club.

'What you want man?' James said, in an arrogant tone as John stood directly in front of him.

'Are you James?'

'Yeah, I'm James, what's it to you man?'

'I'm the new head doorman and you're barred.'

'I'm not barred, who told you that crap?'

'You're barred, because you hit a girl with a bottle.'

'I didn't hit no girl with a bottle, I just pushed her away because she dissed me man.'

'I not going to argue with you, you're barred and I'm not letting you in, so that's the end of it.'

'You think you can stop me?' James said, his anger rising as he tried to side step John.

John being much quicker blocked him. 'I am stopping you and you can try all you like, but you won't get past me,' John told him, looking over his shoulder to check Damon was there as back up and was horrified to see Damon was inside and the door closed.

'I'm not having you Scousers coming up ere and chucking us out of our clubs,' James said, his eyes widening in anger.

'We're not Scousers, we come from Birkenhead and anyway, you're not getting in mate,' John said, as he turned and walked back to the entrance.

As he got near to the door he noticed James was on his mobile and he could hear him screaming at the top of his voice. 'I'm going to shoot the bastard, put a team together cause we can't allow some bloody Scouser coming up here and dissing us.'

'Don't you ever shut the door on me again,' John said angrily as soon as he got back inside.

'Sorry I didn't mean to, the door just shut on itself,' Damon said, feebly.

'Well, make sure it doesn't happen again,' John told him, relieved he was safely back inside.

'So what happened?' Damon asked.

'I just told him he was barred.'

'You know, James used to be a boxer and could have made it to the top if he hadn't got mixed up in crime and drugs. I was watching him on his mobile through the door, did you hear who he was talking to?'

'No, but I did hear him saying he was going to shoot me.'

'Then we're going to have trouble.'

'Oh, I've had those kind of threats before, but nobody's shot me yet.'

'Yeah, but this is Manchester.'

The thought was enough to worry John and he decided to call Brian Philips and explain the situation. Brian told him not to worry as he would take care of it.

To John's total surprise the following night, he spotted James approaching the club, but noticed his step was not so strident, more leisurely, less threatening, but John was not going to take any chances and was out on the pavement ready to confront him.

'Hey man,' James said, raising his hands in half surrender. 'I've come to say I'm sorry I dissed you, I didn't know you were working with Mr Philips.' James explained, offering his hand to shake.

'Okay, so now you know. I'll have a word with the management and maybe we'll let you back in next week, but one thing, make sure you've taken your meds. Behave yourself and cause no trouble, okay?' John acknowledged taking his hand and shaking it, noticing his grip was firm but not aggressive.

'Sure man, I respect that,' James said, as he turned and walked off.

'That's something I thought I'd never see,' Damon said to John as he came back inside.

'You have to sort these guys out at the beginning before they think they can do what they like and you're too scared to stop them.' John said, feeling good that he had proved himself and Damon and Tony were in awe of him and his connections.

It seemed the word had got round that the new doormen were not standing for any nonsense and any trouble makers would be quickly shown the door, but Manchester being what it was, it was inevitable that one of the local gang members would decide to test the doorman by walking in with a gun. The metal detectors picked it up and the alarm went off, alerting John that he had a dangerous situation on their hands, he knew from experience he had to do something quick in case the man pulled the gun and started shooting.

Alex who was working the main door that night, put a restraining hand on John's arm and before anyone realised what he was doing, walked straight up to the man and spoke to him in a quiet voice. 'Look, I don't know who you are, but we know you're carrying. So this is the situation,' he said, guiding the man to the entrance to the dance floor. 'You see those two men in smart suits at the bar? They're Five O, CID, they've got this place under surveillance. So if you're stupid enough to walk in there carrying that thing, then you're going to get nicked.'

The man looked at Alex and his face softened as he said. 'Nice one, man.'

'So go and put the thing in the car and then we'll let you in,' Alex told him.

John waited until the man had left and turned to Alex. 'How the hell did you manage to get away with that? Those two fellas you pointed out are just a couple of ordinary punters.'

'You know that and I know that, but he doesn't. The point is we avoided a confrontation, much better if we can persuade them to leave their guns in their cars than try and bring them in here,' Alex said, a little philosophically.

'I'm impressed our kid, I would never have thought of that.'

'No you wouldn't, that's why I stopped you, because you'd have just tried to bundle him out or tried to smash his face in before he had a chance to pull out the gun, and anyone of us might have been killed,' Alex said, surprising John with his remonstration.

It was two nights later that the same man turned up again this time with a friend and John was relieved the metal detector didn't sound off as they walked through. 'Glad to see you've taken our advice,' John said.

'Yeah man, don't want no trouble, just here to have some fun,' the man said, and John could sense they'd already had a lot to drink or were on some kind of drug.

His instincts were proved right when later on the alarm from the dance floor started flashing. John rushed onto the dance floor to see a fight going on in one corner. Alex had the man in a headlock and was flaying him with heavy punches to his face, but they seemed to be having little effect as the man kept struggling. Alex dragged him to the fire exit and rammed the man's head against the iron push bar to open the door and throw him out while the rest of the team bundled out his mates who were resisting less. John watched amazed as the man was still struggling, flaying out with his legs, trying to kick Alex no matter how hard he was pounding him. Soon Damon joined Alex as he dragged the man out of the fire exit and out into the alleyway. Fearful the man could kick Alex's already damaged leg John joined in, grabbing the man by the legs causing him to lose one of his heavy leather boots in the process.

'That guy must be on something to take that kind of punishment and still get to his feet,' John said, as they watched him get to his feet.

'he was alright earlier and now he's like a psycho,' Alex said, as the man started to run off.

'Some of them don't kick off until something sets them off.' John said, as he watched the man stop and turn back to face them and shout. 'You're all a bunch of knobheads.'

John, already incandescent with anger, picked up the discarded boot and hurled it with all his force at the man and was surprised when the heel of the boot struck the man squarely on the back of the head. The man buckled under the impact and collapsed in a heap on the ground.

'Ever thought of taking up the javelin?' Jay quipped, as they all stood watching the man lying on the ground motionless.

'Very funny, now get back inside, this should never have been allowed to happen so be more alert next time,' John said, the anger still in his voice as he slammed the fire exit door shut.

One night, or rather the early hours of the morning just after the club had closed, Jay took John aside for a quiet word.

'One weekend when I was in the paras, we were on exercise and I had four half pound sticks of PE4 plastic explosives as well as boosters, detonators, a couple of mercury tilt switches and a couple of grenades in my back pack which I 'inadvertently' took home. Do you know anything about explosives?'

'No, nothing,' John said, looking at Jay curiously wonder what was coming next.

'Well on their own their relatively safe, because you need boosters and detonators to set them off...'

'What are mercury tilt switches for?'

'You can put them on a car and wire them up to the detonators, as soon as someone gets in the car it causes a tilt and the mercury rolls down to the switch and BOOM.'

'Bloody hell Jay,' John exclaimed, pausing for breath and effect. 'Why are you telling me this anyway?'

'To be honest I'd forgotten about it and...'

'You forgot!! How could you forget you got a bag full of explosives Jay?' John exclaimed in disbelief. 'So what are you going to do with them?'

'That's what I wanted to talk to you about, because there's no way I can hand them back to the army, I'll finish up back in the glasshouse.

'Where's the stuff now?'

'I've got it stashed in the garden shed.'

'Right leave it with me and I'll figure something out,' John said, thinking this could be a nice little earner.

The first person John approached was Brian Philips, aware that he had some sort of connection with the UDA in Northern Ireland

'You're out of your mind if you think I would touch that stuff, and neither should you, because you could get life for handling explosives, don't ever talk to me about anything like this again, because if you do I'll chop your legs off understood?' Brian said, exasperation hardening his words. 'Take my advice and stay well away from it.'

John didn't take his advice and approached Mick Powell at one of The Nomads meetings. Mick was interested, thinking it could be a useful arsenal to have for protection for the right money and told John he would think about it and let him know.

After the meeting John went to the local pub for a pint, becoming more and more concerned about what he was getting into and bumped into and old friend he hadn't seen in a while. Avril was a petite blonde with short bleached hair and a pretty face, she was a single mum whom had come into Contraband to buy some curtain poles. John had helped her carry them to the till and the pair hit it off and exchanged numbers. Avril was an interesting girl, into Tarot cards and psychic stuff and John was attracted to and curious about the supernatural side of Avril. She was also into the biker scene and John made some interesting new friends through her connections. She dipped in and out of his life and although there was nothing sexual between them they had become close, Avril was quite a spiritual person and John trusted her advice.

'What the blazes do you think you're doing getting mixed up in all that? It's not like you, and do you have any idea what could happen to if you're caught with that stuff, you'd go to prison for a very long time, you'd be an old man when you came out. Think of Jenny and the kids for goodness sake, she's pregnant and will need all the help she can get, so don't be a dickhead and think about what you're doing.'

Strangely what Avril said, had more impact than what Brian Phoenix had said and it made John decide not to have anything to do with the explosives.

'I've been thinking about the situation Jay and I've made a few enquiries about moving the stuff on, it's not worth the risk mate, we're talking life here if I were to get caught. You'll just have to get rid of the stuff,' John said.

'Yeah, I understand, but where, I just can't dump it.'

'Well, you're going to have to do something you can't just leave it in the garden shed.'

'I know, I know, I'll think of something,' Jay said, a cloud of concern darkening his face.

The next thing John knew about what Jay had done with the explosives and the grenades was when he read the newspaper report of a care home having to be evacuated because of a bomb scare. As John read the article it became clear what had happened. Jay had taken the four half pound sticks of plastic explosive, carefully wrapped them in cling film and together with the boosters, detonators, mercury tilt switches and the two live hand grenades, stuffed them into a back pack and had asked his mother to store it, not daring to tell her what was inside. His mother in her innocence decided to store the back pack in her personal locker at the care home where she worked. All seemed well until, his mother became ill and was off work for over three weeks during which time the plastic explosive, being wrapped in cling film and stored in a warm environment began to sweat, producing a liquid which began to seep out of the bottom of the back pack. It wasn't long before the liquid, which also had a peculiar smell was seeping out under the door of the locker. One of the care nurses, thinking it was probably some food that had gone off told the care home manager, who decided they must break open the locker and investigate. They were horrified when they opened the back pack and discovered what it contained and immediately dialled 999; in no time the police and a bomb disposal unit were on site. The fear that the explosives were so unstable and could go off at any time caused the police to evacuate the care home, the disabled residents being hurried out in their wheelchairs having no idea of what all the fuss was about.

As a result, his mother was arrested but released without charge while Jay was arrested and charged with being in possession of explosives. Fortunately for Jay, the court was lenient and he made bail, partly because of his army medical record plus the fact the army did not want to make a big thing of it, it made them look incompetent that a soldier was able to walk out of the barracks with four sticks of explosive and the means to detonate them plus two live hand grenades.

The whole incident caused John to think about some of the decisions he was making and decided he wanted to pull out of the Nomads biker gang.

'Listen Mick, I'm sick of this gang life,' John announced when he went to visit Mick at the clubhouse.

'What's brought on this decision?' Mick asked, looking stunned at the pronouncement.

'It's all becoming a bit too much. The Outlaws in Liverpool barely tolerate us and I can see a war looming.'

'I never thought I'd ever hear this from you John, you turned yellow or something?'

'No, it just that I'm more of a loner mate.'

Mick's expression became grave. 'Well let me tell you. You don't just decide to give up your patch and your loyalty to your brothers in arms. Oh no, we decide when you leave and your patch is ripped from you by us, by force and then you are cast out for your disloyalty,' Mick explained his tone serious.

With anger mounting, John squared up to Mick and said. 'I don't like being threatened Mick, you should know that and if you force me I'll come round and shove some of the plastic explosive through your letter box and blow you and your missus sky high. So let's understand each other I'm walking away from this clean and for your sake I hope that is the end of it Okay?'

Mick knew only too well that if John was pushed hard enough he was capable of anything and decided to err on the side of caution and end the matter there.

WITHOUT CERTIFICATION

1998

John was beginning to get fed up driving to Manchester four nights a week and it was also taking its toll on Jenny, who was worried that eventually John's luck would run out and he would get hurt or killed, especially when she announced that she was pregnant again. So he was delighted when he got a surprise call from Uncle George telling him they were planning to open an adult video shop in Birkenhead and wanted him to run it, they still had a massive stock of VHS tapes and DVDs they wanted to get rid of. Uncle George told him he would front all the costs of leasing a shop and split the proceeds fifty-fifty so they'd be back working together again. It seemed a great opportunity to get off the doors and actually make more money so he explained the situation to Jenny telling her it was all above board and, with a little gentle persuasion, she was happy for him to go ahead and do it.

John quickly found the shop he wanted in Grange Road West, next door to The Cavendish Pub, and signed the lease. He started painting the interior all black and putting up shelves to display the stock, then installed security cameras, so that he was able to see who wanted to come in before he pressed the buzzer to allow them to enter.

For the shop to run efficiently, John needed two assistants, one to work the day shift and one to work the night shift, so asked Alex if he was interested in doing the night shift during the week days. It only took John three weeks before he was ready to open for business, but he needed to find another assistant and it so happened as John was putting the finishing touches to the front of the shop, Michael Edge, known as Edgey, one of his old school mates walked by and stopped.

'Hey John, what are you up to?' Edgey asked.

'Arite mate, long time no see. I'm getting ready to open my shop, what are you doing these days?' John asked.

'Nothing mate, no work anywhere, I'm just off to the job centre.'

'I've got a job for you here if you want it,' John offered.

'Doing what?'

'Come inside and I'll show you,' John invited, assuring Edgy that everything was legit.

The following day John opened for business and was pleased with the amount of punters coming in and the amount of stock moving off the shelves, so much so that by the second day the shelves were almost empty and John had to go back to the little lock up he had rented to get more stock. When he returned loaded down with tapes and DVDs he was shocked to find the shop full of police and Trading Standards officers from Birkenhead Council.

'You're nicked,' a sergeant informed him, taking hold of the heavy carrier bags and handing them to one of the constables.

'What's the charge?' John asked rhetorically, knowing what the answer would be.

'You and your accomplice here, Mr. Edge, will find out when you get to the station,' the sergeant informed him.

Unfortunately at that moment Alex turned up to do his shift and was surprised to see his brother being handcuffed.

'What's going on here?' Alex asked.

'It's a police raid, so you need to leave sir,' one of the constables replied thinking he was a customer.

'Oh, okay, none of my business,' Alex quickly replied, turning to hurry back out the shop.

The sergeant, who had been studying the shop surveillance video, suddenly did a double take as Alex opened the door to leave and called out. 'Hold it right there! You look like the man in this video stacking the shelves. Step over here and let me have a closer look at you sir.'

Alex obediently stepped over towards the sergeant, his head bowed sheepishly. The sergeant raised his glasses to his forehead studying Alex closely, then back at the video and smiled triumphantly as he said. 'You're nicked too.'

Edgy was released as it was clear that he had been duped by John to work there but John and Alex were both charged. To their great surprise they were not being charged with possessing and selling pornography or piracy, but charged with 'Certification,' for unlawfully

257

selling tapes and DVDs without displaying the British Board of Film Censors classification certificate. As a consequence of this, the shop closed down after only two days which didn't please Uncle George, and John had to go back to working the doors in Manchester while awaiting trial.

The case came up at Liverpool Crown Court and it amused John as the judge began his closing statement:

'I have viewed five of these videos and have to state, they are the most pornographic hard core filthy films it has been my displeasure to have to view. It is pornography at its worst. Alexander Lawson, I find you not guilty, you may step down, but as for you John Lawson, I find you guilty as charged and before I pass sentence is there anything you wish to say in mitigation?'

'Yes your Honour,' John said, rising to his feet thinking how pompous the Judge sounded. 'As I understand the charge against me is for selling videos without the proper certification being displayed. Is that correct your honour?'

'Yes,' the Judge answered in his gruff manner.

'Then why was it necessary for you to view all five videos which you have stated you found disgusting to watch?' John asked, and a sharp intake of breath could be heard causing a few sniggers to start to reverberate around the court room.

Cecil, John's brief, sitting beside him, tugged at John's sleeve. 'For goodness sake, sit down before he doubles the sentence.'

The sniggers around the court room were getting louder and the Judge hammered angrily with his mallet calling for silence.

'I would like to know what the content of the tapes has to do with the charge I am facing?' John was determined to ask.

'You have been found guilty of selling videos without the proper certification and I am sentencing you to four months imprisonment. Take him down,' the judge ordered, ignoring John's protests.

HMP WALTON, LIVERPOOL

John wasn't so worried this time as he was driven in the sweat box to Walton Prison, he was only going to be doing eight weeks of the four months and he knew all the procedures, as long as he kept his nose clean it would be a cat walk.

The large reception cell where the prisoners were assessed was much the same as Brixton, stinking of the acrid mixture of body odour and stale tobacco. The area was filled with the usual mixture of common criminals, drug addicts, and a few first timers. As John waited his turn watching the other prisoners being processed, he suddenly heard his name being called. The voice sounded threatening and the stare from the prison officer was so intense it raised the hairs on the back of his neck. This particular officer was huge, very muscular, like he did a lot of body building. He had a strutting jaw and piercing eyes that seemed to dare you to challenge him.

'Don't just stand there Lawson get your arse over here,' the prison officer shouted across at him in the same aggressive manner.

John hurried to the desk and to his surprise the prison officer leaned closer to him and whispered 'you alright John?'

John looked at him shocked by the sudden change in his tone. 'Don't you recognise me? It's Gary, I do a bit of work on the doors with Gary Sandland and you came and worked with us at one of the clubs in Southport.'

John stared at his face trying to remember working with him, but before he could say anything Gary shouted at him. 'Lawson in my office now, MOVE.'

John meekly followed him into the office, wondering when they had worked together if he had done or said something to upset Gary.

John heard the door slam shut as he turned to face Gary and was relieved as he smiled and said. 'Want to phone the missus?'

'Can I?'

'Sure, but make it quick, I'll cover for you and then I'll make sure you get a cell to yourself. There's a lot of smackheads in that lot and you don't want to be mixing with any of them.'

John couldn't believe his luck and decided to call Jenny, allowing himself a smile as the call went straight through without the warning message that preceded calls made from the phones on the cell blocks. He told her things were okay and was careful not to mention Gary. After a couple of minutes Gary opened the office door and John asked Jenny to call his mum and let her know he was okay before he hung up.

'Right outside Lawson,' Gary shouted at the top of his voice keeping up the pretence. 'Let's get you kitted out and into your cell and watch yourself as I'll be keeping an eye on you.'

True to his word Gary had put him in a cell on his own on the fourth floor. There was the usual slopping out and the proverbial run to collect his meals and carry them back up to his cell, but he managed to settle into the routine thinking it wouldn't be too bad doing his stretch with Gary keeping an eye on him. But to John's surprise after only four days, Gary informed him that he was being moved to Kirkham open prison.

Kirkham prison was originally a Royal Air Force base, becoming the main armament training centre before being taken over by the Home Office in 1962 to convert into an open prison. The layout of the prison was very similar to Stanford Hill on the Isle of Sheppey which had also previously been an RAF camp with the billets laid out in regimental style.

The billets consisted of sixteen beds, eight along each side, each with a bedside table and locker. At the end of the billet was a toilet and shower room. There was also a recreation room and television room provided. John was allocated bed one in billet two. John's luck was with him once again when he discovered Jay's dad was working at the jail. Jay was still working at JFK while on bail awaiting trial for the explosives he had stolen from the army. Jay's dad, Allan was working as a civil employee in charge of the canteen and lived no more than three hundred yards from the prison.

All the inmates were offered educational courses such as woodworking, painting and decorating, horticulture or assembling 13 amp plugs, none of which appealed to John. But John's luck was still running when he was offered the cushy job as wing runner, which meant sitting outside the chief prison officer's office waiting to be called to take a message to another prison officer or tell an inmate to report to somewhere or the other. The beauty of the job was that it allowed him to roam around the prison without being constantly checked. When he was checked, he would simply reply 'Wing runner on my way to deliver a message, boss.'

Even better, Jay managed to steal a load of phone cards one day while helping his dad with a prison delivery and arranged to drop some into the prison for John. Jay got a message to John that he was going to pack them in a crushed coke can and toss it over the high fence of the sports field at midnight when security was most relaxed, then all John then had to do, was get up very early, go out onto the field, do some running exercises and retrieve the can. John got up early the next morning and made his way to the field, did a few exercises making his way gradually towards the fence where he spotted the crushed can, tucked it into his shirt and made his way back to the billet.

He was delighted Jay had managed to stuff twenty phone cards inside and John was now rich, not only could he make as many calls as he wanted, but could also buy anything he wanted, it wasn't long before he was wheeling and dealing, even buying himself a Sony Walkman from another inmate for two phone cards.

For some unknown reason the chief prison office had decided he needed another wing runner and to John's surprise a new inmate appeared that morning. He was a huge black guy, over six feet with muscles seeming to bulge from every part of his body. His head was shaved smooth and bald so that it shone in the light.

'Alrite mate, I'm Robbie,' he said, in a Northern accent, offering his massive hand.

'Hi, I'm John,' John said, feeling the strength and power in Robbie's hand as he shook it.

'So what you in for? Robbie asked, settling his frame into the seat next to John.

'Bit bloody silly really, I was running a video shop and got done; not for selling illegal pornography but four months for them not being certificated.'

'The law is a real ass at times.'

'What about you, what you in for?'

'Oh a bit of wheeling and dealing that went wrong and finished up getting six months.'

'You look remarkably fit. You do a lot of training?'

'Yeah, I try to keep fit. I'm a Karate champion, even represented Great Britain a few times but now I'm into property, buying, selling and renting out anything to make a few bob. What about you, you still going to run the video shop when you get out?'

'No, they closed it down and seized most of the stock and we'd only been open a couple of days.'

'So what else are thinking of doing?'

'Well before opening the shop I was a bouncer and had a hard crew that was sent in to sort out clubs where the local bouncers weren't capable of keeping trouble makers out.'

'LAWSON.' John suddenly heard his name being shouted out by the chief prison officer.

'Listen, I know some people who could use you and your mates. We'll talk more when we get a chance,' Robbie said, as John hurried into the office.

October 28th was John's birthday and unbeknown to him, Jay had set up a collection at JFK to buy some booze to smuggle into the prison for John. Jay's plan was to sneak into the prison and drop the booze in some bushes behind a bench in the sunken garden area used for the horticultural courses. The garden was beautifully laid out with flower beds, little stone patios with benches and several clumps of bushes spread around, the ideal place to stash booty.

To John's delight when he found the stash, there was an amazing selection of whisky, vodka and brandy as well as some bottles of beer. The problem now was getting the booze to his room, but having built up a trusting relationship with Robbie, he decided he was the one to help him. John wore his donkey jacket, because of the large pockets which would enable him to carry some of the booty, while Robbie kept a look out he stuffed the beer bottles into the pockets before tucking two bottles of whisky down the front of his jeans and a bottle of brandy for Robbie. Loaded up, they carefully made their precarious way back up the garden and suddenly stopped in their tracks as they saw one of the prison officers walking straight towards them.

'Oh boy now we're for it,' John said, as he felt one of the whiskey bottles beginning to slip and press against the front of his jeans, inadvertently causing the zip of his fly to slide down.

'And what are you two up to, wandering around out here?' the prison officer demanded to know.

'We're both wing runners and we have been delivering a couple of messages for the CPO, we're just on our way back boss,' John answered, as he felt the bottle pressing harder against the zip causing it to slide further down.

As John felt the bottom of the bottle about to protrude from his now almost open zip, he noticed the prison officer glance at his groin with a curious look on his face. The corner of the bottom of the bottle was just peeking out as though John's privates were about to pop out. The prison officer, aware that John was looking at him staring at his open zip, quickly raised his eyes not wanting to be accused of behaving in an inappropriate manner.

'Sorry boss, I've just been to the toilet, forgot to do myself up,' John said quickly, as he pushed the bottle in and quickly pulled the zip up.

'Right lad, make sure you're tidy before you leave the toilet next time,' the prison officer said, as he turned and walked away.

As they walked off, John felt the zipper open again and this time the bottle slipped right out, but he managed to catch it before it hit the ground.

Robbie looked at him in horror. 'Don't you ever do that to me again, we could have got nicked big time for that.'

'Well we didn't, and just think, we can have ourselves a nice little drink tonight and for several nights after.' John said, with a satisfied grin.

With a good supply of booze and the luxuries bought with the phone cards Jay had supplied the rest of John's short stay went smoothly.

John had become fascinated by what Robbie had been telling him about the VAT swindles that crooked businesses were perpetrating on a massive scale, explaining how the crooks would set up a group of companies around Europe and then one company would order a million pounds of electrical goods from one of the others, that company would then export the goods in a large container and claim the VAT back. The trick was that the container contained nothing, there were no electrical goods in the first place. The whole operation was a complete fraud but earning millions for the crooks, elevating them to gangster status until Her Majesty's Customs found about it and closed the loop hole; by then the crooks had got away with millions. Unfortunately some of the crooks in the scheme became greedy and started cheating on their partners in crime resulting in enforcers being called in to try and retrieve the stolen millions.

Robbie seeing the interest being displayed by John warned him that debt collecting at that level was dangerous and involved travelling abroad to wherever the gangsters were hiding out – but the pay more than compensated for the risks.

'Listen Robbie, I'm out next week and you will be out a few weeks later. Let's meet up and sort out some serious business' John said, enticed by the millions up for grabs.

A ROLLING STONE
GATHERS JOHN

1999

It saddened John to learn that Jay got three years in Strangeways prison in the same week he was released from Kirkham, but knew that if Jay kept his nose clean he would only do eighteen month. He resolved to go and visit him once he'd got his own life sorted out.

And that came about in the most unexpected way when coming back from a visit to the shops as he saw Daniel and Siobhan playing with some of the neighbour's children. But the smile drained from his face as he heard one the boys start to swear, using the foulest language as she started to chase one of the girls with a stick, threatening her with what he was going to do with the stick in the most explicit and obscene manner. But the girl was no better as she turned and told him to go away using the same obscene language. John looked on, anger mixed with determination as he rushed forward, grabbed both his children by the hand and pulled them away, dragging them back indoors before they had a chance to protest.

Siobhan was crying and struggling to free herself, as John dragged them both into the kitchen where Jenny was preparing dinner.

'What the devil's going on?' she asked, as John released his grip on them.

'I am not having my children learning to swear and behave in the disgusting way the kids round here are behaving. You should have heard the language, it was foul. I can tell you it was a lot worse than I've heard from some real heavies I've come across.'

'That's the one thing I've always admired about you, even with the strange things you get up to and I don't know the half of it, you don't like to hear people swearing. So what do you propose we do about it?

We can't live in isolation,' Jenny reasoned, as she continued preparing the dinner.

'You're right we can't live in isolation, but what we can do is get the hell away from here and move to somewhere else a little more decent.'

'Such as?'

Scotland, I've always wanted to go back, I hate Birkenhead. It has nothing to offer us and it's riddled with crime and drugs.'

An oppressive gloom gathered about Jenny. 'But we've spent a small fortune on doing this place up. You want us to just walk out and leave it?'

He took hold of her hands and held them tight as he looked into her eyes and said. 'Yes, let's start afresh, you like Scotland as much as I do. I love you and the kids and I don't want anything ever to happen to any of you. We have Daniel, Siobhan and Arran to think about, and the one on the way. I don't like the idea of them being brought up here,' his voice warm, but tinged with sadness.

A look of sympathy flashed across Jenny's face and she broke into a smile as she said. 'You're right, but if we're going to do it, let's do it before I'm too far gone and won't be able to cope with a move.'

'I'll start looking for place tomorrow.'

'How about this one in Wallyford? I know it well and like it there,' she suggested as they looked through the rentals on-line after she had prepared dinner.

John contacted the landlord of the three bedroom house to rent in Wallyford near Musselburgh and in February of 1999 they moved in, leaving Birkenhead behind.

Arran celebrated his first birthday on the 4th March 2000 and a month later, on the 8th April, John had to rush Jenny to the Edinburgh maternity hospital in the early hours of the morning. She went into labour and in the afternoon she gave birth without complications to a healthy boy and just like Arran, Lewis was also named after a Scottish Isle.

'Well that's Arran and Lewis, two islands, what's next Skye?' John quipped overjoyed at the birth of another son.

'You've got to be joking. That's it, I'm not planning for anymore,' Jenny replied, totally exhausted after the birth.

Once they had got themselves settled in and schools sorted out for the children, John had to start looking for work and was lucky to find a job with a company called Rock Steady Security who did a lot of the doors in Edinburgh as well as providing security at rock concerts. His first job was in a nightclub called Club Thirty in Frederick Street, Edinburgh. The job was fairly routine with very little trouble, not requiring John to have to use any of his martial art skills, but the way he conducted himself came to the notice of the area manager who explained they were contracted to provide security for a very special rock concert by the Rolling Stones at Murrayfield Stadium. He wanted John to be part of the security team to bodyguard the Stones at the hotel they would be staying at when they came up in June.

John began to get excited at the thought at being so close to the band and was disappointed when told he was only going to be part of the extra security at the Balmoral Hotel on Princes Street, where the band would be staying. He was pleased however, to be working with Achi who was also at Club Thirty. Achi, the Hebrew name for brother, was a tough Israeli ex-soldier trained in the skills of Krav Maga, the unarmed combat technique developed by the Israel military. Achi was six foot, clean cut, a good physique and shaven head. Someone you wouldn't want to pick an argument with.

The Rolling Stones who were staying for four nights had taken over all the suites on two floors, John was assigned to protect Keith Richards' suite while Achi protected the suite being occupied by Ronnie Wood. The job was a boring twelve hour shift, mainly sitting in the corridor outside the suite making sure no unauthorised person came anywhere near, there was always the threat of crazed female fans, or the press trying to sneak in. It was on the third night that things suddenly happened, the fire alarm went off and everyone was ordered to evacuate the hotel. John sprang into action, banging on the door before guiding Keith Richards and his PA out of the room, down the stairs towards the fire exit. He was about to lead them outside when he spotted the press all waiting with their cameras at the ready.

'I think this is a ruse by the press to get you and the others out onto the street. I think we'll be safer in here,' John said, hustling Keith Richards and the PA into a small corridor and holding them there until the all clear sounded and everybody was allowed back to their rooms.

*

One reporter managed to sneak in but before he could snap a picture, John spun him around and pushed him forcibly out of the fire exit, slamming it shut, then guided Keith back up to his rooms without incident.

Keith thanked John for his astuteness, went into his room and crashed out. John was pleased he had done what was expected of him, but didn't know John McCallum, the head of security for the Rolling Stones, was running around the hotel in a frenzy searching for Keith while John had him downstairs.

The following morning Big John, as John McCallum was known, invited John to breakfast, having been told what had happened and how he had saved Keith from being exposed to the mercy of the waiting paparazzi. To John's surprise, while he was enjoying breakfast in the sumptuous restaurant, Big John offered him a permanent job with the security team.,It was an attractive offer, but having just moved to Scotland and Jenny having just given birth to their second child, John felt touring around the country and abroad with the Rolling Stones would not go down well with her.

So now John had four children to take care of; Daniel, Siobhan, Arran and Lewis, which meant they needed a bigger house. By chance John was introduced to a mortgage adviser who told him for a fee of £500 he could arrange a mortgage – and produce some false pay slips and bank statements. All John had to do was come up with the necessary deposit.

The pay slips and bank statements were good forgeries, but the deposit wasn't going to be that easy, the sporadic work he was getting on the doors wasn't nearly enough with all the other expenses of the rent, feeding and clothing the family. But, as it always seemed to do when John was in need, an opportunity came out of the blue while working the door at Club Thirty. One of the drug dealers got talking to him one night, explaining he was having a run in with another drug dealer who worked for his rival Mikey McGraw. This rival was starting to flash his cash around and encroach onto his territory, he needed to be taught a lesson.

'If you like I can take care of him,' John offered, remembering how Jay had dealt with Pedro and walked away with a tidy sum of money.

'But whatever money I take is mine,' John added, thinking here was a way to make the deposit for the house.

'You're welcome to it,' the dealer agreed. 'I'm not interested in the money, I just want him given a good hiding, okay?'

The target lived on the notorious Niddrie Housing Estate, made famous in the film Trainspotting. It was one of the worst, drug-riddled communities in Scotland and he kept two bull terriers at the house to keep intruders away. John thought it wise not to attempt to take him down where he lived but wait for the right moment when he came to the club and had done the night's dealings. It also meant he would have a good stash of money on him.

The chance came one Saturday night when the rival dealer slipped out the rear exit into the courtyard. 'I've got to make a quick phone call,' John said to the other guy working the door with him and quickly made for the rear exit.

The drug dealer so intent on scrolling through his mobile was not aware of John creeping up on him. Just as the dealer raised his eyes and turned, suddenly aware of movement, John caught him with a solid right to the jaw and he collapsed unconscious to the ground. John was amazed to find his pockets crammed with notes and quickly relieved him of them, then hurried around to the front of the club and strolled in pretending to finish a phone call as though nothing unusual had happened. John went home that night several thousand pounds richer and he knew it would be enough for the deposit. All he had to do now was find the house.

TRAFFICKERS AND PIMPS

John found the perfect house in Port Seton on the coast of the Firth of Forth, four miles North East of Musselburgh. The house was 28 Links Place. It cost £93,000 and John, with the back hand payment of £500 to the dodgy mortgage broker was able to put down a ten grand deposit and obtain a ninety percent mortgage. Jenny was delighted as it was in a respectable neighbourhood, had four bedrooms, with an ensuite master bedroom. The lounge and dining room on the ground floor and been knocked through to make a very spacious living area. The kitchen was also large and was fully fitted. There was even an integral garage where John could store his beloved chopper. The move was relatively easy and they quickly settled down to a new life; it made John happy they were now living in a posh area where there were no kids running around the streets fighting and swearing at each other.

The problem for John was earning enough money to pay the £650 monthly mortgage as well as feed and clothe the family. Arran was fifteen months, Siobhan was nine years old, Daniel was eleven and was little Lewis, the newest member of the family who was six months old. What little financial resources John had in the bank had been used up in the move to Port Seton. So to help with the costs Jenny went back to working as a bus driver with First Bus. John was still doing the odd security job for Rock Steady, as well as working the doors of some of the local nightclubs, but it wasn't enough and he desperately needed another stroke of luck like the Pedro incident. But as always the luck came in a way he never expected. He got a call from Uncle George telling him he had sacked the manager of the brothel he was now running and asked if John was interested in taking over the running of the *massage parlour* as it was called. It was an interesting offer, but having just moved home, John felt he couldn't just leave Jenny and the children and run off down to London again. Uncle George understood and asked if he knew of anyone else who might be interested.

John was now in regular touch with Robbie, who had been released from Kirkham prison and asked him if he knew of anyone. Robbie suggested a friend of his called Gary and so John recommended him to Uncle George. In the meantime John had got a job as a bouncer at a nightclub called Mad Dogs in George Street, Edinburgh. The pay was just enough to meet their outgoings but left very little for anything else and, as always, the urge for something bigger, something more exciting, challenging, intriguing and more money was burning inside John. Three months later, John answered the phone to Uncle George, his voice was thick with rage telling John that bastard Gary he had recommended has been on the fiddle and had run off with over twenty grand and he was now minus a manager and the cash. John felt the weight of his anger and was stunned into silence, not sure what to say.

'I need someone quick and the only person I can trust is you, I understand your predicament, but will you give it some thought?' his uncle pleaded.

'I'll explain things to Jenny and see what she says,' John promised.

Jenny wasn't happy about him working in a massage parlour, which she knew was a euphemism for a brothel, but he explained he had been responsible for recommending Gary and felt he had to offer to help his uncle straighten things out. He also told her that his uncle had agreed he would be provided with a rent free apartment and could go home every weekend and be paid £1100 a week, cash in hand, more than anything he could ever hope to earn locally. That also meant Jenny would be able to give up driving a bus. Reluctantly Jenny agreed, being assured there would be no monkey business with the girls.

The massage parlour was called Steam & Sun and was situated at in Charlton Street, just around the corner from Euston Station in London. What John discovered on his arrival was a mess in every way. The place was filthy, the rooms the girls used for clients were unkempt and the girls, a mixture of nationalities mainly Albanians and Ukrainians were generally unclean, on drugs and paying scant attention to their own cleanliness. John realised he had a major task on his hands to put things right and there was another problem he had to deal with. His uncle was now drinking heavily and smoking vast amounts of hash leaving John to make all the decisions.

John's first decision was to totally refurbish the place, replacing the sauna and showers and more importantly refurbishing the rooms to make them a cleaner and sexier environment. He called his old mate Colin, who was a pretty good all round tradesman, down from Birkenhead to get on with the refurbishment. Having achieved that, John's next decision was to sack all the girls who had pimps. The men were causing trouble, fighting and arguing as they waited outside in the early hours of the morning to collect their girls and take the money they'd earned off them. John also discovered the pimps had been paying Gary £50 a night for each of their girls to work there, earning Gary a nice £500 a night.

The pimps were making up to £1000 a night from the girls that worked the brothel. They were understandably angry when John sacked their girls and tried desperately to negotiate the same deal with John as they had had with Gary. John wasn't interested and told them to get lost, he was determined to go up market and bring in a better class of girl not controlled by pimps. From experience knew his actions could cause a lot of trouble and felt he needed the protection his old friend again; a Browning 9mm handgun and fifty rounds of ammunition would do the trick.

John's instincts were right as around midnight one night there was heavy banging on the door. John looked out the window of his apartment which was directly above the sauna's front door and saw the group of Albanian pimps hammering on the door, shouting for him to come out. John took the gun from its hiding place, tucked it into the back of his jeans and went out to confront them.

'We're not happy what you do sack girls, you listen good, we cut you up if you if you don't let girls back,' one of the pimps called out, producing a knife and waving it about menacingly.

John met his eyes squarely and there was a strong tension about him as he said. 'You don't bring a knife to a gun fight.'

The aggressive look on the pimp's face did not match the anxiety in his eyes. 'You try be funny. I can cut you to pieces with this,' the pimp threatened. 'This is London not Albania, you don't have gun,' he added, flicking the knife from hand to hand.

'Like I said, you don't bring a knife to a gun fight,' John repeated, as he reached behind him and pulled out the gun. The pimps looked at each other all taking a moment to absorb what had just happened.

'You serious about shoot us?' one of the other pimps called out.

'In a heart beat, if you don't get the hell out of here. I hate scum like you who force girls into prostitution and live off their earnings.'

'What about you, isn't that what you doing?' another of the pimps called out.

'Yes, except the girls that will work here now will be doing it of their own free will and will keep all the money they earn. That's the difference between us. You take whatever you can from the girls, but couldn't give a shit what happens to them when you've finished with them. So, you've just got few seconds to put that knife away and piss off or I'll start shooting,' John warned them as he cocked the gun and aimed it at the pimp with the knife. The showdown was over, the pimps just turned and walked away knowing there was no chance of getting their girls back in there.

There was one girl John hadn't sacked. Her name was Nikita, at least that was the name she used. She was an extremely pretty blonde with a demure, innocent face and a beautiful well shaped body to go with it. He began to get curious about how she came to be working there and determined to find out more. Nikita explained she came from a small village in Ukraine. She told him she was from a poor family and her boyfriend who had promised to marry and take care of her, had run off when she became pregnant. Desperate to find a job to support her son and family she found out about an employment agency that were offering jobs as Au Pairs in the UK. It seemed the answer to her problems and soon she was on her way to St Petersburg to meet the people running the agency. They all seemed very nice explaining that would organise everything, arrange her passport and pay her air fare. They even insisted on driving her home so they could meet her family.

Guilt was beginning to prick at his conscience as she told him that when she arrived in the UK everything changed, she was herded into a room along with some other girls and told she wouldn't be working as an au pair but as a prostitute, to pay back the thousands of pounds they had paid for her. She tried to refuse, but was immediately beaten, raped, locked up and refused food until she complied.

'I'd like to help you,' he heard himself offer, hoping she could not read the guilt behind his eyes.

'No you can't help, nobody can,' she said, raising her head and studying him for a moment, trying her hardest to pluck up the courage to tell him before burying it back in her hands. 'They have threatened to kill my family and my son if I attempt to escape. They know where my family live – that's why they insisted on driving me home.' There was an underlying sadness in her voice and a flicker of fear showed in her eyes.

John had seen that look many times before, some things are forced on you and you had to bear the consequences. It was the story of her life and in some ways his own. After the girl had gone, guilt was still hammering at his conscience. It was like a cloak of thorns, pricking at his brain like little electric shocks sparking terrible images of girls being taken from their homes and loved ones, being beaten, raped and forced into prostitution. Then his face changed, darkening a little and his cheeks flared an angry colour as his mind focused on his position. He was running a brothel, so why should he bother or get involved in any of the girl's plights, it wasn't his problem. His problem was to make sure they turned up on time and satisfied the clients, because this was a business, a means of making money.

The first thing you learn is to be strong, because if you're soft anything you've achieved can be easily taken from you, and he wasn't prepared to have it taken away from him whatever the plight of the girls, he told himself as he straightened up, determined to get on with the business of running a brothel.

Things seemed to have settled into a good routine and the business was doing well with the new class of girls until, one Friday evening around seven o'clock, a couple of smartly dressed Eastern European men walked into reception explaining they were looking for the wife of one of them and they thought she might be working there. The receptionist immediately buzzed John explaining the situation over the intercom. John could see the men on the CCTV in his room and rushed downstairs. H studied the two men carefully, guessing they were either Albanian or Croatian. One of the men introduced himself as Nicos, explaining it was his friend Luka desperately looking for his wife who he still loved, but that she had run off after a silly argument and he feared she may have got herself involved in prostitution.

Luka then pulled a photograph from his pocket to show John.

'There's no one here that looks anything like her,' John assured him

'Would it be possible to have a look around and speak to some of the girls who perhaps may have seen her,' Nicos asked. 'She may have changed her appearance slightly, that you perhaps wouldn't notice but Luka would,' he added.

John hesitated for a moment not sure whether he believed them. To him they looked and smelled like they had a military background turned gangster.

John thought pensively as he looked at the way they were dressed in smart Armani suits, expensive highly polished shoes and Gold Rolex watches strapped to the wrists, but there was a hardness in their faces that said be careful how you deal with them.

'Okay, as long as you're quick about it,' John agreed, thinking it would be better to let them see the girl they were looking was not there and if he refused it could lead to more trouble.

As Nicos and Luka started talking to the girls and showing the photograph around, John noticed some of the girls were becoming agitated at the aggressive tones the two men were adopting in their own language.

'Right, that's enough you've seen the girl is not here, so it's time you left,' John told them as he ushered then out.

As they got to the front door, Nicos turned to John and said, 'We don't believe you.'

'I don't care what you believe. You've seen she's not here, so on your way,' John said, as he watched them climb into a shiny black Mercedes with blacked out windows and drive off.

When John asked the girls why they had become nervous, they explained they were not looking for his wife, but for one of their girls who had run off and started working on her own. They explained they were part of a Croatian Mafia gang and it gave him an uncanny feeling that this was not going to be the end of it.

It was only two hours later that feeling was to be proven tight when John looked out the window and saw a fleet of five shiny black Mercedes drive in at the end of Charlton Street. He wasn't surprised when he saw Nicos and Luka get out of the first car quickly followed by others emerging from the other cars. There were about twelve of them, all expensively dressed, but there was one particular man in the middle stretched Merc who was waiting for the door to be opened before he got out.

Obviously the boss, John thought as he watched the other men surround him in a protective shield. *They're coming to break the place*

apart, to teach me a lesson, his unease mounting as he wondered what to
do. What suddenly sprung to his mind was the way he had confronted
the Yardies and got them to back down. *Could it work again?* he had
to try it for there was nothing else. He took the Browning from its
hiding place. *If I go down I'll take a few of the bastards with me,* he said to
himself, as he chambered it with a full magazine, stuck it in the back
of his jeans and made his way out.

John walked purposely towards Nicos and Luka and there was an
uneasy silence, as the men turned, and look at him. Some of the men
instinctively reaching inside their coats for the guns holstered under
their armpits.

'Right you two, come with me and we'll sort this out,' John said,
and there was a note of anger in his voice that made them hesitate
from doing anything as they then turned to the boss. He gave a slight
nod and they moved off, surprised John had recklessly turned his
back on them.

'Look whatever you think is going on, I want to assure we are no
threat to your operations,' John told them, as soon as they entered the
office. 'And to prove we're no threat I am going to take my gun out
and place it on the table and…'

'You're carrying?' Nicos said, surprised.

'Of course you don't think I would have gone out there naked do
you?'

They looked at him with a hint of respect as John pressed the clip
to release the magazine before ejecting the bullet from the chamber
and laying it all out on the small coffee table.

'I don't know who you think we are, but we are a major outfit
in London and we're connected with the Smith family, I guess you
know who they are. We rent these premises from them so I think
they would be pretty upset if it happened to get damaged in any way.
We run the brothel, the sex clubs, the peep shows and the hostess
bars; you run the girls so there is no conflict between us. You came
in here with all the bullshit about looking for you wife when you were
really looking for one of your runaways. I proved she wasn't here or
ever had been. We keep a photograph and ID record of all ours past
and present girls, which you can look at if you wish. The girl you're
looking for has never worked here and if you leave me your details I
will happily let you know should she turn up looking for work,' John
offered.

'We don't need to look at the files, we'll take your word for it and I think that concludes our business,' Nicos said, as they got to their feet.

John followed them out leaving the gun and ammunition where it was on the table.

He watched as Nicos and Luka walked straight to the boss, obviously explaining what had taken place. Eventually the boss looked across at John and beckoned him with his finger, which slightly irritated John but he walked over which gave him the chance to see the man close up. He was shorter than the men around him and John thought he looked a little like Marlon Brando in the Godfather movies.

'You're a brave man, you could have been killed. All my colleagues have served in Croatia or Serbia and won't hesitate to shoot should it become necessary. I respect you for the way you have behaved and I see you as no threat to what we are doing, so this matter is at an end. *Omogu uje dobiti odavde*' he said to his men, as he waited for the car door to be opened and climbed in.

Once safely back in his office John began to shake as he stared down at the gun and ammunition spread out on the table, amazed he had got away with it to a gang that was way out his league, who could have wiped him out and swept him into the gutter without a second thought. The good thing was it enhanced his reputation as word began to spread around, particularly with the girls who started to feel a lot safer.

'O *sole mio, sta 'nfronte a te!, O sole mio, sta 'nfronte a te! sta 'nfronte a te!*,' the voice bellowed out, echoing in the stairway as Giovanni made his way up to his room. Giovanni had been a thorn in John's side since he had become manager. He had been a tenant before the place was taken over and simply refused to move out. Uncle George had tried to ask Giovanni to leave several times in the past, but was unusually frightened to force him out for fear of upsetting the Italian Mafia that operated at the bottom of Charlton Street.

Giovanni didn't have particularly clean habits and the flat was in an untidy state. Hearing him singing away as though he hadn't a care in the world made John angry so soon after his confrontation with the Croatians, he grabbed the gun from the table loaded the magazine and stormed downstairs to the Italian's room.

He hammered on the door and shouted out. 'I want you out of here today.'

Giovanni casually opened the door glared at John as he snarled in broken English. 'You anda o elsa? I ama going nowhere, I ama connected with....'

John raised the gun and said. 'Yes you are, and you're going to be connected permanently with the lead in this gun if you don't get your shit together and get the hell out of here in the next few hours.'

'You willa needa lawyer toa getta me outta here,' he said as he went to slam the door.

'I got the best lawyer there is, his name's Browning,' John said, firing five shots into the framework above the door. 'And if you're going to get a lawyer, you better get a funeral director at the same time, you stupid wop.'

'Okay, okay, Ia move, Ia go tonighta, Ia promise,' Giovanni said, scurrying back inside.

John walked back to his room feeling a little calmer that he'd got rid of Giovanni and now had the room free to accommodate the extra security person he knew he was going to need.

It was on his weekend at home that he met up with Chris, a guy who had worked the doors at Mad Dogs and asked him if he would like to come to London and work for him. Chris was a decent guy and reliable enough, he looked like the stereotypical Scot with his beard and build. He was only five eight, but was stocky and weighed around fourteen stone. Chris had a girlfriend Lauren, who was also happy to move down to London. Lauren was petite with long blonde hair, but tough despite her size. They were both biker types and into heavy rock. John was keen to have Chris working for him so he offered Lauren the job as a receptionist.

Chris and Lauren moved into the flat hurriedly vacated by Giovanni and settled into the operation very quickly. The extra security made the girls feel safer and John felt he could relax more and concentrate on running the business, instead of constantly having to check on everything around the clock.

All seemed well until one evening Lauren buzzed him to tell him there was trouble in reception. John rushed down to find an arrogant young guy with a cockney accent shouting his mouth off that he'd been ripped off. John tried to calm him as he continued to mouth off that he had paid the cab driver the entrance fee and for a girl and why was he being charged again. John tried to explain the cab driver had nothing to do with them and it was the cabbie who had ripped him off, but the man wouldn't have it and was getting more aggressive, becoming a problem for the other clients that were continuing to arrive and who Chris was having to deal with.

John having had enough, hit the man on his left shoulder while pulling his right shoulder towards him, spinning him around before hitting him with a double palm strike to the back, propelling the man forward and inadvertently forcing his face hard against the doorframe, breaking two of his teeth, before grabbing hold of him and throwing him out onto the street. Making sure he would not attempt to come back in, John watched him on the CCTV and was surprised to see the man get to his feet wrench up one of the loose paving stones on the other side of the street, carry it across and hurl it at the window shattering the glass.

That so inflamed John, he dashed upstairs, grabbed the gun, rushed outside, and rage getting the better of judgement, pointed the gun at the man's head and said, 'If you don't get away from here I'm going to blow your head off.' John watched as the man turned and ran off up the street and a spark of fear flared through him as the man stopped took out his mobile and punched in a number. *What an idiot you are John, he's phoning the police.*

John rushed back to his room, frantically unloaded the magazine, wiping them both clean of his fingerprints before throwing them out of the window into the alley behind the building. By the time he'd done that he could hear the sound of sirens wailing.

There were several police cars and they sealed the street off before bursting into the massage parlour.

'Where's the gun?' the armed response policeman asked, as he and other armed response policemen charged in.

'Guns? There aren't any guns around here,' John said innocently.

'You have been reported threatening a man with a gun and…'

'No officer, I only pointed this at him,' John cut in, holding up his walkie talkie. 'In his drunken state he obviously thought it was a gun.'

'Yes well that maybe, but we are going to carry out a search,' the armed police officer told him.

'Help yourselves, but you won't find anything,' John said, with an air of confidence.

Unfortunately they found a replica gun case that Gary used to keep hidden on top of a wardrobe and John was arrested.

What an idiot I've been I just hope Cecil can get me off of this one, he thought, as he was driven off to Camden Police Station.

'We've got the gun case which is being examined by...' the detective constable began.

'And that's all you have an old replica case, no gun, no bullets,' Cecil Watkins cut in angrily, shaking his head causing the dandruff to settle on the shoulders of his crumpled suit.

'And we have the detailed statement from the victim that your client threatened him with a gun,' the detective constable stated.

'Victim?!' Cecil exclaimed, raising his voice more than he intended but managing to calm it before he said. 'The man was drunk and on drugs, causing trouble, even smashing one of the windows, in his violent disturbed mind, as my client attempted to calm him he simply mistook his walkie talkie to be a gun. So you have nothing with which to hold my client and I demand he be released.'

The detective looked at Cecil and then at John who had sat there saying nothing and shrugged knowing he had to let him go.

'Thanks Cecil,' John said, as they drove off in the taxi.

'Bloody fool, what were you thinking brandishing a gun out there in the street?' Cecil admonished him.

'I just lost my rag, he was behaving like an idiot.'

'And so were you. You have to report back in a week and let's just hope the idiot doesn't want to pursue the allegations,' Cecil said, brushing the dandruff off his shoulder.

John recognised the voice as soon as he spoke the words 'You know who I am?'

John instinctively switched the phone to speaker and took the voice recorder from the drawer, laid it on the desk and switched it on as he said. 'Yes I know who you are, what do you want?'

Just thought I'd let you know I am going to have my day in court. You broke two of my teeth you bastard,' the man said, his voice thick with rage.

'Fine by me and I hope your wife will enjoy it too, I noticed the ring on your finger and I guess she'll be very interested to learn you'd come to a brothel all drugged up looking for a prostitute.'

John heard the faint sound of a sharp intake of breath and then a pause before the man said. 'Okay, I tell you what, you bung me five grand and I won't give evidence.'

John gave a little laugh as he said. 'I tell you what, you don't give evidence and I won't play this recording to the police of you trying to bribe me.'

This time there was a loud intake of breath. 'You telling me you've been recording this conversation?'

'Yes, listen to yourself, you plonker. You think the likes of you can get one over on me?' John said, as he pressed the playback button. After a few seconds the phone went dead.

A few days later Cecil phoned to say, the man has withdrawn his allegations admitting he could have been confused in thinking it might have been a gun.

DISHONOUR AMONG THIEVES, MINUS VAT

2000

The council in their bid to close down the peep shows and hostess bars in Soho used a compulsory purchase order to buy the building on the corner of Wardour Street and Brewer Street where Erotica was situated. They also bought the ground floor and basement of the Phoenix in Moor Street. The council paid out millions to purchase the properties but bought them well below their true market value. Uncle Tony and Dave were not too pleased but still made a small fortune in the process.

Uncle George and Uncle Dave still had the apartments above and decided to rent them out to prostitutes to continue to provide them with a steady income. The trouble was Uncle George was drinking more and more and increasing his use of drugs, making him very difficult to deal with, so much so, that it was also upsetting the girls at the Steam and Sun massage parlour. John was particularly upset when his uncle, totally out of his mind on skunk and fuelled by whisky, dropped off a carrier bag for John to look after, containing twelve grand to pay the Smith family.

The situation came to a head when Uncle George came back the next day in total panic that he had lost twelve grand that had been in a carrier bag in the back of his Range Rover. John explained it was in still in the safe after he had given it to him in a drunken stupor the night before and in anger called his Uncle an idiot. Even though he was drunk and drugged up to the eyeballs George didn't like John calling him an idiot and it quickly developed into a violent argument. Uncle George made some serious threats to John, and even though

John knew it was the drink and drugs talking, he realised that if he stayed any longer one of them was going to get seriously injured. John decided he'd had enough and the best thing to do was pack his bags and leave bringing an abrupt and unhappy end to their relationship.

So back in Scotland, again John needed to find work and he knew it wasn't going to be easy. He managed to get his job back at Mad Dogs, where he met up with Michael Chamberlain, an ex South African Special Forces soldier, now living in Scotland with his wife Cara. He was a big man at six foot two, very muscular and with long hair tied back in a pony tail that gave him the appearance of a Samurai warrior, which was quite apt considering his skills in Aikido. John had also got a job at Oscars, a nightclub in Musselburgh owned by Thomas Kelly, Tam to his friends, who had converted the old working men's club into a bar and disco. Tam was a short stocky guy, with a shaven head, who also had a reputation as a tough guy. John had met him one night months earlier at a Charity auction where John had bid for and won a signed Celtic football. It was the time when John had worked with the Rolling Stones and John wanted to give the ballot Mick Jagger who he knew was a great Celtic fan. Tam Kelly was delighted that John was giving the ball to Mick Jagger and it cemented their relationship.

Once again John thought about Robbie and the jobs that he talked about so was keen to make contact with him. Robbie was pleased when John got in touch, because he had a job that he thought John would be very interested in.

Robbie explained there was a businessman, who was simply referred to as 'The German.' 'The German' was a high flyer, very wealthy with a fleet of expensive cars, a mansion and his own helicopter. He was into VAT fraud in a big way, like many others he had found a loop hole in the law and had set up a most sophisticated scam that was to become known as the 'Carousel Fraud', millions of pounds worth of goods, mainly mobile phones or computer chips, went round and round. Purchased free of VAT on the Continent and then sold on in the UK with the VAT added which could be claimed back for the Inland Revenue. However, the goods were never sold for consumption in the UK, but simply passed through a series of companies, some legitimate, some sham, before being exported back out of the UK. The same goods were then re-imported allowing the goods to go round again, enabling the fraud to be repeated many times over. The goods circulated around the companies as many as thirty five times, before the company at the centre of the transactions disappeared from the records – Having by then claimed millions of pounds back from HM Customs & Excise.

The problem, Robbie went on to explain was, The German was working with a local gangster in the North East named Webb, known as Spider, who had got greedy at seeing the vast profits that could be made and decided to do it for himself. He had started up his own companies using The German's identity and making a few million before running off with the proceeds to Benidorm in Spain. Unfortunately, Spider left a trail of his activities which Customs and Excise eventually caught onto, the game was up and the loop hole very firmly closed. Robbie further explained a friend of his, Lloyd, a bouncer, a tall thick set black guy, six foot four, who was the principal contact man with The German, had been to Spider's apartment in Benidorm and said the place was full of shoe boxes stuffed with fifty pound notes, impossible to even guess how much was in each box, let alone how many boxes there were, a hundred at least if not more.

The deal put forward by The German was that he was more interested in Spider being taught a lesson and was happy for whoever carried out the job to keep half the money recovered. This was music to John's ears and he immediately contacted Jay and Michael Chamberlain to see if they were interested in a profitable trip to Spain. They all said yes and went down to meet with Robbie and Lloyd at a service station in Staffordshire. Lloyd explained The German also had two other people living in the North East who owed him large sums of money, one in particular, owing him over £13,000,000 he wanted sorting out and his money back. Lloyd also told them the man had already been pulled in by the police and Customs over his involvement in VAT fraud, The German was worried that he might get arrested and his assets frozen before he got his money back.

'When are we going to meet this German?' John asked, intriguingly.

'Right now, he's been watching us from the other side of the restaurant,' Lloyd said, with a co-spiritual grin, motioning The German to come over.

A smart looking, middle aged man slowly and methodically made his way to their table. John thought he looked a bit like the actor Kevin Spacey. He was of slim build, about six foot, with short, neatly cut but thinning dark hair. He was clean shaven and wearing an expensive tailored suit with a white silk shirt, the cuffs edging out of the sleeves displaying solid gold cufflinks. On his right wrist he wore a Rolex Oyster which immediately grabbed John's interest as most men wear their watches on their left wrist.

'*Guten Tag Mein Herren*, please do not get up, there is no need for formalities. Let us get on with the business at hand, Lloyd assures me you are very capable men,' The German greeted them, studying each of them as he pulled up a chair from one of the other tables and sat down.

He then turned his gaze to John as he reached to the inside pocket of his jacket, pulled out a slip of paper and handed it to him. 'This is the code number to a Swiss bank account which you must guard with your life. You will force *der dieb*, who you will only know as 'David,' to transfer by whatever means £13,000,000 from the accounts I know he has in various banks in South Africa. Anything you find in the house; jewellery, silverware, pictures or cash – he is known to have a large safe with plenty of money in it, you may keep. Also, I will pay you ten per cent of the £13,000,000 once it is confirmed the whole amount has been successfully transferred to the Swiss bank account,' The German explained, in a benevolent manner.

'No disrespect, but you can keep your ten percent, make it twenty and you will have our loyalty' John said, staring intently into The German's eyes.

'Agreed, as I anticipated,' The German said, with a satisfied smug.

John looked at the others to gauge their reaction and was quickly assured by the looks on their faces they were all up for it.

The fact that the job was in the North East, much nearer to home was an added incentive and if successful they would then take on the others like Spider.

The first thing John decided to do was recce the place and the team headed off to start planning the operation. They weren't surprised to discover it was a large mansion set in its own grounds. It was surrounded on three sides by security fencing and walls, the fourth side had a low brick wall bordering a churchyard with a small traditional stone church and cemetery. There was a large back garden with a rear gate giving access to a narrow farm lane covered by CCTV. The main entrance had an electronically operated iron gate with the whole area again covered by cameras. In the driveway was an array of expensive motors; a Lamborghini, a Ferrari, a Bentley, a Rolls Royce and two Range Rovers.

Accepting this was going to be a big job, John felt they were going to need an extra pair of hands for surveillance and got in touch with Darren, the bouncer from Birkenhead, who was very happy to get involved if there was big money at stake. With everything set, Darren crawled behind a clump of bushes in a nearby field to study the property, while John and the team worked out the most effective way of them getting into the house unnoticed.

Jay reminded John of the time they worked as extras on the tv show 'Prime Suspect' dressed as policemen and how the public thought they were real cops. He suggested they do the same again and pretend it's a police raid. John liked the idea, remembering it well, but thought they only needed one of them to dress in full uniform to get them to open the door, the rest of the team could just dress identically in white shirts, dark jackets, black trousers, black baseball caps and black boots, carrying fake police IDs. They would all have walkie talkies so they could communicate with each other if needs be, which would also help in the deception.

One week later the job was on, surveillance permitting, and the team headed back down to the mansion. John, Jay and Michael hid up in a disused building a few miles away to wait for the call from Darren who was hiding in a copse in the field next to the house, giving him a good view of the comings and goings.

Darren however, was unable to get a signal on his mobile from his position and was forced to break with protocol and leave his spot to find a signal to be able tell John that the raid was on. He had observed 'David,' his girlfriend and two of his friends partying all night with booze and drugs and they had now crashed out.

John, Jay and Michael headed down to the churchyard next to the house, when they arrived, John directed Jay to find Darren and tell him to go to the service station by the motorway to monitor police radio signals and let them know if any were coming their way. Jay put on the police uniform that had been acquired while John and Michael dressed in plain clothes. They all pulled stockings over their heads, but not over their faces, keeping the stocking hidden under the baseball caps they were wearing.

Armed and ready, they carefully made their way over the church wall, avoiding the security cameras as they made their way to the back entrance. To their surprise the door was unlocked and they were able to move inside without making a sound or having to pretend it was a police raid. *This is going to be easy,* John thought as they slipped silently into the hallway, pleased Darren had kept a close watch and had chosen the perfect time. The smile dropped from John's face, replaced by shock as he heard the sounds of a television, every pulse in his body starting to speed up as he raised his hand to stop the others moving forward as he recognised the sounds of the Teletubbies and the sound of children laughing. The shock turned to horror as he looked around and spotted children's shoes and some little suitcases on the floor at the bottom of a staircase, as though ready to go travelling somewhere.

John froze for a brief moment, deciding what to do, then turned to the others and ran his hand across his throat as a silent indication to stop what they were doing and get back out. 'We're going back,' he said, it was a statement not a question and there was a lot of resignation in his voice.

Once outside Jay turned angrily to John. 'What the hell was that all about?'

'There are children in there,' John explained.

'So?'

'It's one thing going in there beating a man up and holding him and his friends hostage, but it's another thing if children are involved. You can be certain he wouldn't go to the police on his own account, but threaten or hurt his children then you can bet your life he would squeal. I'm furious with Darren that he hadn't spotted the children,' John said, anger and disappointment written all over his face.

'So what now?' Jay asked, frustration sounding in his voice.

'We'll try again, only this time we'll make sure there are no children around.'

'I don't understand you, you're such a hard bastard and yet you go soft over a bunch of kids,' Jay said, studying his impassive face.

'Trouble comes without going looking for it and children in this situation are trouble, I've seen children hurt and I want no part of it. We will do the job another time and get our rewards.'

'Yeah, but will The German understand we ducked out because of a few kids? He still hasn't got his money and we've got nothing out of it either,' Michael said, exasperations hardening his words

'Yes he will, because as I said, if the kids were harmed and 'David' went to the police, The German could be implicated and then we would be in real trouble. He'll respect us for what we did.'

'John's right, we'll just have to try again and don't forget there are still the other jobs The German wants us to do for him,' Michael said to Jay to try to calm the unease that was mounting.

John was hiding his own unease at the decision, Arran and Lewis' birthdays were fast approaching and Jenny had hinted she would like to go back to the Dominican Republic to celebrate their fifth wedding anniversary. He needed the money as much as they did, probably more so.

John knew they needed a reliable man to take the place of Darren and having gotten to know Tam Kelly well enough to confide in him, agreed with the others to bring him on board. In the meantime John managed to sort out a couple of relatively small jobs robbing drug dealers that produced a few thousand apiece, which was enough for John to take Jenny back to the Dominican Republic for a romantic two week holiday. As soon as they got back, Robbie was waiting anxiously to tell him The German was becoming impatient that they hadn't yet gone back to get his £13,000,000.

John decided they would do the surveillance themselves so as to make sure they acted when no children were there. The same fleet of luxury cars were parked in the driveway. They kept watch throughout the night with a pair of high powered binoculars enabling them to look in through the windows where no curtains had been drawn. They were relieved to see David, a female and the same two males partying, drinking Champagne and sniffing cocaine. With the powerful binoculars they could even watch them, making lines on the dining room table before snorting it. Taking it turns to keep a sharp observation on what was happening in the house, it wasn't until after four in the morning that the party broke up and they slumped off to their rooms.

They could all relax now knowing where the occupants were, happy to wait until they fell into a deep drug and alcohol fuelled sleep. While they waited, Jay got dressed up in the police uniform while John, Michael and Tam put on the white shirt, black trouser, leather jackets, baseball hats with stockings underneath and black boots; around their necks they hung the fake police badges on chains.

Deciding the time was right, they made their way into the grounds the same way as before with no trouble, except this time the door was locked and they were going to have to force it open. With their collective force they soon shouldered the door open, but the noise had awoken 'David' who surprisingly had not fallen into a state of drunken unconsciousness and came tearing down the staircase armed with an air rifle.

'Armed police, put the weapon down,' Jay shouted, raising the pistol at him.

'David' stood frozen to the spot for a few seconds as he stared at the police officer now aiming a weapon at him.

'Drop the weapon and get down on your knees, this is a police raid,' Jay ordered him.

'David' slowly lowered the air rifle and sank to his knees allowing John and Michael to move in and quickly cuff him.

'You were arrested and questioned a few weeks ago regarding our ongoing investigation into VAT fraud and we're here to follow up on that and the fact you have threatened a police officer with a weapon will not have helped your situation,' Jay informed him, keeping his voice calm and formal.

'Right, you hold him there while we search the house for who else might be here,' Jay told John as he, Michael and Tam moved up the staircase to check the bedrooms.

The pretty brunette in 'David''s bed sat up, grabbing the duvet to cover her nakedness as Jay burst in. 'Thank heavens for that. I thought for a moment you were some gangsters that had broken in,' she exclaimed, a look of relief spreading across her face as she stared at the policeman standing infront of her.

'It's alright Madam, we are here as part of an ongoing investigation and I would like you to remain here and not to come out until we have completed our investigations. If you attempt to, you may find yourself being charged with interfering with the investigation, do you understand?' Jay informed her.

'Yes I understand officer, but I need to go to the toilet,' she said, shuffling to the edge of the bed.

'Right, hurry up, I'll wait for you to come out,' Jay told her, and watched as she slipped out of bed dragging the duvet with her in an attempt to cover her modesty. *Another time, another place,* Jay thought, enjoying the sight of her neat rounded bottom as she disappeared into the bathroom.

Michael and Tam found the two other men dead to the world, it took some time to wake them from their drunken stupor enough to slip the handcuffs on. They then hauled them out of bed and dragged them out onto the landing where there were two *chez lounges*. The two men were made to lay face down on the *chez lounges* and told not to move or look up.

'He's got a bird upstairs, but it's alright she really thinks we're the police and I've locked her in the toilet,' Jay told John as he came back downstairs.

'David' strained his neck to look up. 'What do you mean, "she thinks you're the police?"'

'Keep your mouth shut, we'll deal with you in a moment,' John told him, giving him a hefty kick in the ribs before telling Jay to check the security system to see if they had been recorded on any of the cameras.

Jay looked around and found what used to be a pantry where they had installed a bank of monitors and vhs video recorders. To Jay's surprise the more he studied the equipment he noticed the vhs machines were not running so nothing was actually being recorded.

'Great security system you've got, except the recorders aren't running,' Jay said, as he came back into the hall.

'So there's nothing of us on tape?'

'Not a blinking flicker, so we needn't have had to go all the trouble of creeping about to sneak in here,' Jay said, wryly.

'You bastards are not police, you're crooks come to rob the place. Well you won't find much money here. So all your efforts will be for nothing,' 'David' screamed scathingly.

'Well, it may come as a surprise, but we've actually been sent by The German, and I guess you know what he wants,' John said, pulling the stocking down over his face before taking out his Browning and putting it to 'David''s head.

The word German quickly registered and he looked positively stricken and his eyes widened in fear.

'We're a professional team, come to collect the £13,000,000 you owe him. So let's not waste time, where's your computer?' John demanded, pressing the barrel hard against his skin.

'In the study at the end of the hallway,' 'David' told him, his voice trembling with fear.

Jay quickly found the laptop and brought it back to the hallway where John now had 'David' belly down on the floor ready to undo the handcuffs.

'You're going to do a fast track transfer of £13,000,000 from your accounts in South Africa to this numbered bank in Switzerland. Here are the bank co-ordinates,' John explained, as he released the handcuffs and placed the laptop on the floor next to 'David' now down on his knees.

'You've got to be joking. I can't transfer that kind of money just like that.'

'You can't or you won't?'

'I can't just do it on the computer. I would have to speak to my dad in South Africa to make any transfers like what you're suggesting.'

'Then speak to your dad, because understand this. We have gone to a lot of trouble to get this far and if you are going to be difficult, just remember you have got your bird upstairs and your two mates and we won't hesitate to hurt them if we have to, so be sensible and phone your dear dad and tell him you want to transfer £13,000,000 to this account and be very careful what you say to him, one wrong word and you girlfriend will be the first to get it.'

'David' studied John's and Jay's impassive faces feeling the words penetrating his brain as he reached over, picked up the receiver from its cradle, but as he started to tap in the number a buzzer sounded.

'What the hell's that?' John asked.

'David's' face relaxed into a brief smile. 'That's someone at the main gate, so what are you going to do now?'

'I'll go and check the monitors,' Jay said as he hurried off.

'There's a guy with a white van by the main gate, what's he want?' Jay said as he rushed back in.

'He must be one of the painters, we're having the place decorated,' 'David' told them, as the buzzer kept sounding.

'With four of us watching the place, how the hell didn't we spot that going on?' Jay asked.

'That's because they are only starting today,' 'David' said, cockily. 'How are you going to explain your little escapade to him? I tell you what, why don't you lot just slip out and I promise I won't say anything to anyone,' 'David' boldly suggested.

'Well in that case, if the place is being re-decorated it won't matter if there's blood splattered on the walls. So keep your mouth shut while I go and deal with him. Shoot him if he tries anything stupid,'

John said, kicking 'David' in the stomach to knock the wind out of him before hurrying out of the room and rolling the stocking up under his cap.

John slipped in the earpiece as he approached the main gate, 'Bravo two, just checking, suspect at main gate, over,' he pretended, speaking into the walkie talkie and immediately flashed his fake ID badge as he got close to the gate.

The man glanced at the ID badge and looked at the way John was dressed. 'What's happening officer?' the man asked, immediately assuming John was a police officer.

'You must be the decorator scheduled in for this week?' John said, as if it was police knowledge, ignoring his question.

'Yes, yes, that's right, I work for the company doing the kitchen and have come to start doing the prep work,' the man explained.

'I'm afraid you won't be able to do anything today as there is a police operation in progress and the place is sealed off. Just wait there while I radio in the vehicle's registration number,' John said, reading out the number into his radio.

While he was doing this he could hear the muffled voice of Michael talking anxiously to Jay in his earpiece which made it difficult for him to hear what the decorator was saying, so yanked the earpiece out.

'Right, your vehicle checks out, so turn it around and be on your way and I suggest you check whether it will be okay for you to return tomorrow,' John told him, before he turned on his heels and hurried back to the house.

John cautiously pulled the stocking back down over his face and drew his gun before going back into the house, wondering what Michael was going on about.

Unbeknown to John, Michael was talking to Jay about two women who had turned up in the lane at the back gate, finding it locked they had climbed over and were making their way up to the house. Michael was asking Jay what they should do. Jay had told him to keep watch over 'David' while he, being the one wearing the uniform, would go and confront the two ladies just as they entered the hallway.

The two ladies were surprised to be greeted by a police officer and explained they were cleaners that came in once a week to do the general cleaning, but just as Jay was trying to assure them there was nothing for them to worry about, John burst in with the stocking over his face.

'What the hell are these two doing here?' John asked, looking positively stricken at the two elderly women.

The two ladies looked at John's stocking covered face and then back at Jay dressed in a police uniform.

It took them a few seconds to absorb the situation before one of them spoke. 'You're not really coppers are you?' she said, uneasily.

'No ladies we're not, but don't worry we are not here to harm you. The master of the house has been a bit of a naughty boy and we are here to put him straight on a few matters, so unfortunately until we have completed things, we are going to have to restrain you, just as a precaution, we are not going to hurt you, unless of course you do something stupid.' John wanted to assure them, but as they couldn't see his face, it didn't make them feel any easier.

'No, we won't try to do anything, honest,' the other woman cut in nervously, anxious to let him know they wouldn't do anything silly to upset him.

'Good. So if you'll be kind enough to follow me to the lounge.'

'Right ladies, if you each sit in one of the chairs and make yourselves comfortable, I will tie you up and…' John explained as soon as they entered the lounge.

'You're not going to kill us are you?' the first woman cried out apprehensively.

'No of course we're not. We'll just keep you secure until we've finished our business and then it will all be over and you'll be free to go,' John assured them in a quiet gentle manner.

'Right, the two cleaning ladies are taken care of and I don't think they'll cause us any trouble, so let's get this bastard to start transferring the money,' John said, exasperation sounding in his voice as he came back into the study.

'David' looked around at all three of them slowly accepting he had no choice but to do what they asked, picked up the phone and tapped in the number.

'Put it on speaker,' John told him as they waited for it to be answered.

'Howzit son?' they heard a voice answer, John immediately recognising the South African accent.

'Listen dad, I'm in a bit of trouble and I need you to transfer £13,000,000 to an account number I'm going to give you and…'

'£13,000,000! Are you out of your skull, what the hell do you want to do that for?' they heard his father ask.

293

'Listen dad, I don't have time to argue, I'm in trouble and if I don't transfer that money I could be a lot more bother, so just do as I say, we've got more than enough to cover it. Don't make it too obvious, take a bit from each account, okay?'

'Okay, but it will take some time, so I'll try and have it done by tomorrow, okay?'

'No dad, I want it done now, right now?'

'Sounds like you got a gun to your head.'

'In a manner of speaking I have, so just bloody well do it.'

'Can you log in to the accounts on your computer?' John asked.

'Yes I can.'

'Good, so fire it up, so we can see it all happening.'

'There's two more cars pulled up at the rear gate,' they heard Tam's voice blurt out on the walkie talkie.

'What the bloody hell's happening now?' John exclaimed.

'That must be the kitchen fitter, he was also due to start today,' 'David' told them.

'The man's walking up to the house,' Tam's voice echoed out.

'Right we can't take any chances, I'll deal with this,' John said, pulling the stocking back over his face as he hurried out.

John waited just inside the back door for the man to walk in, then stepped out and aimed the gun at his head. 'On the floor now,' John shouted at him.

The man froze, a fearful gaze spreading on his face.

'I said, down on the floor now,' John repeated, and the man complied sinking to his knees.

'Number three, bring me some cuffs,' John called out, using Michael's co-sign.

'We haven't got any left, we've used up what we had on the others,' Michael explained, as he came out of the study.

'Damn, what else have we got we can use?'

'We got some duct tape,' Michael offered.

'Right, I suppose that will have to do. Go and get it and we'll bind him with that,' John told him.

'You're not going to kill me are you?' the trembling middle aged man pleaded.

'Not if you shut up and keep quite, we can't risk you trying to be a hero or running off, so we're going to have to tie you up until we're finished here. It's nothing to do with you, so you won't get hurt as long as you don't try anything silly. Who else is that with you in the other car?'

'My son, it's a family business, please don't hurt him.'

Michael came back with the duct tape and they both set about binding the man's hands and feet, picked him up and carried him into the lounge and dumped him on the floor. The man's eyes widened in horror as he saw the two women tied up in the chairs and let out a scream.

'Shut up,' John yelled at him, giving him a sharp kick in the ribs to quieten him. 'I suppose we'd better tape his mouth shut if he's going to open it like that.'

'No, I won't say anything honest,' the man pleaded.

'Sorry buddy, can't take that chance,' John said, tearing off a strip of the tape and stretching it across his mouth.

'You can't do that, he promised he wouldn't say anything,' one of the cleaners spoke up.

'And so did you two. You'd better tape their mouths up while we're about it while I go and talk to his son.' John told him.

Just before John ventured out, he pulled the stocking off his face and tucked it back under the baseball cap making him appear more like a police officer again.

'Can you get out of the car please sir,' John said to the young man, that he figured to be in his early twenties, as he opened the car door.

'Why, what's going on?' the young man asked, his eyes alive with curiosity.

'Police investigation in progress,' John explained, flashing his fake ID. 'Just follow me back to the house, so we can verify who you are and what your purpose is in being here.'

'I've come to help me dad and...'

'Yes, well you can explain all that when we get to the house. Now get out of the car and follow me,' John said forcefully, raising his voice a little to show authority.

This is beginning to fall apart, John thought as the young man followed him up to the house.

John steered the young man past Jay who was holding down 'David' at gunpoint and steered him into the lounge, where he was confronted with the sight of his father and the two cleaning ladies tied up.

'What have you done to my dad you bastards, you're not police you're just a bunch of thugs,' the young man cried out, swinging round to take a swipe at John who simply blocked the blow and whacked him across the head. The young man was no match for John's blow and buckled at the knees, sinking to the floor.

'Now behave yourself, or you're going to get really hurt, just shut up and stay down, we're going to have to bind you so you don't try and do anything silly.' John explained, as he and Tam set about binding his hands and feet with the duct tape before gagging him.

'You keep an eye on them while I go and see what is happening with 'David'.' John said, hurrying out the room.

'This is getting out of hand mate, we've got seven hostages tied up and we're now running out of duct tape. This could be all over Crime Watch if we're not careful. We need to get out of here fast. How is the transfer going?'

'Alright by the look of things, we're just waiting for the last £4,000,000 to be transferred and we're done,' Jay told him.

'Okay, so all I want now is the combination of the safe I can see tucked away in the corner and then we are done with you,' John said, pulling out the gun, putting it to 'David''s head. 'Better still to save a lot of time, you open it. Number Two can keep watch on the computer,' John added acknowledging Jay, cocking the gun to let 'David' know he hadn't got a choice.

'David' reluctantly got up from the chair and moved to the safe, applied the combination and opened it. John shoved him aside, reached in and took hold of the bundles of money stacked in neat piles.

'There's twenty eight grand there,' 'David' told him. 'I can get another forty grand here very quickly if you don't want to hang about and wait for the rest to transfer,' David offered, 'I only have to make a quick call.'

John thought hard for a moment, 'No thanks. You think we're that stupid to let you make a call. You could be phoning the cavalry for all we know. The twenty eight grand will do nicely. Just get on with transferring the money,' John said, clutching the bundles to his chest as he walked out to the lounge.

'Now, before we untie you ladies and let you go, we would like to offer you some compensation for what you've been through. I'm giving each of you ten grand,' John announced, holding up some of the wads of notes he was clutching. 'That's to help you forget this morning's edification, so you don't go running to the police. 'And you two,' John said turning to look down at the two men. 'I will make sure 'David' gives you an equivalent amount. You can be sure he will, because he'd have too much to lose by not paying you off; but understand if any of you decide to go to the police, then I promise you we'll come looking for you and you wouldn't like what would happen when we found you. Nobody leave here for at least a half an hour, okay? I suggest you sit quietly and count your good fortune. I mean where else could you earn that sort of money cleaning or fixing kitchens?' John said, with a cheeky smile. 'Are you all agreed?' John asked.

'They all nodded their heads as enthusiastically as their restrained movements would allow.

'Good, so now, we'll untie you and I want you to hand over your mobile phones,' John explained. 'Now try to relax while my friend here looks after you,' he added, indicating Michael.

'It's all done, the four mill' has just gone through, so we're done,' John heard Jay say as he came out of the study and followed him into the kitchen. 'This will stop them phoning anyone, and don't forget to cut the land line before we go,' John said, as he placed the plug in the sink, turned on both taps and let it fill before dumping in the collection of mobile phones.

'Right let's get the hell out here,' John said, turning off the taps. 'Just one other thing,' he said to 'David' as they both returned to the study. 'I've taken care of the cleaners, and I suggest when we've gone you get that forty grand to pay off the kitchen fitter and his son, that's the only way you will be able to persuade them not to go to the police. We know you and your mates upstairs won't, but they as sure as hell will if you don't take care of them and you will certainly lose the millions you've still got stashed away.'

'Yeah, don't worry. I'll take care of them,' 'David' said, with an air of inevitability.

'How the hell did we never know about the cleaners and the place being redecorated?' Jay sighed, as they drove away, a tinge of anger in his voice.

'If Darren had done his job properly the first time around then he should have known about the cleaners,' John said, sounding even angrier.

'But they only come in once a week and Darren wasn't there all week and how the hell would any of us known about the decorators?' Michael spoke up in Darren's defence.

I just hope they don't bloody well got to the police, because we could be in for it if they do,' Michael said, worriedly.

'No they won't, I made sure of that, I gave the cleaners ten grand each and the kitchen...'

'You did what, you gave away twenty of the twenty eight grand to the bloody cleaners?' Jay retorted, angrily.

'Eight grand, that doesn't leave a lot for us,' Michael cut in.

'Bloody right after all the effort we've put in,' Tam moaned.

'Listen lads, you've got two grand apiece pocket money. The big money is yet to come. Don't forget we get twenty percent of £13,000,000 – just work it out for yourselves.'

THE SMELL OF FEAR

2001

The German was very pleased with the outcome and assured them they would get their percentage of the £13,000,000. He offered to set up an offshore account for them so he could transfer the money across and give them a code and password to access the account. He also had another job for them, because as well as Spider in Benidorm, there were three other guys, based in the Newcastle area, who had cheated him for around £7,000,000 and he wanted them dealt with. Better still if they were up for it, he wanted them kidnapped and brought to him at his factory in St Austell, Cornwall.

With the promise of another percentage of £7,000,000, John, along with his team were well up for it. Meeting up at Oscars bar, they got their gear and set off for Newcastle. The three guys, The German had told them were known as James, William and Steven. The only address he had for them was James' because that was where all the transactions had taken place. John had bought two old cars that no one would take any notice of and installed a delayed action camera that recorded a picture every minute, concealed in a shoe box on the back shelf of each of them.

James lived in a large semi-detached house, in a rather up market area on the outskirts of Newcastle and John set up the first car outside the house to record the comings and goings of the three men and parked the other car at the street entrance before joining Jay, Michael and Tam at a local hotel where they booked in under false names. Later that evening after retrieving the tapes, the team watched the recordings. 'That one must be James,' John voiced, 'He fits the description The German gave us, short and stocky and dressed like a stockbroker.'

'And that has to be William, really weedy looking bloke with a kind of nerdy way about him,' Michael cut in, as they continued to study the recording.

Steven, the third man never showed up either entering or leaving the house in any of the recordings. This made it easier in a way as they only had two to concentrate on.

John reckoned it would be too risky to attempt a kidnapping in such a closed neighbourhood and decided to send Jay and Michael to follow the two men the next day to see where they disappear to each morning. They were easy to follow as they drove around in a flashy bright red Porsche, which led them to a small factory on the edge of an industrial estate just outside of Newcastle. It was the perfect place for a kidnapping. With the factory decided upon as the best place, the team headed back to Merseyside so John could set about finding a suitable vehicle. He was told about a Scouser who modified vans for bank robbers and drug dealers. Surprisingly, Bill Oakes was not a Scouser but spoke with a strong cockney accent.

'Oakes's the name, hoax's the game, what can I do yer for?' he asked, as John stepped into the tiny hut that acted as his office.

'I want a van with a sliding side door, the inside panelled, the floor as well as the walls and the rear door windows to be blacked out,' John told him.

'Shouldn't be a prob, give me a day or two and I'll see what I can come up wiv,' Bill promised him.

Bill as good as his word, came up with a van a few days later. It was a long wheeled based Ford Transit, fitted out as John had asked, together with fake tax disc and fake MOT certificate.

Delighted John, Jay, Michael and Tam set off back to Newcastle having equipped themselves with handcuffs, duct tape, cable ties, two pillow cases, two decorators white overalls and slip on shoes as well a shotgun, John's Browning 9mm pistol and two baseball bats. They also had the police outfits they had used on the previous raid on 'David.'

The Porsche pulled up outside the factory and the adrenaline began to course through John's veins as they waited until James and William went inside before driving the van up to the entrance. Using the same tactics as before, they charged in with Jay dressed in the police uniform shouting out. 'Stay where you are, this is a police raid, place your hands behind your backs.'

John and the others rushed forward with swift practiced movements and cuffed them both as Jay told them they were being arrested as part of an ongoing investigation into VAT fraud and proceeded to caution them. John and the others had to suppress a laugh, they hadn't expected Jay to do that and he was word perfect.

While Michael and Tam held onto them, John made a quick search of the premises to see if there was a safe or anything worth taking. There was no safe and nothing of any value to be found.

'Right, we're taking you in an undercover van to the police station where you will be questioned. Another team of police and custom officials will come and search the place thoroughly as well as your home. Let's get them out of here,' John said.

'What about my Porsche,' James asked as he and William were marched out to the van.

'Where are the keys?' John asked William.

'In my pocket.'

John felt in his trouser pocket and found the keys. 'Right, I will put the keys on the bench just inside the door and we'll radio HQ and tell them to deal with it when they arrive,' John told him in an authoritive manner.

Both were hauled into the back of the van and made to sit down crossed legged. John and Jay got in and stood either side to keep watch over them. Tam and Michael sat up front with Tam driving.

As they felt the van move James glared at both of them, his eyes narrowing in undisguised malice as he said. 'you're not police, where you taking us?'

'Shut your mouth, you'll find out soon enough,' John shouted at him.

'You bastards tricked us and you'll pay for this.'

'He told you to shut your mouth,' Jay said, getting to his feet, reaching up to the shelf above the two men, grabbing one of the baseball bats.

John restrained Jay's hand, staring into Jay's eyes with a steely glare John said. 'Leave this to me,' he was worried Jay would go overboard.

Like a reprimanded child, Jay let go of the bat and moved back.

'You think you can frighten us with that thing. That's nothing to what will happen to you lot when we get out of here.' James said, vehemently.

John had seen that look before and had learned what it meant to those who were unlucky to be on the receiving end of it, it caused a surge of rage to course through John's body and in an instant he whacked James with a measured glancing blow.

Jay looked at John as he saw blood start to flow from the wound opening up on James's forehead. 'And you warned me to try to keep them in one piece.'

'You lot don't know what you're dealing with and when...' William stuttered, his unease mounting.

John whacked him across the nose and then across the top of his head so that blood was now gushing from his nose and head. William let out a scream as his face scrunched in pain.

'I won't tell you to shut your gob again, open it and you'll get more of this,' John said, caressing the baseball bat watching, his face colouring below where he had struck him.

'I think we should we should put the hoods on them,' John suggested, looking at the two of them with blood gushing from their heads.

'You're not going to kill us are you?' William asked, dread uncurling in his stomach.

'No, we're taking you to meet The German, he's pissed off you stole £7,000,000 from him and he wants it back,' John told him, seeing William's eyes come up and fix sharply on his face, the shock and fear clear to see.

A smile twisted John's lips as he looked at their agitated faces, drawing his gun in a fluid practiced movement. 'Like all thieving bastards, you think you can get away with it. The thing about luck is, eventually it runs out – and yours ran out today,' John told them, watching William's eyes still calculating.

'We can sort it out with The German it's just a misunderstanding, that's all. When we explain he'll understand. You'll see,' James said, but knew as he was saying it, it was a useless thing to say and John could see it in his face.

'Some people don't like to be ripped off and never forget when they are, and The German has a good memory it seems, which I'm sure he will remind you of when you meet up with him and...'

'I've had enough of listening to this, put the hoods on them or I'll beat them to death,' Jay said, gripping the baseball bat ready to swing it. Jay held William by the throat pulling the pillow case over his head. William thinking about what The German was going to be doing to them and sensing Jay's heated aggression almost fainted; he shitted himself.

'What the hell is that smell, have you just crapped yourself? No point in trying to knock the crap out of you now,' Jay said sardonically, lowering the baseball bat from above William's head.

'Bloody hell, it does reek, if you're expecting us to wipe your arse you got another think coming,' John quipped, as he and Jay took out the other pillow case to put over James's head. 'Not another word out either of you. It's bad enough we have sit here amongst this stench without having to listen to you both whining,' John added, as James began to sob underneath the pillow case.

John shook his head at the stupidity and arrogance of them, believing nothing could ever happen to them and now that it has, they're acting like little girl's blouses crying and shitting themselves like animals.

'The cops are coming, you want us to pull off here?' Michael called out on the walkie talkie.

'I know, we can hear it. Just keep calm and tell Tam not to speed up. They can't possibly know about the kidnapping, it's far too early for any reports to have come in.' John told him, as he and Jay moved closer to James and William who had started to shuffle about on hearing the siren approaching from behind.

John shoved the pistol to James's head while Jay shoved the shotgun to William's head. 'Either one of you make a noise or tries to stand up, you're both dead.'

John and Jay listened anxiously as the police siren got louder and louder as it got closer to the van, but to their relief, it sped on past and the noise of the siren slowly diminished up the motorway and into the distance.

After a six hour journey they arrived at The German's factory. Once the van had come to a stop, Tam hopped out and pulled back the sliding door and the smell immediately overwhelmed him, so much so he threw up. 'Bloody hell, what a stink. How the hell did you manage to put up with that?' he asked, as he straightened up, his face ashen.

'We didn't have much choice in the matter,' John said, getting out and breathing in the fresh air.

'I've seen men scared before, but I've never seen a man shit scared,' Michael chuckled, laughing at his own humour, the toxic smell of blood, urine and faeces hitting him as he got out of the cab to join them.

'Yes, I must admit, it's the first time I've seen a man do that. I never realised I had that effect on people,' John said, with a sardonic air. 'Right, can you guys get them out of those smelly clothes and into the white overalls, but keep their heads covered, while I go and see The German,' John told them.

'Does that mean we have to wipe their bloody arses?'

'Do what you have to,' John told them as he hurried off.

As John approached the factory entrance he spotted a hose pipe attached to a tap on the wall. 'Bring them into the factory and when you've stripped them off you can hose the bastards down with this,' he called out. 'Just make sure you keep the hoods on.'

John was impressed as he continued into the factory for it was enormous with heavy machinery lining the floor, but it was quiet, an eerie silence pervaded the area, the machines were idle and there were no workers anywhere to be seen. It was a strange feeling and it made John feel uncomfortable. *Had he come to the right place? Had they got the address wrong? Was it a trap and they were the fall guys, or was Lloyd betraying The German and in cahoots with Spider, maybe it was a set up to get them caught red handed on a charge of kidnapping?* 'he pondered, as he continued to look cautiously around, his ears tuned, listening for any slight sudden movement.

'Ah, you got here at last,' he heard a voice call out and he began to relax as he recognised the voice of The German.

The German was standing by a doorway at the end of the factory with Lloyd by his side. Relieved to see Lloyd smiling as a sign everything was okay, John made his way towards them.

'Where are the two *scheibehauser* scumbags?' The German asked, in his guttural accent. John noticed how smartly dressed he was in another tailored dark blue silk suit, his blue tie knotted expertly, blending perfectly with the pale blue silk shirt, his shoes shining in contrast to the dull grey dirty greasy concrete floor.

'Funny you should call them shitbags, one of them was so scared he actually shat himself,' John told him, which made them both laugh.

'They're still in vun piece I hope,' the German said, worriedly. 'I've things to ask them.'

'Oh, they'll be alright, they're just about to have a shower,' John said, whimsically.

'Very thoughtful of you, sounds like they need it after what you told me,' The German said as he guided John into the room behind him.

It was a large room that may have been a storage area at some point, but was now empty save for a desk with a kettle and cups and other bits on it. There were two swivel chairs in front of the desk facing each other.

'When they're ready bring them in vun at a time, but make sure you keep their heads covered. I can't wait to see those two schnivelling bastards,' The German said, moving across and sitting himself down in one of the swivel chairs.

'When they're ready, we'll take William in first,' John told Jay, as he came back to join them. 'I suggest you and Michael give the van a hose down as we're going to have to travel back in it and I don't want to sit in the back with that putrid smell,' he said to Tam.

John and Jay dragged the struggling William into the room, pushed him down on the empty swivel chair, bound him to it with duct tape and spun him round to face The German.

'You can remove the hood,' The German said.

John yanked the pillow case off and William began to shake as he stared at The German, his chest so tight he could hardly breathe.

The German took a hard measured look at his blood congealed face. 'I want to know what you have done with the £7,000,000 you stole from me and...'

'We didn't steal seven mill'...'

'Shut the schnivelling *Dieb* up,' The German screamed, looking across at John.

'Shut up and listen,' John said, as he whacked him hard across the back of the head.

'Things are going to get a lot worse, if you don't tell me what I want to know,' The German warned him.

William began to shake uncontrollably. 'Look I don't know where the £7,000,000 is. It was something arranged by James and David, you know I don't have anything to do with the bank account and...' he pleaded between frightened sobs of tears.

'Get rid of this *rauber* and bring the other vun in,' The German said, a flare of anger rising in him.

John and Jay ripped off the duct tape securing him to the chair, hauled him up and dragged him out.

'William seems to think you're the one with all the answers,' John said, as he and Jay grabbed hold of James and dragged him off.

'Okay, so William says you know where the £7,000,000 is and what it's got to do what that other *schwindler* David,' The German said, as soon as John and Jay had secured him to the chair.

As they removed the pillow case James looked at The German and a shudder of fear ran through him, then he spotted Lloyd. 'What you doing with this lot?' he asked, giving him an expectant look.

'Never mind about him, tell me where my money is, or you are in *schwierigkeiten sein*?' The German hissed into his face, spittle flying out with every word of his own language. 'Do you think I am a *dummkorpf*, I know what you did.'

John moved over to the table and switched on the kettle making sure James saw what he was doing, as The German eased his chair closer to James. 'So let's not mess around playing games, you know where the money is and I want it back, simple as that, if not, you'll die. I don't have time to waste.'

'Maybe this will help persuade him,' John said, carrying the kettle across and aiming the spout at his groin. 'If you don't tell us where the money is, I'm going to pour this over your crown jewels and the last time I did that, the man was forced to change his sex,' John threatened.

James felt a stab of fright in the pit of his stomach as he cried out. 'No please, its okay I'll tell you, please don't.'

'So tell us,' The German said, beginning to lose patience.

'I can tell you where the money is, but I can't access it, you will have to talk to David, he's the mastermind. He has all the bank details and codes to access the money. I don't care about the money, I didn't want to get involved in the first place, but David told us you had ripped him off and that you were going to rip us off so suggested he put a few million aside for us, honest.'

The German's face darkened with anger. 'You expect me to believe that. How is it you *uneheliches* get so devious to earn the extra buck when you were earning so well with me?'

'Like I said, we believed what David told us, look I don't care about the money, you can have it all, I just want to go home,' James pleaded.

'Damn generous of you since it was my money in the first place, you *gauner*,' The German said throwing him a scornful look before turning his attention to John. 'While he tells me the finer details you two get ready to take the two of them to some quiet place and wait to hear from me that this *uneheliches* is telling the truth, if not you know what to do.'

It was not what John expected to hear, but he was already too far in to argue or disobey. 'Sure,' he said, turning and walking out with Jay.

'You know, when you threatened him with the kettle I had my legs clenched together at the thought. I've known you do some dastardly deeds in your time, but burn a man's nuts off with boiling water. Did you really do that?' Jay asked, as soon as they got outside.

'No of course I didn't,' John said, his lips twisting in amusement. 'And you know what, when I went over and switched the kettle on, I immediately switched it off, so there was no boiling water in it.'

'Well, it certainly convinced him and it convinced me. I really thought you were going to do it,' Jay told him.

'The important thing was, he believed it, and that saved us a lot of trouble.'

'I'd have sooner whacked the *unehelicke*r or whatever it is he called him, over the head.'

'I think it's German for crook or bastard,' John explained, as they came to where Michael and Tam were holding William.

'Right put the cuffs on him and get him in the van, then we need to burn their clothes, as the other one will be out soon and then we'll be off,' John told them.

'Where we going?' Michael asked.

'I don't know yet, depends on what is happening in there.'

A few minutes later Lloyd came out holding onto James' handcuffed wrists. 'You can take him now,' he said, shoving him forward as he turned and looked at John. 'The German wants a quick word.'

'I want you to take them somewhere in the countryside where you can't be seen and wait for my phone call, because if the information he's given me proves to be a con, then I want you to dispose of them, understood?' The German informed him.

John felt his blood run cold, he was talking murder. Kidnapping was one thing but murder was something else.

The German noticed the flicker of doubt dart across his face. 'What's the matter, not up to it?' he asked with cold menace in his voice.

'No problem,' John quickly assured him. 'It's just that, well you're only paying us to kidnap them, you never mentioned anything about...'

'Okay, if you have to do it, I'll double your fee, does that make you feel better?' The German said, with an air of condescension.

It really is the root of all evil, when the thought of making big money can so easily change you' John thought as he came back out to join the others at the van.

It was getting dark as they drove into open country. 'That's looks a good place,' John said, spotting some open fields surrounded by trees.

'Yeah looks good to me,' Jay agreed, surveying the area for any sign of people. 'Just a few cows over there, but I don't think there's any chance of them running to the police,' Jay said, jovially to ease the tension.

'Right, get them out, walk them a hundred yards into that field and lay them down on the grass,' John said to Michael and Tam after he opened the side door of the van.

'What's happening now?' Tam asked, as he got out and looked around the open field.

'We just wait here until we get a call from The German,' John explained.

'Telling us to do what?' Michael asked, a worried frown flickering between his brows.

'Kill the bastards,' John said.

The answer caught Tam by surprise and he froze for a moment letting the word sink in. 'You mean he wants us to kill them?' he asked, a shiver of apprehension running down his spine.

'Oh no, please, don't kill us, we've done what he asked,' William whimpered. He could hear what was being said although they still had the hoods over their heads.

'No, you won't kill us, you're thugs but you're not murderers,' James called out, his voice quivering.

'You better hope so, because if The German says you're to die, then die you will, so keep your mouths shut or I might just do it anyway,' John told James, giving him a whack over the head with the Browning.

Just then John's mobile rang. 'You'd better start praying because if it's The German and he tells me you have given him a load of crap, then it's all over,' he said, as he pressed the green button, listened and a wry smile broke on his face as he clicked it off.

Tam stared intensely at John. 'Look, I want nothing to do with murder, what we've done so far is fine, but killing, no, and...'

'It's okay, we're to hang on, they're still checking out everything and we should know something in the next ten minutes or so,' John told him.

'Yeah well, whatever, I want nothing to do with any killing,' Tam persisted.

John looked at him his gaze sharp, 'Tam whether you like it or not, you're involved just as much as we are and there is no way round it if you want to keep what you're going to earn, if they've got to be got rid of, so be it.'

It was a long agonising ten minutes, the scenario of what he might have to do playing like an endless loop in John's mind. He checked the Browning, cocking and uncocking it, simply for something to do as uncertainty tugged at his sleeve, his heart was beating fast. The urge to go ahead and do what he felt he was going to be told to do and damn the consequences was overwhelming. It was giving him an exhilarating feeling and he had never felt before.

'Do you want to shoot both of them or can I have a pop?' Jay asked, caressing the shotgun he was holding, jerking John out of his revelry.

'No, the shotgun will be too messy, a bullet to the head will be quick and clean, leave it to me,' John told him, his resolve returning, his face curling in determination.

The mobile started ringing, John took a long deep breath, the pulse in his body speeding up as he answered, the rest of them watching his face to try to read what he was being told. His face remained implacable until the call ended and then eased into a soft smile.

'It's your lucky day, The German has told us to let you go. You seemed to have told him what he wanted to know. So this is the thing, we're going to leave you here and be on our way. We're going to take off the handcuffs but leave the hoods on. You wait here for a good fifteen minutes. Don't risk leaving before then, because we could just be waiting to see if you do and then you will get a bullet, okay.'

'Now we've got a percentage of twenty million to split between us. That's what I call a good day's work,' Jay said, reflectively, sitting up front with John driving and Tam and Michael in the back.

CRIME DOESN'T ALWAYS PAY

John's mobile started ringing, making him react with a jolt. He took the phone out of his pocket and pushed the answer button.

'Where are you?' he heard Lloyd's voice ask him.

'Having a celebratory drink with the boys and talking about what we're all going to be doing with the money.'

'Can you go somewhere quiet, I need to tell you something,' Lloyd told him, and John wasn't sure whether he sensed tension in his voice, as he walked out of the pool room at Oscars to find a quieter place to listen.

'Right, I can hear you better now. So when's the money coming through?' John said, hoping that's what Lloyd was ringing about.

There was a long pause before Lloyd spoke, his voice hesitant. 'There's been a problem and...'

'What bloody problem? We've done our bit and want our money.'

'That's the problem, The German's is in no position to make the payment, he's...'

A chill swept over John as he felt the words penetrate his brain. 'Why the hell not?'

'He's been arrested and remanded in custody, his cars are all there in the drive and the place is locked up, they're going to seize all his assets so there is nothing he can do. I've been caught out too, he owes me hundreds of thousands and...'

'He owes us bloody millions. We risked our lives and I was even prepared to kill for that bastard. I'm going to have to come and see you Lloyd, because I'm not sure I trust what you're telling me,' John said, his words heavy with scepticism.

'I have to go,' Lloyd said, before John had a chance to say anymore and a feeling of emptiness engulfed him as he heard Lloyd's phone click off.

John stared at the voiceless phone, feeling the whole weight of what he had been told and it felt like a physical blow, all the hurt and the risks that he and the others had taken, ready to kill if they had to, seemed to flood up his throat, almost choking him as random thoughts flooded his brain. *Nothing worth having is easy. We went into this because the higher the risk, the greater the rewards, but if you play the game you should know the pitfalls. I should have known, these people are crooks and seen the trouble before it arrives. How am I going to tell them it was all for nothing, all those things we were going to do with the money, now just dreams, pipe dreams of what might have been?*

'Come on John, it's your bloody turn, I've played three shots for you while you've been chatting away with Jenny telling her what you're going to be doing with the money,' Michael said jokingly, handing him the cue.

John didn't take the cue, and the intensity of his gaze began to unnerve Michael. 'What's the matter John?' he asked, giving him an expectant look.

'That was Lloyd on the phone, calling to say The German has been arrested and we aren't going to get our money.'

All three stared at him, positively stricken, though unable to process the reality of what he had just told them.

'Is this some kind of wind up?' Jay asked angrily.

'No, Lloyd told me, The German was being held on remand and the CPS are going to seize all his assets, there's no chance of us getting our money.'

The words hung over them like a heavy cloud, confusion and uncertainty written all over their faces.

'This is a rip off,' Tam exploded.

'Yeah, we're being ripped off. How do we know he's been arrested, he could have buggered off back to Germany for all we know,' Michael said vindictively.

'I'll kill the thieving bastards,' Jay screamed, seized by a sense of outrage, snapping the cue and hurling it to the floor with a clatter. 'Come on let's go and find the scheming bastards and sort them out.' Jay said, kicking the broken cue with the toe of his shoe causing the two halves to shoot across the floor, his eyes ablaze with fury.

*

'Know anyone who wants to buy a helicopter?'

'Are you still taking the piss?' Jay said, pulling out his gun and raising it to Lloyd's head. 'We just want to know where our money is and where that shit of a German is.' Jay added forcefully, pressing the gun hard against Lloyd's forehead after he and Michael had pinned him to the ground.

'That's what I was doing when you charged into the garage ready to blow my head off,' Lloyd told him.

'What do you mean, that's what you were doing. It looked to me like you were ready to do a runner?' John said, his eyes narrowing in a disguised malice.

'Searching for the paperwork to do with the helicopter, I've got the keys and I know which hanger it's in, it belongs to one of the companies I set up for The German. It's worth a few million and if we can sell it quick I'm happy to split the proceeds with you.'

'Oh yeah, would you have been willing to do that, if we hadn't come looking for you?' John asked the malice still in his voice.

'Yes, I was going to get in touch with you when I got everything together, the helicopter is the only thing that with a bit of luck the Customs won't be able to get their hands on. If you let me up and point that gun somewhere else, I can explain more,' Lloyd told them, a spark of fear flaring in his eyes.

'Let him up,' John told them.

Jay and Michael released their grip on Lloyd and hauled him to his feet.

'So explain,' John said, his eyes fixed sharply on his face expectantly. 'Just remember I have a rule, people mess with me at their own risk.'

'I'm not messing with you. The German has been arrested and is on remand in Birmingham's Winson Green prison. He's is not only being charged with VAT fraud, but also with the kidnapping of James and William.'

All four of them exchanged horrified looks. 'Is the bastard going to name us?' Tam asked, in anguish. 'Because once you let that genie out of the bottle it's bloody impossible to put it back.'

'No I don't think he will, because it would only implicate him more and link him to other frauds; besides he doesn't know your real names or where you're from,' Lloyd assured them.

'I hope you're bloody right,' Michael uttered.

'Look John, I've been caught out just as you have and I would like to get my money back, which is why I can only think of selling the 'copter. As I said, it's worth a few mill', so do you guys know anyone who wants to buy it?'

'Oh yeah, someone was only asking me the other day if I knew where he could buy a helicopter. Are you kidding, I wouldn't have a clue. How about you guys?' John asked, turning to the others.

'You know the guy you bought the van from, maybe he might know someone,' Jay suggested, with a hapless shrug.

'No, it's not like selling a car, trying to flog a helicopter could raise a lot of suspicion and a lot of questions being asked. No, I think we better leave that well alone.'

'The only thing I can suggest is I try and sell the 'copter and you lot go after Spider. I was over there about four weeks ago taking some paper work for The German and while I was in there Spider showed me a holdall stuffed with Euros and Pounds. He told me there was about a hundred grand just in that bag alone and he still had the shoe boxes crammed full, so I reckon there must well over a million in cash ripe for the taking. It's all yours if you want to go for it. I'll try and sell the helicopter. If I just manage to get a million I'll be happy and disappear out of the country,' Lloyd explained.

FLY TO CATCH A SPIDER

2002

They had been in Benidorm for four days and had met up with Big Jimmy McQuade, a Scouser running the doors at some of the biggest clubs in Benidorm. Jimmy was into running drugs and arms and Jay knew him through his army connections. He was a big brute of a man and good to have on your side. Jimmy managed to get hold of a couple of stun guns, but they weren't Taser guns and needed to be pressed against the body of the victim to be effective. He was also hoping to have a pistol and ammo for them in a couple of days. John asked if he could get four Spanish police uniforms which Jimmy assured him wouldn't be a problem.

As luck would have it John telephoned Lloyd to find out what the situation was with The German, just in case he had been released and was able to transfer the money, but Lloyd told him The German was still on remand and awaiting trial with every prospect he would be going down for a very long stretch. Lloyd asked how things were going with Spider and John told him everything thing was on course, just waiting for a gun in case it was needed.

He heard Lloyd give a little laugh as he explained, 'you don't have to wait, Spider keeps a gun, a Smith and Wesson, I think it's a 357 magnum. He keeps it in a cubby hole by the front door. So you can grab it as soon as you force your way or whichever way you plan to get in.'

With the problem of the gun resolved, the only other problem was the two Rhodesian Ridge Back dogs that Spider let roam around his grounds. Jay arranged to get some heavy tranquilisers from Jimmy, lace them into a couple of juicy steaks and feed them to the dogs by throwing them over the fence; that would put them out of action in no time. To be certain of things, John decided to do one more day of surveillance with all of them walking around like holiday makers out having a good time. By chance they stopped by the local supermarket to get some drinks, John went into the store and while Jay queued up at the cash machine John stood to one side and to his surprise saw Spider walk in and brush past him. John froze for a moment, not sure what to do. Jay was oblivious to the situation as he tried to withdraw cash with the pre-loaded card he had bought in the UK.

You can't take him down here, not infront of all these witnesses, we're not armed, we haven't even got the stun guns, so we could find ourselves in a lot of trouble. John reasoned as he waited anxious for Jay to complete the transaction.

'What the hell's the matter?' Jay asked, looking at John's face as soon as they were out of the supermarket.

'Spider, he's in there.'

'No way, let's get the bastard,' Jay exclaimed, spinning on his heels ready to charge back inside.

John grabbed his arm and held him back. 'No we can't, there are too many people about and we can't risk it.

Jay looked around at the number of people moving around and others just sitting outside their houses watching the comings and goings as they did every day. 'Yeah, I guess you're right,' Jay reluctantly agreed.

'Don't worry we'll get our chance,' John assured him.

'It has to be tomorrow, because we have to get back to Algarve or we will miss our return flight,' Jay reminded him.

'No problem we've got the uniforms and everything else we need, so tomorrow it is and after that we can charter a bloody plane to fly us back if we want to.'

'No, we've still got to behave like tourists to avoid suspicion,' Jay cautioned.

'Yeah, I know I was only joking.'

With everything set they put on the police uniforms, keeping them covered with coats as they got in the car and drove off. The adrenaline was beginning to build, every muscle strained as they pulled up outside the villa.

'This is it guys,' John said. 'Should be as easy as taking candy from a baby,' he added with a chuckle. But the chuckle instantly stuck in his throat as he watched in bewilderment as a minibus pulled up right outside the villa and a whole family of men, women and children, all Eastern European looking piled out. The gates opened and Spider came out to greet them and usher them inside.

'I don't believe it, what the hell is this?' Tam exclaimed, unable to comprehend what was happening after all the careful surveillance they had done.

'What the hell do we do now?' Jay asked, exasperation hardening his words as he stared in total disbelief at the scene unfolding.

'There's nothing we can do,' John said, starting the engine and driving off.

'You mean we've done all this for diddly squat? Michael exclaimed with disbelief.

John could see the confusion in their eyes and knew it was reflected in his own thoughts, of all things he expected to happen today, this was certainly not one of them.

'No, not exactly,' John hesitated to say, looking at their agitated faces. 'We know all we need to know about him and we'll just have to come back and do it another time.'

'Why can't we do it tomorrow?' Tam asked.

'Because if we do we will miss our flights,' Jay cut in.

'But then we'll have more than enough money to pay for our own fares,' Michael interjected.

'We've just seen a family arrive and we have no idea how long they're going to be staying and we're running out of money. Jay's tried the card again, but the machine swallowed it, so if we miss the flight we'll be well and truly stranded,' John explained.

'It's not fair, there's no justice in this world,' Jay said, scornfully.

HAVE THEY STILL GOT THE STOMACH FOR IT?

2003

Christmas had come and gone and it was now February 2003 before John had got enough money together from working the door at Oscars to pay for the trip back to Spain. The plan this time was that he and Jay would fly direct to Benidorm, do a recce to make sure Spider was still at the villa and nobody else was there. Once they were satisfied it was okay to go ahead, they would phone to tell Tam and Michael to come out.

After John and Jay had booked into a cheap hotel, they went out to find an equally cheap restaurant to have a meal. They found a small place that's specialty was paella and decided to share a dish to keep the cost down. As they got back to the hotel and settled down for the night, Jay started to get the shakes.

'What's the matter Jay?' John asked. 'The food wasn't that bad,' he quipped, jokingly.

'I don't know, but I feel bloody horrible,' he said, leaping off the bed and rushing off to the bathroom.

John heard him retching, wondering what the hell could have caused it as he felt perfectly fine. Jay emerged from the bathroom, his face drained of all colour, his body shaking all over as he stumbled back to his bed and collapsed on it as though all his energy had been completely drained from him.

John went to help him and was surprised he was now shivering with fever. He pulled the duvet from under the prostrate Jay and covered him not bothering to get him to undress, hoping his clothing and the duvet would be extra warmth to stop the shivering. In the morning Jay was even worse and in no state to go anywhere, so John decided he would let him rest in bed while he went and did a recce of Spider's place.

John was relieved to discover there was no family there. The only other person he saw coming and going was a pretty young Eastern European looking woman whom he guessed was Spider's girlfriend. *Well, if we have to take her down as well, so be it,* he thought as he studied her walking down to the supermarket. Satisfied this time they wouldn't be any problems, he made his way to the abandoned building site next to Spider's villa. Walking around with a clip board, pretending he was doing a survey, he retrieved one of the stun guns and a small truncheon they had stashed on the previous trip.

As he made his way back to the hotel he had an uneasy feeling in his stomach and began to feel a little sick. By the time he got to their room, he was already starting to shake like Jay. A feeling of coldness enveloping him, he dumped the stun gun and truncheon in the nearest holdall. For three days John and Jay were unable to move out of their beds, sometimes almost lapsing into periods of unconsciousness neither knowing what was causing it. John decided they had to get to a chemist to get some medication, struggling to even get dressed they both headed down to reception. The hotel porter viewed them suspiciously, thinking they were high on drugs, told him of a chemist about a quarter of a mile away.

The pharmacist looked at them in the same way the porter had, thinking they were a couple of junkies needing a fix. With neither able to speak Spanish it was difficult trying to explain what they were suffering with. The pharmacist in an attempt to get rid of them offered some medication, which they took, having no idea what it was as the wording was in Spanish. They left the chemist and hailed a taxi, but the driver took one look at them and drove on. They ended up supporting each other as they made their way slowly back towards the hotel, rattling like a couple of junkies in desperate need of a fix.

'I don't think I'm going to be able to make it back to the hotel at this rate,' Jay said, stopping to take a rest.

Summoning up the energy to continue, Jay spotted a travel agency, turned to John and said. 'It's no good, we can't stay here we need to get back home, the way I feel I could die here.'

'Yeah, I'm beginning to feel the same, let's go in and see if we can change our flights,' John readily agreed, now feeling just as bad as Jay.

With luck and playing on their sickness, the travel agent took sympathy on them and arranged a flight for the next day for a small fee.

With all the effort of getting to the airport and waiting to board the plane their condition was getting as worse as it could be with both of them shivering uncontrollably.

'They'll never let us on the plane in the state we're in,' Jay said, apprehensively, his voice shaking.

'We're just going to have to hold ourselves together until we get on the plane and once it's up in the air we'll be okay,' John told him, trying to convince himself as well as Jay.

'Are you alright?' the stewardess asked as she walked down the aisle checking that everyone had fastened their seat belts.

'Yeah, it's just that, well as it was our last night and we sort of splashed out a bit and had a load too much to drink and now we're paying the price. I've got the hangover of all hangovers and he's no better, we'll be alright when we've slept it off on the flight back,' John said, trying to control the shaking as much as he could.

The stewardess paused for a moment studying them carefully, considering whether they were a health risk to other passengers as well as themselves. 'If you need a blanket let me know,' she invited.

'Yes please a blanket would be great,' Jay said to her.

'I will get some for you,' she said, quickly moving along to check the other passenger's seat belts.

They slept the entire flight and only came awake when the stewardess shook them to tell them to bring their seats back up to upright position and fasten their seat belts. Incredibly, as the plane made its final approach to Heathrow they started to feel better. It was as though they had travelled through a void and been cleansed of their ailments.

As they cleared Customs they were miraculously back to normal with all symptoms of the sickness having gone.

'I don't know about you, but I'm starving, I haven't eaten a bloody thing for four days,' Jay said, as he spotted a burger bar across the concourse.

'I've not eaten for the last three days either, I'm just as starving as you are,' John said, as they both quickened their pace towards the burger bar.

'I don't know how the hell we're going to explain this to Michael and Tam,' Jay said, biting hungrily into his double cheese burger. 'They'll never believe a bloody word of what happened to us.'

'I don't know either, can't even explain it myself. One moment we're near death's door and the next we're sitting here stuffing burgers down our throat as though nothing ever happened. A few hours ago we could hardly stand and were shaking like jellies, try explaining that to someone,' John said, chewing heavily on his burger.

'Trouble is, it aint someone, it's Michael and Tam our partners who are waiting for a call from us to come out to Spain and here we are back in the bleedin' country with nothing to show for it, not even the flu or food poisoning or whatever the hell it was,' Jay said, tucking into his second burger.

'We're going to have to convince them somehow or neither of them will want to come out with us next time,' John said, picking a chip and dipping it into the little dish of ketchup.

'Will there be a next time, we've screwed up twice and it's cost us a lot of money. Can we afford it again?'

'We can't afford not to, not with all that cash just lying there for the taking. We have to go back and as long as they believe what happened to us, then there won't be a problem.'

'Well, let's hope they do. We can make sure we get our story straight on the train back,' Jay said encouragingly, taking a long sip of coffee from the plastic cup he was clutching.

'Yeah, and I'm going to have to think of something to tell Jenny and the kids and that's going to be even worse,' John sighed, a sense of foreboding tightening in his chest at the thought.

DOORSTEP PROTOCOL

'So okay, what the hell happened?' Tam asked angrily, as soon as the four of them had gathered together in the pool room at Oscars, the day after John and Jay had returned from Spain.

'We don't really know, it's a total bloody mystery,' Jay said, deciding which cue to choose from the rack. 'We arrived, found a cheap hotel and went out for a meal. We shared a dish of paella and everything was fine until we got back to the hotel and I started to feel queasy. I started shaking and threw up and as the night wore on I got worse and, it felt like my gut was being forced up my throat or being pulled out of my arse.'

'I was fine at that point,' John continued, 'the following morning I went on my own to recce Spider's place, and everything looked good, there was no sign of the family or the minibus. The only other person I spotted was a pretty looking woman who I guess is his girlfriend. I didn't see there was going to be any problems getting the money. We could take the girl down if we had to, all it needed was for Jay to recover from whatever was making him sick,' John explained, taking a cue from the rack.

'The problem was I didn't recover, I got to the point it took all my effort to get to the bog never mind attempting to take Spider down,' Jay said, lining up to break.

'That night I also went down with the lurgy and we both spent the next three days banged up in the hotel like a couple of junkies going through cold turkey,' John interjected.

'We were still in a bad state when we got to the airport, I was worried they wouldn't let us onto the plane as we were both still shivering like hell and…'

'So when did the miracle take place?' Michael asked his voice heavy with sarcasm.

'We slept all the way back on the plane and when we woke up as the plane came down at Heathrow we both felt better, by the time we had cleared Customs, the symptoms had totally gone,' Jay told him

'And if you think that was a miracle and God was looking after us, I think it was the other way around, God was looking after Spider,' John cut in, grudgingly.

'Talking about miracles,' Jay cut in, 'how's this for a laugh? When I got home and unpacked I found the bloody stun gun and a truncheon lying on top of my clothes. I walked right through Customs without knowing I was carrying them and nobody stopped me. I started to shake thinking what would have happened if I had been stopped.'

'Sorry, that must have been my fault. When I got back from the recce, I was feeling sick and dumped them in the nearest holdall. I just forgot about them after that,' John explained. 'The one good thing is, thanks to Customs, we've got a damn good weapon if we ever need to use it.'

'So what do we do now?' Tam asked, wanting to get back on the subject of Spider and the cash in the shoe boxes.

'We go straight back out, kick the door in and get the bastard and sod anybody else that happens to be there. We've done the recce. You told us it was just him and his tart, so let's just go for it,' Michael cut in, his manner brusque as he hit the cue ball too hard and sending the red bouncing off the table.

'Hang on, let's just think this out. We have to hope for the best, but plan for the worst. I checked all the uniforms and stun guns were still safely hidden in the disused building sight so we won't have any problem with that, but we have to get enough money together for the four of us – this time enough money so that we're able to stay longer should someone turn up unexpectedly and we have to wait for them to leave.' John reasoned, his mouth set in a cautious smile halfway between patience and exasperation.

'John's right,' Tam agreed, 'we can't rush into this. We can't afford to mess up again.'

'So how long is it going to take to get the money together?' Michael asked, irritation beginning to creep into his voice, losing interest in the shot he was about to take.

'There just might be a way to get the money a lot quicker, if you guys are up for it,' Tam surprised them by saying. 'I've got a problem you guys might be able to solve for me.'

'We're all in this together, so if there's something we can do for you and it helps us get the money then count us in,' John hastily said, seeing the worried look on Tam's face.

'Thank you, you're good boys, but it's not quite as simple as that, because it also involves my girlfriend Jan.'

'Yes, I remember you saying something about moving in together.'

'Yes we are, as soon as her divorce comes through from her ex, John Jeromson, a real nasty piece of work, he used to beat her up. He was one of those on-course bookies, that is until he cheated on a heavy bet with a group of gypsies who I gather are still looking for him. After that, he set himself up as a property developer and this where the problem started. He came to Jan to ask her to lend him ninety grand to buy a house to renovate and then sell on at a profit.'

'Didn't know she had that kind of money,' Jay said, surprised.

'She's a smart girl, always taken care of her money, and wasn't very keen to lend it to him, but he promised if she did he wouldn't put obstacles in the way of the divorce, so she reluctantly agreed.'

'Wished I had a woman like that,' Jay said jokingly, laughing at his own humour.

'Anyway, he bought the house, did it up and sold it, but never gave her back the ninety grand. I spoke with him to get him to pay back the money, but he turned really nasty, telling me it was none of my business and if I didn't keep my nose out of it, he would come to the club with some of his heavies, break my legs and smash the place up.'

'The bastard, someone ought to sort him out,' Michael said, his face contorting in disgust.

'I wish someone would,' Tam's voice dropped. 'It's a threat I take seriously and I can't fight it on my own, he's not the type you can beat up and and expect to be left in peace. I'm constantly worrying that he going to come in here with a few toughs and carry out his threat.

John inhaled deeply, wishing he knew what to say, for if he offered to help and sort this guy out, it would mean breaking their protocol. *You don't do anything personal, you don't deal with civilians and you don't crap on your own doorstep,* he thought quietly.

'You want us to sort him out,' Jay spoke up before John had a chance to come to any conclusion.

'I would like someone to put the frighteners on him to make him pay back the money he owes Jan and warn him not to make anymore threats,' Tam told him.

'You realise, if we got involved in this, it would mean breaking protocol?' John cut in.

'I realise that, that's why I hesitated in telling you, I know Jan would be so grateful to get her money back, I'm sure she would happily pay a reward.'

'Listen I don't care about bloody protocol, I'm off back to South Africa as soon as we get the money from Spider. So if sorting that *Skapie* out is going to get us the money to go to Spain then I'm all for it,' Michael said, with quiet conviction.

'Pussy he might well be Michael, but I don't know,' John said, hesitantly. 'It's a rule I've always stuck to.'

'I agree with Michael, let's do what we have to do, the rules can come later,' Jay spoke up, an air of excitement in his voice. 'It's going to make getting back to Spain a damn lot sooner.'

'So are you two are happy to do something to about this?' John asked, looking from Jay to Michael.

'Yes, Tam's one of us and we all have something to gain from this,' Michael happily agreed.

'I agree, no rules are made that can't be broken and the sooner we get back to Spain the better' Jay said, his voice firm and definite.

'Right then, Tam you need to stay out of it from now on. You're too close to the situation and the least you know the better. Oh, I've heard from Lloyd that The German has gone down for seven years, and Customs seized the chopper before Lloyd had a chance to sell it, so he's had his legs cut from under him,' John informed them.

It was decided Jay and Michael would do a recce on Jeromson's flat to assess how easy it would be to gain entry and to their surprise it was much easier than they could have wished for. A window latch is only as strong as the wood it's screwed to and in this case the wood of the window frame was rotting, so it was easy to force the latch, raise the window and climb in. They found nothing, no money or safe anywhere, so climbed back out and eased the latch back leaving no sign they had been there.

John tailed John Jeromson for two weeks and noted that every night after closing the office he would get in his Jaguar with blacked out windows and drive back to his flat and stay home for the night, rarely receiving visitors. The only change to the routine was every Friday, after driving home he would come out about a half hour later, having changed his clothes, get back in the car and drive off. John discreetly followed as Jeromson made his way to his girlfriend's house, where he picked her up and drove to a nearby restaurant before spending the night at her house.

As the area was personal to John and there was the chance he could be recognised, it was agreed Jay and Michael would do the hit and John would wait in the car around the corner ready to drive them off as soon as the job was done. Armed with the stun gun and the truncheon that Customs had so kindly allowed them to bring into the country, they set off with John driving, Jay sitting in the passenger seat beside him with Michael sitting in the back seats holding the stun gun and truncheon. As planned, John dropped Jay and Michael off outside the apartment block and drove further along the road to position himself where he could watch for Jeromson's arrival.

Jay eased back the loose fitting latch, raised the window and they both quickly climbed in. Once inside they looked for a place to hide to wait for John's text to tell them when the Jag was approaching the block. There was a walk in cupboard in the main bedroom and Jay thought this would be the perfect place to hide and wait for their victim. Once John spotted the Jaguar, he drove around the corner so he wouldn't be seen and sent a text to Jay.

'He's arrived,' Jay whispered to Michael as he covered his face with a balaclava. Michael quickly followed suit covering his own face.

They listened carefully as they heard the key turn in the lock, the door open and close and waited until they heard footsteps coming towards them.

Jay and Michael leaped out of the cupboard they were hiding in, with Jay aiming the stun gun at the target.

They both froze as they heard a high pitched scream and found themselves staring at the face of a terrified woman.

Michael moved swiftly towards the woman putting his finger up to his lips indicating for her not to make a noise. 'Don't scream and you won't get hurt,' he said forcefully.

'Who are you and what are you doing here?' Jay asked, looking into her face as he lowered the stun gun.

'Who the blazes are you and what do you want?' she demanded, ignoring his question, her body trembling all over.

'I want to know who you are and what you're doing here?' Jay asked, his anger rising, aiming the stun gun towards her.

'I'm Diane, John's fiancé and came to collect his suit, he's working late and we're going to a dinner,' she explained, a look of terror still on her face. 'What are you going to do to me now?' she asked, wondering whether she was going to be raped, terrified of the way Jay was pointing the stun gun at her.

'Keep your eye on her,' Jay told Michael, as he turned away and walked to the other room to call John.

'Another cock up, it's not him it's his bloody tart, come to pick up a suit, what do you want us to do now?'

'Get out of there as quick as you can. Spin her some line and make out you're friends of the Gypsies come to collect the twenty grand he owes them for welching on the bet,' John told him.

'Right,' said Jay turning to the woman, 'tell your boyfriend we came for the money he owes the Gypsies. Tell him if he doesn't pay up we will come back and kill him. Now walk into that cupboard and stay in there and wait quietly for at least ten minutes. We don't want to hurt you, so be a sensible girl, do as we say and be sure to tell your man what we said. Tell him he had better have the money ready by next week, okay? Now give me your mobile phone.'

The two men put her in the cupboard and closed the doors, not bothering to lock them, then climbed out the window, lowered it back down and carefully eased the latch back so as not to leave any sign there had been a forced entry.

'Talk about expect the unexpected, how the bloody hell did that happen?' Michael said, disbelief and exasperation sounding in his voice as he slid into the back seat of the car.

John gave a deep sigh, his face matching the expression of the others as he said. 'That's just it, in the whole week that I kept observation, I never once saw her or anyone else come to his place.

Maybe we should have held onto her and forced him to come to the house,' Jay reflected. 'I bet she's been straight on the phone to him, we should have smashed her phone up.'

'No, that's what we want her to do, remember we told her to tell him why we were there, which should put the frighteners on him and scare him enough to come up with the money,' Michael said.

'The only problem is it's not the money we went there for. We want the ninety grand to earn the commission, otherwise there's going to be no chance of us getting back to Spain in the near future. We're going to have to work out another plan of action,' John told them.

John stood in the phone box taking a series of long breaths to steady his nerves, then practiced the Irish accent several times before he lifted the receiver from its cradle, tapped in the number and waited for it to be answered.

'Hello,' he heard a male voice answer.

'John Jeromson?' John asked.

'Who's this?' Jeromson asked back, answering the question with a question.

'I'm one of the fellows you ripped off for twenty grand and we want our money. You can't steal from us and get away with it. We sent some people around to warn you, I do hope you've taken their advice seriously and are getting the money together. I will phone you again in a week's time to tell you where to drop the money. We know where you live and where you work, where your ex and your kids live, we know who your girlfriend is and where she lives; so have the money ready, you won't like the consequences if you don't,' John said, replacing the receiver before Jeromson had a chance to say anything. John smiled as he came out of the phone box, pleased with his efforts to scare Jeromson into paying up.

John was justified in feeling he had scared Jeromson, he had, he had scared him a lot, too much. John Jeromson was so scared he reported it to the police, telling them about the raid on his house, holding his girlfriend hostage and the threatening phone call. It was to prove the undoing of all their plans, the truth about breaking protocol, dealing with civilians and of not messing on your own doorstep was about to come back to haunt them.

ENTRAPMENT

It was now coming to the end of 2003. It was Friday October the 31st, a few days after his thirty-seventh birthday and John had got up feeling in a jubilant mood, thinking he'd scared Jeromson enough and he would soon cough up the money, they would get their commission and be able to plan the trip back to Spain. As he was making breakfast for Jenny and the kids, he remained in a jubilant mood, tomorrow was November 1st and he was going out to buy some fireworks for bonfire night. His mind drifted back to when Flemmo took him to the village of Oxton and showed him a series of tunnels that ran under the church and told him about the priests that used to hide there and all about Guy Fawkes and why they lit bonfires to celebrate his capture.

But he was jerked sharply back from his reflections as he heard the phone start to ring, and rushed to answer it, hoping it was Tam calling to tell him Jeromson had been so scared by everything that he had agreed to pay Jan back the money.

'Hi Tam,' John answered as soon as he snatched up the receiver, which was a big mistake as he was quick to discover when a toneless voice enquired 'Mr Lawson?'

'Who's this?' John asked suspiciously, not recognising the voice.

'Detective Sergeant Cowden from Musselburgh police station, I was wondering if you would be kind enough come to the station for an informal chat to help us with some enquiries we are making, regarding certain threats that are alleged to have been made against a Mr Kelly who I believe is someone you are acquainted with.'

John's breathing eased as he thought, *thank heavens for that, at least it's nothing to do with the threats we've been making to Jeromson.*

'If I can be of help sergeant, when would you like me to come?' John asked, adopting a polite co-operative manner.

'Today if that's convenient sir,' sergeant Cowden said, his voice adopting a friendlier tone.

'Bit difficult today, I'm going to be doing the early shift,' John said, making the excuse, thinking he ought to tell Tam about the call before he went to the station.

'No, problem sir, how would tomorrow morning suit you, say ten o'clock?' Cowden suggested, his voice remaining casual and relaxed.

'Fine, sergeant, I will be there at ten o'clock tomorrow,' John volunteered.

'Thank you for your co-operation sir,' the sergeant said, his voice assuming an even friendlier tone.

Cowden hung up and John stared at the phone for a long moment until he heard Jenny's voice asking. 'Who was that on the phone?'

'The police can be such idiots. That was a detective from Musselburgh police station, wanting me to help them about some threats someone has been making to Tam Kelly and Jan his girlfriend,' John explained nonchalantly, as though it was no big deal, which to him it wasn't. The police didn't bother him and he was far too clever to be caught out by them. He was the smart one, they were the idiots.

The police want you to help them?' Jenny asked surprised, always becoming nervous at the mention of the police.

'Yeah running around like headless chickens, they couldn't find a needle in a haystack if it was stuck up their backsides,' John said, almost chuckling at his own dry sense of humour.

'When you seeing the police?' Tam asked, feeling a little uneasy about the situation as he sat with John in his office at Oscars.

John saw the worried look on Tam's face. 'Don't worry, they obviously have no idea about the threats we're making to Jeromson, ironically it seems someone has made a complaint about the threats he's been making to you, maybe Jan did.'

'She hasn't mentioned anything about it.'

'Maybe one of her friends has. Anyway, I'm going to wait until I know what the police have got on Jeromson before I phone him and tell him where to drop the money,' John said as he watched Tam thinking. 'There's nothing to worry about, the police are too busy policing law abiding citizens to have time to bother with criminals like us. I'll just tell them how upset and worried you are about the threats and your and Jan's safety.'

'Just be careful what you say, don't say anymore than you have to,' Tam cautioned him.

John parked his Range Rover in Musselburgh high street and walked the short distance to the police station, feeling he was going to enjoy himself pretending to be a good citizen, helping the police protect the public from criminals.

'Good of you to come Mr Lawson,' Detective Sergeant Cowden said, with a smile as he sat down facing John sitting across the table from him in the small interview room.

John studied the DS, assessing him curiously, guessing he was in his mid forties. He was wearing a tweed jacket over a white open neck shirt, grey trousers and brogue shoes. His face was angular with a strong jaw, large brown eyes with bushy eye brows and a thick head of hair.

'Anything to help the police, detective,' John said, with a slight arrogant air to his voice.

'We are making enquiries regarding allegations of hostage taking and demands for money and wondered whether you know anything about it?' Cowden asked, his large eyes searching John's face for any reaction, as he continued the questioning. 'Do you know a Mr John Jeromson?'

'I thought you invited me here to help you with enquiries regarding Mr Kelly,' John said, putting as much indignation into his voice as possible.

'We'll come to him later. Do you know a Mr Jeromson?' Cowden persisted.

'No I don't,' John said, firmly.

Cowden gave him one of those I know you're lying looks. 'Are you sure you don't know a Mr Jeromson?' he repeated, emphasising the name Jeromson so there could be no mistake who he was referring to.

'I've told you I don't know him,' John repeated, which technically was true as he had never actually met the man, only surveyed him from the car.

'Really, well here's something I'd like you to think about. After Mr Jeromson came to us with his allegations we set up a recorder to monitor all the calls being made to both his home and his office and guess what?'

330

'What?' John asked, his eyebrows rising into an innocent grin.

'We got a recording of your voice,' Cowden said, a look of triumph spreading across his face.

John's eyebrows lowered into a frown. 'You can't have. I've never made any calls, particularly to a man I don't know.'

The look of triumph stayed on the sergeant's face as he said. 'You see we're very lucky these days in that we have the services of an expert speech analyst and he compared your voice with the voice making the threats and guess what?'

John was about to say, *'he couldn't possibly know it was me, I was using an Irish voice,'* but checked himself and just said. 'What?'

'They match. Your attempts at an Irish accent were not that good and what was interesting is that your voice has certain resonances which are unique and helped to define it. The analyst found there was a blend of South African, Scouse and of course Scottish traits in your voice.'

'You're making it up I've never heard so much rubbish. I come here willingly to help you and you're trying to trap me into something I know nothing about. I'm out of here,' John exclaimed, angrily leaping to his feet.

'SIT DOWN,' Cowden shouted, raising his voice to an angry rage.

John grudgingly sat down and glared back at the Sergeant, whose smile had become much broader. Just then a constable tapped on the door, opened it and beckoned. Cowden got to his feet, went over to the Constable and listened to what he had come in to tell him and quickly hurried out, leaving the Constable to watch over John.

'What the devil is that?' Jenny exclaimed almost jumping out of her chair at the heavy hammering on the front door. She was sitting quietly with the children watching television. The hammering was loud and incessant sounding like someone was trying to break the door down.

They were trying to break the door down. It was the police and as Jenny opened the front door she was roughly pushed aside as the police stormed in shouting, 'POLICE!! POLICE!! This is a raid, everyone remain where they are.'

Jenny screamed, so did the children as the police immediately started moving around that house beginning to search every room.

'How many people are in the house?' a uniformed officer who

appeared to be in charge, asked, his voice void of compassion.

'Just me and the children, would you tell me what is going on?' Jenny bravely demanded trying to control her anger.

'We have a warrant to search the house,' he informed her, producing the warrant from his breast pocket and showing it to her.

'I don't understand. Why don't you talk to my husband, he's at the police station now,' she told him, a worried confused look spreading across her face.

'Indeed he is and I suspect he will be helping us for some time. Do you have the keys to the garage?' he asked abrasively, determined to get on with the search.

'They're in the kitchen drawer, I'll get them for you,' she said walking off to the kitchen with him following close behind her.

'I don't know what you hope to find in there,' she said, opening the drawer by the sink, taking out the keys and handing them to him.

She followed him out and went back into the lounge where the children were kneeling on the sofa and staring out the window, red and blue colours from the police lights flashing off their faces.

Jenny looked in the direction of their stare. It was like the circus had come to town, six or seven police cars and vans, their lights flashing, surrounding the immediate area of the house and her and all the neighbours coming out of their houses to goggle at what was going on.

John abruptly looked across as Cowden came back into the room and took a measured look at his beaming face.

'We've just searched your car and...'

'You searched my car? You have no bloody right to search my car without my permission,' John retorted angrily.

'Yes we have and we're also searching your house.'

'You have no bloody right to search my house either. You need a search warrant to enter my property. I know my rights. I will bloody sue you,' John said, his face a mask of anger.

'We have a search warrant,' Cowden told him, watching the changing expression on his face.

John could hear his own breathing. 'You've set me up, this wasn't about me helping you with your enquiries, this was to get me here and keep me here while my property is being searched, you bastards.'

'I would be careful with your choice of language. You are helping us with our enquiries, although I can't say you're being particularly cooperative. However, since the Range Rover can be considered part of your property it is quite in order for us to search it and guess what we found?'

'My spare tyre's flat,' John said copiously, although the cheeky smile on his face did not match the anxiety in his eyes.

'A little more serious than that, although that could be considered a motoring offence. But a stun gun and a truncheon, well that's a different matter, a very serious offence. So what would you be doing with a stun gun, a powerful one at that in the boot of your car, I wonder?'

'I don't know anything about a stun gun or a truncheon, you bastards must have planted it,' John said, contemptuously.

'I bet they've got your finger prints all over them.

A new hope seized him as he remembered he always wore gloves whenever he handled the stun gun or the truncheon. 'I bet it hasn't,' John said confidently, then remembered with a shudder the gloves were also hidden in the boot which made him begin to shift uneasily in his seat.

At that moment the Constable tapped lightly on the door again, entered and gestured to the DS. Cowden got to his feet and walked across to where the Constable was standing and listened to what he had to say, his smile widening as he did so.

John started to drum his fingers lightly on the table in irritation as he watched Cowden come back and resume his seat. 'They have just finished searching your house, quite a house by all accounts, which makes me wonder how the likes of you can afford to live in a house like that on a doorman, bouncer or whatever you guys like to call yourselves, salary, and run two cars. Anyway guess what they found?' Cowden said teasingly, flashing a smile of tobacco stained teeth.

'I'm tired of these guessing games, so why don't you just tell me, so as I can get out of here and get home to my wife,' John said, with an arrogant scoff.

'You're not going anywhere Mr Lawson, a tray of cartridges were found in your garage. What would you be needing with them I wonder and where are you hiding the gun to fire them?' the detective asked in an unwavering stare.

John said nothing, his eyes flickering showing the first hint of fear as he wondered how the hell they had found the cartridges, if he had known there was going to be a raid he would have got rid of them and hidden them where he had buried the Browning, in the wooded area next to Cockenzie Power Station near Musselburgh.

'We've got you bang to rights Lawson, so make it easy on yourself and tell us the truth because we are also interviewing a Mr Thomas Kelly, who we know you work for.'

There was a sharp intake of breath and a shrug of his shoulders as he said. 'Okay detective,' his eyes narrowing in a disguised malice. 'It was me who threatened Jeromson, but it was only a threat, I never intended to hurt him,' John admitted. Thomas Kelly had nothing to do with it. I was working alone, it was just me, I heard the guy had ripped my mate's girlfriend off and thought I could frighten him into handing over some of it,' John added, wanting to protect Jay, Tam and Michael.

After a few days in HMP Edinburgh on bail, both John and Tam were released until their case was ready to come to court. They both headed home in solemn silence at the prospect.

HAIL THE HERO

2004

John leapt to his feet as he heard Jenny's car pull up and rushed out into the hallway to get to the front door and open it. He stood in the doorway, every pulse in his body throbbing, his heart pounding, as he watched her get out of the car, slam the door with more force than was necessary and walk to the front door while trying hard to ignore the twitching curtains of the neighbours.

She fixed him with a steady gaze as she brushed past him. John closed the door and followed her into the lounge. Jenny took off her coat and tossed it heatedly onto one of the armchairs as John stepped forward to embrace her.

'Don't touch me,' she said, shrinking back from him and he could see a distant look in her beautiful eyes as he lowered his hands in submissive surrender.

'Have you any idea what it's been like. Police cars surrounding the house, swarming all over the place, searching every room, cupboard and draw, even the garage, I don't know what they were looking for, *perhaps* you'll be good enough to tell me,' she asked, her voice making it sound more like an order than a question.

This was the moment of truth and guilt was hammering at his conscience as he said. 'They found some bullets in the garage.'

'Bullets!!' Jenny exclaimed. 'Are you completely crazy, what if the kids had found them?'

'No, they couldn't have, they were well hidden,' he said meekly, as he watched her slump down heavily into the other armchair.

'Not well enough apparently, the police found them,' she said, scornfully. 'And what else did they find?'

'Nothing else,' he lied, knowing what the reaction would be if he told her about the stun gun and the truncheon.

'Have you any idea what it was like with all the neighbours coming out and gawking at what was going on, I can't go anywhere now without feeling someone is staring or pointing a finger at me,' she said, her cheeks beginning to flare with anger.

'I'm sorry, I didn't mean for this to happen,' he started to say, not sure at that moment what else to say.

'What did you expect would happen, did you think you could just go on doing what you're doing and it wouldn't catch up with you. I have lived in fear of this happening every time you tell me you're off somewhere debt collecting. So tell me, what terrible things you've been doing this time,' she said her voice acrimonious.

'Depends what you consider terrible,' he replied, defensively and she could see the conflicting emotions on his face.

'Don't bandy words with me,' she cut across him, anger flickering in her eyes. 'Didn't it ever occur to you that at some point your luck would run out, weren't you ever afraid of being caught?'

'Yes, but that was part of it, I'm sorry, I should have been more honest with you,' he began, dropping his voice in acquiescence.

'Yes, you damn well should have,' she cut across him her voice sharp. 'You're so arrogant you think everyone else is stupid. Look what you said about the police, they couldn't find a needle in a haystack if it was stuck up their...I won't repeat the rest of it. Well it turns out they were a bit smarter than you and while you were there thinking in your oh-so-superior way they hadn't got a clue about what you've been up to, they were here ransacking the house, frightening me and the children.'

'Yes, it must have been scary for them, I'm sorry.'

'And me, how could you have been so thoughtless, so reckless,' she challenged him, now almost incandescent with anger.

'I know that now, but I thought what I was doing was to protect you and the kids. To have money to buy you and them all the things you and they deserve and...'

'That's the problem you think money is the answer to everything. Well it's not and never has been, as I would imagine your dear gran would have said. "The love of money is the root of all evil," because look where it's got you, us. You realise we aren't going to able to live here with what's happened. We're going to have to sell this house and find somewhere else to live where nobody knows us.'

To their surprise when they put the house on the market it was valued at £193,000, a full £100000 more than they had paid for it only three years earlier. It sold faster than they thought which meant they had to find somewhere else very quickly. They found a four bedroom ground floor maisonette, below Jenny's friend Katrina's flat at number 166 Pinkie Road. It was in a pretty bad state needing a lot of work doing to it, but it was on sale for only a £110,000.

Knowing they would have a £100,000 profit from the sale of their house, John was happy they would have more than enough money to completely refurbish the maisonette. They put down £55,000 as a deposit and took out a mortgage for the remaining fifty per cent giving them a sizeable surplus to pay for the renovations. John decided to take out £10,000 in cash from the money that had been deposited into their joint account at the Bank of Scotland branch in Musselburgh from the sale of the house, and put it into his other account at the Halifax across the road.

Everything seemed fine and soon the maisonette was full of activity with workers installing the central heating, replacing the floorboards, plastering the walls and ceilings, it was chaos but Jenny was happy watching the transformation gradually taking place. Still on bail awaiting for the date of his trial to be announced, John was determined to keep his nose clean and stay out of trouble. While working the door at Oscars he made good friends with Andy Warburton who he had recruited to come and work alongside him. He had met Andy while working as a security guard at the Princes Mall Shopping Centre and stayed in touch.

Andy lived in Stewart Terrace in the Gorgie area of Edinburgh close to the Hearts football ground, but he couldn't drive, so John was happy to give him a lift home after Oscars had closed, particularly as it was the early hours of the morning. At that time of the mornings the streets were relatively empty as most sensible people were safely tucked up in their beds.

It was Sunday the 28th March 2004 around 2.30am when John turned into Dalry Road as usual, passing the row of tenement buildings with a variety of shops occupying the ground floors. It was as he carried on past the graveyard, and approached the petrol station that he noticed smoke drifting out from one of the shops and two people appearing to be frantically hammering on the doors and shouting up to the flats above the shop.

'What the hell's going on there?' John asked, pulling the Range Rover to an abrupt stop.

'Looks like the nursing agency is on fire,' Andy said, as they leapt out.

'Yes and it looks like it's drifting upwards towards the flats,' John said, looking up to the windows immediately above and was surprised to see some heads poking out and shouting down to tell whoever is messing about with their doorbells to piss off and go and make a nuisance of themselves somewhere else.

'What's happening?' John asked the two guys who had been banging on the door and pressing all the door bells.

'The Scott Nursing Centre is on fire, can't you feel the heat? The idiots in the flats above aren't taking any notice, they thinking we're a couple of drunks. They're going to die if we don't get them out,' one of the guys told him.

John immediately sprang into action and started kicking at the entrance door to the flats. With Andy's help and several hard kicks it eventually gave way. John and Andy tore up the stairs two at a time banging on the doors shouting for everyone to get out as the place was on fire. Smoke was now beginning to pour into the communal stairwell as the flames were taking hold and spreading, seeming to follow them up as they climbed to the second floor continuing to bang on the doors.

Fortunately people now alerted to the danger were hurrying to evacuate themselves from the building. By the time John and Andy had got to the fifth floor it seemed everybody had managed to get out safely. He banged on the last door, but it seemed nobody was answering, he banged heavily again and then looked over the balcony as he waited, he was alarmed to see the black smoke beginning to obscure the entrance, making John think they had to get themselves out before the smoke killed them. Finally the door opened and an elderly man appeared, naked from the waist down wearing only the top half of his pyjamas.

'What's the matter?' he asked, staring at John, his eyes bleary, his voice sleepy, having been woken from a deep sleep, oblivious to his near nakedness.

'You've got to get out, the place is on fire,' John told him, his voice urgent.

It felt like it took forever for the man to understand what John was saying.

'I need to have a pee and find my bottoms,' the man said, as he turned and ambled back inside the flat.

'We need to get you out of here. Is there anyone else in the flat?' John asked becoming exasperated that the man didn't seem to understand the danger they were in.

'I think my wife heard the commotion and is looking around for her cat,' the man replied, still with no sense of urgency.

'I think the best thing to do is for me to barricade us in the flat, put some wet towels around the gaps in the door and open all the windows. You go down and tell the firemen I'm up here with these two elderly people, Okay?' John told Andy on hearing the sirens outside.

Andy pulled his jumper up to cover the lower half of his face and made his way back down the stairs.

As John was about to barricade the door, a man came rushing up the stairs.

'I'm Jonathan Torrance. I live down on the next floor. We have to get them out now. It's too risky for anyone to remain here, it's too dangerous, the building could collapse,' he said, his voice strained with panic.

'It's going to be very risky getting down the stairs,' John said, as he looked over the bannisters down the stairwell at the smoke billowing its way up towards them. 'If I carry the man do you think you could help the lady?'

'I'm sure I can, the sooner the better,' Jonathan said, following John back into the flat.

'What are your names, by the way?' John asked, as the elderly couple stared at him, fear beginning to show on their faces.

'Mr Allison and this is my wife Betty. Are we going to be able to get out of here? I can smell the smoke,' Mr Allison asked, glancing at his wife, clearly concerned for her safety as well as his own.

John was a little surprised by his formality of using the Mr, but at least he was now wearing the bottom half of his pyjamas.

'You can't stay here any longer and you'll never make it on your own, so we are going to carry you out. Go and get a couple of blankets and a couple of towels, we'll soak them with water and can put them over your faces. They'll protect you from breathing in the smoke and we'll wrap you in the blankets as we carry you down the stairs,' John instructed them, keeping his voice calm so as not to cause them to panic.

John, weighing a good eighteen stone of muscle had no problem in raising the man up onto his shoulders in a firemen's lift and carrying him out of the flat. Jonathan took hold of Betty and as she was very slight was able to take her hand and guide her out, before picking her up, even though she kept protesting about her cat.

The descent was perilous as the smoke was now almost at their level, every step had to be a slow and careful judgment. With only one free hand to guide him, John knew one slip and he could send him and Mr Allison tumbling to the bottom. By the time they got safely to the bottom of the stairs the smoke was thick and acrid and John was gasping for air, feeling he was about to faint if he didn't get some fresh air quickly. Almost blinded John was using his free hand to feel his way along the wall. As he reached the front door he saw a haze of light forcing its way through the thick darkness, for a split second it he had a flashback to watching his father drive away through a thick haze of exhaust fumes.

'You're a very brave man. Those two would have died had you not got them out when you did. Good job you lived on the premises,' another of the firemen said, as he guided John out.

'No, I don't live here, me and my friend were just passing and we saw the smoke and…,' John explained, pausing to take deep gulps of the fresh air.

'You're suffering from smoke inhalation, an ambulance has arrived and they'll give you some oxygen,' the fireman told him. 'You mean to say, you just stopped and went into the burning building to rescue people?' he asked surprised as he guided John over to the ambulance. 'You're even braver than I thought, not many people would do what you did. I take my hat, or rather my helmet off to you,' he said, with a real sense of admiration.

'It wasn't only me, there's my mate Andy Warburton and another guy who said his name was Jonathan,' John told him.

'Right, I'll have word with them and leave you with the medics, they'll will take good care of you,' the fireman said, as he walked away to talk to the others.

'Hail The Hero,' many of the customers joked, giving John a pat on the back as they came through the doors at Oscars. It had become a regular thing since the story had been reported in the newspapers and John thrived on it. At least it made him feel good that for once he had saved someone's life, instead of threatening it, and it temporarily distracted his worries about the up coming trial.

But, that period of euphoria quickly evaporated when he got a frantic call from Jenny almost in tears as she angrily exclaimed she had gone to buy some new curtains and was shocked to be told the debit card had been rejected.

'Doesn't make sense, there's over twelve grand in that account,' he said, as much puzzled as she was as to why it had been rejected.

'Well, you better go and sort it out with the bank. I'm embarrassed enough not to be able to pay for a few damn curtains,' she said, raising her voice in frustration.

'Look, don't worry I'll sort it out, I'm sure it's some silly mistake, some idiot in the bank probably pressed the wrong key on the computer. In the meantime I'll go and draw some cash from the other account on my way into work.

'I just hope you're right,' Jenny sighed, before abruptly ending the call.

'I'm sorry sir, the account is frozen,' the bank teller told him, his face a mask of implacability.

'What do you mean it's frozen?' John asked, his temper rising, knowing there was still money in the account.

'I'm afraid it is sir. Do you have any other accounts with us that you can draw from,' the bank teller enquired, with a little raise of his eyebrows.

'Another account, you must be joking. All I wanted was a couple of hundred,' John said, with a fatalistic shrug of his shoulders.

'Sorry, I could not be of assistance sir,' the bank teller said, forcing a customer's smile to his face.

'I'm afraid you are now subject to the Proceeds of Crime Act. I'm surprised you haven't been notified,' Mr McAlister his solicitor informed John when he called into his office to find out why his bank accounts had been frozen.

'What exactly does Proceeds of Crime Act mean?' John asked disconsolately, wondering what the term meant exactly.

'In effect it means The Procurator Fiscal Service, through the Assets Recovery Agency, have seized all your assets which they consider you have benefitted from by your criminal activities, together with a restraint order to prohibit you from dealing with the house you presently reside in, the cars, motorbike, furnishings, anything they consider of value you own. Also, it allows them to recover any property the Procurator Fiscal Service considers represents property obtained through your unlawful activities or which is intended by you to be used in an unlawful way, and to seize all bank accounts so as to prevent any movement of money or possible money laundering,' McAlister explained, in his matter of fact manner.

'How can they possibly do that?'

'Well it would appear that during the search of your house, the police came to the conclusion you were living well beyond your means in terms of what you were reported to be earning as a doorman. The maisonette, the expensive refurbishments, the cars, the motorbike and the other luxuries you appear to have.'

'But that doesn't make sense. We sold the house, because we couldn't afford to live there anymore.'

'But they say you made a hundred grand profit.'

'Yes, but most of that was used to buy the maisonette and refurbish it.'

'Unfortunately that doesn't explain where you got the money from in the first place to buy the house,' McAlister pointed out.

'Does that mean we have no access to our money?' John said, depression beginning to wash over him as worry lines creased his brow.

'That money no, but they will allow you to keep the money you and your wife, are currently earning to pay essential bills.'

'That's generous of them.'

'Not really, because they have issued a demand for you to pay back £100,000, in reparation for your ill gotten gains shall we say.'

'That's rubbish they can't prove I've made all that money.'

'They don't have to Mr Lawson. The onus is on you to prove you haven't. So I suggest you start trying to sort you affairs out before they come and sell the house from under you,' McAlister advised him.

'They can do that?' John said, listening to the surprise in his voice.

'Once they've got their hooks into you, they can do almost anything.'

After the meeting John walked along Musselburgh High Street opposite the police station where he'd been arrested and noticed a man climb up onto one of the benches at the bus stop and begin preaching holding a Bible in his hand. 'You are all going to face God one day. You are going to face the final judgment. Now is the time to repent.'

John gave him a discerning look and as he turned to walk on he couldn't believe his eyes as he spotted a wallet lying in the gutter. In his practiced way he swiftly moved over, snatched up the wallet without anybody noticing, shoved it in his pocket and hurried off to a darkened doorway.

His heart began to beat fast as he opened the wallet to see how much money there was in it, but his heart quickly slowed when he discovered the wallet wasn't real, but a gospel tract that read.

If this was a real wallet, packed with real money, would you: A. Keep it? B. Take it to the police? C. Give some of the money to the poor?

You have been underpaid for years. There's a big mistake in your pay cheque to your advantage, would you: A. Tell the boss? B. Keep quiet? C. Give some to a church?

If telling a white lie would save a friend's job, would you: A. Tell the truth? B. Act dumb? C. Lie?

Do you consider yourself to be a 'good' person? A. Yes. B. No.

Have you ever told a lie for any reason (including 'fibs' and 'white' lies--be honest)? A. Yes. B. No.

Have you ever stolen something--irrespective of its value (listen to your conscience)? A. Yes. B. No.

Would you consider a person who admits that they are a liar and a thief, to be a 'good' person?

Who do you think will enter Heaven? A. Those who say they are good when they are not? B. Liars and thieves? C. Those whom God has forgiven and cleansed of sin?

Did you realize that the Bible warns that thieves, liars, fornicators (those who have had sex out of marriage), idolaters (those who create a god to suit themselves), effeminate, adulterers, and the covetous (the greedy), will not enter the Kingdom of Heaven?

John shoved the wallet and the tract back in his pocket and started to laugh as he made his way home thinking, *I don't think I would have got a single one of them right.*

It was a tough ten months waiting for the trial date and John and Jenny's marriage was stretched to the limit with the pressure mounting as the day finally approached.

'Why is my trial taking place here?' John asked, anxious to know, sitting facing his solicitor, Mr McAlister, and Mr Gilbert Rawlings QC, across the small table in the interview room at the Dunfermline Sheriff Court in Fife.

Mr Gilbert Rawlings his Solicitor Advocate was dressed in a silk gown over his normal business suit, but not wearing a wig, in line with Scottish court tradition.

He was a little above average height, rather plump and reminded John a little of Cecil Watkins, although this man was thinning on top so there was no problem of dandruff. He was clean shaven and his face was a little severe though John was not sure whether it was simply part of his act as a counsellor.

Gilbert Rawlings drew in a deep breath as he studied John, before looking down at his notes and looking back up into his face as he said. 'As far as I can gather they have chosen to try you here to avoid any complications with the trial of your colleagues Thomas Kelly, Jason Davies and Michael Chamberlain, whose trial is due to be held in Edinburgh in a couple of months time. It seems the police had been building the case against the three of them after forensic investigation of the sim card in your phone which they seized revealed incriminating evidence against them. They also found text messages to Jason Davies and Michael Chamberlain at the time of the crime, triangulation of phone mast positions placed them firmly in the frame. CCTV footage of the route you drove to Jeromson's flat and images of Chamberlain and Davies getting off the train at Edinburgh's Waverly Station on the day of the crime all add weight to their guilt. So it is clear to me they want you to be tried and convicted before their trial comes up.'

'They're determined to get us all. They're more devious than I thought.'

'They can be when they want to be and they certainly are in this case,' Gilbert Rawlings said, perceptively.

'As you are probably aware, the jury's verdict is by majority vote, so I hope I can appeal to their good natures, showing you have been working regularly with no reports of any misdemeanours – and of course you have the police commendation and meritorious awards for your bravery over the fire escapade. When you get into court

I want you to behave as though you are a reformed man who has renounced his criminal activities, I might just manage to split them, then who knows, we might even get a not proven verdict or the judge might order a retrial,' Gilbert Rawlings told him.

'Well I guess there's some hope there,' John said, not convinced by his words.

'The good news is they have agreed to drop the stun gun charge, on the basis that we claimed the search of your car was illegal because your vehicle was parked on the High Street and not covered by the warrant to search your house, therefore they needed your permission to search your car which they did not ask for. Also, the tray of bullets turned out to be a tray of blank cartridges, as you obviously knew they were, making them inadmissible. So the only admissible evidence is the voice recordings of you making the threats.

'Huh, I should have practiced my Irish accent a bit more,' John scoffed with a shrug of his shoulders.

'You go into court with that attitude and I tell you now, the jury will return a majority verdict and the judge will throw the book at you. So be smart for once and play the good reformed citizen,' Gilbert Rawlings rebuked him.

'You have been found guilty of attempted extortion,' the judge pronounced after the jury had given their majority verdict. 'I have taken into account all the facts of the case. Mr Jeromson admitting he did owe certain monies to his ex-wife and you admitted your part in this although you pleaded not guilty to the charge. However, one cannot take away the seriousness of the threat and the fact you solicited two men to carry out that threat. One has to wonder what would have happened had Mr Jeromson turned up instead of the young lady. I have also taken into account that no one was hurt physically and that you are to receive a commendation and meritorious award for your bravery in rescuing people from a blazing fire, which is commendable, but that also demonstrates a tendency to be impulsive and reckless in that you don't consider the consequences of your actions. I am going to remand you on bail for a period of four weeks to ascertain physiological and family reports. On receiving those reports, you will be summoned back to this court to be sentenced, and I should advise you, you can expect a custodial sentence.'

DOWN FOR A THIRD TIME

John had now been in HMP Glenochil Prison near Stirling for six weeks and all was going well until he was told his solicitor was coming to see him. He became slightly worried ash he had an inkling of what it might be about. That inkling was confirmed when McAlister explained Jay, Michael and Tam's cases were coming up at the High Court and he had been made a compellable witness.

John's immediate reaction was, 'No way will I give evidence against them.'

'If you refuse, there could be severe consequences and you could be charged with contempt of court,' McAlister warned him.

'I was always told, never open your mouth about anyone unless you intend to benefit by it, and I certainly don't intend to benefit by giving evidence against my friends,' John said, stubbornly.

In the High Court, John was led up from the holding cells to the witness waiting room, not knowing when he was going to be called, his mind playing havoc over what McAlister had advised him yet again when he had come to see him in the holding cells. Asking himself if he had the arrogance to defy the court and stick to the villains code, you don't welch on your fellow villains.

'Right Lawson, it's your turn,' one of the prison officers guarding him said.

They ushered him through a door and before he knew was happening he was standing in a witness box on an elevated platform surrounded by high rails.

As he became accustomed to the sudden bright lights he looked around the court and spotted Tam, Jay and Michael looking back at him.

John looked around the rest of the court and it seemed everyone was staring at him and it made him angry as he turned his eyes to the left to look at the judge.

The clerk of the court came forward and handed John a Bible and said, 'Repeat after me, the truth I give, shall be the truth, the whole truth and nothing but the truth, so help me God.'

John stood firm and there was a strong tension about him as he refused to take hold of the Bible saying, 'I don't need that as I won't be giving evidence.'

'Mr Lawson, you are a compellable witness and as such you are summoned here to give evidence in this trial and...'

'I didn't ask to come here and I don't want to be here. I am not prepared to be a witness. I've had my trial and been sentenced and that's the end of it as far as I'm concerned, so you can stick your evidence up your...,' John cut in and there was an angry arrogance in his voice.

'Mr Lawson,' the judge interrupted him, banging his gavel heavily on the bench. 'Your behaviour is shameful and in contempt of this court and if you continue in this manner and refuse to give evidence I will have no alternative but to...'

'You can do what you like. I'm still not going to give evidence,' John cut across him in a supercilious attitude.

'Very well, I hold you in contempt of court. I will deal with you later, take him down,' the judge ordered, his face colouring, his voice thick with anger as he banged the gavel down heavily with a resounding thud.

John was taken down to the holding cells to await the long drive back to Glenochil Prison. John discovered later that because of his refusal to testify, Tam was released without charge for lack of evidence but Jay and Michael were found guilty as the evidence was heavily stacked against them. Jay got five years and Michael four.

John was pleased his actions had got Tam off, but was hurt when he began to hear rumours that Jay and Michael thought he had stitched them up, implicating them in some way when he confessed while doing a deal with the police that let Tam go free of all charges.

Four weeks later John once again endured the sweat box from Glenochil to Edinburgh. Contempt of court is a civil offence, not a criminal one and as a consequence such cases are held in a Civil Court not the High Court. As John stood facing the judge, he looked across the court and saw Jenny sitting in the public seats and smiled at her, but before he could measure her reaction the judge spoke up.

'Mr Lawson, you have been charged with contempt of court and you need to understand that in doing so you have interfered with the courts ability to properly administer justice to those who are accused of breaking the law and brought before it. Contempt of court is a serious offence and if we were to let it go unpunished then the courts would cease to function effectively and as a consequence the punishment must reflect the seriousness of your refusal to give evidence when summoned to court to do so, together with the disrespectful manner in which you conducted I am left with with no alternative but to impose a custodial sentence that takes into account your language and your behaviour. I therefore sentence you to fifteen months imprisonment, the sentence to run consecutively with your current prison term, in that when you have finished serving that term you will then begin to serve the second term of fifteen months. Take him down,' the judge pronounced.

John looked across at Jenny, her face flushed and furious and felt he saw hatred in her usual beautiful sparkling eyes as she shook her head despairingly at him as if to say, *'how much more do I and the children have to suffer because of your arrogance and stupidity?'* It made him feel sick for he knew at that moment his marriage was all but over.

SETTLING IN

They say the first few months of a prison sentence are the hardest while you get adjusted to the routine, and as Alfie told him on his first stretch inside'. *'one fing I've learnt is, yer av ta try not ta fink of what's appening on the outside. Yer world until yer done yer time is prison, and the bleedin' day ta day routines yer just av ta get used ta. Yer start finking about anyfink else and it'll start ta drive yer bleedin' crazy. Do yer bird and that way yer survive.'*

It had held him in good stead, he'd knuckled down, kept his nose clean and accepted he was banged up for the next two and a half years at least, the only thing that constantly nagged at his conscience were his kids and Jenny.

Christmas and the New Year were well and truly over and life was settling back into the normal daily routine of prison life, but John was determined he would not let it get him down. He would survive whatever it took. Having got the cleaners job in the prison library he joined the art class and found he had a passion for clay modelling, making all sorts of models, putting it into the kiln and firing it, then painting it. It was while doing his daily cleaning chores in the library he was approached by a small stocky Nigerian who had the broadest smile John had ever seen.

'Do you have any books on religion?' he asked his voice polite and respectful.

John was taken by surprise by both his manner and the fact he was interested in books on religion.

'Haven't got a clue mate, no one ever asked before, you a Christian?'

'Yes I am a Christian and have faith in the Lord, he is all powerful

349

and has delivered me from my sins and made me see the true faith,' the Nigerian explained, in a magnanimous gesture, his wide grin stretching his mouth.

It was not the answer John expected and it took him completely by surprise. 'If he's that powerful, why hasn't he delivered you from this hell hole?' John retorted as he continued dusting the shelves.

'Unfortunately I fell from the path of righteousness and the Devil took hold of me and I slipped into wicked ways.'

'Really, so it was the devil huh, that's a new one on me mate?' John retorted in a supercilious manner.

'So what were the wicked ways that brought you to this hell hole?' John asked, in a supercilious manner.

'I got involved in credit card fraud and now I must pay, justice must be served as it will be served on Judgement Day before the Lord. But know one thing my friend, I have been already set free by Jesus,' he said, not upset by John's caustic remarks.

'I don't know about him setting you free, but the law as sure as hell won't, because the only time they'll set you free is when you've done your time, mate.'

'I'm in God's hands now and I am happy,' he said, his smile broadening again.

'Well good luck mate, as long as it keeps you smiling but to me there is something childish in the belief that there's somebody up there that has these supernatural powers to suddenly change your life around. Going from being a villain to becoming holier than thou, it only happens in books and you've obviously been reading too many of them,' John said with heavy sarcasm, sweeping his arm around indicating the array of books stacked on the shelves.

'The only book I read is the Bible and books to do with religion,' the Nigerian said, in a demure manner.

'I'd rather read a book about the Krays or gangland. Anyway what's your name? I've seen you walking around the exercise yard, but you don't appear to mix with anybody.'

'My Name is Tony and I come from Africa, Nigeria to be precise.'

'That's interesting I lived in Africa, South Africa actually.'

'Not a good place for a black man to live.'

'No, I guess not, certainly not when I was there.'

'Why did you leave?'

'My father abandoned us, it's a long story and I'd better not go into it now, the screws will be along any time and they won't like to see us talking, maybe I'll catch up with you in the exercise yard,' John suggested, anxious they could get into trouble and he could be put on report and lose his privileges.

'Of course, I must not stop you working,' Tony said, the broad smile still on his face as he sauntered off.

John met up with Tony in the exercise yard many times, 'Hello my friend how are you today?' he would greet John.

'I'm fine thank you,' John would politely reply and hope they could have a conversation without talking about religion.

Tony had this quiet open approachable demeanour, never swore and tended to keep himself to himself, he wasn't not on drugs, never scrounged or tried to borrow or cadge, teabags, coffee, cigarettes or anything else.

Every Monday the prisoners were handed a canteen sheet on which they could order whatever they liked; tobacco, sweets, toiletries, within the limits of the money they had earned from the job they were given. What they ordered was then delivered to their cell on the Friday. It was inevitable that some of the prisoners would use up what they had chosen well before the next Friday and would then go on the scrounge.

'You know what day it is today my friend?' Tony asked as they walked together around the exercise yard.

'Of course I know what day it is, it's Thursday, it comes after Wednesday and before Friday,' John said, in his sarcastic manner.

'No my friend, it is not Thursday today, it is Christian Fellowship day today,' Tony said, the broad smile stretching his face as usual.

'Tony, you tell me this every Thursday and I tell you the same. I'm not interested. If it was a Villains Fellowship day, I'd be more interested,' John said, derisively. 'If you want to believe in all that rubbish, that's up to you, but don't expect me to. I've seen what religion did to my gran, she believed in God, but it didn't stop her being mugged, where was your God then? I also saw what it did in South Africa, men would go to church and pray for goodness and their sins to be forgiven, but as soon as they came out of church, the men would strike out at the first black man they saw. So don't preach to me about religion,' John said, trying to control his anger as he had come to like Tony and didn't want to upset him.

'But that is not of God's doing, that is the Devil's work,' Tony insisted. 'I will pray for you tonight my friend and hope God sends his blessing upon you.' Tony told him, just as the exercise period came to an end and they were ushered back inside.

Another inmate John got to know was a Russian called Vadim, a quiet man with a gentle way about him who spoke very good English.

Vadim, as John learned in conversation had got the nickname of 'Vlad the Impaler.' He was tall just over six feet tall, slim with dark hair and pointed features; le looked a bit like the actor John Cusack.

'Howt did you do to get a name like that, if you don't mind me asking,' John asked once they had started talking together.

'You may ask, I had a very successful business which arranged for students of wealthy Russian families to obtain places in some of Britain's most prestigious public schools. We would make of all the arrangements, paper work, visas, travel, accommodation and for their well being and safety while studying here,' Vlad explained.

'So what happened that you ended up in here?' John asked, curious that a man clearly well educated should be in here amongst the villains.

'I was driving to a business trip in Scotland with my mind concentrating on what was going to be discussed at the meeting. I was not familiar with the narrow roads and I clipped the kerb. The car went into a spin and hit a car coming in the opposite direction, that car spun out of control down an embankment and crashed into a fence. Unfortunately the driver and the passenger, two elderly people were killed; the passenger was impaled on the fence, hence the nickname I've been given. I got five years for causing death by dangerous driving. I've never been in trouble before, never been a police station before, let alone a prison and have lost the business in the process.'

'With luck you'll only do two and half,' John said, by way of offering some kind of consolation.

'Yes, with luck, but I'm worried about some of the hard liners, the ones that stuck the nick name on me. They can cut up rough when they want to and I wouldn't fancy my chances against them,' Vlad said, mournfully.

'Unfortunately it happens in every prison, its part of the system when violent criminals are locked up together, particularly lifers who don't care what they do or who they hurt because they've got nothing to lose,' John said, with a hapless shrug.

'Listen if you get any trouble from anyone, you let me know because I'm more than well equipped to deal with them. Besides, the way I feel sometimes, I would like to vent my frustration out on some of those bastards,' John offered, puffing himself up to his full size to let Vlad know he was quite capable of doing what he said.

'Thank you, that that makes me feel a little better. So what are you in for?'

'Kidnapping and extortion, but I made one mistake.'

'What was that?'

'I got caught.'

'I think I'm going to like you,' Vlad said, offering his hand to shake.

It was kind of strange that after having talked to Vlad about the aggressiveness of some prisoners as John walked along the narrow corridor back to his cell, he accidentally bumped into one of the inmates walking in the opposite direction. He quickly glanced at the other inmate, apologised and continued on his way.

'Oi you,' the inmate called after him.

John stopped and looked round, 'What?' John asked innocently, not wanting to get into any argument as he studied the man. He was huge, about six feet tall and looked like he carried some twenty stone of muscle.

'You just barged into me,' the inmate said, accusingly.

'Yes and I said sorry,' John said, offering an apologetic smile, but felt the inmate staring at him beginning to make him feel uneasy.

'You looking for trouble?' the inmate challenged, regarding him with a look of disfavour.

'I'm not looking for anything, just making my way back to my cell, no big deal,' John said, turning to move on.

'You'd better start to show some respect man, or else.'

John stopped in his tracks and turned back, the hairs starting to rise on the back of his neck. 'Or else what?' he asked, a tiny spark of anger flaring in him.

'You'll find out if you don't show respect the next time you walk past me.'

John said nothing, just turned and carried on along the corridor.

'I saw you having a few angry words with that body builder, McLean I think his name is,' Vlad said as he pushed his plate aside, sitting at the same table in the canteen with John and Tony having their evening meal.

'Yeah, ignorant bastard thinks he owns the place, another one of the morons looking for trouble.'

'Yeah, and have you seen the way he treats his cellmate, like a slave forcing him to do all sorts of things. He's only young, about twenty two I think,' Vlad told him.

'Yeah, Vaughn's his name, the kid arrived the same day as me. What's he in for again?' John asked, finishing his meal.

'A bit like me really, death by dangerous driving, he crashed his car and his girlfriend was killed in the process. McLean treats him like a servant, makes him clean the cell, clean his shoes and do his ironing and if he refuses, McLean threatens to beat him up. Nobody seems to want to help him, if the screws know, they don't care or want to do anything about it, so the poor guy continues to suffer,' Vlad said, and there was pity in his voice for the young man's plight.

'Maybe when I bump into the man again I'll maybe have a quiet word with him,' John said, as they got up from the table.

'I don't know of any easy way of saying this, I want a divorce,' Jenny said, as she sat facing John across the table in the family visiting room. 'I can't take it anymore, everything is collapsing around me, my world is falling apart and I can't cope anymore. I feel drained, I can't touch the bank accounts and the constant threat of the house being taken away, there's nothing left of our marriage. I think it's the best thing for us to part.'

He looked into her eyes and could see the sorrow and tried to give her an understanding smile but it could not hide the anxiety on his face as he said. 'I've been expecting this, I've let you and the kids down badly so I don't blame you for how you feel. If this is what you really want, I won't contest it.'

'Thank you, I don't think I could stand it if we had to fight, there has been enough unhappiness and the children have suffered enough. I won't stop you seeing the children and as I promised I will continue to bring them to see you.'

'What will you tell them?'

'I will tell them we are separating, but will stay good friends and they will still be able to see their daddy whenever they like.'

'I'm sorry it's come to this and…'

'It's no good being sorry it's too late for that. Getting four years was bad enough, but you couldn't stop there, you had to go and make it worse by getting yourself done for contempt of court with no thought the consequences. You're going to be inside for nearly three years,' she said and there was a deep underlying sadness in her voice.

A look of sympathy flashed across his face as he struggled with what to say, he knew everything she felt and had said was true. 'I will tell the kids the same and I will always be there for them and you. Please call them over so I can give them one last hug before the visit ends,' he said, his voice warm, but tinged with sadness.

Jenny called the children over from the play area where they had been happily rolling around and playing with the large assortment of toys.

John experienced his first prickle of uneasiness as he cuddled the children, knowing that soon they would no longer be a family in the true sense of the word, it hurt and the misery was vivid in his eyes.

If you're looking for trouble you can always find it, but sometimes when you're not looking for trouble it will find you, as it did when John walked along the passage to meet up with Vlad and heard the commotion coming from one of the cells further along the landing. One of the inmates was shouting at someone telling them to clean the floor or he would kick their useless head in. John immediately recognised the voice of McLean, the body builder and guessed what was happening. He was bullying his weaker cell mate and it enraged John, still upset about the divorce.

As young Vaughan rushed out of the cell to get a mop, John dashed into the cell, charged at McLean, shoving him hard against the cell wall and gripped him by the throat as he said, 'I don't care how big or hard you are mate, but you don't scare me. If you ever threaten that young lad again or make him do your chores then I will come back and break your jaw.' McLean was so surprised he stared into John's angry face before he tried to use all his strength to force him off.

John knew McLean was the stronger, so smartly stepped back allowing McLean's momentum to carry him forward and gave him his well practiced sideway sweep with his leg. McLean crashed to the cell floor and stared up as John grabbed the front of his shirt, his face a mask of anger, John raised his fist and was about to smash it into McLean's face when something stopped him, it was like a powerful force clutching at his wrist restraining him.

John released his grip and lowered his arm as he spat out the words. 'Make sure next time you pick on someone your own size, because the trouble with you bullies, you know how to dish it out, but you're cowards when it comes to taking it. And be careful not to barge into me whenever we pass on the landings, I might get upset, and I can promise you wouldn't like me when I get upset.'

John had been in Glenochil now for just over five months and it was coming up to Arran's birthday, pangs of guilt rose up again that he wouldn't there for his birthday and wouldn't see him until the following Saturday. It was on that Saturday when Jenny delivered another shock, for while Arran, Lewis and Siobhan played around with the toys in the play area it gave Jenny a chance to speak quietly with John.

'You'll never believe what Arran did the other day. They had a book fair at school and each child was allowed to choose a book to take home and I was shocked when I discovered the book Arran had chosen,' she said, and there was an edge of nervousness in her voice, as she looked at him wondering what his reaction was going to be when she told him.

Some book about gangland and gansters, the thought rushed through John's mind as he looked at her apprehensively.

'It was called '*When Parents Separate*',' Jenny told him, and saw the shock on his face as he turned his head to look across at Arran innocently playing with the toys.

'It has to tell us something, when a seven year old picks up a book like that, while we've been naively thinking we were protecting them from the horrors of the divorce,' she said, a look of bewilderment on her face.

It took John a moment to absorb what she had said and kept his face blank. 'Kids grow up so quickly these days. It would be interesting to know what he expected to find in the book that we haven't already told him,' he finally said.

'He knows we are separating, but I have been very careful in telling the reasons why and maybe that is what he's looking for,' Jenny said, raising an eyebrow sceptically.

He took a deep breath and let it out slowly as he said. 'I suppose the time has come to tell him and the others the truth, it will all come out eventually.'

'The truth, they know you're in prison, they're here now for goodness sake,' she said, struggling to keep her voice calm, using all her self control to maintain it. 'But what they don't know or rather don't understand is what brought you here and why I can't live with it anymore and I don't know how to explain that,' she said, shaking her head in despair.

'Do you want me to tell them?' he asked, in an attempt to redeem himself.

'No, this is something I am going to have to do, here is not the right place and I have to choose the right moment before he gets too deep into that book,' she said, turning her head to look across at the children, but more to hide the tears and hold herself together.

IF A WICKED MAN

2005

'Hello John, glad you decided to come my friend, you will enjoy tonight,' Tony said, the broad welcoming smile stretching his face as usual.

John's attention was drawn to a man who was going around embracing all the inmates and saying 'Welcome brother,' and John stiffened as he saw him turn and approach him.

'Welcome brother,' the man said, with a beaming smile, his arms outstretched to embrace him.

John instinctively took a step back and held up his hand with his palm face out, to stop the man in his tracks. 'I'm not your brother and I don't like anyone embracing me, particularly a man in prison,' John said, looking at him with hostile eyes.

'My apologies, you are new here, may I welcome you to our gathering. My name is Duncan Strathdee, I am a pastor and…'

'You don't look like one,' John interrupted him, looking at the way his was dressed in a white tee-shirt, jeans and trainers.

'It is not how a man is dressed, but what is in his soul, that matters,' the pastor said, not phased by John's aggression.

I'm more interested in what's in my stomach, John thought as he looked across at the table where there was tea bags, sachets of Nescafe, plates of biscuits and cakes invitingly laid out.

John looked around at the other inmates, some he knew and was surprised to see many of them were long term, hardened criminals, serving life sentences for murder, bank robberies, drug dealing.. What surprised John even more was they seemed to be so relaxed and friendly towards each other, it gave him an uncanny feeling.

'Right everybody,' the pastor called out, 'Shall we take a seat and we can begin.'

The group moved across to a group of chairs assembled in a circle with one chair set apart with a guitar resting against it. John held back, wondering why he had allowed himself to be talked into coming, then looked across at the food, remembering the only reason he agreed to come was because of the good quality coffee and biscuits on offer. He reluctantly moved to the circle of chairs and sat down.

'Right guys tonight were gonnae start by saying the Lord's Prayer,' the pastor announced.

The group bowed their heads and closed their eyes as they began to pray, all except John who looked around, shifting uncomfortably in his seat, knowing he was stuck here whether he liked it or not for there was nothing he could do about it. After the prayer one of the inmates started handing out laminated song sheets which made John think, it's bad enough with all the prayers but having to sing hymns as well is beyond a joke. *I just thought we would be sitting around drinking tea or coffee and eating some nice cakes*, the thought making him even more miserable.

John watched as the pastor picked up the guitar and strum it like he was a rock star, the inmates joined in clapping their hands in rhythm and a blues beat developed as they began to sing.

> *'Open the eyes of my heart Lord*
> *Open the eyes of my heart*
> *I want to see you, I want to see you*
> *See you high and lifted up*
> *Shining in the light of your glory*
> *Pour out your power and love*
> *As we cry Holy, Holy, Holy'*

Throughout the singing, John stared at the words and they were beginning to chip at his hard shell, the aggression he had been feeling slowly slipping away, being replaced by a sense of warmth enveloping him, guilt hammering at his conscience.

It was like nothing he had ever experienced before and it frightened him. He felt a panic growing inside him and it made him feel nervous, his whole way of thinking being plunged into uncertainty, his whole world shifting. As he tried to hold himself together, a blanket of sadness fell over him and he felt indecision creeping up on him. *Was something happening, was the Devil putting him to the test, was this a contest between good and evil?* he wondered and tears began to form in his eyes.

As the tears seeped from his eyes, he raised the laminated song sheet to his face in an attempt to cover the shame his was feeling of everyone looking at him, a big tough guy crying. Everything was now flashing through his mind asking himself why he was feeling like this, what was it in the singing and the words that were making him react this way. *This stupid silly way,* he thought, and it started to make him angry bringing back some of his aggression. He lowered the song sheet and wiped away the tears with the back of his hand and it made him feel better.

'Are you alright my friend?' Tony asked, seeing the troubled look on his face.

John glared at him, trying to regain his hard composure, annoyed that Tony may have noticed him crying.

'I'm fine,' he said defiantly. 'I just don't understand all this stuff. You're all singing away as if there's no tomorrow, but there is a tomorrow and the day after that there will be another tomorrow and another one after that. Which makes me wonder if there is there a God and if there is, why does he let these things happen?'

'You have to have faith my friend, only then can you hope to find the answers.'

'Faith in what, why is there so much evil in the world. If there is a God why does he make people suffer, destroy human lives, let children die of hunger and disease?'

'Those are questions the greatest human minds have been struggling with since man was created,' the pastor intervened, as he came across to join in the conversation. 'Life in itself creates all manner of problems. We think we know how life should be, but things have a habit of changing, the unexpected, things we have no power over.

'But you say God is all powerful?' John cut in, confused by what the pastor was saying.

'You're not the first to ask these questions John, just last week an inmate asked me, if there is a God, why is there so much pain and suffering in the world?'

'And what answer did you give him?'

'I said ok, let's remove God from the equation for the sake of argument, the same question remains, considering there is no God, why is there so much pain and suffering in the world?'

'And what was his reply to that?'

'He simply replied, 'Because of man. You see John, the pain and suffering is caused by man and the free will that God gave him. There is much we can't control in life,' the pastor said, reverently.

When John got back to his cell, he lay on the bunk, his head buzzing with all that had happened. *Why had he been so affected by the hymn, was it the words or the music and why had it made him cry?* The thought making him cringe and it made him think of the song *'Big Girls Don't Cry.'* But *what about big boys, or big men and he was a big man, a tough man and he hadn't cried since he was a lad when his dad deserted him.*

John continued to toss and turn throughout the night unable to sleep, unable to blank the troubled thoughts from his mind. Everytime he closed his eyes, he saw the image of the sign hanging outside the Charles Thompson mission.

> **'It is appointed unto men to die once**
> **and after this the judgement'**

Then the next moment he would see his Gran's face waving her finger at him as she said, *'What will it profit a man if he gains the whole world, but loses his soul?'*

No sooner had that image gone when another would comet, the wallet he'd picked out of the gutter and the questions the tract asked:

> *'If there is heaven, do you believe you are good enough to get there?*
> *Have you ever told a lie in your life?*
> *Have you ever taken something that didn't belong to you?*
> *Have you ever used God's name in vain?*
> *Have you ever committed adultery?*

For the first time in his life he was troubled that he could only answer, 'yes.'

The following morning he opened his weary eyes as the cell doors opened to do the head count before breakfast. John however was not in a mood to eat or do anything, for he was still struggling, his thoughts in a turmoil, angry he had allowed himself to be drawn into something so alien to him, against everything he believed in, or rather everything he didn't believe in.

'Good morning John, how are you today?' Tony asked as he appeared in the cell doorway.

'If you don't mind I'd much rather be on my own,' John said, not wanting to talk to anyone about how mixed up he was feeling.

'I brought something for you my friend,' Tony told him as he produced a Bible from behind his back and offered it to John.

John looked contemptuously at the offered Bible, remembering the court clerk offering him the Bible to swear on. 'I told someone else what they could with their Bible, including the judge, so don't tempt me to say the same to you.'

'No my friend, you need this. I saw how you reacted last night. I saw you crying, trying to hide your tears from the rest of us.'

'I wasn't crying,' John retorted angrily.

'There is no shame in crying. It takes a brave man to cry.' Tony said, compassionately.

John reluctantly took the Bible, turned and threw it onto his bunk, before closing the cell door and going off to work in the library.

Because of staff shortages, Friday was always early bang up day. In turn this meant all prisoners having had their evening meal at four o'clock and their canteen order delivered, were back in their cells by five o'clock and locked up until eight o'clock the following morning. It would be a long solitary night and John had never felt so lonely as he felt at that moment, the prison was quiet as it could be, the hollow sounds of inmates moving about in their cells, talking and moaning, generally settling down for the night could be heard. He sighed in the loneliness of his cell, confusion running riot in his head, anger mixed with sorrow, hatred mixed with love. He needed something to make him feel whole again, make him feel part of something, but the problem was he no longer knew what that something was.

Had he found something that he didn't understand or didn't want to understand or was frightened to understand? It gnawed at him.

He looked at the Bible he had taken off the bed and stuck on the top of his bedside locker, reached out and picked it up. He felt the soft leather binding, opened it and began to thumb through the pages, not knowing where to look or what to look for. He had never properly read a Bible, except in Sunday School one time, which he hated and only went because he was forced to. He stopped thumbing about midway through and casually glanced at the page. It was the book of Ezekiel chapter eighteen and verse twenty seven, a feeling of warmth like a soft white cloth began to engulf him as he started to read the verse:

*'But **if a wicked man** turns away from the wickedness he has committed and does what is just and right, he will save his life. Because he considers all the offenses he has committed and turns away from them, he will surely live; he will not die. Yet the house of Israel says, "The way of the Lord is not just." Are my ways unjust? O house of Israel? Is it not your ways that are unjust? Therefore, O house of Israel, I will judge you, each one according to his ways declares the Sovereign LORD. Repent! Turn away from all your offenses; then sin will not be your downfall. Rid yourselves of all the offenses you have committed, and get a new heart and a new spirit. Why will you die, O house of Israel? For I take no pleasure in the death of anyone, declares the Sovereign LORD. Repent and live!'*

He turned his head away from the page, the words '*if A wicked man*' cutting deep into him, hurting him, for he knew he was a wicked man. The judge had told him he was a wicked man and hadn't his mother once told him that, the first time she came to visit him when she said, '*I will pray that God will steer you away from being a wicked man. She was right he was a wicked man and he would continue to be one, only a better and more determined wicked man,*' he thought as he placed the Bible face down on the bed.

He lay there, trying to blank his mind, but what his mother had said would not clear from his mind, the words Wicked Man seeming to flash before his eyes, but then the flashes stopped assailing him as he thought, *it didn't say I was a wicked man, it said 'if a wicked man,'* making him reach for the Bible again. He picked it up and found it was still open at the same page.

Suddenly so full of emotion yet still not quite understanding, he slid off the bed and crumpled to his knees wanting to say something, wanting to pray as he had seen the others do, but not knowing what to say or who to say it to. *Who is this God, why am I so affected by Him, what does he want from me'* the thought screaming out in his head.

The images of some of the terrible things he had done, the kidnapping, the beatings, the robberies, the willingness to kill, flashed like lightning through his mind. He stayed on his knees for a long time, frightened the feelings he was experiencing would evaporate and disappear before he knew what they meant. He didn't want that, he wanted it to remain so he could begin to understand it, for he had never ever felt this good, felt so uplifted, his heart beating with a new found enlightenment. The more John studied the words the more questions it evoked, which made him anxious for Thursday to come around so he could seek some of the answers from the Pastor, of how could he get this new heart and new spirit.

As they gathered in the chapel on the Thursday evening, Duncan warily approached John, not spreading his arms ready to embrace, but was surprised when John spread his arms ready to embrace the Pastor.

'Welcome brother,' the Pastor said, embracing John. 'I am pleased to see you are more relaxed, ready to embrace the spirit of the Lord.'

'I am Duncan, but I have many questions.'

'Then ask and I will try to answer them.'

'Where do I find this new heart, this spirit of the Lord you preach so much about?'

'Why do you want a new heart, a new spirit?'

'I believe now there is a God, he is real and I am going to have to stand before Him on judgement day. I believe there is a Heaven and Hell and I am heading for Hell if I don't change my life.'

The Pastor studied John, a compassionate smile easing onto his face. 'The first thing is to admit to God you are a sinner. All people have sinned against God, some more than others, but a sin is a sin.'

'I want to make good and when I get out of prison I want to help people, do some charity work or something.'

The Pastor narrowed his eyes as he said. 'John you cannot buy your way out of sin, you can't earn forgiveness. As you have found out in your own court case, you couldn't bribe the judge by telling him you rescued a couple of elderly people from a fire. If that judge had let you off because of that, then the judge would have failed in his duty to uphold the law and so it is with God, you can't bribe Him either. You can't redeem yourself in the eyes of the Lord because you've done some good deeds, that is not enough.'

'So what do I need to do to?'

'The first thing is, you have to be genuine, and you've probably heard the word repent many times. Repent is a very real thing. Repent means more than just saying sorry, sorrow without repentance leads to death.'

'What do you mean by that?' John asked, not sure he understood.

'Ask yourself how many times your children have said sorry to you about something they've done, but keep doing it again – which means they are really not sorry for what they're doing, just sorry they got caught. Repentance is actually turning away from what's wrong in God's eyes and doing your best to not go there again. Then you must put your faith and trust in Jesus Christ for as He says, 'I am the way and the truth and the life and No-one comes to the Father but through Me.'

'Forgive me Pastor, but that's easier said than done. What do you mean by that?'

'God realised there was a problem with humanity and that problem with humanity was sin and sin brings death; the Bible says the wages of sin is death. That's why when you go through that list of broken laws you realise your need for a Saviour. The law just points to your brokenness and the Holy Spirit convicts your heart John. By God's Grace He sent Jesus to Earth, Jesus lived without sin to be the perfect sacrifice that God required and willingly laid down his life for you and for me. Jesus went to the cross and God allowed that to happen. God allowed Jesus to be crushed for our iniquity, He allowed His son to die on the cross so that justice could be served and God's wrath was poured out on Him instead of you and me. Jesus took the hit for you John, your fine was paid by Christ on the cross. He bled and died for you and after three days God raised Him from the dead, defeating death itself. God declared that all who sin will die, both physically and spiritually. This is the fate of all mankind. But as I said John, God, in His grace and mercy, provided a way out of this dilemma, by shedding the blood of His only Son on the cross. Jesus died for your sins, but unlike the judge in your court, God will not punish you and you will be saved if you are willing to repent of your sins and put your faith in Jesus.'

'What do you mean by being saved?' John asked.

'It means being saved from your own sins, leading to an eternity separated from God in hell. John 3:16 says, "For God so loved the World that He gave his only begotten son Jesus Christ that whosoever believes in Him shall not perish but have eternal life," but John you have to be genuine, you have to want to repent and put your faith in Christ, I promise you, God will give you a new heart and spirit within you when you turn from your sin and surrender your life to Jesus.'

'Ok, I am beginning to understand, so I can only be redeemed because of what Jesus did? I can't earn this new heart and new spirit, it's freely given by God when I repent and trust in Jesus, right?'

'That's right John, and it's more than just saying a quick prayer, it's so much more than that. It's giving up on your self-reliance and putting all your trust in Jesus. You have to be willing to surrender to Him, let the Gospel change you John. Cry out to God with a sincere heart and let Him begin a work in you that he began in me many years ago.'

When John got back to his cell he was so overcome with what the Pastor had said that he fell onto his bed. Images of the terrible things he had done rolling out before him like an endless series of slides, the beatings, the kidnapping, the robberies, the hurt to his family ballooning up inside him bringing tears to his eyes.

The suffering of Christ on the cross and the realisation that in some way John was responsible for hammering the nails into Jesus caused tears of sorrow to stream from his eyes. The fact that Jesus gave His life for someone that cursed His name and spat in His face overwhelmed John and he fell to his knees.

'Jesus please forgive me for the sins I have committed and the people I have hurt. I am so sorry for the things I have done and I want to turn away from them now and I want you to be my Lord and I believe in my heart God raised you from the dead and you are alive today and I surrender my life to you. I am yours do with me as you will.' John prayed aloud, the tears streaming down his face.

How long he remained on his knees he could not remember or care for he was overcome which such a feeling of well being that he felt no pain just a tremendous sense of happiness. He knew it was about to change him in a way he could never have imagined.

A NEW CREATION

When John woke up the following morning he felt different, everything felt different, the prison felt different, the cell felt different it is was as though there was an overpowering sense of peace and gentleness pervading the air. When the cell door opened, John walked out a different person, a man now at peace with himself.

'You look cheerful this morning Lawson,' the wing officer, quipped as John strode purposely past him.

'I have found something at last, that I think is making me happy.'

'As long as we don't have to start searching your cell for drugs, I'm pleased for you,' the wing officer said, with a smile as he watched John head off for his breakfast. Things were now happening in John's life, bringing about all manner of challenges. He was busy doing his daily chores at the library and had just finished cleaning one of the classrooms and was about to close the door when he heard someone walk in.

'Hello John,' Michael Chamberlain said, but there wasn't a welcoming smile on his face.

'Michael,' John exclaimed, surprised at seeing him standing there.

'Why are you looking at me so surprised John? You're the reason I'm here,' Michael said, looking at him with hostile eyes.

John felt the weight of his anger like a physical blow and winced inwardly as he said. 'We need to talk.'

'You're damn right we do,' Michael retorted as he followed John back into the classroom.

'Look, I'd heard rumours you think I stitched you up and...'

'You did, you did a deal with the Procurator Fiscal to get Tam Kelly off and get yourself a reduced sentence.'

'You got to be joking. I got another fifteen months for refusing to give evidence.'

'Good on you that you never gave evidence, but it was strange that Tam was released the very day you came to court.'

'Look they had me bang to rights, they had recordings of my voice making the threats, they had the sim cards from my phones, they had us all on CCTV, you arriving at the station. They had all the evidence they needed and if I hadn't put my hand up I would have received a much longer sentence. Okay, I know by pleading guilty that I dropped you and Jay in it but remember Michael, you and Jay dropped yourselves in it too by denying you were in Edinburgh that day when they had you both on CCTV. You did the crime just like me and now you gotta do the time just like me.'

Michael continued to stare. 'Yes I dropped you and Jay in it in it by pleading guilty, but what would you have done?'

Michael continued to stare at John, a hard silent stare.

'And you tell me Michael, who got the longest sentence eh? You got four and Jay got five years, but in the end I got five years and three months, and have either of you been hit with a Proceeds of Crime act?'

'No, I haven't.'

'Well I have and I'm going to lose my house, my cars, my banks accounts have been seized and I'm about to lose my wife. So you tell me who came out worse on the so called deal?'

'Yeah well I've lost my wife as well, Cara decided she had had enough and ran off back to South Africa. But when you put it like that I guess you didn't get off so lightly, but you should not have put your hands up in the first place.'

'Maybe you're right, but it is something we have to live with and we can stay friends or become bitter enemies and I wouldn't want that, because I now have a new heart and a new spirit, I've become a Christian.'

Michael stared at him amazed at his words and it showed on his face. 'You a Christian, when the hell did this happen?'

'Only recently since I've been going to Bible classes and I feel a different person. I'm beginning to be at peace with myself and it feels wonderful.'

'You're serious aren't you? So what about Spider, you still on for that when we get out?' Michael asked, as he continued to look at John in amazement.

'No, I'm a changed man and I'm never going back into crime. That life is behind me and all I want to do now is know God more, know his ways and serve him.'

'You're bloody serious.'

'Yes I am and I would love you to come to the Christian Fellowship meetings,' John heard himself saying.

'Well, I don't think I will ever become a Christian. As I think you know, I'm into Apache Shamanism, but I think it would be interesting to come if nothing else to see how it has affected you.'

On his mother's last visit before she went back to Birkenhead she felt she had noticed a change in John, he appeared to be more relaxed, she hadn't sensed the anger in him so much and it gave her hope that the strict regime of the prison was beginning to have an effect on him and she prayed it would continue. The prayer was answered when John rang her, there was the usual silence as she listened to the recorded massage silence, '*the phone call you are about to receive is from an inmate of Her Majesty's Prison, Glenochil. Please hang up now if you do not wish to receive this call.*'

There was a breathless wait until he heard mother say. 'Hello son.'

'Hi mum, did you get back safely?' he asked rhetorically, because she obviously had, but it was really just something to say to begin with as there was something much more important he wanted to say.

Jose noticed that he called her mum instead of the usual ma.

'Yes fine, the train was a bit late but, it usually is, I don't think I've ever known them to run on time. Anyway how are you?' she asked in her casual manner.

'Fine mum…I've…'

'You seemed a little more relaxed on the last visit,' his mother said, interrupting him. 'Maybe prison is at last teaching you a few things.'

'I don't know about prison, but you are right I am a more relaxed person now.'

'I'm pleased to hear it, so what has brought this about?'

'I am more relaxed because I have found peace at last. I have become a Christian mum.'

He heard a sharp intake of breath and then silence.

'Mum, are you there?' he asked, anguishing over the silence. 'Mum, are you there? My card is going to run out soon.'

'Sorry son,' she suddenly spoke up and he realised she was crying.

369

'I've been praying for this day and have never given up hope that you would give up the wickedness that has ruined the lives of you and others. Jesus carried our sins in his body on the cross so that we can be dead to sin and begin to live for what is right. By his wounds you are healed,' she said, as she fought to control her emotions. 'I can tell you now, after my first visit, I telephoned Pastor Duncan Strathdee and told him about you and we prayed together that someone in the prison would search for you and guide you to God.'

He felt the shock of what she was telling him travel through his body to his face and he was glad she wasn't able to see it. 'Then your prayers have truly been answered for someone did find me and lead me to the Bible study. I have found the true meaning of life. I mean Jesus has changed me. I have found God and surrendered myself to Him to do with as He will.'

Happiness was now sounding in his mother's voice. 'I am so happy for you, for you have been blessed and now you have to live it out, keep surrendering to Jesus every day,' she said, with urgent passion now in her voice.

'I know mum, I'm so grateful for the Lord's forgiveness for the hurt I have caused you, Jenny and the kids.'

'You must also ask forgiveness for all those people you hurt you are now in prison being punished for,' his mother reminded him.

'I have mum and I know now that Jesus has already forgiven me,' he said, his voice unwavering.

'I will continue to pray for you son, but with God protecting you, I can now relax without worrying whether you will get into an argument or a fight.'

'The only time I will ever raise my voice now mum is to sing the praises of the Lord.'

'Then you have made me whole again and I have got my son back, so praise the Lord for he is just and forgiving,' she said, struggling to hold onto her emotions. 'I went on a visit to a ship called Logos Hope in Liverpool, it's run by O M Ministries and I met George Verwer the man who founded the organisation. He's got such faith and he told me the aim of the ministry is to bring knowledge, help and hope to the people of the world I bought you a book while I was there, it's called *Taming the Tiger*. I'll post it to you tomorrow.'

Please mother, don't start Bible-bashing me, let me do it my way in my own time he thought silently. 'I'll call again next week mum. Take good care of yourself and love to everyone, God bless,' John said, also struggling to control his emotions as he replaced the receiver to its cradle.

Because of John's change in character and behaviour the screws began to see him in a different light and allowed him to move around more freely, trusting him with jobs that they would have earlier never thought of assigning to him. One of the jobs they gave him was to go to the main stores to collect cleaning materials for the offices and other supplies, which also meant he had to go out into the prison yard to help unload the lorries making deliveries. One day John stood waiting with the civilian in charge of the stores for a delivery due any minute. As the large truck drew to a stop and the driver scrambled out of the cab, John did a double take at the same time as the driver.

'Kenny.'

'John.'

They stood staring at each other before Kenny said. 'What's going on John, what are you doing here?' Kenny, the son of Auntie Betty and Uncle Tommy asked, surprised to see his cousin standing there.

'What do you think I'm doing here? This is a prison and I'm in it, don't you recognise the uniform?'

'Nobody told me you were in prison. Does your mum know? Do my mum and dad know?'

'Yes Auntie Betty and Uncle Tommy know and obviously my mum knows, but you know what gossip's like and it could put pressure on the family so we decided to keep it quiet.'

'Yeah but what about Jenny and the kids, do they know?'

'Of course they know, but Jenny is divorcing me and I can't say I blame her and…'

'Lawson, there's no talking with drivers, there's work to be done, the truck needs to be unloaded so get the barrow,' one of the screws called out watching what was going on.

'Give my love to the family,' John managed to say before he moved off.

As John started unloading the supplies he glanced up at Kenny sitting in the cab staring straight ahead and smiled looking at his bemused face and thought, *I guess now everyone will know.*

*

'Lawson, after breakfast get you gear together and wait in your cell, you're being moved,' the wing officer told him as John made his way down to the canteen.

'Where are they moving me to boss?' John asked.

'Wait and see, just make sure you're ready,' the wing officer told him, but it was said with a warm smile.

John was relieved when they told him he was being moved to the newly built block and was even more relieved when he entered the new wing, it was a palace compared with D wing. The wing was L shaped with two rows of cells, some single, some double, facing each other across a much wider landing. A series of aluminium tables were bolted to the floor along the middle of the landing, where the prisoners could sit and eat their meals instead having to go down to a communal canteen. The meals were served through the hatch of a small kitchen at the end of the landing where the food was kept warm after being brought up from the main kitchens. The cells themselves were clean and neat, fitted with a proper toilet, sink and a much more comfortable bunk and even a television set. At the end of the landing there was a shower block and a small recreation room with a pool table and table tennis table, as well as a separate small gym with running machines and fitness equipment. John was allocated his own cell on the fours, which overlooked the exercise yard and football pitch and also gave him a fantastic view over the Ochil Hills all the way to the William Wallace Monument that stood tall and proud overlooking the place of Scotland's victory over the English at the Battle of Stirling Bridge. He also had a scenic view of Stirling Castle, one of the largest and most important historic castles in Scotland, where several Scottish Kings and Queens have been crowned, including Mary Queen of Scots. John enjoyed gazing at the landscape through the barred window and it added to his new found sense of contentment, freed from the anger and pain of the past that faith had gifted him. As he continued enjoying the view it made him think of the verse from the book of Luke:

'The spirit of the Lord is upon me, because he hath anointed me to preach the gospel to the poor; he hath sent me to heal the broken hearted, to preach deliverance to the captives and recovering of sight to the blind, to set at liberty them that are bruised.'

It was now August 2005 and John had been in prison for just over a year and was a completely changed man, preaching the Gospel to any prisoner who would care to listen, though many avoided him, turning away the moment they saw him approaching, thinking he was mad or on some kind of drug. But John remained determined, repeating to himself after every rejection verses from the second letter to the Corinthians:

'To the one we are the aroma of death leading to death, and to the other the aroma of life leading to life. And who is sufficient for these things? For we are not, as so many, peddling the word of God; but as of sincerity, but as from God, we speak in the sight of God in Christ.'

Jenny surprised John on her visit with the children when she handed him a letter for which had been given permission to bring in and pass to him. John wondered what it was as it had clearly been opened by Jenny but he guessed had also been opened and checked by the prison security.

'Aren't you going to open it?' Jenny asked impatiently waiting to see his reaction.

'What's in it?' he asked, worried it could have something to do with the divorce.

'You won't know unless you open it,' she said, irritably.

John opened it and a broad smile spread on his face as he read the contents, it contained one letter from the police stating he had been awarded a meritorious award for his bravery in saving two elderly people's lives and another letter from The Society For The Protection Of Life From Fire, awarding him a commendation for his bravery in rescuing nine people including carrying two elderly people from the fire, the ceremony to take place on 21st November at the Gallery in Fettes College.

'Fettes College, that's where Tony Blair went wasn't it, doesn't say much for the college does it? How the blazes do they expect me to attend when I'm banged up here?' John said, looking up at Jenny.

'Surely they'll let you out to receive the awards. I mean they can't be that strict, particularly now you've changed your ways and become a Christian.'

'I can ask I guess.'

'Show them the letters that should encourage them. You should have seen the reaction from the kids when they saw the letters, they felt so proud of you and want to be there when you receive the awards,' Jenny said, and he noted there was a hint of pride in her voice.

'I'll see what I can do, I would love the kids to be there proud of what their dad had done and proud of what he's become,' John said, stifling back the emotions swelling up inside him.

'I'm told the Governor, Kate Donegal, is due to visit the library on Monday so I may get a chance to ask her.'

John waited nervously while going about his chores for the Governor to appear so that he could try and have a word with her.

'Excuse me Governor, may I have a quick word with you please?' John ventured as the Governor came close to where he was working.

She stopped in her tracks and looked at John, her face implacable almost as though to say, '*how dare you address me.*'

'I have received these letters Governor and I was wondering whether I might be granted permission to attend the award ceremony, I think it will be good for my future.'

The Governor took the letters from his hand and studied them. 'This is wonderful Lawson, congratulations.'

'Thank you Ma'am.'

'However, you are a long term prisoner in a high security prison, for you to attend we would have to arrange for a private security van to transport you to and from the event and assign a prison officer to escort you. Also, you need to know that as a high security prisoner you will be handcuffed and remain handcuffed the whole time, that might cause you some embarrassment particularly if your family were to attend,' she advised him, in a formal, but not too unfriendly manner.

'I understand Governor, but I would still like to put in an application to attend if I may.'

'Very well Lawson, put in an application, but I don't want to raise your hopes too high as this is a most unusual case, but I will do my best,' she promised, as she turned and walked away.

CASTLE HUNTLY

The morning began well, as did every morning; there was no better feeling now than waking up to God. But the day wasn't to be blessed it seemed when he was called to the wing office and handed a letter informing him that his application had not been approved due to the high costs of transporting and guarding a long term high security prisoner.

As he walked back to the library to start his daily chores, he thought about the verse he had read in the Bible that said something like, *'don't be anxious about anything, let your requests be made known to God,'* and it made him a little feel better.

Later that day his solicitor Mr McAlister came to visit him.

'The Asset Recovery Agency has finally agreed on the final sum and you'll be pleased to hear they have settled on forty grand and...'

'Forty grand,' John exclaimed, 'What makes you think I'd be pleased I've got to give away forty grand?'

'You seem to forget they wanted £90,000 to begin with, so on the face of it I think you've got a good deal,' Mr McAlister reminded him, as he removed the paperwork from the briefcase he was carrying and placed it on the small table of the private visiting room.

'A good deal, and when do we have to pay that?'

'If the court is satisfied that time to pay is required it will allow you up to six months and up to a further six months if you can show exceptional reasons to justify the extension. So that means in effect with a bit of luck we can delay the selling of the house and...'

'If I were to take full responsibility for the money, could we avoid having to sell the house?' John asked, dejected at the thought of Jenny and the children having to move out of the house they had so lovingly refurbished all because of his arrogant stupidity. 'I'm the criminal, it was me who got the money and should be punished. not anyone else.'

'Unfortunately the law doesn't see it that way. They look at who else might have jointly benefitted from the proceeds of your criminal acts. They consider the house was purchased with the proceeds of your criminal activities and as a consequence your wife is considered equally culpable and therefore cannot be exempt from the Proceeds of Crime Act. As I was saying, I will endeavour to give Mrs Lawson time to find suitable alternative accommodation for her and the children, but I should warn you, twelve months is the absolute limit and after that interest will be charged and that can push the charge up considerably,' Mr McAlister explained.

'The longer we can give Jenny to find something suitable the better and I will take full responsibility for any outstanding amount if any, once the house has been sold,' John informed McAlister.

As he made his way to his cell after his evening meal, he decided to check the notice board at the end of the landing by the wing officer's desk to see if his name was there indicating there was mail for him.

There was and he approached the wing officer. 'I see my name is up on the board, is there some mail for me boss?' John asked.

'Yes Lawson, there's a letter and a package,' the wing officer told him.

John took the letter and the package and hurried off to his cell. He opened the letter leaving the package to last, guessing it was a Bible from his mother.

The letter was from Jenny's solicitors outlining details of the divorce proceedings which did nothing to lift his spirits, so he turned his attention to the package, ripped off the wrapping and was surprised to see it was not a Bible but a book, '*Taming The Tiger*' written by Tony Anthony. The words '*From The Depths Of Hell To The Heights Of Glory,*' emblazoned at the bottom of the cover page caught his eye.

John was so taken by the book that he read it in two nights, especially the chapter where the preacher Michael Wright had heard about the plight of Tony Anthony being banged up in Nicosia's notorious Central Prison. He enjoyed the pages where Michael Wright comes to visit Tony in prison and Tony asks in a not too friendly manner, what made him want to come and visit him. Michael simply answered that he believed God had sent him to Tony to tell him about Jesus.

It reminded John of how Nigerian Tony had sought him out and guided him to Jesus. By the time John had read the book a second time he determined he would try and make contact with Tony Anthony to tell him how much the book had inspired him when he was released. John even gave the book to a Muslim inmate called Bash in the hope it would inspire him to think about Christ in a different way. The book had encouraged him in his faith and he was beginning to feel better about himself and God and this became concrete when the wing officer came to the table where John was sitting having his evening meal, to tell him to get his things together for the following morning he was going to be moved to another prison. It was 17th November 2005, and John had been in prison now for thirteen months. John busied himself gathering his stuff together, looked around the cell and crossed over to look out the window one last time at the view he had become so used to surveying every morning. Wherever he was going to be sent to, he knew he was going to miss the comfort of his little cell that he had become so used to. He knew he would also miss the new friends he'd made as well as Vlad and Michael, of course. But most importantly he would miss going to the Bible classes.

'Where am I being moved to, boss?' John asked anxiously as they came to collect him.

'Castle Huntly open prison, you'll like it there Lawson, it's a holiday camp compared to this. You deserve it, you've kept your nose clean and stayed out of trouble,' the wing officer told him with an encouraging smile.

Bash had been sent to Castle Huntly two weeks earlier, so at least there would be someone there he knew. As well as John, five other prisoners were being transferred with him, two of which he was pleased to see were Rooney and Vaughan. They were all taken down to reception, signed out, then handcuffed and loaded into the prison van, the sweat box, and driven out of Glenochil prison.

The journey was an eye opener, to see the outside world after thirteen months of brick walls and barbed wire was breathtaking. To catch glimpses of the people moving freely around and to spot the latest makes of cars speeding along, it reminded him of the difference when he was being transferred to Stanford Hill Open Prison on the Isle of Sheppey, except now they weren't handcuffed and were travelling in a coach with big windows so that they could just sit back and enjoy the scenery. As they approached and turned into the prison drive, John could see the North Gate entrance, which was just a simple barrier between what looked like two Gothic towers. The barrier was raised without much preamble and as the van continued its journey John could just see the castle up on the hill and noticed, as he strained his neck to see, that there appeared to be great open area with fields and woods, with no walls, let alone high walls surrounding the prison. The van pulled up alongside the reception, a clean modern building where they were unloaded and still handcuffed, led into the building. Once inside they were guided into a fairly large room, the handcuffs were removed and they were told to sit down and wait. After a short while a senior prison officer walked in, looked around at them, then looked at his watch and said. 'It's almost lunch time, so the other prisoners will be heading for the dining hall for their meal, so I suggest you all go and have a look around the place, see where everything is, then go to the dining hall, get something to eat and be back here at one thirty, Okay?'

Nobody moved, surprised by what the prison officer had said, that they could just get up and walk around the place.

'Go on, off you go and be back here by one thirty,' he said, ushering them out.

John walked out with Rooney and Vaughan staring around in amazement at the vast area of open ground with well manicured lawns, trees with the leaves in the last of their Autumn shades, landscaped gardens, walled off areas with bedding plants, green houses and long plastic hot houses growing all sorts of plants and vegetables.

'You could walk out of here, you wouldn't even need to scale a wall, there aren't any,' John said, as they all sat down and started feeling the grass as though they had never seen it before.

'No, only an idiot would think of absconding from here, that's why there are no walls or barbed wire. You get caught and they bang you back up and you lose your remission, not worth it,' Rooney said, as he pulled out a handful of grass and smelt it.

'How long you got to do John?' Vaughan asked.

'About another eleven months on my current sentence, but I've got a contempt of court to serve as well, but no one has said anything about that so I don't know what my dates are going to be,' John told him.

'I think we'd better find the dining hall and get some lunch,' Rooney suggested as he scrambled to his feet.

The dining hall was large, clean, and well furnished and there was a good selection of food that looked appetising – and indeed it was. The three of them having queued up, selected what they wanted, took their meals to a table and tucked in to the best meal they had had in prison.

'Better than some of the meals I have outside,' Rooney joked, shoving the food down as fast as he could chew and swallow it.

'Right we'd better get back before someone comes looking for us,' John said, getting up from the table and grabbing his dirty plates.

Once back in the room at reception the prison officer was waiting for them and was pleased to see everyone had returned and on time.

'Right, well I guess you all know the prison rules from the time you've served already, and although this is an open prison the same rules apply here and appropriate action will be taken if any of you break them. So, no mobile phones, no drugs. You will be subjected to urine tests and anyone failing the test will be punished, fail the test twice and you'll be immediately sent back to a closed prison. As you've already seen there are no walls or barbed wire and you are free to move around within precincts of the prison, but don't think you can just walk out, because you will be caught and the punishment is severe, you will lose all your remission and may have your current sentence added to.'

John was assigned to a block and told to report to the wing office. The block was constructed of a series of porta-cabins linked together in a long row. There were fifteen rooms on each side with a central corridor running the entire length between them, at the end of the corridor was a large shower room. John reported to the wing officer who assigned him to room 12 as he referred to it and issued him with a key as he said. 'Go and have a look at your room and then go to the stores to collect your bedding.'

He opened the room with the key and was surprised by its clean condition. It was reasonably spacious, equipped with a television and furnished like it had come from Ikea. There was a nice desk and another table on which stood a kettle and the other paraphernalia for making tea and coffee. In the far corner was a little room which John discovered contained the toilet and that really pleased him. However, he was a little disappointed to see there were bunk beds, the top one with the bedding laid out, clearly occupied by another prisoner's stuff which meant he was sharing a cell. It was four o'clock by the time he had collected his bedding and made up the bottom bunk when he heard a key being inserted and the door flying open.

'Hi pal, Shaun's the name, drugs the game, welcome,' Shaun announced as he sauntered in, not showing any surprise someone else was now sharing the room with him.

John looked at Shaun and all his fears of sharing a cell were realised. He was a big guy, overweight and bloated. He had thick black greasy hair, a pale complexion and displayed a row of rotten black teeth when he smiled, showing all the hallmarks of drug addiction.

'So what are you in for?' Shaun asked, which was the standard question every prisoner asked a new inmate.

John told him as briefly as he could as he was already beginning to feel uncomfortable about having to share a cell with this man.

'Do you want to chase the dragon?' Shaun offered.

'No thanks, I don't touch the stuff,' John was quick to tell him.

'Want a smoke?'

'I don't smoke either,' John curtly replied.

'You some kind of goody two shoes pal?'

'No Shaun, far from it but I have become a Christian mate and Jesus has changed me and I know He can set you free from your addictions if you will only...'

'Aye, aye, aye I've heard it all before pal and I'm no interested in your Jesus, but if you change your mind there's plenty of drugs around,' Shaun told him

'I thought drugs were banned.'

'Nah, you don't take any notice of that there's plenty of it around.'

'Seriously?'

'Sure, I can score you a bag for a tenner and I can get you a mobile phone if you want,' Shaun offered, taking out a cigarette, lighting up and blowing out large clouds of smoke.

This was too much for John as he began to cough and walked out and made his way to the wing office.

'Sorry boss, but you've put me in with a smoker, I don't smoke, never have. I need to move or you need to move him,' John told the wing officer.

'There's nothing I can do about it, that's the cell you've been assigned to and that's the end of it, so make the best of it,' the wing officer told him in an unflinching manner.

As John walked reluctantly back to his cell he noticed a small lounge area and to his amazement he spotted his Muslim friend Abdul Bashir sitting on one of the sofas. He looked in a terrible state, rocking backwards and forwards staring blankly into space. His eyes was sunken like two deep black holes, his body frail from having lost so much weight, his light brown skin taking on a grey appearance having lost its firmness hanging loosely around his chin and neck.

Shocked to see him in this state John went over and sat down beside him. 'Hi Bash, what's going on what's happen to you.'

Bash stopped rocking and slowly turned his head, his eyes blinking while his drug fuelled brain struggled to recognise who it was that was sitting next to him.

'Bash, it's me John, don't you recognise me?'

'John, John,' he repeated, his brain still struggling to function as he at last managed to focus his eyes. 'Sorry John, I'm on the smack, I'm on the hard stuff and I can't get off it.'

John looked at him sadly but compassionately. 'I remember you telling me your sister ran off with a drug dealer and you had to go and kidnap her to get her away from him and drugs, which is why you finished up here, so what happened for you to become hooked on drugs?'

'I don't know John, this place is boring and I haven't got any friends like I had with you in Glenochil, they stuck me in with some serious drug user and I just gave in one night after he kept offering it to me for free. I was feeling lost, and the only consolation was drugs, they're so easy to get your hands on and before you know it you can't do without them,' Bash explained, his voice slow and slurred. That night John spent the worst night he'd ever experienced in his whole time in prison, his cellmate was constantly in and out of the cell scoring drugs, using the little enclosed toilet without closing the door, so John could hear him doing his business by the sound of him straining to force his bowels open, which when they eventually did was followed by a series of loud farts. With the stench drifting out from the toilet and his constant smoking the cell was soon stinking and it began to make John angry. Fury simmered at the back of his mind, making him want to grab hold of Shaun, shove him hard against the wall and beat the hell out of him; but as before something held him back and he laid down on his bunk closed his eyes and prayed that God would find a way for him to be moved. Extraordinarily, the following morning Shaun arrived back in the cell looking rather angry with himself.

'What you doing back here, you're supposed be at work aren't you?' John asked surprised to see him there.

'I've just been sacked off my job and now I have been told to move, so I'm changing cells, one of ma pals has got a space in his cell so I'm moving in with him,' Shaun told him, as he started to gather up his things.

It made John feel as though his prayers had been answered and as soon as Shaun left he started cleaning the cell up, opening the windows to let out the smell that still pervaded the air. As John could now spread some of his own stuff out on the desk, he came across the letters inviting him to the award ceremony, the problem as he quickly realised reading the letter again was that it was now Friday 18th November and the ceremony was on Monday 21st.

Thinking there might just be chance now that he was in an open prison he made his way to the wing officer and showed him the letters. The wing officer studied the letters then looked up at John and said. 'You know Lawson you have to be here at least a week before we can assess whether you are suitable to be allowed out for visits, so since you only arrived here yesterday I doubt that this can be approved.'

'Please boss, this is a big thing for me and could really help me with my future when I'm released, particularly with me having a criminal record,' John pleaded.

'You should be congratulated on your bravery,' the wing officer said, and there was an air of respect in his voice.

'Thank you boss.'

'I'll take these letters up to the castle and see what I can do, but don't hold out too much hope.'

IF THEY ONLY KNEW

Once again his prayers had been answered as they let him out of prison for the day. It was an odd feeling being back in his old flat in Pinkie Road and John felt remorse, he apologised to Jenny that she too was subject to the proceeds of crime act.

'Look John, what's done is done and yes I am angry and yes we are going to have to find somewhere else to live, but hopefully there will be enough left from the sale of the flat for me and the kids to start over again,' Jenny replied brusquely. The words 'start over again' made John realise that their relationship was truly over and he couldn't hide the tear in his eye as he thought about the children, especially as he was at home now while they were in school. Jenny could see that he was hurting and told him more compassionately to hurry up and change as they had to meet Daniel at Dreghorn Army barracks. John was shocked as they entered the gallery at Fettes College where the ceremony was to take place. Two lines of chairs filled the room. On one side there were rows of uniformed police officers and it made him smile, wondering who was left to police the streets. There were members of the fire brigade sitting alongside the police, while opposite, members of the public were seated. At the end of the gallery there was a table at which the Lord Mayor of Edinburgh, the Chief Police Constable, the Chief Fire Officer and other dignitaries were seated. Members of the press could be seen moving around talking to people and taking photographs.

John, Jenny and Daniel, who was looking very smart in his army uniform, were ushered to seats where the members of the public were sitting and just managed to sit down in time as the Lord Mayor rose from his seat and began to speak. By now John was watching warily, becoming over awed with the situation. He suddenly felt a hot damp flush of panic, feeling his strength drain away as he wondered whether any of the police had recognised him, the words the Lord Mayor was speaking became a blur as he continued to scan the faces of the police.

'Ladies and Gentlemen I would like to welcome you to this award ceremony to honour both members of the emergency services and members of the public whom have gone beyond the call of duty and shown exemplary courage in putting their own lives at risk to save others.'

John watched with a dispassionate interest as the Lord Mayor rambled on until finally the awards began with the Master of Ceremonies announcing the people to be honoured. Award after award was handed out until he was nudged hard by Daniel; John had not registered his name being called out. John got to his feet and made his way to the front as he heard the Master of Ceremonies announce:

'Mr Lawson is to receive a meritorious award for his bravery in saving the lives of nine people from a burning building, personally rescuing two elderly people from the top of the building at great risk to his own life and also alerting the other residents of the building to the dangers with the help of his friend Andrew Warburton who, although not present, is also to receive a meritorious award.'

The Chief Constable handed John the framed award and as they shook hands and posed the cameras clicked away. The Master of Ceremonies then announced,

'Mr Lawson receives a commendation from the Preservation of Life Society for his actions in the same incident.'

The Chief Fire Officer presented John with this award as well and once again they shook hands and posed for the photographers.

With the ceremony over, everyone was invited to enjoy some light refreshments, but John held back taking a quick glance at his watch, knowing he had to get back to the flat, change out of his suit and for Jenny to drive him back to prison.

'Won't you join us Mr Lawson. That was a very courageous thing you did in rescuing those people, you deserve the award so do come and have a drink,' one of the police officers invited.

'Thank you, but unfortunately I can't stay, I have to go.'

'You have to go back to work?'

'In a way yes.'

'You mean to say your boss wouldn't give you the time off for such a special occasion?'

'Well I'm with Her Majesty's services at the moment and have to dash back,' John said, sheepishly.

'At least that's something, anyway well done. I just wish there were more public spirited citizens like you instead of the increasing number of criminals we have to deal with these days, keep up the good work,' the police officer said, shaking John's hand.

'I'll do my best,' John said, looking at him thinking, *if only you knew the reason I have to go is because I have to be back in prison by five o'clock or I'll be in trouble.*

FREEDOM INSIDE

2006

The perk of being in an open prison was the home visits every month and John was thrilled to be able to spend Christmas with Daniel, Siobhan, Arran and Lewis, but was upset that Jenny told him, after they had opened the presents, that she would be spending the rest of the day with her new boyfriend, Kenny. At least John had the pleasure of watching Arran and Lewis play with the Hot Wheels set, with Lewis whooping with excitement as the cars did a loop the loop, while Siobhan sat quietly on the sofa dressing her Bratz doll with the collection of clothes that came with the set. What really interested John was the present he had given Daniel, a Bible protected by a metal casing, designed specifically for military personal to carry with them into battle,. His heart swelled with pride, as he watched him flick through the pages, and then look up and smile a thank you.

'This is going to be very useful to take with me to Iraq,' Daniel said, holding the Bible up.

John was peeling the potatoes for lunch and dropped the knife as the shock of what he had just heard struck home…

'What did you just say?'

'Sorry Dad, I was going to tell you. Our battalion is being sent to Iraq for a six months tour at the end of January.'

'You see there is God working His miracles. He must have been guiding me to buy you that Bible,' he said, as the shock eased on his face into a reassuring smile. 'Hold on to it and keep it with you always son, I believe it will give you strength and reassurance when you need it.'

'Yes, I will take it with me Dad, because it will remind me of you and that you will be praying for me and my safe return,' Daniel said, giving the Bible a gentle rub.

'I'll pray for you every day son, that Jesus brings you home safely, and the rest of the men that are going with you,' he said, fighting back a tear as he finished peeling the potatoes.

The Christmas meal was a great success and John was so happy as he looked at everybody sat around the table and tucking heartedly into the turkey. On New Year's Eve, John popped down to Oscars to wish Tam a Happy New year. Not wanting to stay long, he stayed for just one drink and then headed out the door. It was the wrong moment. The new bouncer Grant was on his own, trying to hold back a drunken mob of youths causing trouble. As Grant was dealing with two of the mob, another one sneaked up behind him gripping a beer bottle and raised it ready to smash it over his head. John instinctively reacted and shoved Grant out of the way, inadvertently placing himself in line with the descending bottle which caught him squarely on the head. Fortunately the bottle never smashed and John quickly disarmed the man. The mob recognising John and knowing his reputation quickly turned and ran off. Grant was so grateful when he realised what John had done, that he shook his hand warmly saying, 'if I can ever return the favour, you just let me know okay?'

John returned to Castle Huntly on Monday January 2nd and was soon settled back into the prison routine. It was then that John decided to join the Bible study group and it was during one of the discussion periods he spoke about the book *Taming the Tiger* his mother had sent him.

To John's amazement a couple of weeks later as he was walking around the prison he spotted a poster announcing the author of *Taming The Tiger*, Tony Anthony, was going to be visiting the prison in two weeks time to share his story. John could not believe what he was reading, this was the man whose book had so moved him that he had determined to seek him out when he got released and yet here he was, coming to the very prison he was in. He couldn't wait to phone and tell his mother the news.

'You see son, how God's connected everything, how I got the book from George Verwer, then sent it to you, you read it and now he's coming to the prison. These things don't just happen, it's not a coincidence, it's a God incidence,' she said, and there was great passion in her voice. 'God works in mysterious ways, always remember that son,' she added.

The night Tony Anthony came to the prison to talk to the inmates had a profound affect on John, adding to the opportunity to re-shape his life with God's help. But as Tony made clear in his talk, 'prison takes many shapes and forms and you don't have to be behind bars to be in prison. Many of you were in a prison before you ever came here, a prison to violence, to addiction to stuff you look at on the internet, in prison to anger or self abuse. My friends, prison takes many shapes and forms, but only Jesus can truly set you free.'

Tony's talk had so moved John that he rushed up to shake his hand, telling him he had read his book and it had such a positive impact making him begin to take accountability of his life before God. It pleased Tony to hear John say that and he gave him his card, inviting him to make contact when he was released from prison parting with the words, 'Just remember everyone suffers in life at some point, but Jesus will see you through.'

Those words stayed with John and helped him in his struggle to find the courage to understand the changes that were happening within him. *As Christ said, become a new creation and let the old self die,* his mind told him, realising it only takes one person to share the Gospel and change a life, as Michael Wright had done for Tony Anthony and as Tony the Nigerian had done for him. He determined that when he was released from prison he would find people to share what Jesus had done for him.

By now Daniel was serving the second half of his tour of Iraq and John spent many nights praying for God's protection over his son. It was tough being in prison knowing Daniel was in a war zone, but once again felt a great sense of peace as he sat reading his Bible, believing God would protect him. John's job application to work in the community was approved and he was assigned with two other prisoners, Matt and Dave, to work at an old people's day care centre in Dundee. John along with the other prisoners working out in the community were bussed into the City centre and dropped off at their various places of work. It was good because it gave John the opportunity to be away from the prison and be amongst the community, feeling he was doing some good and it also kept his mind occupied which helped to make the days go quicker. Life was even better when Daniel returned safely from Iraq and was stationed back in Edinburgh, which meant he could he could visit John and they could meet up on the days John was allowed out; particularly as John was now allowed out on a Sunday to visit the Perth Christian Centre.

John had been told that Jay was being transferred to Huntly Castle and had heard the rumours that Jay was out to get him, even Alex had warned him that Jay had sworn revenge and told everybody that when he caught up with John he would do him in and make sure he paid for selling him and Michael down the river. And it was on one of his walks around the prison that his faith was to be tested in a way he hadn't expected, when John spotted Jay in the reception area with a group of heavies. Whatever his inner feelings were, he knew he had to face Jay and sort it out.

'We need to talk,' John said, confronting Jay. 'I suggest we got to my cell.'

Jay was thrown and not sure how to react. He knew John to be a violent man and had forgotten how capable John was of doing him more harm than he had been threatening to do to him. The atmosphere was heavy and he felt one wrong word or move was all that was needed to set John off.

'No, it's alright John. I don't harbour any grudges, it's in the past let's forget it,' Jay said, as he turned and walked away, with all the heavies staring at him in surprise at his apparent surrender.

'No Jay,' John called out. 'I suggest we go to my cell so we can talk, not fight.'

Jay, realising he had no choice, followed John gingerly to his cell with the others looking on.

'Listen Jay I've heard all the rumours that you think I did a deal and stitched you and Michael up. Well let me tell you that if I did, then I made the worst deal in history, not only did I get four years, but another fifteen months for refusing to give evidence against you, and on top of that I've been done under the Proceeds of Crime Act, they have seized all my assets and are forcing me to sell the house to meet the costs. On top off all that I've lost my wife, so Jay you tell me who's come off worse out of all of this?' John said, without anger and with a quiet dignity as soon as they got to John's cell.

It surprised Jay and he took a long measured look at his face still trying to calculate what John had just told him. 'Sorry, I didn't know.'

'No you didn't, and another thing, you'll be out of here long before me.'

'Yes I guess I will, so I suggest we forget about it and put it behind us.'

'Fine by me, but you've made a rod for your own back,' John told him.

'Why is that?'

'Well, you've announced to everyone you were going to do me in, so you could lose face if we don't handle it well.'

'So what do you suggest?'

'We keep our distance in here and tell everybody you are going to wait until you get me on the outside,' John suggested.

'Even better, because the other thing I wanted to sort out with you is going back to Spain and getting our hands on Spider's money. We spent enough time and money, so it's ours by right and I imagine you're still up for it,' Jay said.

'No Jay I'm not, I've done with all that, I've changed, I'm a Christian now.'

Jay shook his head as though he was mishearing what John was telling him. 'Are you serious?'

'Yes very,' John assured him.

'This is not one of your cons to get early release, you know, what do they call them, "prison Christians"?'

'No, it's no con, it was only when I let go of my past and died to myself that I could begin to become what I now want to be – a servant of Jesus.'

Jay shook his head again. 'I don't know what to say.'

'Then say nothing, but remember Jesus changed me mate and he can do the same for you, he knocks at your door Jay, but you must be willing to open it.'

'Yeah well, another time maybe, but I can't handle it now it's all a bit cranky to me. If it makes you happy then fine, but watch out for some of the guys that came in with me, a couple of them are loose cannons and would love to have a pop at you, they think you're some kind of fruit cake,' Jay warned him.

IT IS FINISHED

2007

John was due for release in October 2006 on his first sentence, but having met the conditions for parole he was unusually paroled back into prison, to serve his civil offence for contempt of court. As a consequence it was seven and a half months later, on May 17th 2007, that John was finally granted parole on his second prison term and released from Castle Huntly prison. Tam Kelly was waiting to pick him up with a broad welcoming smile on his face, as John walked out of the main gate carrying his only belongings in a black plastic bag.

'How does it feel to be free at last?' Tam asked as he opened the boot of his green BMW and piled John's belongings in.

'I've been free for quite some time now,' John told him.

Tam gazed at him distantly, a puzzled expression spreading over his face. 'I don't understand you've only just been released,' Tam said, in surprise slamming the boot shut with an air of exasperation.

'You forget Tam, I was set free by Jesus, I told you I am a Christian now.'

'Yes sorry, I forgot, I thought that was just for the prison authorities and once you were out then…'

'The only thing I knew was that I knew nothing until I found God, and Tam until then I was nothing,' John said, and there was warm tone to his voice.

'Right well, we'd better get you to the probation office so they can sort you out and when they've done that and got you settled come over to the club and we'll have a celebration drink, you can pick up a bird and…'

'Tam, you're not listening to me, I'm not into that anymore, I must follow my Christian beliefs.'

'Which I guess means you're still not interested in going after Spider's money?' Tam said, despairingly.

'No I'm not, we've been through that already and I haven't changed my mind.'

'Well, maybe when you've been back outside in the real world for sometime, you might change your mind,' Tam said, wistfully as they drove away from the prison.

John didn't look back, for the past was behind him and he was now journeying into the future.

The future though did not get off to a good start, the room he was allocated by the local council was a small bedsit in a run down block of flats near the Musselburgh racecourse, mainly occupied by down and outs, junkies and alcoholics. There was the recognisable acrid smell of unsanitary conditions that were just as bad, if not worse ,than he had experienced in prison.

Well at least I am in the right place to share The Gospel with lost souls, he thought to himself as he dropped his meagre belongings to the floor and slumped down on the small single bed, However, with none of his prison friends to talk to and feeling completely alone it felt more like a prison cell than Huntly Castle. Alone with his thoughts his mind drifted to the nice flat he and Jenny had, the new furniture, his Range Rover, his motorbike, money in the bank – all gone.

The flat had been forcibly sold a few months earlier and John agreed to shoulder the full burden of the £40,000 owed to the crime department from his share of the profits. Fortunately Jenny was left with enough money to rent a new house in Prestonpans for her and the children, leaving him sitting in a dump of a bedsit with very little money and it made him feel sad. He lowered his head into his hands and prayed.

'How are things going, you settled in alright?' Tam asked as John walked into Oscars.

'Not really I've been given a miserable little bedsit in a block of flats that quite frankly should be knocked down and I was wondering if you knew of anyone who might have a flat to rent?'

'As it happens I do know of someone who is looking for someone to rent his flat. I'll give him a ring and see what he says. Order yourself a drink,' Tam offered, as he made off to the office then stopped and turned back. 'Sorry, I forgot you don't drink anymore.'

Tam was back quickly with a happy smile on his face as he said. 'You're in luck, he was doubtful as first until I mentioned your name and then said to tell you to pop round and see him right away. Grant seems to like you for some reason.'

'Grant, you mean the bouncer that got into a spot of bother here that night when I was on home leave?'

'Yes, he's been offered a great job in Canada and wants someone to take over the lease of his flat, so go and see him. It's his night off so he's there now, it's 11 Graham Street up the toon, here I've written it down,' Tam said, handing him the address. John stood on the pavement looking up at the massive modern, grey stoned apartment block in Graham Street with its large windows, wondering for a moment whether Tam had given him the wrong address. But when Grant answered the intercom and told him to come up to flat 10 on the fourth floor John was relieved and full of expectation. The apartment was well beyond John's expectations, a spacious lounge with floor to ceiling windows that provided a panoramic view of the Edinburgh skyline. The flat was well furnished throughout with a fully equipped kitchen.

'So what do you think?' Grant asked.

'Fantastic.'

'I've spent over six grand on the furniture, all from Ikea, and kitted it out with everything you need, so it would be nice to get some of it back and…'

'Look Grant, I've just come out of prison and there is no way I can afford any of this, as much as I'd love to, the flat is fantastic, but it's well beyond me,' John said, his voice trailing off with disappointment.

Grant took a long hard look at him and a shadow of a smile crossed his face as he said. 'I owe you John, you saved me from me being smashed over the head with a beer bottle and if that bottle had hit me, I probably would have been injured badly and as a consequence not be in a position to take the job in Canada; so as long as you take over the rent, you can start paying me for the furniture when you've got back on your feet and if you can't, well don't worry about it; like I said I owe you.'

His words were so unexpected that it left John speechless not sure how to respond. 'I don't know what to say,' he finally blurted out.

'You don't have to say anything, here are the keys, the flat's all yours,' Grant said, handing John the keys. 'I've moved in with my girlfriend, she's got a flat just along the block and is coming to Canada with me. I'll need to pop back with the lease for you to sign and pick up a few things before I go, so get your things and make yourself at home.'

After Grant had gone John sat down on the black leather L shaped sofa and looked out of the huge windows at the panoramic view of Edinburgh. Arthur's Seat, the extinct volcano that dominates the city skyline directly in front of him with Edinburgh Castle in the distance, the only movement across an endless sky was an occasional bird or plane. John had despaired at the thought he was going to be stuck in that terrible bedsit for a long time, but as he looked up to heaven he realised his prayer had been answered and God had done more than he had asked or could ever have imagined. It was a week later that Grant popped in to see how John was getting on and surprised him with a proposition by saying. 'I know you're short of money John so I have something that might interest you.'

John looked at him expectantly, already grateful for what he had done to help him and was ready to listen to anything he had to offer.

'There's a job I'm thinking about doing with a couple of mates of mine which will give me a nice big wedge to go to Canada with and I was wondering with your track record if you'd be interested in coming in with us?'

'What is it the job exactly?' John asked, worry beginning to shadow his face as he continued to look at Grant.

'There's this guy that owns a scrap yard and is reported to have around £200,000 stashed away in a safe. If you're willing to do the surveillance work so we can work out the best time to make the hit and then be ready with the getaway car, you could earn yourself a nice fifty grand,' Grant explained.

The worried look stayed on John's face as he said. 'Sorry Grant I'm not interested, I am a Christian now and have turned away from crime and turned to God and He's my saviour now, not money.'

Grant studied his impassive face and screwed up his eyes in vexation as he said. 'I don't believe this, you really mean this stuff don't you? It's amazing what prison does to some people, but I never thought it would change a hard man like you.'

John smiled gently at him. 'It wasn't prison that changed me, it was God and I have given myself to Him. Let me give you an example, remember at the club when I pushed you out of the way and took the hit for you, the bottle that was meant for you?'

'And I'm grateful, which is why I was happy for you to have the flat.'

'Well, Christ took the hit for me when he sacrificed himself on the cross and my sins nailed Him to the wood. He paid the price for me Grant. He gave His Life for me and there is no greater love than one that sacrifices their life for another, and I owe Him in a much bigger way than you said you owe me.'

A cagey look crept onto Grant's face. 'Well I didn't expect to hear all this, but as I said there's fifty grand in it for you so I'll give you some time to think about it and I'll pop in and see you in a week's time. It's a lot of money John and you're skint, so think hard on it because you'll never get another chance like this,' Grant said, before turning and walking out. John slumped down on the sofa his mind beginning to spin, fifty grand was a lot of money and it could set him up for the future and as Grant said he would never get another chance like this. He got to his feet, crossed to the window and stared out at the skyline before raising his eyes to heaven praying for an answer. Temptation doesn't always come in your weakest moments, but will attempt to weaken you in your strongest. Leaning wearily against the glass with his eyes closed he seemed to hear a still quiet voice in his head, *'But those who desire to be rich fall into temptation, into a snare, into many senseless and harmful desires that plunge people into ruin and destruction.'*

Slowly he opened his eyes and studied his worried reflection in the window and saw the question etched on his face, *'am I really a new creation, have I truly been given a new heart and new spirit?'*

The words 'If A Wicked Man' springing to mind once more, John breathed a sigh of relief as he began to comprehend what that truly meant. The violence, the kidnappings, the beatings, the sex clubs, the blood on his hands, all wiped clean. There was that voice again, but a little louder this time, 'IT IS FINISHED.' In that instant his eyes filled with tears, wiping his eyes with both hands he heard himself say to his reflection:

'Believe your beliefs and doubt your doubts for with God all things are possible,'
and it made him feel good, cleansed, knowing in that moment of

temptation he had truly turned his back on the past, let go of what he had been and whatever the past, his future was now in the hands of God.

About the Author

John Lawson lives in East Sussex with his wife Carolyn. He currently works in a full time voluntary capacity as director of a charitable organisation where he is invited to speak in some of the toughest prisons on the planet, schools, colleges, universities, youth clubs and anywhere else that he is needed.

To contact John you can email him: john.lawson@ifawickedman.com

John Sealey lives in Essex with his wife Shelly. Since retiring from the film industry as an editor, producer and director, John started writing and has had several books published with many more in the pipeline. He is also working on several screenplays including If A Wicked Man.

To contact John Sealey john.sealey@ifawickedman.com

For more information visit www.ifawickedman.com